Perception with an Eye for Motion

Perception with an Eye for Motion

James E. Cutting

A Bradford Book
The MIT Press
Cambridge, Massachusetts
London, England

This book was set in Palatino by The MIT Press Computergraphics Department and printed and bound by Halliday Lithograph in the United States of America.

Library of Congress Cataloging-in-Publication Data

Cutting, James E.
  Perception with an eye for motion.

  "A Bradford book."
  Bibliography: p.
  Includes index.
  1. Motion perception (Vision) I. Title.
BF245.C88 1986   152.1'425   85-29788
ISBN 0-262-03119-1

For Gunnar Johansson, who taught me about motion, and Wendell Garner, who taught me about structure

Contents

Acknowledgments

I have had a lot of help hatching these ideas. A partial list of people who contributed in important ways includes Judith Bernstock, Susan Brennan, Lynn Cooper, Michael Kubovy, and Ann Marion for sharing their knowledge of art and perception; David Carpenter, Frank Restle, and James Todd for triggering my interest in graphical projections; Scott Fisher and Michael Naimark for revealing things I thought not possible in photography and cinema; Kristina Hooper for trying to shelter me in Silicon Valley, a world without tenure; Carol Krumhansl for many things, the least of which was her patience in teaching me patience so I could try to solve math problems; and Daryl Lawton, Herschel Leibowitz, Ulric Neisser, Hugh Priest, Martin Regan, and Susan Volman for piquing my interest in optic flow.

Many people read and commented on various forms of various chapters. In addition to some of those above these include Mark Detweiler, William Epstein, Jennifer Freyd, Norma Graham, Julian Hochberg, Paul Kolers, Robert Millard, Stephen Palmer, Christopher Peacocke, Irvin Rock, Sverker Runeson, Mark Schmuckler, Robert Sekuler, Roger Shepard, and Kent Stevens. What is here has been vastly improved by their efforts; I thank them all.

This work was supported, in part, by National Institutes of Mental Health Grant MH37467 and by the ATARI Sunnyvale Research Laboratory before its demise.

Introduction

This book is about information. The information of interest is used in visual perception, its locus is in the world as projected to the eye, and it is revealed through motion of objects or movement of an observer. In an effort to stir things up a little, I like to use the term *external representation* to stand for information about objects and events. Such information represents them and is ready for use by a perceptual system. The notion of *internal representation*, so common and useful to all fields of cognitive science, has little currency here. Proper consideration of external representation, I claim, is logically prior to internal representation and to information processing as well; we must know what information is used before we can understand how it is processed.

The study of perceptual information needs a methodology. Much effort has been expended in that of classical psychophysics, but it is now almost common to say that this was misguided, at least as an attempt to understand the match of perceptual systems to biologically important dimensions of the world. I do not entirely share this view. To be sure, the selection of variables most easily defined by the physicist, rather than by the perceiver's needs, may lead to nowhere of general interest. Information for a perceiver is not *in* frequency, intensity, mass, extent, or time; it is distributed across them. Nonetheless, psychophysical methods are without parallel for revealing information used in perception. Moreover, these can be applied to computer graphics, which, with their ability to control and simulate visual environments, has freed us forever from the necessity of using simple stimuli varied in simple ways.

I think it suits us best to couch information in mathematical terms. The math itself provides formless and timeless expressions of what the world offers its inhabitants; math is the essence of structure. But care is important here. Mathematics is too powerful to provide constraints on information; it models truth and drivel with equal felicity. Thus constraints are needed. In visual perception constraints on information are found in geometric optics, cast in terms of projected angles between points and lines. But even here there are problems: All projections produce distortions, a fact that has seemed by many to falsify the idea that information in optic relations is sufficiently trustworthy to guide perception. Yet I claim that this is a misconstrual of the natural situation. Although distortions can be found in static cross sections of the optic array, they seem less noticeable (or less disruptive) in dynamic images. There, movement of the observer, motions of an object, or both reveal three-dimensional relations. Projective geometry is the body of rules for that revelation, and the perceptual system appears to know some of them.

The typical notion about information in proximal images is that information is *correlated* with affairs in the distal world. Discussions of this view date at least from Berkeley and have continued to the present. Issues are rehearsed in terms of signs or cues to the perception of this and that, and we can almost imagine a huge covariance matrix for every possible proximal-distal co-occurrence. All entries in this matrix are typically thought to be nonzero and nonunity; in particular, entries of 1.00 are forbidden. If this restriction is true, perception and the perceptual theorist are in tough straits: Perceptual process can be only *inferential*, where some grounds (or premises) for each inference are based on mental construction rather than on what is presented to the eye and constrained by the biology of the visual system.

An opposing view is that *some* entries in this proximal-distal matrix are unity. These are *invariant* sources of information that *specify* the object or event in the external world. The visual system needs only to be constrained through evolution to pick it up (process it). For every invariant that may exist, perception gets easier to understand and to implement on a machine. With sufficient numbers a perceptual system that does not need cognition to work properly can be both imagined and (at some point) built. Large stores of correlational information are not needed, and large general-purpose processors are freed for other tasks. Thus in my view perception is largely data driven, bottom up, in everyday life. But this is not to say that *all* perception must function this way, nor that all entries in this matrix need be 1.00. I claim only that there *are* perceptual invariants and that their number turns out to be nontrivially small. Gibson, of course, presented essentially this same view. What is unusual to my approach is that I take information to be richer than even he allowed: For any object or event there may be *more than one invariant* associated with it.

This book is divided into four sections. In the first five chapters I consider some philosophy, psychology, and intellectual history behind important concepts in visual perception—information, projections, the optic array, pictures, space, and invariants. In chapters 6 through 9

I discuss one type of optic flow, that for a moving object and a stationary observer, and focus on a particular invariant from projective geometry and a correlate of it. A surprise finding is that observers seem to use this invariant, the cross ratio, in some situations but shun its use in others. In chapters 10 through 13 I discuss a second type of optic flow, that of a stationary environment and a moving observer, and address the problem of how an individual might find his or her way. Evidence is reviewed against the general use of a topological invariant, the focus of expansion, and formalisms and empirical evidence are summoned in favor of another, differential motion parallax. And in the final two chapters I revert to the style of the first five to consider classes of perceptual theory, *direct* and *indirect perception*, and their historical roots. A new class of theory is then proposed: *directed perception*, which considers the world so rich in information, even invariants, that discussions of algorithms and informational processing again become central to perception. In essence, information overspecifies perception but underspecifies process.

And basically that is what this book is about. Because the history of perception is so rich, I often delve into what many will regard as ancient sources in the hope of making contemporary points. And many contemporary works I gloss over or discuss not at all. This book, then, takes on a somewhat idiosyncratic air. For this I apologize, but my goal is not to be representative; instead, I wish to present some foundations for a new view of perception.

I

Information for Vision

Nothing can be known concerning the things of the world without the power of geometry.
Roger Bacon (1260; in Burke 1928, p. 234)

1

Information

The world is a plenum. It is lavishly furnished with things that are informative and meaningful to its inhabitants at every turn. In particular, the visual world for humankind is rich with objects and events to which we are attuned. Our visual system collects information about what is optically displayed and does so according to our needs as they have evolved from our earliest forebears. It is largely through vision that we know our environment and our physical place within it.

But how is it that we understand the visual patterns that surround us? Why does our visual system work so well? What is the nature of the surrounding information such that it has meaning for us? These are some of the difficult questions that face anyone who studies perception. In fact, there was an almost uninterrupted stretch of more than two thousand years when all philosophers worth their salt felt it necessary to consider them.[1] The reason for their long-term interest is that such questions tap some of the deepest issues of philosophy. Indeed, they run to the heart of metaphysics.

Metaphysics and Perception

The term *metaphysics* means "what comes after physics."[2] This handy phrase sets an interesting stage. Consider a rough sketch for a highly desirable, albeit impossible goal—a complete understanding of perception. At a minimum, such an understanding wants, first, a description of what is perceived and, second, an explanation of how we perceive it, even act on it. The first entails discussion of objects and events in our surround, and those can be discussed in physical terms appropriate to the organism.[3] What comes after the physics is *perception*. In this manner, the study of perception is the study of metaphysics.

To say that perception is metaphysics is, of course, a ruse. Yet it is not a play on words to suggest that perception and metaphysics are intimately tied. Metaphysics divides many ways. Older traditions divide it into ontology, cosmology, and epistemology.[4] These terms can be rephrased as three simple queries: What is there? Where did it come from? And how do we know it? Anyone interested in these questions is bound to be interested in perception, and anyone interested in perception should be interested in these questions. Of course, I cannot consider them in broad scope, but I will focus on them with regard to a central concept in perception—information.

What Is There?

Ontology is the study of things. It is almost inescapable that, if we perceive a particular entity, it should count in our ontology. Why do we perceive it as we do? This is yet another deep query, posed most clearly by Koffka (1935) and picked up by Gibson (1950, 1971b) and many others. Any respectable answer to Koffka's question must suggest that we are predisposed to parse the world into the kinds of objects and events that are meaningful to us. This is a fine start, but a perceptual psychologist cannot stop here. Such an answer, if the author's intent is for it to stand as final word, is nearly as anti-intellectual as it is glib. Unsatisfyingly, it hints that ultimate answers to questions of perception are found in other fields. In turn, it suggests that psychological approaches to perception are a peripheral scientific enterprise to be swept up in answers of biology. To me, this seems unsavory and unlikely. Thus the psychologist and others interested in perception, such as the philosopher or computer scientist, must go further. Any answer to basic ontological questions, I suggest, must consider information about objects and events.

Information *informs*. The roots of this idea mean *to instill form within*, and I like this idea a lot. But therein lie myriad traps; perhaps no word in philosophy is more slippery than the word *form*. Nevertheless, let me take it to mean the three-dimensional shape of an object. Following from definition, then, geometric shapes are instilled in visual information. Instillation in turn invokes the idea of essences or abstractions that represent objects. Later I will claim and try to demonstrate that such abstractions *specify* the objects that they represent. But here I claim only that perception is the process of picking up that information, with the end result of having the form, in some sense, instilled within the perceiver. Thus visual perception is the study of the mapping from perceptible external objects, through optic information that represents them, to the observer who uses that information for his or her purposes. Geometry is the vehicle of this instillation. Not only is geometry useful in describing the object, encoding it in equations for the purposes of description by the experimenter, but also, I suggest, observers can decode that information along lines which demonstrate that the human visual system is a sophisticated geometry-analyzing engine.

Returning to metaphysics, my emphasis on information makes it a special ontological category. One way to coordinate discussion of the particular categories I am interested in—perceived objects and perceptual information—is to be vigilant in use of terms. A handy way to hold onto the difference is to remember that we *perceive objects*, but we *pick up information*. By this I mean that our experience is full of objects and events but that our visual system responds to mathematical, typically geometric relations.

Where Does Information Come From?

Cosmology, or the study of origins and the nature of the universe, is well beyond the normal scope of psychology. Nonetheless, regardless of how silly it may seem, I must ask about the origin of information. It seems to me that any answer must contain reciprocal parts. *Information comes from the environment* during a given perceptual act but also must be tailored to the perceiver, constrained and reduced from the indefinitely large number of possibilities by the perceiver's ability to pick it up and find it useful. Thus the *adequacy of classes of information to perception comes from the perceiver*, shaped by evolution and learning. In sum, information is shaped by the mutuality of perceiver and environment (Gibson 1979).

Information, I claim, is found in the geometric relations of parts of objects to each other and to their surrounds. Rules of geometry govern these relations presented to a perceiver, and it is the discovery of those rules applicable to visual perception that is a major psychological task. Among the most important, I suggest, are the ones allied to laws of optics and projective geometry, which I begin to discuss in chapter 2 and continue to elaborate in following chapters. The problem of projections is one familiar since Kepler and Descartes: The world has three dimensions but our retinas only two. Preservation of information through such dimensional reduction can be discussed only in terms lawful to projections. Thus how we come to perceive dynamic projections in a tractable manner stems from the fact that two-dimensional projections of three-dimensional environments change in lawful ways. A central task of the study of vision is to discover those ways.

How Do We Know about Visible Objects?

Epistemology, or the study of the nature and grounds of knowledge, is the branch of metaphysics easiest to relate to perception. We *know* the objects around us in part because we can perceive them. In fact, it is sometimes said that to perceive is to know.[5] I have deep sympathy with this idea, but it rankles many. To warrant the name, knowledge ought to be true. But is what we perceive true? Answers to this question typically entail justification of belief about reality. And these answers go beyond what is perceived into what can be known without doubt. This latter realm, I believe, is an utter morass best left to philosophy. Nevertheless, there is something cogent about the idea that knowledge and perception are intimately tied. Without perception it is difficult to know how and where any study of epistemology can begin or end. The mind would be an entirely solipsistic organ, blowing its notes in a strange unreality.[6]

In summary, questions posed by ontology, cosmology, and epistemology are fundamental to perception, and perception is fundamental to them. Nevertheless, they are not the kinds of questions psychologists try to answer by dropping all and scurrying into their laboratories. For the experimentalist these questions and the answers they engender are less than completely satisfying. Our usual court of appeals—that of experiments and data—cannot be in session to deliberate on them. And we grow impatient, and rightfully so, when those outside (and inside) our discipline tell us the proper answers and even the proper questions to consider. Nonetheless, some questions of a metaphysical nature show more promise from an approach rooted in empirical psychology. I suggest that one is the last question posed at the beginning of this chapter: What is the nature of information such that it informs us? This question is at the intersection of psychology, philosophy, and artificial intelligence. An answer to it is, I contend, a necessary beginning to any account of perception.

Three Approaches to Information

In general, three classes of visual information have been discussed: From philosophy came sense data, from engineering came information theory, and from psychology has come an application of geometric optics. I have already tipped my hand strongly in favor of the last, but it is instructive to consider each in turn.

Information in Sense Data
Philosophers often use the concept of *sense data*, sometimes called sensa or sensibilia. Sense data are the unanalyzed sensations from sense organs as sent to the central nervous system; they are a rather curious outgrowth of the early analytic philosophy of this century. Sense data became the tool for discussing how perception might be possible and fallible at the same time. The initial utility of the notion was based on the need to consider foundations of knowledge. It was argued, for example, that we cannot know with complete assurance what we perceive without first knowing the conditions under which

we perceive it. This reduces to the idea that we can be assured of perception if and only if we can be assured of what we perceive, a style of argument that convinces few.

Early discussions began with *sense contents*, a notion introduced by Moore (1905–1906). It was transformed into sense data,[7] then adopted by Russell (1914) and Price (1932). Thereafter it became popular as an attempt to provide a metaphysically neutral term for describing what is presented to the mind of the perceiver. Sense data are caused by but are not identical with physical objects. They are private and subjective, bound to the receptive capabilities of the perceiver. Thus a red traffic light causes different sense data for drivers of adjacent automobiles.

An interesting progression took place in the development of the sense data concept. Objective fact began to play a part in sense data talk. Sense data are different for different people, in part because no two individuals can occupy the same viewpoint. For vision, then, sense data began to take on the meaning of optic projections of a physical object and its surround. Thus sense data became both information and sensation, public and private. From my perspective the sensory, or private, nature of sense data serves no purposes here; in fact, with Dretske (1981), I suggest that information must be objective and public, without private parts. Making information partly subjective impedes progress, giving it a nebulous status between the mental and the physical.

Ignoring this issue, philosophers had their attention elsewhere when developing the sense data concept; they were addressing the foundations problem in epistemology. It was argued that observers could be assured of their sense data because it is not in the nature of sense data to be correct or incorrect; sense data simply are what they are—phenomenal impression. On the other hand, it was thought that observers could not be assured of their perceptions. This led to a situation that begins to sound familiar to psychologists: It was said that observers can *directly* perceive the sense data, because those data are firm, but *indirectly* perceive the objects to which sense data are referred. Instead of considering the direct/indirect debate here, I defer it until the last two chapters. Here I wish only to state the reason behind sense data talk— the justification of belief. It has often been said that perceivers can never be assured that they are not being deceived by some omniscient, slightly mad being. The mere possibility of illusion, hallucination, or electrophysiological intervention causing percepts identical with those that occur normally makes the sureness of perception unjustified, or so the philosopher thinks. Now it is clear to me that such circumstances are offbeat if not implausible. But the philosopher is ever-worried about counterexamples to normality, no matter how unlikely.

In summary, two ideas are important about sense data: Information for perception is unsure, and the conditions for perception cannot be known a priori to be normal. My counterclaim is, first, that information *is* trustworthy under normal conditions. That is, even if at the current time the sense data are ambiguous and nonspecific as to what should be perceived, later instants will disambiguate those states, typically— as suggested by my title—through motion of the object or movement of the observer.[8] Second, justified true belief in the normality of perceptual conditions can also be litigated over time. If an observer explores an environment by moving through it, viewing conditions will become apparent. The probability of abnormal conditions giving rise to normal perceptions when an unfettered perceiver roams through a cluttered space is so small as to be nonexistent, even for the philosopher who traffics in surety.[9]

Information in Sets and Set Size

From engineering came information measured logarithmically by the number of members in a set to which an object belongs. Typically, the base of the scale is 2, and the unit is the *bit*. A choice between two equiprobable items, then, is one-bit choice; that among four items, a two-bit choice; and that among eight items, a three-bit choice. The seminal work behind this idea is *The Mathematical Theory of Communication*, by Shannon and Weaver (1949), a book about the electrical transmission of signals and not at all about perception. Information theory was popularized within psychology by many people, but most successfully by Miller (1956; Miller and Frick 1949) in research on language perception, an area reasonably close to its origins. Shortly thereafter it spread to perception, where it thrived.[10] It is not so popular now as it once was in experimental psychology, and in several ways this is the field of perception's loss. The ideas that it addressed, albeit inadequately, are important for understanding perception.

The information-theoretic approach has much quantitative precision and elegance. For example, if I tell someone that today is in the month of January, I have given him or her more information, excluding 11 of 12 possibilities (and therefore $\log_2(12)$, or 3.585 bits), than if I say today is Thursday, thereby excluding 6 of 7 possibilities ($\log_2(7)$, or 2.807 bits). Such analyses were applied to almost any action or percept (see Quastler 1955), and ensuing calculations gave the appearance of deep understanding. To be sure, there was always something odd about the idea that the information about an entity is contained in a measure of the *number* of things in its class or set. It would seem, instead, that information would somehow be in what a thing *is*. But the information-theoretic approach has other problems. Consider the following seven.

One problem is a classic puzzle for perception—ambiguity. An entity may appear to be one thing but not the same thing at all times. Multistable visual illusions are salient cases in point. From an information-theoretic point of view, two things can be said: (1) At any given time an ambiguous figure is singular, and (2) even though there may be a class of objects implied by a stimulus array, that class still excludes a large number of others. In this manner, the approach sidesteps the question of why there was ambiguity in the first place, although the approach remains self-consistent and adequate for other goals. But whereas there can be great power in an approach that systematically ignores a side issue,[11] ambiguity has not traditionally been regarded a side issue to perception.

A second problem is that information-theoretic analysis initially ignored the state of the organism. Consider again the example given above; at any given time it seems likely that more people know the month than the day of the week. Thus by definition the statement about month is more informative, but in terms of what an individual might not already know, the day is probably more so. Surely new knowledge is more informative than old knowledge. The most important response to this problem was Garner's (1962), who spoke of information based on a priori *uncertainty*. From his perspective, if someone already knows that it is the first month of the year, being told that it is January offers no information; it reduces no uncertainty. Garner thus distinguished the received amount of information from the *value* of the received amount. In the month case, the value is zero because of the state of the individual. But, a priori, how do we know this state?

A third problem is truth, or verifiability. We would think that information should reveal the true status of affairs, but no such claim has been made. Consider again the day and month case. Suppose that in fact it is January but not a Thursday or Thursday but not January, or suppose that it is even a Monday in May. These facts do not change the information measured. But it seems wrong for incorrect and correct information to have the same status or for incorrect information to be considered information at all. This issue, and the explanations that ensue, drag us sideways into philosophical issues of justification. We are then torn away from our goal of explaining how information informs.

The next four problems are even more difficult and deal with the nature of categories and conceptual sets. The fourth problem is that, whereas all members of a set are counted equally by the theory, natural sets are rarely homogeneous. As Rosch (1973, 1975) amply showed, some members are more representative than others. Robins, for example, are rightly considered by North Americans to be more birdlike than ostriches, and thus we should think that they would count more in bitwise assessment. The prototypicality of robins over ostriches suggests that natural sets can be fuzzy. Because of fuzziness, it is not clear how to allot membership: Should we count all members equally or weight them according to their typicality in a class? These are questions to which there may be answers, and much intellectual effort has been focused on them,[12] but to me they do not offer solid ways to measure information for everyday perception.

A fifth problem is that the objects or events around us rarely imply *single* sets to which they belong, and a sixth problem is that they do not imply the *size* of those sets. Consider a pencil. Does a pencil imply all writing implements, all things that fit into a briefcase, all artifacts, or something else? And how many types of writing instruments, brief-caseable items, and artifacts are there? Is a charred piece of wood a writing implement to be counted in the first set? It depends, of course, on the intentions of the individual. Is a computer an item that fits in a briefcase and therefore a member of the second set? It depends on the sizes of the computer and of the briefcase. Is a dinner an artifact and of the third set? It depends on construal of the term "artifact"; a dinner is human prepared but rarely completely synthetic.

But perhaps the most difficult problem with sets is the seventh—relativism. Items belong to different sets at the convenience of the individual. A pen can be a writing implement at one point in time, a sharp object for cleaning shoes at another, and a bookmark at yet a third.[13] Because all aspects of all contexts cannot be known for every potential situation, it is not clear what sets should be involved in any given information calculation.

Problems of heterogeneity within sets, multiple membership across sets, unspecifiability of set size, and relativism confound the application of information theory to perception. Moreover, it is not clear that their resolutions can bring us closer to an understanding of how information is used. Answers can tell us only about the proper ways to *represent* information once objects are perceived. Ultimately, the problem with the information-theoretic approach to perception is that objects that belong universally to single sets of fixed size and composition are not the stuff of which our world is made.[14]

Information in Geometric Structure
A third measure of information concerns relations among objects and object parts. Unfortunately the nature of real-world relations, like that of real-world sets, is manifold and multidefined. Which are we to consider? To begin with, there are structural and functional ways to relate

objects. My bias is toward the structural, but discussions of both are fraught with difficulties.

Relations entail formats, and many psychologists have been concerned about the format in which the relations are expressed in mental activity. Putatively, this is an issue about the architecture of the mind.[15] But whatever the merit of the debate over format, its resolution is not crucial to my discussion. I use both popular formats to discuss the information important to the observer: On the one hand, I need equations that specify the layout of objects in the visual world and hence use a propositional format that is easy to implement in a computer program; and on the other hand, I need two-dimensional analog figures that represent the relations of geometric optics in order to explicate these equations for the reader.

The basis of information about spatial relations that I consider is quite concrete—*angles*. I start with angles because of the nature of light. As Euclid stated, and as will be considered at some length in chapter 2, the line of sight from the eye to an object is straight.[16] Between lines of sight are angles, and within angles we can find much information about the geometry of surfaces. Geometrized information escapes some problems of the other two forms. First, unlike sense data, spatial information does not change or require change with the state of the organism. In fact, no organism need be present at all for the situations I discuss. Second, truth enters into discussion only as mathematical truth—proof of theorems and geometric relations. There is no need to delve into problems of justification and belief because they do not arise. The mathematics that I use is sufficiently closed that proof and truth are unproblematic.[17] What needs proof, or at least corroboration, is that perceivers use this type of information. And third, by definition, there is no problem of size, composition, overlap, or context of sets. Plainly put, based on angles the form of information central to this discussion is mathematical relations about *distance*.

To many, it will seem outrageous to consider angles as a basis for information about distance. They will suggest that, if I thought the problems of sense data and information-theoretic analyses were numerous, then the problem I have set myself is enormous; it flies in the face of nearly three hundred years of philosophical tradition.[18] But I am not claiming that distance information is registered at the eye without transformation. Instead, I claim that *relative* distance can be recovered from information in the optic array and that the recovery process is inextricably tied to movement of the observer or motion of objects. There has, of course, been much debate within psychology and philosophy over the nature of these transformations. Some appear in later chapters. One major conceptual tool that allows for recovery is *invari-*

ance, the topic of chapter 5. The invariance that concerns this work is information about a rigid object's shape or about rigid relations among objects that does not change with point of view, lighting, or other transformations. Such information provides the firm foundation for perception that philosophy has shown we desperately need.[19] One might find invariance in many ways. Here I will be eclectic, discussing information in three forms, taking the lead from machine vision.

Three Approaches to Structure through Motion

What sources of visual information are available to a perceiver when making judgments about a moving object? Ullman (1981, 1983) characterized three approaches for unrestricted motion.[20] All three attempt to derive unambiguous three-dimensional solutions from two-dimensional projections, either over time or as seen from different viewpoints. Increasingly in both machine vision and psychology, mathematical proof of geometric relations and demonstration that human perceivers use them govern what constitutes solutions to problems. The research presented here is in this tradition.

Discrete Points and Views. The first approach considers relations among discrete elements from different views. Ullman (1979) based his structure-from-motion theorem on it and proved that four points in three-dimensional space seen in three different parallel projections suffice to determine rigid spatial arrangement. He also suggested that five points seen in two different polar projections may suffice. I discuss these projection techniques in chapter 2. This approach is most closely connected with the set of studies presented in chapters 7 and 8. My goal there is to determine if the observer can recover a certain aspect of object structure, namely coplanarity of a surface, from relations among parallel lines over time. Although I consider a continuous view rather than discrete ones, my emphasis is still on *spatial* structure, rather than *spatiotemporal* structure. Because I limit myself to planar stimuli, my approach (when mapped back onto Ullman's) is that of considering four points in a minimum of two discrete perspective views. When considering other measures, three points may suffice and may do so in as few as two views.[21]

Discrete Points and Displacements. A second approach has been quite popular in machine vision.[22] Instantaneous displacements of points in space are indicated on a proximal image as vectors, or arrows that point in a particular direction for a particular distance. These are then used to determine the arrangement of objects under the assumption that the layout is rigid. Prazdny (1981a), for example, suggested that five points and their displacements in a single perspective view are sufficient to reconstruct a three-dimensional array. This second approach is closely related to my analyses in chapter 9. There, discrete points (or parallel lines) are considered, each with a particular displacement vector at every instant in time. Again, the stimuli are presented continuously. Results suggest that four parallel lines and their displacements are sufficient to register a planar surface. Three may do as well.

Displacement Fields. The third approach is probably the most common. Many researchers have used many different formalisms about displacement fields to describe linear and curvilinear translations through rigid space.[23] One of their goals is to describe global flow generated by observer movement. In chapters 11 through 13 I use a hybrid of this approach and the second. That is, rather than starting with discrete points and displacements for an observer moving over a plane, I consider the displacement field and from it generalize to fields of discrete points as projected to the eye. This pattern of motion is commonly called *motion parallax*, sometimes motion perspective.

Overview

Questions of perception are intimately tied to metaphysics. This tie is both welcome and ensnarling. It is welcome because it demonstrates the profundity of the questions. It is ensnarling because our tools for finding out—experiments and their data—help us little in providing metaphysically appropriate answers. But setting these questions aside, we can address issues of how information informs.

In the study of visual perception, we could begin with sense data. These are thought untrustworthy as representing objects in the environment and thus ill-provide a foundation. To shore up the system, conceptual elaborations are needed to take us out of the perception and into cognition. We could also begin with information-theoretic analyses, but these proceed most easily only when the sets are of known size, homogeneous in composition, nonoverlapping, and unvarying across contexts. Most interesting sets in the perceptual world are none of these. On the other hand, we could consider—as I do—a third kind of information, the geometrical structure of spatially distributed objects and object parts as they are projected to the eye. The epistemological position that I am proposing is little different from that of Roger Bacon, quoted at the beginning of this section: Geometry is the foundation of vision. Going beyond Bacon, invariance is to be found in geometrized information, and the pursuit of trustworthiness in perception may prove fruitful through it. This information can be couched in many ways, and following an eclectic path, I use several—discrete points and views, discrete points and their instantaneous displacements, and displacement fields.

Before approaching that end, however, many intermediate steps must be taken. Because optic information has been much maligned, in chapter 2 I consider the nature of projections and the optic array. In chapter 3 I analyze pictures as projections of three-dimensional environments; I discuss in chapter 4 the intellectual history of objects in space such that they might be projectable, and I address invariance as a mathematical and psychological tool that might serve to discuss projections in chapter 5. By then we will have the tools to explore particular invariants in particular perceptual situations.

2

Projections, Optics, and the Optic Array

My goal is to offer concrete reasons why visual perception can be trusted. My claim is that the trustworthiness of perception is built on the trustworthiness of information. Time and motion turn the trick, fortifying the information on which the perception is based. And if information is the key to understanding perception, then projections are the key to understanding visual information. Projections, in turn, are based on optics. In later chapters I consider changing optic projections as *proximal* stimuli, whether at the eye or on a film screen, that contain information about the *distal* layout, the arrangements of objects in the real world. Before that, however, I must discuss the static optic array. But because its geometry is somewhat tricky, I start with static planar projections, tracing their discovery and use. This analysis touches on pictorial art, mapmaking, and graphic design in an effort to gain appreciation for the plurality of projection techniques more or less similar to what the visual world presents to the eye.

Projections in Art and in the Eye

Projections are the core of visual art. The impact of architecture, sculpture, painting, and photography depends on what is seen. Arrangements of surfaces—constructed, carved, painted, or filmed—are projected to the eye, and to understand them, we must address their arrangement. Consider some comparative optics.

Eyes and Cameras

It was once fashionable to compare eyes with cameras. The analogy is particularly apt for the vertebrate eye (Helmholtz 1868, Wald 1950): Both the camera and the eye have dioptric lenses focusing bundles of light rays to a point, both have pupils primarily to adjust focal depth but also to modulate light, and both rely on laws of projection onto surfaces. The eye-camera analogy is old, developed well before modern cameras, and is due to Leonardo da Vinci (Richter 1883). Experiments followed shortly thereafter by Aranzi in 1595 and Scheiner in 1619 on the optics of enucleated ox eyes (Pirenne 1970, Polyak 1957). Kepler and Descartes popularized these studies and specifically discussed their optics in terms of *cameras*, or chambers that admitted light through a small opening. Much later, with the work of Niepce and Daguerre in the nineteenth century, those principles were applied to photography.

More recently, however, the eye-camera analogy has fallen out of favor.[1] Important distinctions have been emphasized. For example, the eye has neither shutters nor exposure time, yet the visual system allows us to see a moving object clearly, whereas a still camera would register blur. In addition, the shape of the projection surfaces are different. Despite flaws in the analogy, however, the intended domain of the comparison remains—the facts of lenses, pupils, and projections are still valid. These must be considered in order to understand the lawfulness of structural information in the visual world.

Medieval artists and almost all who went before used many devices to represent spatial relations among objects. For example, the height in the picture plane, the relative distance of the base of a depicted object from the bottom of the picture, was commonly used to represent distance. But such devices, although effective, were relatively crude. With the development of Renaissance art arose a new tool of depiction for naturalistic representation—linear perspective.[2] Early hints can be seen in the paintings of Duccio and Giotto in the fourteenth century. Much of the action, however, took place in fifteenth-century Florence. There, Brunelleschi made the first perspective sketches in 1425 with the aid of a mirror, Massachio and Donatello took his ideas and applied them to painting and sculpture, and Alberti codified and extended them in his rules of composition, *Della Pittura*. Published in 1436, it is the oldest extant document on linear perspective. In it, a half century before Leonardo, Alberti encouraged the artist to imagine the picture plane as something "transparent and like glass" to be drawn on (Edgerton 1975, pp. 87–90; White 1957), as shown in figure 2.1.[3] The study of linear perspective then burgeoned, unifying medieval optics, mathematics, and the technology of depicting.

From medieval optics came another important tool that advanced Renaissance art. It was a different kind of camera, the *camera obscura*, or dark chamber. Its principles were first sketched by Alhazen at the end of the tenth century (Lindberg 1967, Polyak 1957), and it was adopted by Alberti and others as an instructional device for young artists. This camera is a light-tight box with a pinhole at one end and an opaque or translucent flat surface behind it on which the image of the world projected. The projection, like any focused image, is upside down and reversed, a condition Leonardo tried to correct with double

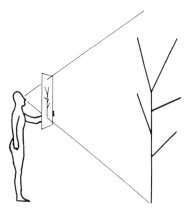

Figure 2.1
A schematic diagram of projection onto a planar surface, known as Alberti's window.

lenses. Later, in 1604, Kepler reported that this inversion took place on the retina, a fact that led to centuries of quandary.[4] What is important here, however, is not the quandary but the fact that artists discovered and worked with projections. The pinhole camera obscura was the first tool, earlier even than Brunelleschi's mirror and Alberti's window, for drawing and measuring images.

Because light travels in straight lines, the only rays that can pass through a small aperture the size of a pinprick are those traveling straight from some part of an object through the pinhole and onto the projection surface. The optimum pinhole is about 0.4 mm in diameter (Pirenne 1970); smaller apertures are subject to proportionately too much diffraction (bending of light waves around edges) to register an image of reasonable quality, and larger holes allow multiple sources of light to reach each location on the projection surface. The pinhole creates a one-to-one mapping between what is present in the visual world, unoccluded by other objects, and what is on the projection surface.[5] That surface can be a plane, a curved surface of a sphere, or surfaces of any shape whatsoever; photographs are examples of planes, what bathes the cornea at the front of the eye or the retina at the back of it are examples of curved surfaces, and certain works of photographic art are examples of the third type of surface—discontinuous and object shaped.[6] The first two are shown in figure 2.2. For any point on one surface, one can find an equivalent point on the other such that the points that surround have the same ordinal arrangements. Betweenness is everywhere satisfied.

But the projection surfaces are different in important ways. The photograph, the canvas, and the sketch pad are flat; the retina conforms

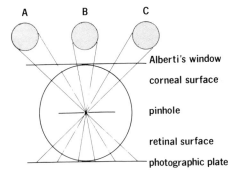

Figure 2.2
Projections of columns in front of and behind a pinhole aperture onto flat and curved surfaces, elaborated from Leonardo da Vinci (Richter 1883). Notice that even though the exterior pillars (*A* and *C*) are farther from the pinhole than the middle pillar (*B*), flat projections of them are larger. Curved projections yield what Leonardo called natural perspective. All points on the human retina are not equidistant from the nodal point in the cornea-lens system as shown here.

nearly to a section of a sphere. Plane geometry is appropriate to the former, spherical geometry to the latter. The differences were first outlined by Leonardo (Richter 1883), who was troubled by the difference between natural perspective (that seen with our eyes) and artificial perspective (that used to construct a painting). In general, pictorial distortions are introduced when any region of the plane is not orthogonal to the line of sight between object and image. Spherical objects, for example, project as ellipses, not circles, when the camera lens is not focused directly on them; and in a line of pillars parallel to the plane, those on the periphery project wider images than those directly in front of the lens. Neither of these effects occurs with a spherical projection surface, but the discovery of such planar distortions led to their playful use.

Anamorphosis
Certainly the most extreme and striking projections are those of anamorphic art. Begun by Leonardo and Dürer and fully developed by the seventeenth century, these minor artworks are the camera obscura obscured or gone haywire.[7] They are representational but composed so that they can be discerned only when viewed from extreme positions or with the aid of a cylindrical mirror. They are important to perception because they demonstrate that a projection surface need not be orthogonal to the line of sight and that the relation between distal object and proximal image is not fixed except by convention.

Rather than pursuing projections in art and photography, however, consider next the development of projection systems in an area of applied mathematics—mapmaking. Here a special kind of anamorphosis was embraced; it is informative because it projects from a sphere (the earth) onto a plane (a map). The mapping of elements in the optic array onto a picture is exactly of this form. I end this section, then, with an analysis of planar projections.

Projections, Navigation, and Graphics

Projections from globe to map are at least as old as Ptolemy's *Geographia,* but systematic interest in them was not rekindled until the sixteenth century.[8] Then came the pursuit and subsequent discovery of new tools for representation. The practical matter was to introduce as little distortion as possible in areas of the world deemed important (typically Europe), while transforming a continuous two-dimensional surface (the globe) into a discontinuous one (a map) that could be folded up and stored easily. Early solutions projected a sphere onto a cylinder. The most famous is the stereographic projection of Gerhardus Mercator, published in 1554 and shown in figure 2.3. There, points along any longitude (north-south meridian) are mapped as straight lines on the cylinder by means of a common pole. Hence I call it a *polar* projection.[9] The location of this pole is on the equator. A vertical fan of rays is passed from it through the opposing longitude and beyond until it strikes the surface of the cylinder. To create the map, the pole is moved continuously along the equator, wrapping around the globe covering all longitudes. Once all projections are completed, they form a cylinder to be slit and unrolled into a flat, two-dimensional surface.

Two kinds of distortion are evident in the Mercator projection. First, the map expands the latitudinal (east-west) distances away from the equator. The cause of this distortion is that longitudes project as parallel lines. At the extremes, the North and South Poles become lines stretched across the top and bottom of the map. Because of these distortions and because of the uninhabitability of these regions, latitudes above 80° are usually omitted. Second, the projected north-south distances between latitudes become increasingly greater near the poles. Thus, on the map but not on the globe, the distance between the seventieth and eightieth parallels is considerably larger than that between the equator and the tenth parallel. Together, these effects create the misimpression that Greenland is larger than South America. In fact, it is less than one-eighth the size.

Another cylindrical projection is orthographic, so called because projectors (lines used to construct the projection, emanating from the de-

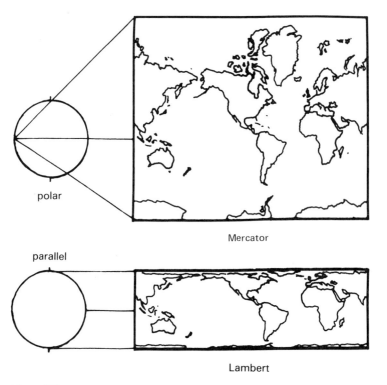

Figure 2.3
Mercator and Lambert projections of the world and an indication of how they are generated. For my purposes the Mercator is a type of polar projection and the Lambert a parallel projection.

picted object and intersecting the image) are orthogonal (at right angles) to the projection surface. This map is *parallel projection*, also shown in figure 2.3. It was first drawn by Lambert in 1722 but was never as popular in cartography as the Mercator.[10] Despite its relative obscurity, its consideration here is instructive. The Lambert projection takes every point on the globe and maps it to the *nearest* point on the cylinder. For all longitudes, projectors between sphere and cylinder are parallel. This map has the same latitudinal distortions near the poles as does the Mercator but has the opposite distortions in longitude. They are compressed rather than stretched, yielding a Greenland that retains its relative area but at the cost of being severely misshapen.

Two features are important about these projections. First, as should be obvious, they have been extremely useful to navigators and political geographers. They represent the topography of the globe quite well.

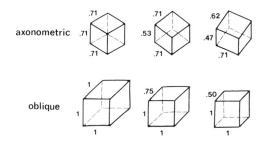

Figure 2.4
Parallel projections of cubes, in which hidden edges are shown as broken lines. The axonometric projections are, from left to right, isometric, dimetric, and trimetric. The three oblique projections of a cube are the cavalier on the left and the cabinet on the right, which essentially is a Necker cube. Foreshortening ratios (projected length divided by real length) are given for each side.

But second, because *all* such projections introduce distortions, there is no possibility of a flat, distortionless map. It is the nature of the projection process, when transforming spherical to planar dimensions, that such vagaries occur.[11] Polar and parallel projections, however, are only the first division of a hierarchy of planar maps, used in both art and science.[12] In general, parallel projections attempt to reproduce metric (absolute) distances in an object but do so at the cost of appearing somewhat strange and distorted. Polar projection, on the other hand, presents a situation more like that found in everyday vision. The rays of light project, not in parallel, but as a solid pyramid.[13] Oddly enough, as line drawings, these too can look distorted.

Parallel Projections
Parallel projections parse into *orthographic* and *oblique*. Orthographic projectors intersect the plane at right angles. Their projections include the multiview, or top-front-side, renderings so often used in mechanical drawing. These have the advantage of showing *no* distortions on a planar surface but have the obvious disadvantage of being unable to portray a three-dimensional object in depth in a single view.

Other orthographic projections are *axonometric*, as shown in figure 2.4. Here, the various axes of the object must intersect the projection plane at any angle so long as it is not 90°. The angles determine *foreshortening ratios*, the values of which are the projected length of a given set of lines divided by their true length. Comparison of ratios further divides axonometrics. In an *isometric* projection all axes intersect the picture plane at 45°. The wire-frame cube, first shown by Kopfermann (Koffka 1935) and investigated by Hochberg and McAlister (1953), is of this kind. Interestingly, it is a graphical object that does not appear depthlike. All foreshortening ratios are 0.707, the cosine of 45°. In a *dimetric* projection two axes intersect the picture plane at the same angle and hence have the same foreshortening ratio, but the third axis intersects at a different angle; in a *trimetric* projection none of the axes intersects the plane at the same angle.

The other type of parallel projection is the oblique, also shown in figure 2.4. Oblique projections have one face of the object parallel to the picture plane and projectors intersecting the plane at *oblique* angles. Such projections provide a metric representation of one face of an object but not of the other faces. Oblique projections come in many kinds, but the most common are the *cavalier* and the *cabinet*. Cavalier projectors intersect the image at 45°, and the cabinet's at 64°. The cavalier projectors project the sides of an object at full value, with no foreshortening. Because these look odd, overemphasizing the depth of an object, cabinet projectors are often preferred. Their depth dimension (or z axis) has a foreshortening ratio of 0.50, the cotangent of 64°. Unfortunately, these projections often look too thin. Notice that the Necker cube is a wireframe object in cabinet projection.

Polar Projections
Polar projections divide into one-, two-, and three-point perspectives. These correspond to the number of poles at which distal parallel lines converge in the image, a feature never found in parallel projections. As a result of these poles, two other distinctions emerge: diminution of projected size with distance from the projected plane and nonuniform foreshortening along various axes of objects. Both are caused by projectors intersecting the image plane at nonuniform angles. Typically there is one projector, the centric ray, at or near the middle of the image that intersects the plane at a right angle. All others intersect it at increasingly acute angles around that ray.

One-point perspective is the technique developed by Brunelleschi. Although fourteenth-century painters flirted with views from orientations other than the front (and parallel to the image plane), fifteenth-century artists almost exclusively presented faces of buildings and other objects in this orientation (Edgerton 1975). *Two-point perspective* allows an object to be viewed at any position in which no face is parallel to the image plane, and *three-point perspective* has parallel lines converge along three axes. Three-point perspective often comes as close to "natural perspective" as can be obtained on a planar surface.[14] Examples are shown in figure 2.5.

If information for visual perception is to be found in the study of projections, it should now be clear that the study is a complex one.

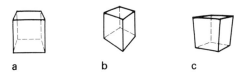

a   b   c

Figure 2.5
Three polar projections of a cube in (a) one-point perspective, (b) two-point perspective, and (c) three-point perspective. The cube in (a) also demonstrates Albertian perspective.

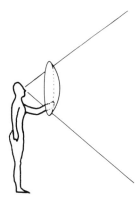

Figure 2.6
A spherical projection surface for measurement of visual angles in the optic array. I call this Leonardo's window.

The problem is the plethora of projections, each distorting an object in a different way. Fortunately, planar projections do not apply to everyday vision. The optic array is a spherical projection, and thus we need to consider its properties before comparing the perception of pictures, cinemas, and experimental stimuli with the perception of three-dimensional objects laid out in space.

The Optic Array and Its Measure

The central concept in vision is the *optic array*, the projection of the world presented to a single eye.[15] The optic array is a "flowing sea of energy, in which the organism is immersed, whose variations of order are mathematically analyzable" (Gibson 1959, p. 466). More concretely, it is the spherically projected, geometric pattern of ambient light around a station point, or point of observation. It necessitates a projection window of different shape than Alberti's. I call it Leonardo's window, after his analyses of natural perspective. As shown in figure 2.6, this projection surface is spherical rather than planar because no plane can intercept at right angles all projectors from all directions. The projection is also polar rather than parallel because projectors must converge; otherwise, only things the size of the eye's pupil could ever be seen at a given time. Finally, the optic array at a projection point need not have an eye placed there; it is completely objective and can be recorded with a camera, obscura or otherwise.

When an eye is placed at the projection point, the image on its receptors, called the *retinal image,* strongly corresponds to the optic array—rotated through 180° but otherwise nearly identical. Nevertheless, there are three important differences. First, the retinal image is incompletely spherical; movable eyes must be anchored in their sockets so that they can rotate. Those sockets, and the skulls from which they are composed, necessarily obliterate much of the array. Second, the retinal image suffers degradation because of imperfections in the cornea-lens system.[16] Third, and most important, there is motion on the retina with any eye movement. The retina moves *under* the optic array, causing global transformations in retinal coordinates but few changes in the optic array.[17]

Some Assumptions

To determine information about objects in the optic array, a researcher must make measurements that, in turn, are based on assumptions. These assumptions were made explicit by Todd (1984) and apply to my analysis as strongly as anywhere. First, light is reflected from all surfaces in all directions; there are no holes in the optic array from any vantage point. Second, the structure of the optic array can be described mathematically by solid angles intersecting a projection surface, which can also serve as information for the perceiver. Third, within any cross section of the optic array there are distinguishable units, called optic elements, between which angles are measured.[18] And fourth, the environment surrounding the point of observation is subject to physical constraints. The particular one of interest here is rigidity, a property of most objects and the ground. With these assumptions acknowledged, consider next the units of measurement.

Some Units

Useful units of the optic array are visual angles, arcs traced out on an imaginary spherical surface (or the not-so-imaginary retina). Throughout my discussions I measure these arcs in degrees. They could also be measured in radians, where those angles are divided by $360°/2\pi$ (57.29°), the curved length of the radius laid out on the circumference of the circle. But radians lack the common appeal of degrees, so I stick with the latter. Areas of projected surface—variously called the cross sections of bundles of rays, pencils of arc, cones of light, or visual pyramids—can be measured in *solid* visual angles. Such measures, however, are tricky. They take place not in the accustomed planar geometry but in spherical geometry,[19] measured in steradians, where 4π steradians equal a sphere. But because I do not need to measure the area of these solid angles, only their projected heights and widths, steradians are not needed.

The trigonometry of visual angles is as follows: If h is the total height (or width) of an object whose central flank is at right angles to the line of sight and d is the distance to the midpoint on the flank, the visual angle α subtended by that object is

$$\alpha = 2\arctan(h/2d). \tag{2.1}$$

For small objects, α is well approximated by $\arctan(h/d)$. (Here and later, *arctan* is the function *arctangent*.)

Rules of Thumb and Fist

Because units of visual angle, as yet, may have little intuitive appeal, consider a literal rule of thumb from Helmholtz (1868). If one's thumb-nail is, like mine, 1.4 cm across and if the distance from eye to thumbnail with one's arm fully extended is 56 cm, then the thumbnail subtends $2\arctan(1.4/112)$, or $1.4°$.[20] Thus the width of my thumb at arm's length, adding the fleshy surround, is about $2°$.

A rule of fist can be added to the rule of thumb. If one's fist, measured from the base knuckle of the small finger to the base knuckle of the index finger, is 7.8 cm wide, then it subtends about $8°$ of arc. When extended to include the fleshy parts on either side of the knuckles, excluding the thumb, the visual angle of the fist is about $10°$. Of course, arm lengths, hand widths, and thumb sizes vary, particularly across males and females, adults and children. Nonetheless, because relevant body proportions across people are nearly ratio scaled, these measures generally apply to all. With rules of thumb and fist in hand, we can set out to measure the visual world. This is precisely what Euclid set out to do.

From Euclidean to Ecological Optics

Twenty-three centuries ago, Euclid wrote his *Optics*. It is the earliest extant work on mathematical relations presented to the eye and is a straightforward application of geometry, given in his *Elements*. Like that work, *Optics* is replete with definitions, theorems, and proofs. This fact is important for philosophical reasons because it demonstrates the tenure of the relation between what is presented to the eye (and hence perceived) and physical space: Geometry is earth measure, and the eye is its fundamental measuring instrument. Euclid's juxtaposition of geometry and optics established perception as the basic route to knowing, an idea I consider in more detail in chapter 4. But here let me review what Euclid said, as translated by Burton (1945), the first English translation of *Optics*. (In what follows, parenthetical page numbers refer to Burton's translation.)

Euclid's Axioms

Optics begins with axioms (or definitions). These set out assumptions that we are familiar and comfortable with. The first and most important is the rectilinearity, or straightness, of light rays,[21] and the second is that rays of light between object and eye form a cone.[22] The third axiom concerns occlusion and interposition; objects that have rays connecting them directly to the eye are seen, but others are not. These three axioms have what Ronchi (1970) called "physicophysiological" content in that they deal primarily with the physical, more natural-science aspects of optics. The remainder have "physiopsychological" content and deal with facts relevant to perception.

The later axioms define relations among visual angles and form bases for discussion of layout. The fourth axiom is that, all other things being equal, those objects seen within larger visual angles appear larger, those within smaller appear smaller. The fifth axiom is that objects whose visual angles are higher off the ground plane appear higher, those lower appear lower; and the sixth axiom states that those things within visual angles to the left or right appear left or right, respectively. These three ideas set up the projective character of the optic array. The seventh axiom states that those "things seen within several angles appear to be more clear" (p. 357), where clarity is a correlate of the number of rays that exist within (or more concretely, the size of) all visual angles available.[23]

Euclid's Theorems

Following the axioms, Euclid made sixty statements with proofs about optic relations. Many appear quite modern, and they are eminently sensible in all the possible meanings of that word. Some are less relevant to optics than to the geometry of circles and other conic sections; others are redundant or symmetric to one another, but many are central to visual perception.

1. Thresholds. Euclid's third statement explains threshold detection: "Every object seen has a certain limit of distance, and when this is reached it is seen no longer" (p. 357). This is a straightforward application of the idea that, although lines and angles are infinitely divisible, the perception of size is not. Things phenomenally disappear when their visual angles get too small. Euclid also explained that blurring, an intermediate state between clarity and disappearance, is a natural phenomenon: "Rectangular objects, when seen from a distance, appear round" (p. 359). His proof was that the angles disappear before the sides because they are relatively smaller.[24]

2. *Constancies and the Convergence of Parallels.*   Interspersed among ideas about limits to perception are statements about convergence of parallel lines as they recede into the distance. Associated with these are discussions of relative size: "Objects of equal size unequally distant appear unequal and the one lying nearer to the eye always appears larger" (p. 358). There is a problem here and elsewhere as to what Euclid meant by the term translated as "appearance." It would seem that he emphasized the measure of objects in the optic array, rather than their perception. If this is true, then the problem of size constancy of objects is not directly addressed by Euclid. On the other hand, it is difficult to believe that he was unaware of size constancy simply from looking at his diagrams. His third to last statement is that "objects increased in size will appear to seem to approach the eye" (p. 372).

3. *Distortions.*   Euclid also discussed compression distortions in polar projection. For example, "If an arc of a circle is placed on the same plane as the eye, the arc appears to be a straight line" (p. 361), which is accompanied by a diagram showing all points on the arc equidistant from the eye. He also stated, "The wheels of the chariots appear sometimes as circular, sometimes distorted" (p. 367). And in related observations, "of a sphere seen in whatever way by one eye, less than a hemisphere is always seen" and "when the eye approaches the sphere, the part seen will be less, but will seem to be more" (p. 362). In this latter statement, Euclid noted that the observer will see, on approach, less and less of the spherical surface but that the visual angle subtended will become larger and larger.

4. *The Horizon and Motion Perspective.*   Most important to this work are Euclid's statements about information during locomotion. Several deal with the height of the eye above (or below) the ground plane (pp. 359–360):

> In the case of flat surfaces lying below the level of the eye, the more remote parts appear higher. . . . In the case of objects below the level of the eye which rise one above another, as the eye approaches the objects, the taller one appears to gain height, but

as the eye recedes, the shorter one appears to gain. . . . In the case
of objects of unequal size above the eye which rise one above the
other, as the eye approaches the objects, the shorter one appears
to gain height, but, as the eye recedes, the taller one appears to
gain.

Eye height and the horizon play important roles in the experiments
and discussion in later chapters. Euclid also discussed motion parallax
and motion perspective (pp. 370–371). If an observer moves through
the environment and looks generally ahead,

objects move at equal speed, and have their ends on the same side
of a straight line which is at right angles to their course, as they
advance toward a line drawn through the point where the eye is
located, which is parallel to the straight line before mentioned, the
one farther away from the eye will seem to be ahead of the nearer
one, but when they have passed (the direct line of vision), the one
that was in the lead will seem to follow, and the one that followed
will seem to be in the lead.

And, more simply with respect to looking to the side, "when objects
move at equal speed, those more remote seem to move more slowly."
Finally, perhaps Euclid's most blatantly psychological statement is about
induced motion: "If, when certain objects are moved, one is obviously
not moved, the object that is not moved will seem to move backward"
(p. 371).

Assessing Classical, Modern, and Ecological Optics
Euclid's work is a clear mix of what we now know as physics and
psychology. Classical optics changed with Alhazen, John Pecham, and
Roger Bacon. They replaced Euclid's psychology with more and more
systematic statements about physiology. The trend continued, and now
students almost never find any psychology in modern textbooks on
optics. Although more knowledge is always welcome, the loss of concern
over the original issues has not pleased all students of optics.[25] For
example, Ronchi (1958, p. 173) stated that:

Optics, properly understood, is not a part of physics, but the science
of vision. The process of vision contains three components: physical,
physiological, and psychological. The last of these is predominant,
because a universe full of rays, waves, and photons would be dark
and colorless in the absence of a living observer's mind. Without
mind there may be rays, waves, or photons; but there can be no
light. Hence light is not a physical phenomenon, and the study
of it does not belong to physics, whereas the study of rays, waves,

and photons does. This new way of viewing the subject of optics is applied to images, both virtual and real. These are mathematical or psychological entities, with nothing physical about them.

Thus there are three different approaches to optics: classical, of which Euclid is the best example; modern, typified by Hecht and Zajac (1974); and ecological, represented by Gibson. Classical optics is best summarized as a series of statements in three domains of study: mathematics (particularly geometry), the physical world (pyramids of light reflected off surfaces), and perception (relative size, motion parallax, and so forth). Modern optics, beginning with Alhazen, has also been primarily concerned with three domains, but they are slightly different: mathematics, physics (and increasingly with minutia, such as photons), and physiology (substituted for psychology).[26] Ecological optics reverts to the concerns of classical optics, away from photons and receptors toward geometry, layout, and perception.

Boynton (1974) may have been first to realize the similarity between classical and ecological optics and set as his task their comparison. He alleged two shortcomings of these approaches stemming from physiological optics. First, he suggested that the quality of the retinal image is always worse than predicted on the basis of geometry (see also Haber 1980), and that to ignore degradation of the image is to ignore inherent information loss. Second, he suggested that geometrical and ecological optics have nothing to say about intensity of light and that perception is vastly influenced by that variable.

I can recast Gibson's (1974) reply, which was weak, in the stronger terms of Euclid. First, in the third theorem of *Optics*, Euclid stated that, through threshold considerations and blurring of images, geometry and perception would diverge at the limits of acuity. Physiological optics explains this divergence in a rigorous way, but the elements of this fact have always been a part of classical optics and, by extension, of ecological optics as well. The retinal image is not a construct that is necessary in a psychological sense simply because it is a degraded form of the optic array. Second, although Euclid made no statement remotely suggesting that illumination is important, he obviously assumed daylight conditions, which are well above threshold for detection of light. Gibson (1960a, 1961) also made this assumption, and it seems fully warranted if we are concerned with how perception serves everyday activity. Thus Boynton's remarks were in the first case wide of the mark and in the second not directly relevant to the task that ecological optics has set for itself. Boynton's position seems based on the common confusion between information and energy and on a set-theoretic pun on the word *in*: Information is *in* the light, light is measured *in* quanta, but it does not follow that information is *in* quanta. Information is spread out across patterns of quanta typically so far above threshold that their individual registration does not constrain discussions of normal perception.

"Ecological optics" is the term that Gibson (1961, 1979) gave to the study of environmental information for vision. Unsatisfied with optics proper, he borrowed the term *ecological* from Brunswik (1956), who in turn had borrowed it from Lewin (1943). Put simply (Gibson 1966, pp. 221–222), ecological optics "purports to be a new basis for a science of vision, put together from parts of physical optics, illumination engineering, ecology, and perspective geometry." There is no question that Gibson went beyond Euclid, but I contend that it was in the same direction and with the essentially same goal in mind: describing geometric relations in the optic array. Photometric concerns—particularly those of shading and illumination—were important additions by Gibson and more recently by many researchers in artificial intelligence, but their main contribution is to aid the understanding of the observer's environment.

Overview

Pictures are planar projections of a three-dimensional environment, and these planar projections come in many kinds. Distortions perfuse all, and Leonardo da Vinci decried the problems of linear perspective in representing natural scenes. Polar projections onto a plane are most like natural perspective when constrained in appropriate ways, but they are still not like the optic array. The optic array is a spherical projection and is the central concept in the analysis of visual information. It is my task, and that of others, to measure projections of objects in the optic array in search of information that perceivers might use.

Euclid's work demonstrates that classical optics was scaled to the viewer, but as optics became sophisticated through the Middle Ages, the Renaissance, and beyond, interest in perception dropped out. Ecological optics is not so much a new field as a rekindling of interest in an old one. Euclid was on the right track; extension of his views begins to make a theory of perception tractable and builds our understanding of the perception of objects laid out in space.

3

Pictures

The studies of projections and optics intersect in two areas: perception of the environment and perception of representational pictures. Although the former is the major focus of this book, the latter raises important issues. The psychology of picture perception is also a fertile ground for assessing adequacy of general theories of perception, and in this chapter I touch on these. The central reason for this digression, however, is pragmatic. In the experiments described in later chapters, images are presented to viewers on a computer-driven display. These stimuli are pictures—flat cinematic images. Because I plan to make theoretical statements about the perception of the real world on the basis of perception of computer-generated moving images, I must consider the relation between the two. Let me begin with an overview of some theoretical views of picture perception.

Approaches to Picture Perception

Nearly all who have contributed to perceptual theory agree that photographs are special cases in which the optic array is truncated and frozen in cross section. They disagree, however, when it comes to projection surfaces, and it is here that the divergence of thoughts on perspective begins. Some of the issues were forecast by Jacques Rivière, who in 1912 (Fry 1966, p. 77) wrote:

> Perspective is as accidental as lighting. It is the sign, not of a particular moment in time, but of a particular position in space. It indicates not the situation of objects, but the situation of the spectator.

Is perspective really accidental? Does it not reveal the layout of objects? And if not, how does it reveal the place of the observer?

Conventions

One school, generally composed of artists and art historians, suggests that the devices used to represent depth in paintings are fabrications of culture. They are *conventional representations*. Panofsky presented this view in 1926. Concerned with the difference in projection surfaces, he noted that "the eye actually projects not on a plane but on the inner surface of a sphere" (Carrier 1980, p. 286). He reasoned further that, because the projections of art are planar, they are a result of cultural convenience and convention. Since Panofsky, many have shared this view. Its force is captured by Goodman (1968, p. 33), who told a story about Picasso and his depiction of Gertrude Stein. On hearing a complaint that the portrait did not look like the subject, Picasso replied, "No matter; it will."[1] Goodman, however, was more careful than this quote might first appear. His intent was to pursue Panofsky's lead concerning projection surfaces. Goodman suggested that we have become acculturated to planar projection, where that plane is held vertically. This convention creates the optic facts of converging railroad tracks and parallel vertical poles. But Goodman (1968, p. 16) noted:

> The rules of pictorial perspective no more follow from the laws of optics than would rules calling for drawing the tracks parallel and the poles converging.

Thus, when a low-flying aerial photographer takes pictures of a local terrain, railroad tracks would remain parallel and telephone poles converge. Convergence of certain parallels but not of others is as "accidental" as Rivière suggested.

Despite these facts, I find the choice of the word *convention* unfortunate. It can mean too many things. The roots of the word connote a *contract*. Applied to the perception of paintings, the contract must be between painter and perceiver, with emphasis placed on the relative arbitrariness of the conventions, as if any artistic group could decide on any tools of depiction, provided that percipients of art agreed to their efficacy.[2] I suggest that constraints on such contracts seem far too loose for picture perception to work as well as it does, and following long tradition I suggest that the idea of conventions is incomplete at best.[3] Devices for depiction are conventional only insofar as their bases are *not* in optics. Put another way, the ultimate contractor is the evolution of the human visual system. Linear perspective, even with a conventionally held vertical plane, is intimately tied to optics.

Surrogates

Gibson (1954b) suggested that the success of representative pictures lay in *surrogates* to the optic array that capture Rivière's "accidents" at a particular place and time. Surrogates come in two varieties, conventional and nonconventional, the latter of which are the most critical to realistic pictures. These are the sources of information in the picture that mimic those in the optic array. Gibson proposed that the similarity relation between the representing (the surrogate) and the represented (the optic array) be called *fidelity*.[4] Some artworks have greater fidelity to the optic array than others, but none are identical to it. Pictures represent many, but never all, characteristics presented to a single eye. For example, in photography and in film, in which fidelity is greatest, the range of reflectance values are orders of magnitude less than that found around us during the day. In paintings the reflectance constraint is even greater (Hochberg 1978a).

Helmholtz (1871) and Hochberg (1979) explained how some surrogates work. One is in *chiaroscuro*, a sixteenth-century technique that uses subtle gradations of shading to enhance contrast. In particular, regions of a painting or woodcut that should have the same reflectance are often given widely differing values to make adjacent and contrasting areas appear darker or lighter. Chiaroscuro is not a tool for fidelity but a method to enhance what cannot be captured in etching, ink, or paint. Nevertheless, such shading is not conventional; it takes advantage of a perceptual phenomenon, the Craik-O'Brien illusion (Cornsweet 1970), in which smooth gradations of reflectance are seen as a uniform field. Thus the artist can fool the eye of the observer over a section of canvas by gradually changing image intensity where no such change would occur in the optic array. More generally, surrogates have theoretical importance for perception when they take on a new name—cues. But I find the term "cue," like the term "convention," unfortunate. It has implications that go against the theoretical perspective that I wish to present. These implications concern the trustworthiness of optic information; I return to them at the end of this chapter.

Mental Constructions

How the perceiver deals with surrogates in pictures has caused much controversy.[5] One idea from Helmholtz (1871) is easily allied to the sense data approach of philosophy. It is perhaps best represented in art by Gombrich (1960) and has been called a *constructivist* approach. Here, emphasis is placed on cognitive elaboration of pictorial surrogates and the development of schemata for picture perception.[6] Those taking this approach believe that we learn to perceive cues in the image for the purpose of composing an internal representation of the depicted scene. Stripped bare, this process must entail two types of associations; First, cues (surrogates) are associated with (have some probabalistic connection to) properties of the real world as they are reflected in the optic array; second, those elements are associated (through habit strength or the like) such that they compose a whole scene. I find the latter idea curious, but it is not unique to picture perception. It can be found in many accounts, from Mill (1843) to Wallach (1976b) and Rock (1983). The former idea, however, is the most intriguing. It suggests at least two stages in perceptual learning. At first, those who have no experience with pictures should be baffled by them, seeing them as two-dimensional surfaces with odd marks; then with practice they should come to see pictures as representing objects in a three-dimensional world. The developmental evidence in favor of this sequence is quite unconvincing. In fact, if anything, the evidence supports the opposite view. I consider that evidence in the next section, but from it Haber (1979, 1980) suggested that children have little difficulty in treating pictures as revealing objects in depth. On the contrary, they have early difficulty in treating pictures as two-dimensional objects.

Theories of picture perception in broad sweep are not directly relevant to the discussions of motion in the optic array. Central issues of caricature and abstract (nonrepresentational) art are beyond my scope. One issue of depiction, however, is central to representational images on computer-driven displays.

La Gournerie's Paradox

Perspective, from its roots, means "to look through." It is only a small step, then, to consider perspective as the view through Alberti's window into the real world. *Linear perspective* is the technique, developed by Brunelleschi and codified by Alberti, for portrayal of objects receding in depth to a vanishing point. It is a polar, planar projection meant to be viewed such that the vanishing point is at the same height as the eye (Edgerton 1975). Lines radiate from the pole at the horizon, forming a pyramid of rays. The obvious question is: How does Brunelleschi's pole at the horizon relate to Euclid's pole at the eye? In some sense, they are at opposite ends of the visual world. The answer can be conceived of in two ways, one as a demonstration with mirrors and the other as an analysis in projective geometry.

In the mirror demonstration, conceived by Brunelleschi (Edgerton 1975), a drawing is made on a flat surface in one-point perspective, and a hole is drilled through the vanishing point. Next the observer holds the drawing and a mirror such that they are parallel, with the drawing closer.[7] The observer looks through the hole from the *back* of the drawing at the mirror and sees the reflected surface in it. What is seen is *exactly* the same, except mirror reversed, as if one were looking at the drawing from the front at twice the distance between the mirror and image. The importance is that in this demonstration the eye and vanishing point are in the same location, not a virtual world apart.

Thus there is something similar about Euclid's cone of light and Brunelleschi's convergence of rays.

The geometric explanation of Brunelleschi's experiment concerns the projective nature of parallel lines and the relation of the image plane to lines of sight. When the painting is constructed to be viewed as an orthogonal cross section of the optic array, the eye should be aligned with the perpendicular to the picture surface at the location of the vanishing point. Thus the vanishing point and the station point are not really the same; they are simply opposite ends of the centric ray, sometimes called the "prince of rays." When the eye is not there, the geometry of the depicted space is distorted.

Linear Perspective from the Wrong Station Point

The crux of Brunelleschi's experiment is that the eye is fixed in one position. The hole in the back of the picture constrains the viewpoint, making lateral excursions impossible. Appropriate placement of the parallel mirror at half an arm's length ensures the correct perspective if the image is originally constructed at arm's length from the station point, a convenient distance from which to paint.

When viewing most pictures, however, eye position is not fixed. Indeed, gallery folk wander about and look at pictures from many different locales. The paradox is that linear perspective is mathematically correct for only one station point,[8] yet almost any position generally in front of a picture will do for the layout in the picture to seem relatively undisturbed. This phenomenon is fortunate, for without it the utility of pictures would be vanishingly small. But it is unpredicted by the theory of perspective drawing. This paradox was first discussed by La Gournerie in 1859 (Pirenne 1970, 1975). In what follows I call it *La Gournerie's paradox*; Kubovy (1986) calls it the robustness of perspective. It is useful to discuss the paradox in two forms: The first concerns viewing pictures along the centric ray but at a distance either nearer or farther than the proper station point; the second and more interesting concerns viewing pictures from the side.

To consider such distortions, we must reconstruct the geometry of pictured (or virtual) space on the premise that the image is, like Alberti's window, invisible and that observers look through it to make sense of the depicted world.[9] The possible transformations of viewing position are along the z axis and along the x or y axis. The former creates a collapse (or expansion) in depth; the latter causes shear or twisting of the depth axis against the frontoparallel plane. Observer movements that generate collapse are called *normal displacements* because they occur along the surface normal, or perpendicular, to the picture plane; those generating shear are *parallel displacements*, occurring parallel to

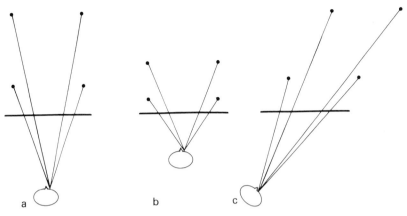

Figure 3.1
The distortions of virtual space in a picture. (a) Four points in the environment projected onto an image plane, a situation that mimics a photograph. (b) Compression transformations in pictured space caused by an observer moved closer to the image plane than the proper station point. (c) Affine shear of virtual space caused by lateral displacement of the observer. The xz planes are thus affine transformed; the xy planes stacked in depth are perspective transformed.

the image plane. Both are *affine transformations*. They preserve collinearities among points but do not preserve most distances or, most particularly, many angles. All possible viewpoints of a pictured surface are additive combinations of collapse and shear of the virtual space.

In figure 3.1a four points are projected onto the image plane as might be seen in a large photograph. When the observer moves closer to the image, undergoing normal displacement (as shown in figure 3.1b), the projected points stay in the same physical locations on the image, but the correct geometry in the virtual environment must change. Notice that the distance between the front and back surfaces is relatively compressed, a collapse of depth like that found when looking through a telephoto lens. The effects of parallel displacements of the observer on virtual space are shown in figure 3.1c. The same arrangement of image points is shown, with the observer moving to the side. If the image represents the virtual environment behind it, that space must change. In particular, points shift over by differing amounts. Parallel lines remain parallel but right angles change into acute and obtuse angles. This result is related to the oft-noted effect in portraiture, where if the portrayed subject appears to look out at the observer when he or she is in front of the painting, the subject also appears to follow the observer around the room.[10]

Pirenne's (1970, p. 99) account of the perception of a picture viewed from the side is in sympathy with Helmholtz.[11] When the surface characteristics of a picture can be seen or when binocular disparities grade uniformly across the surface,

> an unconscious intuitive process of psychological compensation takes place, which restores the correct view when the picture is looked at from the wrong position.

Overall, Pirenne's notion and that of others (Green 1983, Kubovy 1986) suggests that unconscious inference unpacks the deformations through some process akin to mental rotation.[12] What is most interesting to me, however, is that compression and shear in the depicted environment are not normally acknowledged by the observer. Within broad limits, affine transformations seem to preserve most of the character of most objects to a satisfactory degree. What we need, however, are assessments that address this issue.

Static Displays
Empirical investigations of La Gournerie's paradox are relatively few. Consider first those relevant to viewing pictures at right angles but at different station points along the picture normal. Adams (1972), for example, presented perspective line drawings of tiled floors to observers who viewed them from one, two, and four feet with either one or two eyes. The amount of depth imputed to the displays varied appropriately with viewing distance, but in all cases depth was underestimated. One reason for this underestimation, however, may be the fact that accommodation and convergence (weak information sources for depth) are effective within this range. The major point to be emphasized, however, is that the extent of virtual space is always a function of viewing distance.

Similarly, Hagen and Elliott (1976) presented line drawings of geometric figures to perceivers in polar perspective appropriate for their viewpoint, in parallel projection, or in between (closer than infinity but farther than normal viewing). All images were normalized to the same physical size and mounted on poster board. Hagen and Elliott asked viewers to indicate which version among paired comparisons looked more like an "accurate drawing" or a "realistic picture." Surprising to me is that their viewers generally preferred the images in parallel projection. Hagen and Elliott called this the "zoom effect," where the results appear to indicate that observers, when looking at pictures, would rather have them taken with a telephoto (zoomed) lens than with a normal one. This, they claimed, makes the image most neutral with respect to the station point and, somehow, best serves when the image's flat surface is perceivable. Some are critical of Hagen and Elliott's work,[13] but, possible qualms aside, an important point

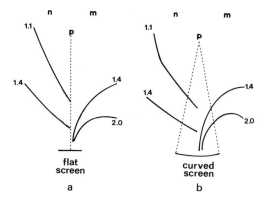

Figure 3.2
Isodeformation contours proposed by Meister (1966) for (a) flat and (b) curved cinema projection screens. Index *n*, on the left-hand side of each panel, measures static distortions; index *m*, on the right-hand side of each, measures distortions resulting from motion. Both *n* and *m* are based on affine transformations causing compression in the width of an image.

remains: There is something perceptually right but logically wrong about parallel projection.

Viewing pictures from the side has an equally interesting set of analyses and results. Meister (1966, p. 179), for example, suggested that in every cinema auditorium, there

> will be an area of viewing in which the distortions are not noticeable; another area in which distortions are noticeable but tolerated; and finally, a third area in which the distortions will not be tolerated.

Meister then analyzed the distortions of images projected onto flat and curved screens when viewers sit at various places in an auditorium. Consider flat screens first. Because by Leonardo's analysis distortions are greatest at the edge of a planar projection, Meister's metric *n* denotes the maximum affine distortion at the far edge of a screen from any viewpoint. Thus, if a viewer sits down front and to the right, distortions of the left edge of the screen are measured. The metric is similar to the foreshortening ratio in axonometric projection: It is the visual angle for the width of an image seen from a point along the normal to the edge of the screen divided by the angle of that image when seen from any other equidistant point. Static isodeformation contours for a flat screen are shown in figure 3.2a. A similar calculation is used for curved screens, and the results are shown in figure 3.2b. Although no empirical data are reported, Meister suggested that distortions are not noticed when *n* is equal to or less than 1.1, tolerable when *n* is less than 1.4, and intolerable when n is 1.4 or more. From figure 3.2 these estimates seem sensible, if somewhat conservative, and they are generally supported by experimental results.

Perkins (1972), for example, showed that rectangular and nonrectangular parallelepipeds (boxes with parallelograms for sides) can be discriminated accurately when line drawings of them are seen in full face (90° to the picture plane). Moreover, when viewed from 41°, he found that discrimination judgments are no less accurate but that performance deteriorates considerably when that angle is 26° (Perkins 1973, 1982, 1983). In the latter case but not the former, performance was clearly influenced by distortions in virtual space. Elaborating this scheme, Hagen (1976) showed slanted pictures to children and adults. Her results show that size judgments are unaffected in slanted pictures and that the results hold for both adults and children.[14] Together, these results suggest that affine- and perspective-transformed information in slanted pictures may be as easy to pick up as untransformed information in the optic array. They can also be taken as indicating a certain tolerance of the visual system for plastic deformations, a topic in chapters 4 and 7.

Dynamic Displays
Little experimentation relevant to La Gournerie's paradox has been conducted with dynamic stimuli, a situation bemoaned by Hochberg and Brooks (1978) and by Haber (1983c). We are probably all familiar with sitting near the front and side of a movie theater but fully enjoying what is displayed. We often do not notice that the virtual space is collapsed in depth along the z axis and that objects in virtual space behave as if they were nonrigid when undergoing rotation and translation.

Braunstein (1962, 1976) investigated the perception of coherence (rigidity) and depth in dynamic displays. Viewers were presented with displays in parallel projection and in three degrees of polar perspective, where the computed station point was 2-, 4-, and 16-stimulus radii from the object. Most interesting was the fact that with higher perspectives (that is, with the station point closer to the rotating dots), the object appeared more depthlike, but that with lower perspectives, it appeared more rigid. These results support Hagen and Elliott's "zoom effect," generalized to dynamic displays. In order to perceive rigid objects, parallel projection may be preferred when information about the display surface is salient (typically from stereopsis). In movie theaters, however, the distance to the screen is much greater and stereoscopic differences much diminished.

Meister (1966) also investigated distortions for moving objects on flat and curved projection screens. A new index was calculated for the image of an object moving across the screen; m is the ratio of the visual angles of the image width at the near versus the far edge. The m values for planar and curved screens are also given in figure 3.2. Again, no empirical data are reported, but Meister suggested that at values below 1.4 distortions are not noticed; values between 1.4 and 2.0 produce tolerable distortions, and values above 2.0 produce intolerable distortions. These isodeformation contours curve away from the screen in an odd manner, but they may properly reflect esthetic judgments. Nevertheless, Gibson's (1947) motion picture testing data give no support for such contours. Gibson's study showed no diminution of perceptual abilities for viewing cinema clips far off the midline of the theater.

La Gournerie's paradox is important if we are to understand the effectiveness of cinema—distortions may or may not be less disruptive than those for static pictures. Such effects must be better understood if we are to have a coherent theory of visual perception. One resolution of the paradox is to suggest that there may be invariants preserved in dynamic affine-transformed images and that perception uses these invariants. Such a sketch, however, does not solve the problem. We must discover what these invariants are and determine if and how they are used. The four experiments in chapter 7 are devoted to this pursuit.

Perception and Cues

More important to perceptual theory than La Gournerie's paradox is the concept of cues. This notion is quite old and has almost always been used in the discussion of the perception of layout in pictures. The term *cue* derives from sixteenth-century theater documentation. It was the abbreviation q for the Latin *quando*, meaning "when." It was used in a script as a prompt for an actor in the performance of actions. It was a single bit but entailed other information only hinted at. The cue was a coded signal, or symbol, and only the well-informed could decode it. It demanded a store of knowledge on which to act. By analogy, cues to perception are coded, nonspecific sources of information associated through learning with the layout of objects in depth.[15]

To discuss cues to perception is to accept perception as an inferential process that proceeds from impoverished information. As in theater, a cue signals the perceptual system to do something, to carry out a process that is well learned and prestored. Cues for depth are thought to hint at the layout of objects, from which it was thought that the perceptual system might make systematic inferences, performing some

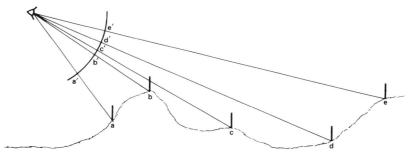

Figure 3.3
The height of the base of an object on the projection surface, in this case Leonardo's
window, within a vertical column of the optic array yields perfect ordinal correlation
with distances in the environment.

calculation or remembering some relation from experience. In this manner, the cue concept handily fits that of sense data. Cues are thought
to have some probabilistic value between 0.0 and 1.0, but generally
not at the certain extremes (Brunswik 1956, Gibson 1957b). Guarded
inferences about distal stimuli, it was thought, must be based on the
relative trustworthiness, or cue value, of proximal information.

It turns out that these inferences for perception, or whatever they
are called, need not be so guarded. Indeed, many cues to layout of
objects in depth are hardly subtle: They hammer home to the perceiver
certain relations among objects in the visual world. They *specify* certain
aspects of what is perceived, and they allow for few, and at most times
no, alternatives. Under many circumstances there is a one-to-one mapping between what is displayed in the optic array and the physical
relations among the objects and observer. Consider two so-called cues
to the perception of the layout of objects in depth. ,

Two "Cues" to Layout in Depth
One source of information about layout comes from Euclid: *height in
the projection plane.* If we consider Alberti's window and the projections
of those objects on it, then we have a situation like that shown in figure
3.3. Because an observer's eye is always some distance above the surface
of support and because almost all objects in the real world are planted
firmly on that surface of support, the angle at the eye between the
horizon and the base of an object on the ground is always smaller the
farther it is from the observer. In other words, this cue is really an
invariant, an ordered relation between distance in the environment
and height in the plane (below the horizon). It is a trustworthy source
of information perceivers use (see, for example, Dunn et al 1965). The

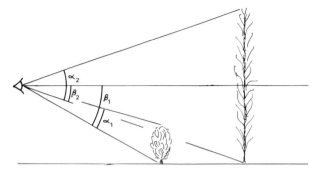

Figure 3.4
The angular height of the projected image of an object divided by the angle of its base to the horizon can be used to judge its height relative to the observer. The bush is marginally less than half the eye height because α_1 is exactly half β_1; the height of the tree is exactly twice the eye height of the observer since α_2 is twice β_2.

world simply comes furnished this way, and this law of optics is seldom controverted.

A second source of information is the *horizon ratio*, first implied by Euclid, discussed by Gibson (1947, 1950), and worked out in detail by Sedgwick (1973, 1983). The horizon ratio compares the height of objects in the environment to the height of the observer's eye. The basis of the calculation is that the horizon is functionally at an infinite distance.[16] It follows, then, that horizon and eye are at the same height, a fact Edgerton (1975) called *horizon-line isocephaly*. The horizon ratio works as shown in figure 3.4. Because the line from eye to horizon can be considered parallel to the ground plane, any point on any object that intersects the line of sight to the horizon is exactly one eye height above the ground. Thus, if the top of a bush is the same height as the horizon, that bush is as tall as the observer's eye is above the ground. If the top of the bush does not come up to the horizon, it is shorter, and if it goes above the horizon, it is taller. What is useful about this formulation is that certain metric information is roughly preserved. If the height of an object is equal to the angle from the top of the object to the horizon, then that object is 0.5 eye height tall. If, on the other hand, the portion of the object that projects above the horizon is equal to that portion below, then it is two eye heights tall. This information is precisely what makes the horizon ratio useful in scaling the environment.

Overview

Pictures inform us about objects and events in our environment. The fact that the visual system seems to accommodate picture slants and other distortions suggests either that cognition rectifies the affine changes of virtual space, as Pirenne suggested, or that such distortions are not noticed to the degree that we might expect. The former view suggests that we must be acutely attuned to orthogonal dimensions in real space and modify our perceptions of virtual objects in slanted pictures, whereas the latter entails neither. Although little that will be presented later hangs on a decision between the two, my bet is on the latter. I suspect that we are more concerned with satisfying betweenness than with preserving right angles and right corners.

The final discussion compared the notions of cues and specification. Embedded in this distinction are several important philosophical and theoretical issues. The most important is the relationship between information and objects: Information can either hint at an attribute of an object or specify it. I take the latter view, which is bound in the idea of invariants for perception, the topic of chapter 5. I discuss cues again in later chapters. Those cues not tied to relations among projected elements in the optic array I call nonrelational cues. But let me now turn from a discussion of pictures and pictorial space to a discussion of real space and its philosophical underpinnings.

4
Space

Projections and photographs must have something "behind" them—objects laid out in space. In this chapter I discuss various epistemological views of three-dimensional layout and its perception. These divide three ways. The first view is a set of philosophical issues relating space, perception, and geometry; the second is what I regard as the misuse of certain facts of optic projections to build theories of visual perception; and the third is a sidelight on non-Euclidean geometries and perception.

Antinomies of Space, Perception, and Geometry

Space has almost always been considered an abstract container into which the physical objects of the world are poured. In *Timaeus*, Plato presented an early version of this idea (Jowett 1952, p. 457):

> Wherefore, the mother and receptacle of all created, visible, and in any way sensible things, is not to be termed earth or air, or fire, or water, or any of their compounds, or any of the elements from which these are derived, but is an invisible and formless being which receives all things, and in some mysterious way partakes of the intelligible, and is most incomprehensible.

The view creaks with age, but its stated relation of space to objects is not only acceptable but also essential. Plato provided no basis for the unfortunate but common phrases of "space perception" and "depth perception." That is, we cannot perceive space, only the objects in space. Similarly, because depth is but one dimension arbitrarily picked out of the dimensions of space, we cannot perceive depth, only objects laid out in depth.

Plato's views led to many issues that taxed later philosophers. Some that caused particular concern were place versus space, where the former delimits the boundaries of an object in the latter; extension, the way in which matter occupies space; vacuum, what happens to space when no matter is present; impenetrability, the fact that two entities of the same kind cannot occupy the same space;[1] and the relation between physical space and mathematical space. It is only the last of these that I pursue. In the many ways in which space, perception, and geometry interrelate, there is a set of inherent antinomies, or paradoxes, that stem from a series of premises:

1. Geometry is about space.
2. Geometry ("earth measure") governs relations among physical objects.
3. Geometry is among the most trustworthy bodies of knowledge.
4. Space is known through the layout of objects we perceive.
5. Perception is untrustworthy.

For the purposes of this discussion the major paradox of the group is found in the juxtaposition of statements 1, 4, and 5: It seems odd that our perception of objects in space can be both infirm and a basis for a branch of mathematics. Broader than this antinomy, however, are the puzzles broached by the whole set. Their enormity has engaged philosophers steadily for the last four centuries.

Most philosophers agree that the integrity of statements 1 and 3 is to be preserved at all costs. There have been several solutions to paradoxes that have arisen concerning the relations of statements 1 and 3 to the other statements. I discuss them in more detail later, but in précis, consider two. The first decouples statements 1 and 2: Physical space and mathematical space are not the same and should not be confused. This view is older than the existence of non-Euclidean geometries and has a certain appeal. Nevertheless, it denies some important history. We should not forget that Euclid's *Elements* was the generalization of the layout of objects in physical space (Hempel 1945). A second solution is to falsify statement 4, suggesting that space is an a priori, purely Platonic entity. On this view, our perceptions of objects in space usually corroborate our intuitions about space, but they do not establish them. This notion makes some sense, and because it removes perception as a direct foundation for space (statement 4), it removes it as an indirect foundation for geometry. But his solution raises a question about statement 5 that is rarely asked: Why is perception considered so untrustworthy? If perception corroborates intuitions of space and if space is mathematically specifiable, how could perception be so infirm? One answer is simply that it is not.[2] Error in perception, it seems to me, has been overemphasized. This view was perhaps first espoused by Reid (1785, pp. 199–200):

> Complaints of the fallacy of the senses have been very common in ancient and in modern times, especially among the philosophers.

If we should take for granted all they have said on this subject, the natural conclusion from it might seem to be, that the senses are given to us by some malignant demon on purpose to delude us, rather than that they are formed by the wise and beneficent Author of nature, to give us true information of things necessary to our preservation and happiness.

With Reid, and in line with the Epicurean school of ancient Greece, I claim that a span of continuous perception accrued over time with motion and movement is a bedrock on which we can build anything, on which evolution can continue and societies develop. For centuries that bedrock was conceived as natural geometry.

Natural Geometry from Kepler to Kant
The term *natural geometry* was first used by Kepler in 1604. The only psychological remnant handed down from Euclid's *Optics*, natural geometry is an internal "distance measuring triangle" used to compute distance and size of an object (Maull 1980, p. 36). Elaborated somewhat, natural geometry suggests that mental space and, to extend the idea even further, mental transformations have many of the features of physical space and physical transformations—an idea popular today.[3] Kepler's notion, however, attracted less attention than it might have. It was only with Descartes and his *Dioptrics* of 1637 (Anscombe and Geach 1954) that the concept aroused interest in how spatial relations are perceived. For Descartes, natural geometry was not about space itself but was an innate psychological algorithm (Epstein 1977), even a mechanism for unconscious inference.[4]

In espousing the idea of natural geometry, Descartes was most concerned with the inversion of the retinal image, noted earlier by Leonardo and Kepler, and with the different projections to the two eyes. Nevertheless, the recovery of spatial relations in the environment was central to his wishes. Natural geometry was a means by which the mind could interpret spatial relations, meshing perceived and physical space. It was as if, according to Descartes and going somewhat beyond him, the mind used rules of projection to recover relations among objects projected on the retina. How these rules were used and what they might be was never made clear.

Descartes's position was roundly criticized by Berkeley in his *Essay towards a New Theory of Vision*. Berkeley argued that natural geometry was a spurious conflation of math and nature (1709, para. 14):

Those *lines* and *angles* have no real existence in nature, being only an hypothesis framed by mathematicians, and by them introduced into *optics*, that they might treat of that science in a *geometrical* way.

Berkeley also claimed that any idea that was not itself experienced, such as natural geometry, could not be used as the means of perceiving any other idea. This second retort seems archaic and unconvincing today, but his first struck deep at the foundations of geometry.[5] Gradually, it became clear that something was desperately wrong with statements 1 through 4. Berkeley was among the first since Plato to suggest a form of statement 5, that visual perception is infirm.

These ideas generally festered until Kant. For Kant, human experience of the world is largely constructed by an active mind. He said little about how we perceive objects in space, but his ideas were central to all later thought: Space is transcendental, the first principle of our perceivable world; it is subjective and ideal, continuous and undelimited, arising not through algorithm but preexisting as a framework into which the layout of objects in physical space is fit. His basic tenet was a response to Berkeley's first criticism of Descartes; he removed geometry from the experiential realm. Geometry became an odd hybrid, both synthetic and a priori. It was synthetic in that it brought together new notions that did not simply result from logical analysis, and it was a priori (or prior to perceptual experience) because it would not be trustworthy otherwise. Following Berkeley, Kant placed geometry in the domain not of the physical but of the mental, where proof and obviousness rule rather than measurement. Nonetheless, geometric relations in the world are real. In fact, following Euclid, Kant was quick to add in his address of 1770 that "the laws of sensuality [perception] will be the laws of nature *so far as it can be perceived by our senses*" (Eckoff 1970, p. 66).

After Kant, the concept of natural geometry fell on hard times. Its decline was unfortunate for the study of perception. Left unexplicated was the problem recognized by Descartes but swept aside by Kant: How do we know the layout of objects in space from the information given on our retinas? Space may be a priori, but layout is not. The fall of natural geometry was made even more precipitous in the nineteenth century with the discovery of non-Euclidean geometries. These new systems drove stronger wedges between statements 1 and 2. Seemingly horrible questions arose: Is perception so untrustworthy, as suggested in statement 5, that it cannot be used to decide the nature of physical space? Cannot perception at least corroborate geometry, in a weakened version of statement 4?

Physical Space and Non-Euclidean Space

In the nineteenth century, alternative geometries were discovered.[6] These substituted for Euclid's fifth (or parallel) axiom a different one, starting with a line and a point not on it. These geometries allow either more than one straight line through the point parallel to the first line (Lobachevskian) or no parallel lines through it (Riemannian). Another way to consider them is with regard to the sums of the angles of a triangle: In Euclidean geometry the angles always sum to 180°, but in Lobachevskian geometry they always sum to less, and in Riemannian geometry, to more. The degree to which a particular non-Euclidean geometry deviates from this value is a measure of its curvature.

Kline (1980) attributed the fall of mathematics from a central position in Western epistemology to these discoveries. It is easy to imagine the enormous stir, within and without mathematics, created by the plurality of geometries. From within, this stir was exemplified by Gauss, who began to question statement 3 (but not statement 2) as early as 1817 (Torretti 1978, p. 55):

> Maybe in another life we shall attain insights into the essence of space which are now beyond our reach. Until then we should class geometry not with arithmetic, which stands purely a priori, but, say, with mechanics.

Gauss worried extensively about the implications of these new geometries. In a letter to a fellow mathematician, he wrote (Daniels 1974, p. 21):

> Exactly in the impossibility of deciding *a priori* between ... Euclidean geometry ... and S [Bolyai's, and later Lobachevski's, geometry] lies the clearest proof that Kant was wrong to maintain that [physical] space is only the form of our intuition.

Because of this affront to Kant, Gauss encouraged mathematicians to keep their geometry-shattering discoveries in low profile until foundations were secured.[7] He feared most the "uproar of the Boeotians" (Torretti 1978), in reference to the loose confederation of outsiders that threatened Athens and Sparta before Alexander the Great. The Boeotians were quiet for nearly fifty years, but eventually they did roar.

Not surprisingly, psychologists and philosophers roared most. Wundt, for one, was furious. Appealing to statements 1, 2, and 4, he suggested in his *Logik* (Torretti 1978, p. 292) that

> the order of the objects of the real world according to the laws of our three-dimensional flat geometry ... is the factual expression of the real order of phemomena, which cannot, as such, be replaced by any other order.

Lotze (1878, p. 276), for another, was more curt. He thought these new geometries were "one huge coherent error." And Frege (1884, p. 20e), unwilling to give up any of the first four statements, attacked the nonintuitability of these new geometries:

> Empirical propositions hold good of what is physically or psychologically existent, the truths of [Euclidean] geometry govern all that is spatially intuitable, whether existent or product of our fancy. The wildest visions of delirium, the boldest inventions of legend or poetry . . . remain, so long as they remain intuitable, still subject to the axioms of geometry. Conceptual thought can after a fashion shake off their yoke, when it postulates, say, a space of four dimensions or of positive curvature. To study such conceptions is not useless by any means; but it is to leave the ground of intuition entirely behind. If we do make use of intuition even here, as an aid, it is still the same old intuition of Euclidean space, the only space of which we can have any picture.

Others were more careful, seeing that the philosophy of perception, space, and geometry must change. For example, Helmholtz (1870, 1878b) became interested in the general nature of our knowledge about space and particularly in the extent to which the axioms of geometry have empirical reference. Like Gauss, he realized that Kant's conception of space was three dimensional and Euclidean. To Helmholtz it seemed unlikely that all mathematical spaces could be a priori, so he made three suggestions. First, contrary to Frege, he stated that all the new geometries were conceivable and imaginable by the mere fact that they had been formulated. Thus no geometry could be truer than another either as a closed system of postulates or as a reflection of intuitive space. Second, on the basis of personal experience, it was not possible to determine which geometry best reflected the *physical* space of our world. If space is infinitely extended, has only three dimensions, and has a constant curvature of zero, then no geometry but that of Euclid is true for the physical world. But if the space were sufficiently curved, then, Helmholtz (1878a, p. 403) stated:

> As an exponent of the empirical theory of perception, I believe that anyone, in passing from Euclidean to pseudospherical space, would at first believe that he saw apparent movements of the objects around him but that very soon he would learn to adjust his judgments of spatial relations to the new conditions.

Third, Helmholtz suggested that the value of the curvature of physical space must be constant and that it can be determined only empirically with instruments that extend experience. It cannot be a priori, because there are no a priori constraints on curvature. Helmholtz (1878b) ultimately concluded that Kant was right on one count but wrong on another: Space is a necessary form of intuition, but Euclidean axioms are not part of it. In this manner, he freed physical space, and with it natural geometry, from the bonds of the abstract. Furthermore, he tried to make their bases empirical. It was an excellent gambit, but it met with opposition.

Russell (1897) presented the most broad-based reply, criticizing Helmholtz on three counts. First, he chastised Helmholtz for assuming that measurement of curvature is completely empirical, involving no a priori assumptions. Measurement, according to Russell, can take place only within an assumed geometry; thus empirical research cannot be the grounds for deciding the true form of physical space. Later, however, Einstein (1922) would defend Helmholtz's position. Second, Russell discussed, as many others had previously, the imaginability of geometries. Most "Boeotians" aligned themselves with Frege, suggesting that intuition was Euclidean in form.[8] Helmholtz (1878b), however, had suggested that any space that can be described can be imagined. Russell thought this was a poor choice for a criterion of imaginability. Psychologically, however, it seems odd for Russell to have placed so much emphasis on images in proof or refutation of the form of space: Images, worse than percepts, are not foundation-making material. Russell's third critique was the one he thought most damning: Helmholtz, perhaps following Gauss implicitly, based his notions of geometry on the mechanics of rigid bodies mobile in space. Noting the inherent circularity of such a position, Russell (1897, p. 81) suggested that

> to make Geometry await the perfection of Physics, is to make Physics, which depends throughout on geometry, forever impossible. As well might we leave the formation of numbers until we had counted the houses in Piccadilly.

Most felicitously for this work, however, Russell (1897) went on to describe projective geometry as the basis of space and perception. He later recanted this view (Kline 1980), but the position remains attractive in that it allows continued close connections among geometry, physical space, and perception.

Three Views: Apriorism, Empiricism, and Conventionalism
By the end of the nineteenth century, three views of geometries and space had emerged, two of which have already been discussed. They can be treated as a nested set. The oldest and most influential is *apriorism*, stretching from Plato to Kant and beyond to Russell and to Wiener (1922). Apriorism proposes that geometry and space are simply given.

This view was so strongly held for so long that even Hume, an otherwise archempiricist, regarded geometry as a nonempirical discipline in which proof lies in the relations of ideas rather than in those of physical stuff.[9] But in the nineteenth century, particularly with the discovery of non-Euclidean geometries, other views emerged.

The second view was *empiricism*, founded on the success and methodology of science. Euclidean geometry could be regarded as a compelling theory about physical space: It was corroborated by experience (perception) and experiment, but like all good theories it remained eminently falsifiable (subject to disproof). Non-Euclidean geometries were also viable theories, but less plausible on the basis of experience. Such a view was held by a wide variety of thinkers. These included Helmholtz, who was actively engaged in empirical endeavor; Gauss, Lobachevski, and Riemann, who established the new geometries; and John Stuart Mill and Ernst Mach.

Mach (1906) proposed that geometry has three roots: biology, perception, and logic. That is, we are biologically predisposed to know space (the aprioristic root), we arrive at geometric concepts as an idealization of what we perceive, and we systematize these ideals into a mathematics. Amplifying the last two, Mach (1906, pp. 124–125) stated:

> Geometry, accordingly, consists of the application of mathematics to experiences concerning space. . . . Just as mechanics can assert the constancy of masses or reduce the interactions between bodies to *simple* accelerations *only within limits of errors of observation*, so likewise the existence of straight lines, planes, the amount of the angle-sums, etc., can be maintained only on a similar restriction.

Thus Mach suggested that the roots of geometry can be only as sound as those of perception and that statement 5 must be false.

But of all empiricists Mill is most interesting. His position was little different from Mach's stripped of Kantian features. It was proposed more than a half century before, apparently without knowledge of non-Euclidean geometries (Torretti 1978). Mill (1843, p. 147), affirming statements 1, 2, and 4, denied the existence of most geometrical objects:

> There exist no points without magnitude; no lines without breadth, nor perfectly straight; no circles with all their radii exactly equal, nor squares with all their sides perfectly right.

Sidestepping statement 5, which in other contexts he also believed to be true, Mill suggested that we smooth out the natural irregularities of geometrical objects. These objects, he said (1843), have a "capacity of being painted in the imagination with a distinctness equal to reality: in other words, the exact resemblance of our ideas of form to the sensations which suggest them" (p. 154). An anti-Platonist at heart, Mill (p. 404) suggested that geometry was one of the natural sciences, as much subject to natural law as physics:[10]

> Every theorem of geometry is a law of external nature, and might have been ascertained by generalization from observation and experiment, which in this case resolve themselves into comparison and measurement. But it was found practicable, and being practicable, was desirable, to deduce these truths by ratiocination from a small number of general laws of nature, the certainty and universality of which are obvious to the most careless observer, and which compose the first principles and ultimate premises of the science.

The third view is *conventionalism*. This position was expounded most clearly by Poincaré (1905), and it builds on both previous views. Science, according to Poincaré, is a domain of hard facts, known through the senses and their extension, scientific instruments. But in order to report these facts, scientists must agree on the format in which they are to appear. The format is chosen by convention, tacitly agreed on by the members of the discipline. A geometry, in Poincaré's view, is just such a format. All physical facts of the world could just as well be placed in non-Euclidean geometries with small but continuous curvature as within a Euclidean system. To make this idea more concrete, Poincaré (1905, p. 51) generated the following possible-worlds argument against Helmholtz:

> Beings whose minds were made as ours, and with senses like ours, but without any preliminary education, might receive from a suitably-chosen external world impressions which would lead them to construct a geometry other than that of Euclid, and to localise the phenomena of this external world in a non-Euclidean space, or even in space of four dimensions. As for us, whose education has been made by our actual world, if we were suddenly transported into this new world, we should have no difficulty in referring phenomena to our Euclidean space.

Thus for Poincaré it was through happenstance and a concern with certain geometrical problems that we stumbled on a Euclidean description of the physical world. Others stumbling on different problems from a "suitably chosen" array might happen on other geometries. Through cultural tradition these geometries spread as conventions, or contracts, about dealing with the real world, and they are interconvertible when dealing with the same physical space.

In other words, some biological givens are necessary to perceive objects in spatial relation, consistent with apriorism. And, consistent with empiricism, geometry arises with experience. But the *particular* geometry does not arise invariably from what we perceive: Historical accident and cultural tradition pick out important observations, and these are systematized into a geometry, which provides a formal description of our intuitions and perceptions. Ultimately, Poincaré's position is one of espousing all the first four statements listed and regarding the fifth as inconsequential or false. His view assumes a predisposition to perceive and know spatial relations, and his epistemology is based on the perceived layout. Geometry simply becomes a conventionalized system in which to capture experience.[11] But Poincaré did not have the last word. In 1902, Hilbert formally removed perception and reality from the foundations of geometry (Kline 1980). Since Hilbert, the axioms of geometry begin with statements about what we imagine—always a less constrained psychological concept—not with what we perceive. With this change the tie between mathematics and natural phenomena was broken, as Berkeley would have wanted, and statements 1 and 2 were separated.[12] This odd result was perhaps best captured by Einstein (1922, pp. 28, 31), who said:

> As far as the laws of mathematics refer to reality, they are not certain; and as far as they are certain they do not refer to reality. . . . Yet on the other hand it is certain that mathematics generally, and particularly geometry, owes its existence to the need which was felt of learning something about the relations of real things to one another.

First Overview

There is an idea in the philosophy of space that physical space can be geometrized (measured exactly by mathematics) and that objects in it are perceived in geometric relations (measured inexactly by the eye). The conundrum for two thousand years was that the foundations of geometry seemed experiential, that our experience was inexact, but that geometry was exact and pure. Eventually, perception was removed from the foundations of geometry. But its removal as a pillar of geometry should not deter us from considering its reverse: *Mathematics may have its origin, but not its basis, in perception, but visual perception can still have its basis, but not its origin, in geometry.* In turn, epistemology can then have both its origin and basis in perception and can have it more firmly planted there than has typically been allowed.

But space is not the exclusive province of philosophers. Among many others, psychologists have a central interest in space in their effort to understand perception of objects in the world. In the next two sections I approach theories about the perception of objects in space in two ways: historically, from the notion of ambiguity in projections, and geometrically, from the notion of non-Euclidean visual space.

Perception, Projection, and Theories of Space

Discussion of projections and projection techniques has been central to theories of visual perception for more than three centuries. These techniques, although as old as Euclid and Ptolemy, were incompletely understood when Berkeley put forth his theory of vision. They were nonetheless influential. A central argument came from Molyneux (1690, p. 113):

> For *distance* of itself, is not to be perceived; for 'tis a line (or a length) presented to our eye with its end toward us, which must therefore be only a *point*, and that is *invisible*.

This analysis, known as *Molyneux's premise* (Pastore 1971), fascinated Berkeley (1709), and he used it in his essay as its second statement. At base, it is a discussion of projective distortions of a line at the limit. The problem with Molyneux's analysis, however, is that the length of a single optic ray is irrelevant to perception; it is the cross-sectional relations among collected contiguous bundles of rays that is important. Vanishingly few real lines in our environment are ever seen end on, projecting down their length. As Euclid realized, systematic patterns of convergence are created through recession in depth of multilined environments.[13]

After Molyneux, projections continued to intrigue philosophers. One of the more widely discussed illusions of the eighteenth and nineteenth centuries was the windmill illusion. Smith (1738) and Helmholtz (1866), among others, discussed it in detail. The illusion occurs at dawn or dusk when a windmill is seen in silhouette from relatively far away and in half-profile. The blade spins and, even though the polar perspective is appropriate for seeing the windmill from the front, spontaneous reversals occur, as if the windmill suddenly faced away from the observer. The illusion is sufficiently compelling, according to Miles (1929), that selling windmills was at risk: New owners often complained that theirs turned the wrong way.[14] We are more familiar with spontaneous reversals of figures shown in parallel projection, such as the Necker cube discussed in chapter 2. Windmills show that illusions of motion and of configuration are not wholly foreign to real life and that the optics of polar perspective are not so incontrovertible that the visual system might prefer an object in reverse orientation. If allowed to walk around the windmill, the observer will find the illusion unstable, and if tried at midday, the illusion will not occur at all. Veridical perception will win out.

Despite the fascinations of Molyneux, Berkeley, Smith, and Helmholtz, projections and perspective played a small role in perceptual theory until the middle of this century. Then it suddenly assumed a leading role, ironically as a blackguard and villain. Rather than providing the foundation for realism, perspective was assumed to demonstrate a kind of surrealism, which in elaboration of Poincaré could be made sense of only through the conventional bases of society.

Adelbert Ames
The first systematic study of perception and projection was that of Adelbert Ames. Promoting a *transactionalist approach* and subsumed by the philosophy of Dewey, Ames compiled a series of striking demonstrations promoting the idea that we bring a rich set of expectancies to every perceptual situation.[15] These were thought to demonstrate the degree to which the *assumptive world*, a contractual by-product of our culture, is overlaid on the physical world. The two best-known demonstrations are the Ames room and the rotating trapezoidal window. The Ames room is a chamber that, when viewed from a small peephole, looks like a perfectly normal room. In fact, it is carpentered as an irregular sexahedron with no visible right angles. The effect, however, is so compelling that, when people walk around within the room, from the peephole view they may appear to change size. The transactionalist account of this effect is that we come into the situation *expecting* to see a regular room and therefore we see it. This is a wonderfully elegant, if overly persuasive, demonstration of Cartesian natural geometry. The rotating trapezoidal window is simlarly successful but this time includes motion. The window is actually a trapezoid but constructed and painted to have the general look of a rectangular window frame seen from an oblique angle, say 45°. When rotated on a vertical axis and viewed in rather dim light from a distance of about ten times its radius, the window appears to oscillate, moving back and forth, rather than rotate. The optics of polar projection are violated when interpreting the window as oscillating, but the percept is robust and almost irrepressible.

Neither illusion works well under somewhat altered conditions. In the Ames room, for example, if the observer looks from a point displaced from the designated viewpoint or, even better, if the observer moves around while looking into the room, its true shape becomes apparent.[16] In the trapezoidal window illusion, if the observer views the apparatus from closer up, the perceived oscillation ceases and rotation takes its place. Ames and his followers suggested that our knowledge about the way the world *ought to be* governs our percepts in ambiguous situations. I suggest, however, that what the transactionalist work demonstrates is that experimenters must be quite clever in devising situations both rich in information *and* illusory. Polar perspective viewing, the kind that we do in everyday circumstances, is almost completely satisfactory in revealing the layout of surfaces and objects around us.

James Gibson and Gunnar Johansson
Gibson (1950, 1979), of course, espoused almost exactly this view. He was continuously interested in projections and in a geometric under-standing of them.[17] But he also had a deep skepticism about the ultimate explanatory value of projective geometry (Gibson 1970). His rationale seemed a good one: Projective geometry knows only lines; it does not know surfaces, and it does not deal with occlusions of one surface by another. Johansson (1970, 1974, 1975, 1978), on the other hand, like Russell and Poincaré before him, suggested that projective geometry is the basis for visual perception. For Johansson, vision makes no sense outside of this framework. He emphasized the role of projections in the same way Kepler emphasized natural geometry: The rules of pro-jective geometry are *decoding principles* applied to the optic array. I have more to say about the positions of Gibson and Johansson in chapter 9.

Projective geometry, then, is a wire-frame description of the world without filled-in surfaces. Gibson recognized that opacity is an important property of surfaces and that projective geometry could not deal with it. My solution to this dilemma is pragmatic. Rather than discarding projective geometry, I try to use it as much as possible under the assumption that the problems of occlusions and projections are inde-pendent of one another. In particular, I assume that occlusions can be dealt with later on their own terms and do not jeopardize this discussion.

Perception and Geometries of Curved Space
Euclid assumed the rectilinearity of rays and hence of uncurved space. But maybe space, or at least its perceptual counterpart, is not rectilinear at all. Thomas Reid (1764) appears to have been the first to suggest that "the geometry of the visibles" is a spherical rather than a Euclidean geometry. Implicit in Reid's view is that the surface of the cornea and retina are curved projection surfaces and that these measure the visible world. Certain analyses following from this fact reveal apparent co-nundrums for a Euclidean geometry of vision. Modern observations

stem from Helmholtz (1866), and in general two approaches have been
made to the curvature of space.

Rudolf Luneburg and Absolute Visual Curvature

Luneburg (1947), working at Dartmouth with Ames, proposed that
"visual space" is curved, following a Lobachevskian geometry. Many
have followed this line of thinking.[18] The theory is one of *binocular*
perception, specifically dealing with the coordination of projections at
the two eyes. Evidence gathered in support of a hyperbolic visual geometry is based on elaborations of an experimental paradigm generalized
from Helmholtz and explored by Hillebrand in 1902 and Blumenfeld
in 1913. The experimental situation is called the alley problem, in
which a square matrix of lights is shown to an observer. All lights are
arranged in the horizontal plane of the two eyes and placed a small
distance from them. What is interesting about this arrangement is that
the observer can achieve alternating, conflicting impressions: The lights
can be seen in a square configuration, and also both the columns of
lights extending outward and the rows stretching across may appear
curved. The last phenomenon is related to horopters of equal disparities
on the two retinas, known at least since Helmholtz. Coupled with the
curved columns of lights, they serve as the basis for measuring the
putative curvature of visual space.[19]

It seems to me that this experimental situation is a good example of
where effort after experimental control through stimulus reduction has
led to a circumstance from which it is difficult to generalize back to
normal perception. The most important problems with Luneburg's work,
in my opinion, are that the observer cannot move through the environment and that the stimulus does not move.[20] In particular, if the
observer could move, he or she could almost certainly discern the
difference between potential layouts, just as he or she could accurately
discern the real shape of an Ames room if left to wander about. A
second problem is that these experiments are generally run in the dark
and that the configural properties of the stimulus are the reduced relations among a few luminous points.[21] Following Gibson (1950), this
is an air-theory approach to perception because the objects are disembodied from surfaces of support. And third, I question the motivation
behind this type of experiment. Luneburg and associates seemed to be
in search of the inherent shape of the Platonic vessel of space into
which visual objects are placed, or perhaps in search of the axioms of
the a priori geometry of a Kantian intuitional space. Apparently, this
space can manifest itself only when almost empty. If this non-Euclidean
space were really the fundament of vision, important questions arise
(Grünbaum 1973): Why, for example, does this curved space seem to

straighten out when it is filled with many objects? How does Loba-chevski become Euclid, and why?[22]

Assessments of Relative Visual Curvature
Not everyone who has proposed a non-Euclidean geometry for vision has come out of the Luneburg tradition. Other curved-world theorists include Foley (1964, 1966), who considered one problem in detail. Since Helmholtz, most discussions of the possible curvature of space have considered curvature to be constant, an assumption made by Luneburg. Foley, on the other hand, showed deviations from constant curvature in alleylike experiments. Striking asymmetries, as well as large individual differences, were found.

Watson (1978) also proposed a non-Euclidean geometry for vision to account for the perception of certain illusions. His motivation is quite attractive: Illusions, rather than being examples of the kind of misperception that philosophers and psychologists are so concerned with, may actually be examples of veridical perception in a Riemannian framework. Moreover, Watson addressed some of the questions left unanswered by Luneburg and his associates. In particular, Watson offered an account as to why we do not notice curvature in everyday life: Real-life situations do not provide the circumstances within which one can perform the analytic experiments necessary to distinguish a Euclidean from a curved geometry. These can be done only under laboratory control. Watson did not explicitly discuss amount of curvature; instead, he proposed that curvature is illusion dependent.

Although I have genuine sympathy for Watson's account, his evidence suffers some of the same difficulties as that of Luneburg. First, his stimuli are laid out on a plane, although in Watson's cases it is the frontoparallel rather than the horizontal plane. But it seems odd to generalize from an analysis of two-dimensional curvature to three dimensions, particularly when we know that most drawings provoke perception of three-dimensional virtual spaces. Second, Watson's examples, like those of Luneburg, are stimuli of few components, reduced and impoverished when compared to the real world. Although he considered many different types of illusions, his selection of two-dimensional line drawings raises issues about sampling. We can generalize to almost anything from a cagey selection of exemplars. And third, and most important for this work, Watson's stimuli are static pictures. Such a visual space—planar, reduced, and rigid in viewpoint—is not the space within which we roam. It seems plausible that the visual system struggles to do its best with minimal information. Moreover, it may be that these struggles are modeled best by some non-Euclidean geometry. But when the visual system is flooded with information, it seems difficult not to suggest that it reverts to principles best modeled by Euclidean geometry and projections of it.[23]

Second Overview

Two aspects of the perception of space have been considered in the latter part of this chapter—the role of projections in perceptual theory and the possibility of a non-Euclidean geometry for vision. Projections have played an odd role in theories of layout perception. Some theorists, such as Berkeley and Ames, have suggested that projections prove the infirmity of perception. Others, such as Gibson, seem overly worried that projective geometry cannot deal with occluding surfaces. I think neither of these positions is most prudent. Following Russell, Poincaré, and Johansson, I suggest that projections are the foundation of vision and that to understand them is to go a long way toward understanding the trustworthiness of perception. Curved geometries have occasionally been considered as best for representing visual space. This idea is interesting because it forces reconsideration of major issues. Insofar as can be determined, however, curved geometries in visual space can be demonstrated for only extremely close viewing (Helmholtz 1866) or in planar projections and in impoverished conditions with planar surfaces. Given these results, my bet is that the Euclidean nature of human-scaled space does just fine for analyses and theories of vision.

5

Invariants

Heraclitus thought the world was ever changing; Parmenides thought it ever constant.[1] In truth it is some of both. There are those things that change and those that do not. The former can be called *variants*, the latter *invariants*. From mathematics we get the idea that some aspects of an object or event can be invariant even while others change: Such things are said to be invariant under transformation.

This idea has sparked new interest in a central question in perception—how do we perceive things to be constant when their projected images continually change?[2] This question is a version of Koffka's "Why do we perceive things as we do?" Invariance under transformation, the lack of change within a sea of change, could be the key to explaining constancies in perception. Gibson (1967, p. 162) captured this idea as follows:

> If *invariants* of the energy flux at the receptors of an organism exist, and if these invariants correspond to the permanent properties of the environment, and if they are the basis of the organism's perception of the environment instead of the sensory data on which we have thought it based, then I think there is new support for realism in epistemology as well as for a new theory of perception in psychology. I may be wrong, but one way to find out is to submit this thesis to criticism.

Gibson championed this idea in perception. In recent years it has seen increasing popularity, and there are, I think, good reasons for this upsurge. One is dissatisfaction with the cue concept, discussed in chapter 3. But more important is the realization that traditional stimulus analyses have not been as sophisticated as they ought to be. The search for invariants is, in part, a search for more sophisticated types of information available to a perceiver.

Underlying Gibson's cogent statement are many assumptions. In this chapter I investigate these and others. Because the term "invariance" is mathematical in origin and because psychologists use it to huckster ideas under the aegis of the Queen of the Sciences, the first four assumptions deal with the intersection of mathematics and perception. The last three concern invariance as information. Before I discuss them, however, consider a brief history.

Invariance in Perceptual Theory

The current importance of the concept of invariance is due entirely to Gibson. Its use in perceptual theory, however, is much older. Invariance has appeared in the tool chest of nearly every perceptual theorist. Consider Helmholtz (1878a, p. 384):

> I should like, now, to return to the discussion of the most fundamental facts of perception. As we have seen, we not only have changing sense impressions which come to us without our doing anything; we also perceive while we are being active or moving about. . . . Each movement we make by which we alter the appearance of objects should be thought of as an experiment designed to test whether we have understood correctly the invariant relations of the phenomena before us, that is, their existence in definite spatial relations.[3]

Although Helmholtz said much more than this, here he promoted the idea of an active organism exploring the invariants of an object undergoing transformation caused by exploration. That invariants were important to Helmholtz has not been lost to students of perception,[4] but this fact is rarely emphasized.

Gestalt psychologists also used the term. Koffka (1935) mentioned it in many contexts, although he used it differently than did Helmholtz and Gibson. Missing was the idea that aspects of the environment are invariant *under transformation*. Invariants for Koffka were constancies without mathematical implication.

Gibson (1967), in the given quote, suggested that this concept necessarily brings forth a new theory of perception. What should be clear, however, is that this theory is not wholly new. What is new to Gibson is the full emphasis on invariants and deemphasis on conceptual elaboration. Such a view contravenes Helmholtz's unconscious inference and Koffka's discussion of the non–structure-preserving mapping from distal to proximal stimulus.

In *The Perception of the Visual World*, Gibson (1950) introduced invariance as it influenced his later work. It is interesting, however, that he used the concept little there and only in connection with a particular invariant from projective geometry—the cross ratio, the subject of chapters 6 through 9 here. It was Boring (1952) who picked the idea out of Gibson and emphasized its importance. Boring was strongly influenced by Stevens's (1951) discussion of invariance as central to all scientific endeavor.[5] Gibson then worked hard on the idea (Gibson 1958, Gibson et al. 1955), and the first full-scale treatments appeared a few years later (Gibson 1959, 1960b). Afterward, although much of the rest of his theory changed, his discussion of invariants generally did not. He stuck fairly close to the idea from mathematics that invariants should be abstract and formless (Gibson 1973b). The question remains, however: What assumptions are made when this term is used in perception?

Assumption 1: Mathematics Is an Appropriate Descriptive Language for Visual Perception

One assumption, broached by Gibson and myriad other students of perception since Herbart, is that the best descriptors for visual perception are those of mathematics. This assumption transcends goals of elegance, formalism, and precision and has its basis in two ideas: The spatial layout of our visual world is best described by some form of mathematics, and the human mind is attuned to that description because it is attuned to the layout. The first idea is as old as Euclid; the second is Galileo's *mathesis universalis*, a Renaissance notion that seems quite modern. Echoed by Pylyshyn (1972, pp. 547–548), scientists believe that

> the secrets of the universe (both physical and psychological) are, as Galileo said, "written in the language of mathematics." But this must not be misunderstood to mean that it is only accessible to a mathematician. Even less does it mean that everything of importance can be measured and subjected to calculation. It means that those aspects of the universe that are ultimately comprehensible to the human mind are comprehensible because one can see in them a structure that is *essentially mathematical*.

Although Pylyshyn was more concerned with the relation of linguistic formalisms to language, his statement applies equally to perceptual theory and perception. Many of us believe that an explanation of the perception of layout is partly understood through the mathematics of how things are arrayed before us and how their optics change when we or they move. Together, then, these twin ideas—that the structure of the world is mathematical and that this structure is comprehensible because of its mathematical nature—form an assumptive base for realism in perception and epistemology. It is the promise of tractability in the mathematics of the optic array that makes realism tenable.

Nevertheless, to say that mathematics is an appropriate descriptive language for perception is a global statement. It makes no commitment to any particular type of mathematics. Thus I know few who would overtly disagree with this assumption; it is weak. Mathematics is so varied that it is difficult to believe that this assumption could be false. Math can be used anywhere; its formalisms can be used without prejudice in both astronomy and astrology; it can model equally truth, trivialism, and falsehood.

Assumption 2: Mathematical Truths Are Transportable into Perception without Change of Meaning

It is one thing to say that the world and its perception are essentially mathematical. It is quite another to say that the tools of a particular branch of mathematics can be safely transported out of a rigorous and tightly circumscribed domain into an entirely different, less rigorous, and comparatively disordered domain like visual perception.[6] Cassirer (1944, p. 11) noted this when discussing group theory and perception:

> The precision of mathematical concepts rests upon their being confined to a definite sphere. They cannot, without logical prejudice, be extended beyond that sphere into other domains.

Cassirer warned us that importation of mathematical ideas into perception can be a problematic course of action. The structure and problems of a particular branch of mathematics may bear no resemblance to those of perception. The implication is that if any aspect of math and perception is anisomorphic for a particular problem, then application of mathematics will be misleading.

Cassirer, however, made the strong claim that the principles of invariance and groups are the basis of both perception and geometric thought. In fact, he stated that mathematical and psychological thought could be brought together under group theory. This claim may be true, but it is not without question, as I discuss later. What should be clear, however, is that assumption 2 is stronger and more particular than assumption 1: A specific kind of mathematics is asked to work for a specific problem in perception—that of how we perceive constancies in the world. Thus we must assess whether "invariance" means the same thing in mathematics as it has come to mean in perception. To do this, we need more background on the term's use in mathematics.

Notes on Invariance, Transformations, and Groups in Mathematics
Invariance is a term born of mid-nineteenth-century mathematical thought. It was first used by Boole, Cayley, and Sylvester from 1841

to 1850 in algebra.[7] As its use developed and spread, invariance came to mean "anything which is left unaltered by a coordinate transformation" (Thomas 1944, p. 7). Thus, if the three dimensions of a rectangular room can be represented in Cartesian coordinates (x, y, and z), moving a block through that space, changing its coordinates, does not change its shape; that remains invariant. Later, in the nineteenth century with the work of Lie and Klein, invariance and transformation became interlocked. Psychologists have heard most about the early history of invariance in the context of Klein's Erlangen program of 1872,[8] which defines a geometry as a system of definitions and theorems that remain invariant under a given group of transformations.

If invariants are those things in a geometry that are unaltered by coordinate transformation, we need to know more about them and how they form a group. The key concept here is *group*, in its mathematical, but not commonsense, meaning. There are four postulates true of a group (see Bell 1945 and Stevens 1951):

1. *Closure*. If a and b are members of a set of operations (transformations), then $a * b$ is also a member of the set. (The symbol * denotes combination.) All members of the group can be related to all other members; the group is also closed.

2. *Association*. For any three operations in the set, $(a * b) * c = a * (b * c)$. Order in pairwise combination of a string of operations is irrelevant.

3. *Identity*. There is an operation i such that $a * i = a$. The group includes a null operation, called the identity transformation.

4. *Inversion*. There is an operation a' such that $a' * a = i$. The existence of one operation implies its inverse.

Now consider a small exercise in group theory—what one can do with a block of wood on a desktop. One can push it to the right (operation a) and push it backward to the same extent (operation b). One could start again and push it diagonally at 45° until it rests in the same position, $a * b$. If operation c is turning the block over, one can move the block diagonally and then turn it over, $(a * b) * c$; or one can move it to the right, then move it backward an equal amount while turning it over, $a * (b * c)$. And, of course, one can do nothing, i, and do the opposite of a, b, and c. In addition, if the operations are also commutative (a fifth postulate), $a * b = b * a$, then the group is Abelian. The small group of operations just listed is an Abelian group, although spatial translations and rotations in general are not.

In Euclidean space, a rigid object like our block of wood can be moved around without changing its shape. All possible motions (or transformations) form a continuous group—the "group of displacements" (Poincaré 1905, 1907; Piaget 1970)—that is infinitely dense in potential operations along its various dimensions. Helmholtz (1894, p. 504) was the first to try to use this in an account of the perception of objects in space:

> Being acquainted with the material form of an object, we are able to represent clearly in our minds all the perspective images we expect to see when we look at it from different sides; and we are startled if an image we actually see does not correspond to our expectations, as can happen, for example, when a change in the form of an object accompanies changes in its position.

Cassirer (1944, 1945) developed this idea in an attempt to coordinate perception and geometry. It is this coordination, if possible, that legitimizes the importation of the terms "invariance," "transformation," and "group" into perception without changing their mathematical meaning.

Assumption 3: Mathematical Imports Are Useful in Explaining Perception

It is one thing to import a term from a different discipline, but it is yet another to make it work for you. As an entrée into this discussion, consider again Klein's Erlangen program and its later efficacy within mathematics. Basically, two things happened: The program ultimately failed and, where some of its ideas generalized, the results seemed trivial. With regard to the first, many new geometries did not fit the program. In particular, the concept of space developed such that its intrinsic structure generally could not be defined in terms of transformation groups. But more relevant is the matter of trivialization. The Erlangen program flourished for a while, and its ideas were applied to nearly everything imaginable. This brought problems (Bell 1945, p. 446):

> The success of the Erlanger Programm was also partly responsible for another tendency that did mathematics no particular good. When it was shown that a certain theory satisfied the postulates of a group, it seems to have been assumed as a matter of course that the theory was thereby significantly advanced. To cite a trivial instance, when it is gravely announced that all of the rational integers form a group with respect to addition, common sense will not stand open mouthed in dumb admiration, but will demand, "What of it?"

Like the application of groups to rational integers, any application of invariance, transformations, and groups to perception *may* be trivial.

This is not to denigrate the power of groups per se, as they have provided powerful insights in other arenas, but only to warn against the presumed utility of such application. For example, reconsider the case of moving the block of wood: It is true that everything one can do with it by moving it around in space does not alter its shape and that these transformations satisfy the postulates of a group. But it is not clear that such a fact elucidates a theory of the perception of or action with that block. Instead, it appears simply to obfuscate the obvious.

Consider a case in which these concepts do not help. At the heart of group theory is the null transformation i. When applied to perception, all possible objects and events are invariant under the null transformation. But this truth seems empty. To counter this, we might try to remove the null transformation from the group, stating that we perceive invariants as revealed under all nonnull transformations. But then we no longer have a group: Identity and inversion postulates are violated. Moreover, it is not simply the null transformation that is problematic; i is completely surrounded by infinitesimal transformations that are also useless to perception. I return to this idea under assumption 4. Once the notion of invariants under transformation is applied to perception, it is an empirical matter as to whether it will be useful to perceptual theory. The link begins as a codification that may be circularly rooted in geometry and perception (Cassirer 1944), but unless we can specify why some invariants are used in perception and some are not, the use of the concepts of group, transformation, and invariance may offer us little.

A Note on Overgeneralization of Invariants in Perception
The members of the group are transformations related by the postulates given earlier. Invariants are one class of entities they operate on. Thus there are two species of mathematical entities: invariants and transformations. Recently, Shaw and Pittenger (1977) and Michaels and Carello (1981) called invariants and transformations two varieties of the same species—invariants. Shaw and Pittenger (1977), for example, spoke of transformations or symmetry operations as *transformational invariants* and what they operate on as symmetries or *structural invariants*. Even though I have suggested a similar distinction,[9] I think that the term "transformation invariant" is misleading. My reason is that if we can make these terms useful to psychology, we ought to do so without changing their mathematical meaning. Invariants are invariant because they survive transformations unchanged. But transformations are not invariant simply because they are unchanged by the entities on which they operate. In other words, there is an asymmetry

between the two concepts. Transformations operate on both invariants and variants and are changed by neither; invariants are operated on by transformations and remain unchanged, whereas variants are operated on and changed. Another way to look at this, provisionally accepting application of invariant to an operator, is to suggest that the term "transformational invariant" is uninformative because there appears to be no such thing, mathematically, as a "transformational variant." Objects, for example, do not operate on transformations such that they can change them. Pushing a block to the left does not become pushing it to the right or turning it over as a result of the character of the block.[10] The overgeneralization of the term "invariant" can also be found in Gibson, as I discuss under assumption 7.

Assumption 4: Mathematical Invariants Are Absolute and Those for Perception Are Not

Previously I suggested that the null transformation is not psychologically useful and that it is not a special case; it is simply the center of a region of transformations in a continuous group that are so small as to be undetectable by a perceiver. Thus there is likely to be an indefinitely large number of transformations of an object too small to reveal any invariants not revealed under the null transformation. This point was made implicitly by Luchins and Luchins (1964), explicitly by Hochberg (1981, 1982), but made earlier by Cassirer (1944, p. 16) in a statement that weakens his argument on the parallel between geometry and perception:

> It goes without saying that this analogy between the formation of invariants in perception and in geometry ought not to make us overlook the thoroughgoing differences which are very important from the epistemological point of view. These differences may be characterized by an expression which Plato used to define the opposition of perception to thought. All perception is confined to the "more or less". . . . Only approximative, not absolute determinations are attainable in perception. This characteristic is also exhibited by perceptual *constancy*. Its realization is never ideally complete, but always remains within certain limits. The fixation of these limits constitutes one of the most important tasks of psychological research. Beyond these limits there is no further "transformation."

The anisomorphism between group theory and perception, then, is that in mathematics all transformations reveal invariants, whereas in perception only sufficiently large ones do. This latter idea is the crux

of the experiments and discussion in later chapters. Without acknowl-
edgment of threshold considerations, a theory of perception based on
invariants is simply a stimulus theory without necessary relevance to
the organism.[11] This is much more than a quibble. We must not assume
that we are simply dealing with necessarily minute changes in optic
flux. Threshold determination for perceptual invariants is an empirical
matter, and some thresholds may be so high as to render questionable
an invariant's use at all.

A Note on Invariants in Pictures
One of the most puzzling applications of the concept of invariants can
be found in Gibson's (1979, p. 271) account of picture perception. He
suggested that a picture is

> *an array of persisting invariants of structure that are nameless and
> formless.* . . . Ordinarily, these invariants underlie transformations
> and emerge most clearly when the persisting properties separate
> off from the changing properties; but they can also be distinguished
> in the limiting case of an unchanging structure.

Pictures are putatively full of invariants that continually undergo the
null transformation. Although such a statement may make mathematical
sense, logically it makes none. As Arnheim (1979, p. 122) pleaded:
"The notion of invariance loses its meaning where nothing variable
can exist."[12] By the logic outlined, invariants that undergo no perceptible
transformation in time cannot be revealed to the perceiver at all. Variants
and invariants alike are unchanged by the null transformation. Thus
in a frozen picture it is not clear how the structure of the virtual world
is apprehended. It is possible that transformations in virtual space can
be registered, but as gradients, not as invariants. More is said about
this in the discussion of assumption 7.

First Overview

In this first section I have tried to explicate four assumptions underlying
the application of invariance to perception. In essence, I have considered
whether invariance has survived importation into psychology, whether
importation has forced a change in its meaning, and whether it is a
useful citizen. I believe that the first assumption is valid, perhaps only
because it is almost completely nonrestrictive: Mathematics is an appropriate descriptive language for perception if only because its formalisms can take on a nearly infinite variety of forms.

I believe that the second and third assumptions are valid if one is
careful. Certain mathematical truths are transportable into perception

without loss of meaning, and they can be useful to us. If these assumptions are to remain valid, however, psychologists must guard against contamination of the transplanted idea. Careful specification of invariants can help retain the rigor of the term, and wariness about overgeneralizations can keep it from differentiating beyond recognition. The term "invariant," and the term "transformation" as well, I believe, should take hold and grow in perception, but these terms do not guarantee that the term "group" will be useful just because it belongs to the same alien family. Group theory, I believe, is not easily applied to perception as more than an empty formalism.[13]

And I believe the fourth assumption to be true: Because of the "more or less" of perception, perceptual invariants cannot be absolute. This fact skews the parallel between geometry and perception and suggests that invariance may not always be able to do the yeomanly work in perception that some of us want. At best, invariants work for perceivers only some of the time, and the determination of how well they work for psychologists is an empirical question. Consider next three assumptions about invariants and sources of information. Like the four that went before, these are statements I believe are true.

Assumption 5: An Invariant Is Information, Not an Object Property

Invariance as applied to perception has meant at least two things. The one I wish to concentrate on is information in the sense of the chapter's first quotation: "Invariants *correspond* to the permanent properties of the environment" (Gibson 1967, p. 162, my emphasis). The other sense, and the one I think problematic for perceptual theory, is invariance as an object property. This idea seems to have come from the gestalt psychologists (Koffka 1935, Heider and Simmel 1944). Consider two examples.

First, Gibson (1966, p. 8) suggested that "the earth 'below', the air 'above' " were simple invariants. But they are not; they are permanent features of the layout. They do not *correspond* to properties of the environment; they *are* its properties. They are not information; they are substances. Helmholtz (1878a, p. 387) was clearest separating the two:

> That which, independently of any and everything else, remains the same during all temporal changes, we call a *substance*; the invariant relation between variable but related quantities we call a *law*. We perceive only the latter directly.

Second, consider a flat surface. That surface may be invariably flat; flatness can be said to be its invariant. Although I do not wish to impugn either constancies or perceived properties, a problem arises as to how we are to account for the perception of this surface. In ecological optics we typically assume that the information (the invariant) specifies the object or event perceived; that is, we pick up (process) the invariant and as a result perceive the object properties specified. But here we must be extremely careful. It is illegitimate to say that we can perceive a flat surface because it is invariably flat. This is the fallacy of assuming the consequence: The *explanandum* (that which is explained) is the same as the *explanans* (the means by which the explanation occurs). To state that flatness specifies the perception of a flat surface is to use a logic that runs in circles. Unfortunately, Gibson (1979, p. 271) slipped into this tautology. For example, he noted:

> When the young child sees the family cat at play the front view, side view, rear view, top view, and so on are not seen, and what gets perceived is the *invariant* cat. . . . It is not that he sees an abstract cat, or a conceptual cat, or the common features of the class of cats, as some philosophers would have us believe; what he gets is the information for the persistence of that peculiar, furry, mobile layout of surfaces.

This is loose logic. If invariants are information, a cat is a cat and not an invariant. There may be some mathematically specifiable information that specifies a particular cat, but it is not the cat itself. The information about an object or event cannot be of the same form as its perceived properties. Invariants in theory and in perception must be formless—they cannot be shapes or geometric figures.

My approach is hard nosed, and my goal is to explore specific, formless invariant relations that specify flatness and rigidity and observer direction. I investigate flatness and rigidity in chapters 6 through 9 and observer direction in chapters 12 and 13. The information, to be formless in the physical sense, is couched in terms of mathematical expressions. Such invariants are often proposed for perception but less often stated with precision.[14] The general dearth of known perceptual invariants is recognized as a problem even by the staunchest proponents of ecological optics. For example, Neisser (1977, p. 24) said:

> In Gibson's view some characteristic *must* be invariant over time, to specify the unvarying shape of the real object.
> Unfortunately, these crucial invariants have not yet been isolated. The claim that they exist is the largest outstanding promissory note in ecological optics.

Assumption 6: Invariance Does Not Entail One-to-One Mapping between Information and Object

Fundamentally, invariance is about mapping. Following Palmer (1978) the mapping is between a *representing set* of relations and a *represented set*. For my purposes the representing set is the geometric relations measured in the optic array, and the represented set is the distances among objects and object parts in the world. In visual perception invariance maps any token of relations in the image set back to a single token of the real-world set. The mapping remains true even when accompanied by transformations of the object, caused by the object's motion or the observer's movement. But notice, I make no claim about the reverse mapping from real world to proximal image. I claim the real world entails a many-to-one mapping from information to objects but not a one-to-one mapping. *The main purpose of this book is to explore this difference.*

In direct perception it is often said that an invariant specifies the object or event perceived. That is, information is associated with *one* particular object or event, or a coherent class of them, and none other. Likewise it is often assumed—and the quote by Neisser stated this— that for every object or event there is one and only one invariant. Like Neisser, Eleanor Gibson (1967, p. 464) has also made this assumption:

> The search for an invariant—the relation that remains constant over change—is the essence of object perception. The stimulus invariant that keeps its identity despite the transformations of stimulation caused by motion of the object or a movement of the observer is the basis for perception of that object.

And James Gibson (1966) also made it. He discussed the relation among environmental source, stimulus invariant, and percept. The first two are related by physical law and the second two by psychological resonance. One-to-one mappings are implied at each juncture.[15] Similarly, Gibson (1967, p. 166) said:

> How can the child separate the variants caused by external events from the variants caused by his bodily movements? How can he know that the whole world has not moved, for example, whenever he moves his eyes? This is an old and controversial question in psychology. A possible answer is, by extracting a still higher order of invariant. The uncontrollable variation, the one that cannot be reversed by reversing an exploratory movement, is information for an external event just as the invariant that remains after a controllable variation is information for an external object.

It is clear in these quotations, and generally throughout the body of literature on direct perception, that there is an assumed one-to-one mapping between invariant and object.[16] But such a mapping, attractive as it appears, cannot generally hold.

Assumption 7: Gradients Are Not Typically Invariants

Many descriptions of surfaces and of optic flow deal with *gradients*. This term was first used in visual perception by Koffka (1935, p. 248), who suggested that "the qualities of perceived objects depend upon *gradients* of stimulation." Gibson (1947, 1950) picked up this idea, and gradients have since been explored by many.[17] They are measures made on a projection surface of the stochastically regular properties of the environment. Gradients *grade*, or change, as objects project from different regions of the optic array and, most typically, as one traces them out from one's feet up to the horizon.

The link between invariants and gradients has been made, but not always with care. This has led some critics to suggest that it is too vague to be useful. Topper (1979, p. 136), for example, pleaded that Gibson "should be more precise in defining what are and what are not invariants." Ullman (1979, p. 378) quoted Gibson (1972, p. 221), noting that

> the definition of invariances in the theory of direct perception is in fact so broad that almost any rule, once discerned, can be reformulated in terms of invariances: "A great many properties of the optic array are *lawfully* or *regularly* variant with change of observation point, and this means that in each case a property defined by the law is *invariant*."

And Gibson (1979, p. 272) further argued that

> the gradient of size and the gradient of density of texture are invariants; the horizon considered as the line where sizes and textures diminish to zero is an invariant. There are many kinds of invariants.

Gibson's statements here, I believe, are off the mark. Unfortunately, many of us have slipped into this error.[18] Let me explain why it is wrong.

Perceptual invariants denote a constant mapping between the representing domain (information about the world in the optic array) and the represented domain (the physical world). For an invariant to warrant the name, it must not depend on the spatial relation of the object to the perceiver. That is, coordinate change of the viewer or of the object should not change the information. If information varies with viewer or object position, as it does in a gradient for any nonplanar surface, that information is not invariant. To pursue this a little, let me note that Gibson suggested that the *property* the variant specifies—the layout of the surface—*can* be invariant across changing points of observation. There are, as I see it, two problems with this analysis. The first, as suggested by Ullman, is the vagueness of the concepts of "lawfulness" and "regularity" in variants. What are the laws? What kind of regularity qualifies? Second, this analysis is a retreat from the notion of invariants specifying objects or events. Instead, the variants (gradients) specify the invariant property that is perceived. Thus the variants are said to specify the object, and the invariant, rather than being the information that specifies the object, is the property of the object perceived. What is needed for a theoretical account of perception is an invariant that specifies both the gradients and the object perceived. One such entity is considered in chapter 9.

Second Overview

The last three assumptions dealt with how the term "invariant" should be used as an explanatory device in perception. All, I believe, are true, but opposite claims have been made. The fifth assumption is that the term should be reserved for discussion of information and not include the constancies of objects or object properties. The rationale is twofold: If invariants are formless, they cannot also be object properties, and if perception is to be explained nontautologically, we should not try to explain what is perceived by means of the pickup of what is perceived.

The sixth assumption concerns the mapping between information and objects. This point may appear abstruse at present, but I hope the next eight chapters make it clearer. Briefly, however, we should recognize the following possibility: Two sources of information can specify the same object or object property and yet not be the same—not even notational variants of one another. In forecast of how multiple specification can occur, let me say that if information is the combination of relations among optic elements, combinatorics can be quite different, even though the base elements are the same.

Finally, the seventh assumption is that gradients are not invariants. I suggest this first merely on the basis of semantic analysis. Gradients, if anything, must be variants; invariants, if anything, cannot grade. But the rationale for this separation is deeper: Gradients for all nonflat surfaces do not survive unchanged the transformations of observer position. I assume further that an invariant can underlie some gradients and that the information used in perception may often be the invariant rather than the gradient.

All these assumptions are about the class of entities called invariants. It is almost time to consider a particular one—the cross ratio. Before that, however, let me define the class.

A Definition of a Perceptual Invariant

Throughout this work I use the word "invariant" as a noun, not an adjective. As a noun it is a source of information about an object or event that remains constant during transformation; as an adjective it simply connotes constancy.

I suggest that a perceptual invariant must be mathematically specifiable in one of two forms—as a real number or as an ordered relation among reals.[19] In the first case that number may be dimensionless, one formed by a ratio with numerator and denominator measured in the same units, which cancel. The invariant considered in chapters 6, 7, and 9 is one such number. In the second case, inequalities or rankings can be considered. In later chapters this is explored in optic flow: in chapter 9 as a uniformity (or lack of ordering) and in chapters 12 and 13 as a set of inequalities. Reduction to numbers is a strong check on invariance. I claim that if such numbers are not equal or orderings not constant, invariance is not present.

To be an *optic* invariant, all information about an object or event must be present in the optic array, measurable at a particular place and time, and valid at all places and times. Thus the invariant is a constant mapping from the proximal image and distal stimulus, where relations between image (or eye) and stimulus are not fixed. More simply, all perceptual invariants for vision are projective.

Finally and most important, an invariant is not *perceptual* unless it is demonstrated that the observer can use the information in a perceptual task.

II
Competing Invariants of Configuration and Flow

In the geometry specifying perspective transformations, i.e. projective geometry, metrics has no meaning. Instead certain relations, the so-called projective properties, which remain invariant under perspective transformations of a figure, are abstracted. One example [of] such an invariance under form change is the cross ratio . . . .

Johansson et al. (1980, p. 31)

6
Cross Ratios

In chapters 1 and 5 I suggested that the lawfulness of visual perception is due, in part, to invariants. In chapter 4 I suggested that this source might be projective geometry. One rationale for assuming that projective geometry is fundamental to vision was given by Poincaré (1905, p. 49):

> The properties of light and its propagation in a straight line have also given rise to some of the propositions of geometry, and in particular to those of projective geometry, so that . . . one would be tempted to say that metrical geometry is the study of solids, and projective geometry that of light.

If information for perception is in the light, then invariants may be in projective geometry.

What is needed, of course, is a concrete example. Here, I investigate the *cross ratio*. My goals are modest. I do not suggest that the use of the cross ratio in perception solves fundamental and sweeping epistemological problems. It is merely one example, perhaps not even a prototypical one, that can be used to promote realism as a perspective in perception and epistemology. One invariant is not enough on which to build a theory. But one is better than none, and this one is among what I believe to be a large number that can be investigated; vision researchers have already begun to look at a few of these invariants. They are trustworthy sources of information, underlying Rivière's vicissitudes of lighting, position, and time.

The rationale for choice of the cross ratio is fourfold. First, it has the distinct advantage of being an invariant in mathematics based on an important theorem. In a straightforward way, this fact allows me to apply the concept of invariance to perceptual situations. No one can quibble as to whether or not the cross ratio is an invariant. Second, the cross ratio has face validity when applied to a perceptual problem: It is about straight lines and easily generalizes to planar surfaces— both of which are found in our perceptual environment. Third, although Gibson (1950) and Johansson et al. (1980) suggested that the cross ratio

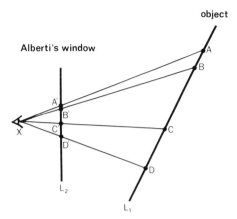

Figure 6.1

A schematic display of the cross ratio. Four elements are on a line L_1, point X is an element not on L_1, and all elements are connected to X, creating line segments AX, BX, CX, and DX. Line L_2 passes through these segments (or their extensions in either direction). When segment lengths are placed in ratio form, they create an invariant mapping from L_1 to L_2.

might be useful to perception, neither provided data in its support. E. J. Gibson et al. (1978) and Simpson (1983) also discussed this ratio, but again neither provided a direct test of its efficacy. Fourth, the cross ratio addresses, somewhat obliquely, issues of processing. Many regard the registration of invariants as a view that simplifies perceptual process. Ullman (1980, p. 380), for example, argued that

> if processing is trivial or nonexistent, then one is led to search "immediately registerable" information, such as the simple cross-ratio in the perception of three-dimensional structure in motion.

Although Ullman would disapprove, this research is such a search. With my rationale in place, consider next a description of the properties of the cross ratio.

The Canonical Cross Ratio

The cross ratio concerns the polar (or as a special case, the parallel) projection of four collinear points. Consider the situation in figure 6.1. Let A, B, C, and D be four points on the same straight line, L_1. Let X be a point not on that line, and connect all points to X. This creates the new lines of which AX, BX, CX, and DX are segments. Let line L_2 intersect these new lines at points A', B', C', and D'. Projective geometry tells us that the cross ratios of segments bounded by the points $ABCD$

and $A'B'C'D'$ are the same. In particular, the following segment lengths form the following equal ratios:

$$(AD \cdot BC)/(AC \cdot BD) = (A'D' \cdot B'C')/(A'C' \cdot B'D'). \tag{6.1}$$

This cross ratio—the product of the longest segment (AD) and the inner segment (BC), divided by the product of the segments connecting non-adjacent exterior and interior pairs of points (AC and BD)—is invariant under any projection to any point not aligned with A through D. Stated in another way, its value does not change, regardless of the location of point X or of the orientations of lines L_1 or L_2, so long as X is on neither line.

As it turns out, there are many ways to permute segment relations among the points A, B, C, D on line L_1. Given four elements and four places within a ratio, there are 24 different cross ratios, 6 of which are numerically different. All these are invariant under rotation and displacement of line L_1, change of position of line L_2, or movement of point X. Following most mathematical discussions, I consider the cross ratio given in Eq. (6.1) to be the canonical form and use it throughout the next chapters. After proving its invariance and showing some of its properties, I return to the other five cross ratios.

Two Proofs of Cross Ratio Invariance
Proof of cross ratio invariance is typically given in vector algebra (see, for example, Gellert et al. 1977 and Seidenberg 1962). The two proofs I present here, however, are given in trigonometry, adapted from Ayres (1967). The desirability of two proofs stems from the different aspects of the cross ratio that are seen as important. What has been of most interest to mathematicians is proof that the relations of segments AC, AD, BC, and BD are invariant on each possible projective line (all L_2's), what I call the *projected-segments proof*. Vector algebra is well suited to it. Of the most interest in vision, however, is the invariance of the optic angles subtending those segments as one moves around an object or as the object changes position. I call this the *projected-angles proof*. Schematic layouts for both proofs are shown in figure 6.2. The importance of the projected-angles proof is that, when considering angles rather than segments, the shape of the projection surface becomes irrelevant. Thus the projection surface can be a plane, as in a movie theater, or a curved surface, such as the retina or the cornea of the eye.

Presentation of the proofs entails three steps. First, I define the cross ratio $(AD \cdot BC)/(AC \cdot BD)$ in terms of the three angles α, β, and γ that subtend the lengths AB, BC, and CD, respectively. These are shown in the top half of figure 6.2. This step is necessary for the two that follow. Second, I define the cross ratio $(A'D' \cdot B'C')/(A'C' \cdot B'D')$ in terms of those

projected-segments proof

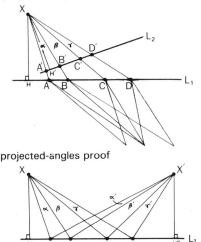

projected-angles proof

Figure 6.2
Two schematic displays for the proof of invariance in the cross ratio. The projected-segments proof shows the arrangement for different projection lines, the proof usually given in projective geometry; and the projected-angles proof shows the arrangement for different station points or changes in the orientation of the object, the situation relevant to these studies and to visual perception generally.

same angles. Thus, given that both quadruples yield the same cross ratio of angles, the situation shown in figure 6.1 and in the top half of figure 6.2 is proven. Third, I preserve the original segment lengths, but move the station point to X', thus creating three new angles α', β', and γ'. Given that this new arrangement of angles has the same form as the old, the situation shown in the bottom half of figure 6.2 is also proven.

Step 1: Conversion to Cross Ratio of Angles.   As before, collinear elements A through D are connected to a noncollinear element X. In addition, however, a perpendicular from X is dropped to line L_1, intersecting it at point H. This point will prove useful later. Also, the three important angles are drawn: α subtending segment AB, β subtending BC, and γ subtending CD. The cross ratio $(AD \cdot BC)/(AC \cdot BD)$ can be rearranged as the division of two ratios, AD/AC by BD/BC. At this point we can set up some proportions, multiplying each segment by a constant, $0.5 \cdot HX$. It happens that $0.5 \cdot HX$ times each segment is equal to the area of each triangle formed with the station point. Thus the original cross ratio of line segments is equal to a cross ratio of triangular areas. This set of substitutions can be shown as

$$\frac{\dfrac{AD}{AC}}{\dfrac{BD}{BC}} = \frac{\dfrac{0.5 \cdot HX \cdot AD}{0.5 \cdot HX \cdot AC}}{\dfrac{0.5 \cdot HX \cdot BD}{0.5 \cdot HX \cdot BC}} = \frac{\dfrac{\text{area of } \triangle AXD}{\text{area of } \triangle AXC}}{\dfrac{\text{area of } \triangle BXD}{\text{area of } \triangle BXC}} .$$

Now we can express the area of each triangle as a function of component side lengths and the angle that subtends the original length on L_1. Or we can consider the area of each triangle as half the area of a parallelogram, also shown in the top panel of figure 6.2. Its area is the product of the length of adjacent sides times the sine of the angle between them. Thus the relations shown above are expanded and then simplified as

$$\frac{\dfrac{0.5 \cdot AX \cdot DX \cdot \sin(\alpha + \beta + \gamma)}{0.5 \cdot AX \cdot CX \cdot \sin(\alpha + \beta)}}{\dfrac{0.5 \cdot BX \cdot DX \cdot \sin(\beta + \gamma)}{0.5 \cdot BX \cdot CX \cdot \sin(\beta)}} = \frac{\dfrac{\sin(\alpha + \beta + \gamma)}{\sin(\alpha + \beta)}}{\dfrac{\sin(\beta + \gamma)}{\sin(\beta)}} .$$

Rewriting the last expression by reinverting the ratio in the denominator yields a cross ratio of angles:

$$[\sin(\alpha + \beta + \gamma) \cdot \sin(\beta)] / [\sin(\alpha + \beta) \cdot \sin(\beta + \gamma)]. \tag{6.2}$$

Step 2: Conversion to Same Angles from Different Segments.   The second step is to convert to these same angles from different line segments, those on line L_2 labeled A' through D'. Notice that a new perpendicular from X is dropped to L_2, intersecting it at H'. Now it should be obvious that the eventual cross ratio of these angles should be the same as in the previous step, as exactly the same angles are involved. But what is not so obvious is that these second line segments should be able to achieve the same goal. If they can, then their cross ratio is the same as that for L_1. The proof begins in the same manner, where the expression $(A'D' \cdot B'C')/(A'C' \cdot B'D')$ is broken into two ratios and substitution of areas of triangles is made:

$$\frac{\dfrac{A'D'}{A'C'}}{\dfrac{B'D'}{B'C'}} = \frac{\dfrac{0.5 \cdot XH' \cdot A'D'}{0.5 \cdot XH' \cdot A'C'}}{\dfrac{0.5 \cdot XH' \cdot B'D'}{0.5 \cdot XH' \cdot B'C'}} = \frac{\dfrac{0.5 \cdot A'X \cdot D'X \cdot \sin(\alpha + \beta + \gamma)}{0.5 \cdot A'X \cdot C'X \cdot \sin(\alpha + \beta)}}{\dfrac{0.5 \cdot B'X \cdot D'X \cdot \sin(\beta + \gamma)}{0.5 \cdot B'X \cdot C'X \cdot \sin(\beta)}} .$$

In the right-hand side of these equations, as before, all the segment lengths of rays from point X and all values of 0.5 cancel, leaving

$$[\sin(\alpha + \beta + \gamma)\cdot\sin(\beta)]/[\sin(\alpha + \beta)\cdot\sin(\beta + \gamma)]. \qquad (6.3)$$

Notice that the ratio given in expression (6.3) is identical with expression (6.2), proving that

$$(AD\cdot BD)/(AC\cdot BD) = (A'D'\cdot B'C')/(A'C'\cdot B'D').$$

Step 3: Conversion to Different Angles from Same Segments. This final step is most important. Here, a new station point is chosen, X'. Points A through D are then connected to X', and the perpendicular to L_1 dropped from X' intersects L_1 at H''. We start with the same cross ratio as in step 1, $(AD/AC)/(BD/BC)$, and expand it into areas of triangles, then parallelograms:

$$\frac{\dfrac{AD}{AC}}{\dfrac{BD}{BC}} = \frac{\dfrac{0.5\cdot X'H''\cdot AD}{0.5\cdot X'H''\cdot AC}}{\dfrac{0.5\cdot X'H''\cdot BD}{0.5\cdot X'H''\cdot BC}} = \frac{\dfrac{0.5\cdot AX'\cdot DX'\cdot\sin(\alpha' + \beta' + \gamma')}{0.5\cdot AX'\cdot CX'\cdot\sin(\alpha' + \beta')}}{\dfrac{0.5\cdot BX'\cdot DX'\cdot\sin(\beta' + \gamma')}{0.5\cdot BX'\cdot CX'\cdot\sin(\beta')}}.$$

Simplifying and rearranging the rightmost expression yields

$$[\sin(\alpha' + \beta' + \gamma')\cdot\sin(\beta')]/[\sin(\alpha' + \beta')\cdot\sin(\beta' + \gamma')]. \qquad (6.4)$$

Because the leftmost expressions in steps 1 and 3 are identical, the expressions given in expressions (6.2) and (6.4) are identical in value. Thus the cross ratio of angles at station points X and X' is the same and will be invariant for any station point not on line L_1.

A Reflection on These Proofs
Cross ratio invariance at all possible cross sections of the optic array is, in part, formal proof of the multiplicity of possible layouts for any given *static* optic array. The Ames demonstrations discussed in chapter 4 are specific examples of how such layouts can present the same optic array, and many psychologists have taken this fact as prototypic of how perception is underdetermined by stimulation.[1] This is unfortunate because it emphasizes the wrong facts. Indeed, the cross ratio (and most likely other information as well) is invariant at all cross sections of the same optic array, but it is also *invariant across all cross sections of all optic arrays containing arrangements of collinear elements A, B, C, D.* Thus, rather than demonstrating the inadequacy of stimulus information for a static view, the cross ratio demonstrates the adequacy of stimulus information in a series of static views or across time in a continuously changing view.

To understand how I test for the perceptual efficacy of the cross ratio, I must demonstrate how its properties change with variations in positions of the four elements. These are beyond (or perhaps beneath) the projective mathematics found in any text, but I use them in the experiments that follow.

Properties of the Canonical Cross Ratio

It is helpful to begin consideration of the canonical cross ratio with equally spaced elements. The invariance of the cross ratio is not confined to equidistant points, but these serve as a simple beginning. Consider the top panel of figure 6.3. The cross ratio of these elements is 0.75. If one of the four elements is displaced and the other three left unchanged, the cross ratio changes. What is important is the amount of change in the cross ratio when each of the elements A through D is displaced an equal amount in either direction along the line. If elements are spaced one unit apart, then all the changes in figure 6.3 involve left or right shifts of one-third unit.

Notice first the effects of shifts in point A. These displacements change the cross ratio by differing amounts: When point A is displaced to the left by 0.33 unit, the cross ratio decreases to 0.71, an absolute change of 0.04. This decrease in due to the proportionally greater increase in segment length AC in the denominator than in AD in the numerator. On the other hand, when point A is moved to the right by the same amount, the cross ratio increases to 0.80, an absolute change of 0.05. This increase is caused by the greater proportional decrease in AC than in AD. Because proportional decreases for rightward change in point A are greater than those for leftward change, absolute change in the cross ratio in the former case is somewhat greater.

Consider second the shifts of point B. Again, changes in the cross ratio are different according to direction, but they are also much greater than for point A. A rightward shift of 0.33 unit increases the cross ratio to 0.86, an absolute change of 0.11; and leftward shift decreases it to 0.60, a change of 0.15. The increase in cross ratio in the leftward case is due to the proportionately greater increase in BC than in BD, and, similarly, the decrease in cross ratio in the rightward case is due to the respective decreases in BC and BD. The greater absolute change in the cross ratio with rightward displacement stems from the greater proportional decreases rather than increases in segment lengths.

As seen in figure 6.3, changes in C and D are the same as those in B and A, because the elements are symmetrically arranged. Notice that equal changes involving interior elements B and C alter the cross ratio

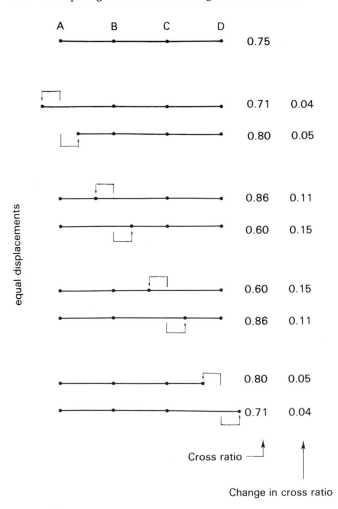

Figure 6.3
The effects on the canonical cross ratio of moving each of the four elements A, B, C, D an equal amount in either direction.

roughly three times more than do changes in the exterior elements A and D. With unevenly spaced elements the same general pattern recurs.

Other facts about this cross ratio are also important. Its range varies from 0.00 to 1.00, provided that ordinal exchange of elements is not allowed, for example, $ACBD$ or $BACD$. Lowest values occur when B and C are close together. At the limit, if B and C are at the same location, line segment BC is zero, the numerator zero, and the overall value zero. The highest values occur when A and B are close together, C and D close together, or both. At the limit, when A and B are in the same locations, $(AD \cdot BC)/(AC \cdot BD)$ reduces to $(AD \cdot AC)/(AC \cdot AD)$, or 1.00. In addition, the values of this cross ratio are not normally distributed: Equal distribution of the four elements yields a value of 0.75, which is the mode of all possible cross ratios. Cross ratios of 0.75 can also occur when elements are not equally distributed.

Finally, consider a situation complementary to that of figure 6.3. In figure 6.4, rather than showing equal displacements and unequal changes in cross ratio, I show unequal displacements that generate equal changes in cross ratio. For comparison's sake, the four elements are again equidistant before any is moved. Arbitrarily I have chosen absolute changes of 0.06. This is a value in the upper range used in the experiments to follow, but any value yields the same pattern so long as it is not too extreme. Increases in cross ratio are thus limited in the figure to 0.81, decreases to 0.69. These changes are indexed by displacement of each element needed to generate the new cross ratio. Normalized to the smallest displacement in the group, which is set to unity, the changes present a pattern complementary to that of figure 6.3. The leftward displacement of A necessary to alter the cross ratio 0.06 is 4.3 units; rightward change, 2.6 units. The leftward change in B necessary to alter the cross ratio by 0.06 is 1.2, and the rightward change is the smallest and therefore 1.0. A symmetric pattern is seen for C and D. Overall, the displacements necessary for A and D are roughly three times those for B and C.

Other Cross Ratios
The canonical cross ratio is not alone. All possible projective segments can be included in these measures—not only AD, BC, AC, and BD, but also AB and CD. Thus there are six numerically different cross ratios, given in table 6.1. The canonical cross ratio is listed first and has several desirable characteristics. One not shared by the others is that its range is constrained between 0 and 1. All others become infinite as segment length AB, BC, or CD goes to zero. This is unfortunate because many of the stimuli that I use have small segments that could cause extremely large changes in cross ratio. Another property of the canonical cross

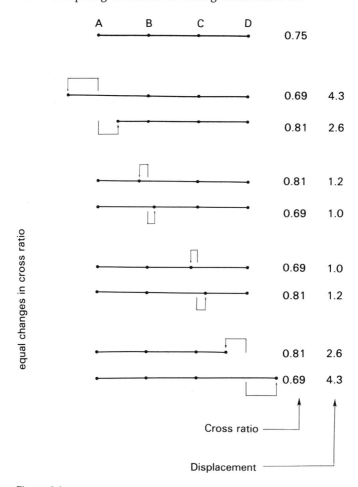

Figure 6.4
The complement of figure 6.3. Here, holding the change in cross ratio fixed determines the displacement of particular elements.

Table 6.1
Six Classes of Cross Ratios

Cross ratio	Range	Value for even distribution	Change with interior shift	Change with exterior shift
1. $(AD \cdot BC)/(AC \cdot BD)$	0.0–1.0	0.75	0.13	0.04
2. $(AC \cdot BD)/(AD \cdot BC)$	1.0–∞	1.33	0.25	0.07
3. $(AD \cdot BC)/(AB \cdot CD)$	0.0–∞	3.00	2.24	0.49
4. $(AB \cdot CD)/(AD \cdot BC)$	0.0–∞	0.33	0.25	0.07
5. $(AC \cdot BD)/(AB \cdot CD)$	0.0–∞	4.00	0.68	0.68
6. $(AB \cdot CD)/(AC \cdot BD)$	0.0–∞	0.25	0.04	0.04

ratio, shared with those numbered 2 through 4, is that changes in the position of interior elements change the cross ratio more than those for exterior elements. This is a good feature, not only for interpretation of the data, but also for methodological reasons as well. Cross ratios 5 and 6 do not discriminate between the two hypotheses to be discussed, in which change in the cross ratio is pitted against change in position of a single element.

There is a problem with the selection of the canonical cross ratio over the others. Why should it be perceptually important and the others not? A priori, of course, there is no real reason to choose it. I have temporarily eliminated all others because of their undelimited ranges, but I consider them again in chapter 8. Range considerations are independent of invariance; they are basically an aesthetic concern.

Two Hypotheses

Suppose that elements *A* through *D* are parallel lines placed on a transparent plane. Suppose further that the plane is set in motion, with two types of motion present—rotation or translation of the entire plane (*primary motion*) and, nested within it, a smooth lateral displacement of one line, oscillating back and forth (*secondary motion*) as the plane rotates. The question is, then, when secondary motion is relatively small, is an observer's ability to detect nonrigidity in the planar object governed by the element's displacement or by the amount of change in the cross ratio that it creates?[2]

Figure 6.5 shows competing pairs of predictions from complementary hypotheses. The horizontal axis indicates which of the four elements is displaced; the vertical axis indicates performance at detecting nonrigidity in the stimulus. The left-hand panels portray potential outcomes of one condition of interest, where the size of displacement is the same

If displacement is picked up. . .

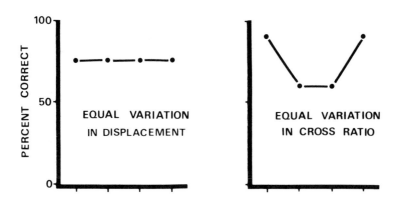

If cross ratio is picked up. . .

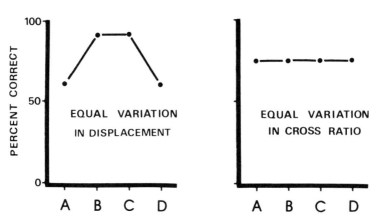

Figure 6.5
Two alternative hypotheses concerning the perception of dynamic displays consisting of four elements moving uniformly (primary motion), but with one having an additional component of motion (secondary motion). In the left-hand panels are predictions from the stimulus changes shown in figure 6.3, and in the right-hand panels are the predictions from the stimulus changes in figure 6.4.

no matter which element is moved (as in figure 6.3), and the right-hand panels show a second condition, where all cross ratio changes are held constant (as in figure 6.4). The upper panels portray results predicted on the basis of what I call the *displacement hypothesis*. It assumes that the perceiver can detect only the magnitude of change in position of a single element. Throughout, I call the displacement of the rigidity-violating element a *nonrelational cue*. The lower panels depict outcomes from what I call the *cross ratio hypothesis*. It assumes that the perceiver picks up the magnitude of cross ratio change but is otherwise insensitive to the changes in single-element positions.

Predictions are straightforward. If the displacement hypothesis is true, then under the condition that equal displacements occur across elements, detection of nonrigidity ought to be uniform across them. Using a staircase procedure (Cornsweet 1962), where trial difficulty is varied by block, we can set the overall performance level at approximately 75%. But when cross ratios are varied uniformly within a block, performance ought to be better when A or D have secondary motion rather than when B or C move. If, on the other hand, the cross ratio hypothesis is true, a different pattern of results ought to emerge. Under a condition that varies displacement equally within a block, secondary motions of B and C ought to be detected more easily than those of A and D precisely because they change the cross ratio more. And in a complementary fashion, a condition that produces equal changes in cross ratio, regardless of the position of the element, ought to yield equal performance across positions.

Two good features arise out of this design. First, the hypotheses and the conditions are dually complementary: The condition that tests the null hypothesis under one theoretical position tests the experimental hypothesis under the other. If the results are tractable, I am not limited to accepting the validity of the null hypothesis when possible competing hypotheses might make nearly the same prediction. If some third hypothesis is tenable, then it must make a set of predictions different from these. Second, the two theoretical positions—the displacement hypothesis and the cross ratio hypothesis—are ones that pit a local, nonrelational *cue* (discussed in chapter 3) for nonrigidity against a global *invariant* (discussed in chapter 5). Thus this procedure provides a test for the efficacy of projective geometry and invariants in the perception of rigidity and nonrigidity.

Four Cases for the Cross Ratio: A Preview of Experiments 1 through 8

In figure 6.6, four cases are presented in exploration of the possible utility and generality of the cross ratio for perception. Case 1 presents

Case 1: Rotating object
top view

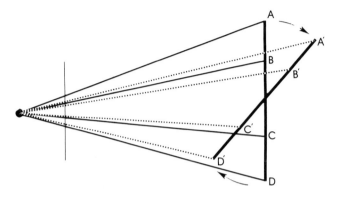

Case 2: Toppling object
side view

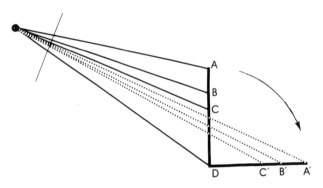

Figure 6.6
Four cases in which the cross ratio could be used to determine the rigid flatness of a moving plane. Case 1 shows four points on a rotating object seen from a stationary viewpoint. Case 2 shows four points on a toppling object seen from a stationary viewpoint. Case 3 shows four points on a surface of support from a translating viewpoint. Case 4 shows a circling object that keeps its face oriented toward a stationary viewer.

Case 3: Flowing surface of support
side view

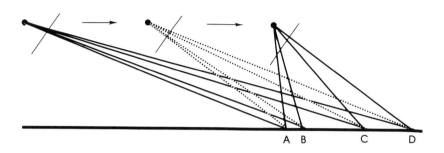

Case 4: Circling object
top view

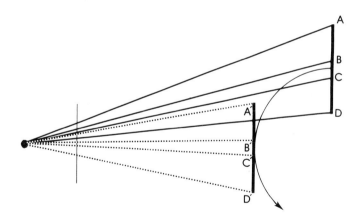

four parallel lines on a plane that rotate around a central axis. Viewed from the fixed station point indicated, or from any point at all, the cross ratio of elements A, B, C, D remains the same throughout their rotation. Thus, if viewers can perceive the rigid flatness of a rotating plane, it might serve as information on which that judgment is made. Case 2 presents four parallel lines on a plane that topple away from the viewer, much like the rungs of a ladder that is falling down. Again, if rigid flatness of the toppling object can be discerned, the information used may be the cross ratio. Case 3 presents four coplanar parallel lines located on a surface of support with the observer moving over them, and case 4 presents the same four lines on a circularly translating plane in front of a stationary observer. Again, in these cases the cross ratio could be used to make rigid planarity judgments. In the course of discussing the experiments, rotating, toppling, flowing, and circling are called primary motion.

Eight experiments were designed to explore viewers' ability to discriminate presence or absence of *secondary* motion within each of four *primary* motion cases. Experiments 1, 2, 4, 5, and 6 concern case 1, experiment 3 considers case 2, experiment 7 explores case 3, and experiment 8 investigates case 4. The first four experiments are discussed in chapter 7, the next two in chapter 8, and the final two in chapter 9.[3]

All stimuli were computer generated and shown on a computer-driven display. In each case the stimuli had four coplanar, randomly spaced parallel lines. In case 1 these lines appeared in vertical orientation, and the plane rotated in depth around a vertical axis. In case 2 the four lines were horizontally oriented, like rungs on a ladder that is toppling, falling away from the viewer in depth along the z axis. In case 3 these lines were again horizontal, like markers on the floor of a dark hallway as the viewer approaches and then recedes from them. In case 4 the lines were like those of case 1, but they traversed a circular path. Thus in case 1 the *primary* motion was rotation through 360° around a central vertical axis, in case 2 it was rotation through a projectively specified 90° around a peripheral horizontal axis, and in cases 3 and 4 it was translation plus expansion and compression for continuously changing observer to object relations.

Secondary motion, if present on a given trial, could always be thought of as independent motion within a moving plane. Half of all stimuli displayed only primary motion. They were rigid and maintained a constant cross ratio for the duration of the trial. The other half displayed both primary motion of all elements and secondary motion of one. These were nonrigid and varied in cross ratio throughout. Observers were encouraged to scan displays thoroughly. All stimuli were generated in polar projection for an optically specified station point. All subtended about 8° of visual angle in both horizontal and vertical directions. Different sets of observers participated in each experiment.[4] Eye movements and head movements were not restrained in any way. The testing room was moderately lit, and the surface and edges of the display screen could be clearly seen.

Overview

The cross ratio is an invariant from projective geometry that might be used in the visual perception of moving surfaces. In this chapter I proved the invariance of cross ratios and sketched their application to four perceptual situations: rotating and toppling surfaces, surfaces that might support a locomoting observer, and a circling surface. I also considered the properties of the canonical cross ratio and five other cross ratios. Noncanonical cross ratios have been temporarily set aside for purposes of experimentation because of their range of values. Finally, I considered two hypotheses to be used in the experiments in the next chapters. One is that observers can pick up the cross ratio, and the other is that observers are attuned only to the displacement of one element as it disrupts the rigidity of four elements on a moving plane.

7

Cross Ratios and Motion Perception

In this chapter I put an invariant to experimental test, assessing its usefulness to perceivers. Four experiments are discussed. The first two investigate the utility of the cross ratio for judging rigidity in rotating objects, described as case 1 in the previous chapter, and the third experiment assesses its utility in judging rigidity of toppling objects, described as case 2. These are then followed by an application of the cross ratio to La Gournerie's paradox and to the perception of film and by a fourth experiment on dynamic projections seen from the side. The results of all four are similar, support the cross ratio, and as a collection rule out some competing hypotheses about how perceivers might discern rigidity in a plane.

Experiment 1: Cross Ratios and Rotating Planes

Each stimulus consisted of four equal-length, vertical parallel lines on a transparent plane. The plane rotated around a vertical axis at a projected distance of six times its width. Optically these might correspond, for example, to lines 0.75 m in length, with outer lines an average of 1 m apart and the axis between the middle lines at a distance of 6 m from the observer. Placement of the lines within the plane was random within fixed regions.[1] Every trial presented one stimulus, which rotated with the nearest lines moving leftward. Within a block, eight stimuli were rigid and eight were nonrigid. Rigid stimuli had no lines move from their randomly assigned placements within the plane during rotation. Nonrigid stimuli had *one* of the lines move laterally *within the plane*. Two such trials involved each line, A through D. In one, the line moved first away from the axis of rotation, then back, and in the other it moved first toward the axis, then away, but in both it remained parallel and end aligned with the others.[2] Four frames each of two typical stimulus sequences are shown in figure 7.1. The stimulus on the left-hand side is rigid, that on the right-hand side, nonrigid.

Three viewers participated—two students and me. Under condition 1, the total displacement of the rigidity-violating line in each nonrigid

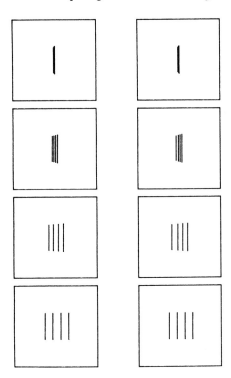

Figure 7.1
On the left-hand side are four frames from a trial presenting the rigid stimulus in experiment 1. The cross ratio is 0.763 in all frames. On the right-hand side are the equivalent frames from a nonrigid stimulus, where the cross ratio changes from 0.713 to 0.763 as a result of the rightward movement of the leftmost line. In a motion sequence viewers can readily see the right-hand stimulus as nonrigid.

trial was fixed within a block. If the average stimulus was 1 unit across, a typical session began with a total lateral displacement of this line of 0.10 unit.[3] If the observer was correct on more than 12 out of 16 trials in that block, displacements were reduced to 0.025 unit. If the observer then got fewer than 12 correct, they were increased to 0.05, and so forth. Under condition 2, the displacement of the rigidity-violating line in each nonrigid trial was predetermined by the amount of change desired in the cross ratio. A typical session began with a cross ratio change of ±0.100. If the viewer got more than 12 correct, then the ratio-change value was reduced to 0.025; if the viewer then got fewer than 12 correct, it increased to 0.050, and so forth.[4]

Results
Of most interest is each observer's performance on nonrigid trials as a function of the element moved, A through D. Different viewers did differentially well at various displacements and cross ratio changes, but there were no systematic interactions that impeded interpretation of the patterns of performance after collapsing across all blocks. As noted in figure 6.3, if viewers pick up secondary motions as displacements of single elements, then under the condition of equal displacements we would expect no difference in accuracy across the four positions. If, on the other hand, viewers perceive changes in the stimuli according to changes in cross ratio, then performance ought to be worse for displacements of lines A or D than for B or C. In fact, this latter pattern occurred for all three participants,[5] as shown in the left-hand side of figure 7.2. These results are consistent with the idea that perceivers are attuned to differences in cross ratio when judging whether or not coplanar lines remain rigid during rotation.

As noted in figure 6.4, a set of predictions is also made for the discriminability of stimuli that undergo equal changes in cross ratio. If viewer accuracy were a function of displacements (already falsified by condition 1), then they ought to be able to detect secondary motion in nonrigid stimuli better when those motions involve lines A or D than when they involve B or C. If, on the other hand, perceivers are attuned to cross ratios (as the results suggest above), then no performance differences ought to accrue. Indeed, as shown in the right-hand side of figure 7.2, the results of all three viewers show essentially flat functions,[6] with threshold detection of cross ratio change at about 0.025 to 0.037. Of course, to observe no systematic differences is not to prove the null hypothesis, but I take such effects in conjunction with those of the previous condition as evidence in support of cross ratios.

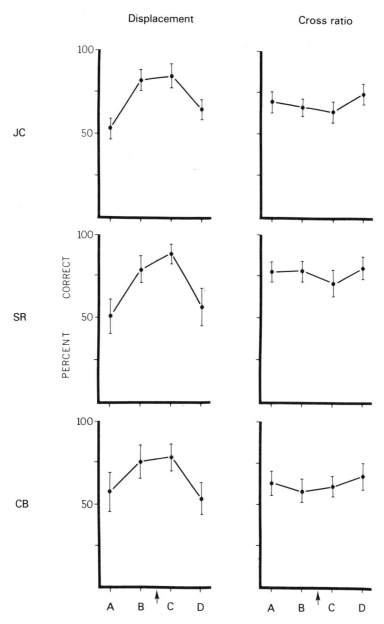

Figure 7.2
Results of experiment 1 for viewers JC, SR, and CB. The stimulus was a rotating object. The left-hand panels are the data for condition 1, where rigidity-violating elements had equal displacements across positions *A* through *D*; and the right-hand panels are data for condition 2, where rigidity-violating elements move to create equal changes in cross ratio. The data shown are those for only the nonrigid trials. The standard errors of the mean are shown, and the arrows indicate the mean axis of rotation. These results support the cross ratio hypothesis.

An Alternative Hypothesis
The data for both conditions are consistent with the idea that the cross ratio is an invariant used to detect rigid flatness under rotational transformation. There is, however, at least one design feature that could abrogate this claim: All stimuli rotated about an axis between lines *B* and *C*, and mean distances of these lines from the axis of rotation was one-third that for *A* and *D*. Reconsideration of figure 6.4 shows that, while maintaining equal changes in cross ratio, mean displacements of *A* and *D* under condition 2 were almost three times those for *B* and *C*. Perhaps it is not the cross ratio that is important to perception of these displays but only the proportion of radial motion of the line in question to its distance from the axis of rotation. This idea suggests that there may be a Weber fraction for the detection of secondary to primary motions. A Weber fraction compares the stimulus change along a particular dimension against its magnitude along that same dimension. Thus it may be the coincidence of displacements and distance from the axis that creates the uniformity of results under condition 2, rather than equal changes in cross ratio. And, similarly under condition 1, the relatively small motion of lines *A* and *D* as a function of axial distance, as compared with those for *B* and *C*, may have caused the curvilinear trend in the data. This is a serious problem, and it prompted an additional test of the cross ratio in rotating planes.

Experiment 2: Cross Ratios and Asymmetrically Rotating Planes

The results of experiment 1 may reflect cross ratios, but they may be attributable to a Weber fraction of secondary to primary motions instead. The obvious test is to displace the axis of rotation from the center of the rotating stimulus to the side. Two predictions arise: If the cross ratio serves for rigidity judgments, then results should not change. If, on the other hand, the Weber fraction serves for rigidity judgments, then performance ought to be better for those elements nearer the axis of rotation than for those farther away. Only one factor was changed from experiment 1. Rather than objects rotating around an unseen axis midway between lines *B* and *C*, they rotated around one between lines *C* and *D*, displaced slightly toward *D*. All else was the same. Again, two conditions were employed, one that held single-element displacements equal within a block and one that held cross ratio changes equal. Three viewers participated, two of us from the previous study and a naive observer.

Results
The data show the same patterns as in experiment 1, as seen in figure 7.3. Under condition 1, where within-block displacements were held

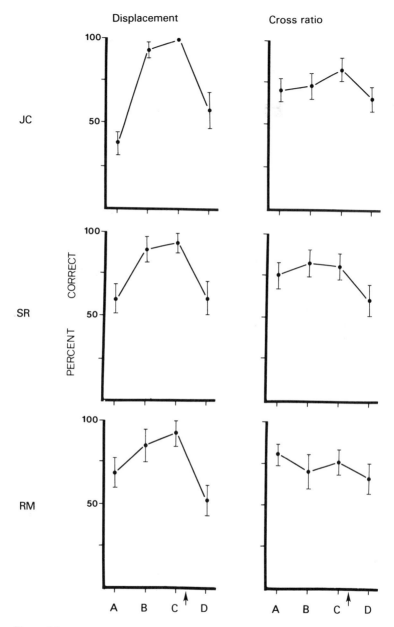

Figure 7.3
Results of experiment 2 for viewers JC, SR, and RM. The stimulus was a rotating object. The left- and right-hand panels correspond to conditions 1 and 2, respectively. Arrows indicate the mean axis of rotation. Again, these results support the cross ratio hypothesis.

constant, observers did much better on central members of the array. Under condition 2, where within-block changes in cross ratio were held constant, observers had essentially flat functions. Thus these data are consistent with the cross ratio hypothesis and provide no support for a Weber fraction of secondary to primary motions.[7] Again, the threshold for cross ratio change was about 0.025.

Experiment 3: Cross Ratios and Toppling Planes

A new set of stimuli and a new experimental paradigm were employed to explore the generality of cross ratios as a perceptual invariant. The new stimuli were toppling objects, shown as case 2 of figure 6.6. Each looked like a falling ladder with four randomly placed rungs. The rungs were equal-length, coplanar parallel lines. Unlike the stimuli of experiments 1 and 2, however, these lines were accompanied by an orthogonal pair bracketing their ends. The six lines together formed a rectangular lattice with bars at the ends and two others in the middle. The boundary pair was oriented vertically before the stimulus began to move. Optically, this object was seen as if looked down on with its base (line D) at a distance of two eye heights. The height of the object varied with the placement of the highest bar, but 0.60 eye height was average. Thus it is as if one viewed an erect 6 × 1.2 m ladder, with all but four rungs knocked out, from the front from a horizontal distance of 20 m and a height of 10 m. Again, all these measures are proportional, not absolute. The motion of the stimulus was the object's falling to the ground away from the viewer, as if support were suddenly removed. Placement of the four parallel lines within the structure was again random with certain constraints.[8]

For generality's sake, the paradigm was also varied. Every trial presented *two* stimuli simultaneously, side by side, falling in complete synchrony. They were equally spaced from the middle of the projection plane. Every trial presented one rigid stimulus and one nonrigid stimulus, whose nonrigidity was determined by motion within the plane of the toppling object toward *or* away from the axis of rotation (line D). In eight trials the nonrigid stimulus was on the left, and in another eight trials it was on the right. In the nonrigid stimuli, some had line A, B, or C moved either upward or downward. Because line D could never move, the other nonrigid stimuli had *all* the other lines move, holding their rigid relations.[9] Viewers indicated which stimulus, that on the right or left, was rigid throughout the trial. Four frames from a sample sequence are shown in figure 7.4.

Under condition 1, the up- or downward displacement of the rigidity-violating line was fixed by block, as in the previous studies. A typical

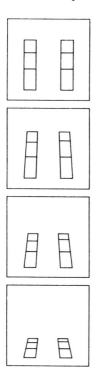

Figure 7.4
Four frames from a sample trial from experiment 3. The stimulus on the left-hand side is rigid with a constant cross ratio of 0.752; that on the right-hand side is nonrigid because of the upward movement of the second rung from the top. The cross ratio change was from 0.752 to 0.822. The right-hand stimulus is easily seen as nonrigid in a dynamic sequence.

session began with displacements of 11.4% of the ladder height. These values were reduced and increased according to the scheme outlined. Under condition 2, like before, displacements were determined by the amount of change they caused in the cross ratio.[10]

Results
The data for each viewer were again collapsed across blocks. Under condition 1 the same pattern recurred, as shown in the left-hand side of figure 7.5. All data show distinct, downwardly parabolic trends across line positions. Again, these results are entirely consistent with cross ratio utility in perception, not the Weber fraction. As before and as shown in the right-hand side of figure 7.5, the data for all three viewers under condition 2 are essentially flat with a cross ratio change threshold at about 0.025. Although the data are slightly more variable, the overall pattern is the same and supports cross ratios rather than Weber fractions.[11] The results of these first three studies provoke a new analysis of the perception of film and La Gournerie's paradox.

Cross Ratios, Cinema, and Television

Why is it that rigid surfaces in film look rigid? In particular, why is it that, when a viewer sits near the front and to the side of a movie theater and watches a movie from a point at which a rectangle projects as a trapezoid, an object does not appear to deform when it or the camera moves? And what about television with its curved projection surface? Consider a conjecture and a few analyses.

Film and Flat Screens
The results of experiments 1 through 3 suggest that viewers can make judgments about the rigidity of planar moving objects on the basis of cross ratios. This invariant specifies collinearity and, when applied to parallel lines, coplanarity. Suppose that these results generalize and that viewers are able to use this information not only in general but also when actually watching film from the wrong station point.

Cross ratios have some interesting properties when applied to La Gournerie's paradox. One is seen in figure 7.6. Imagine a large-screen cinematic version of the stimuli presented in experiment 1. Shown are the relations of cross ratio measured on the virtual object, on the movie screen, and on an imaginary plane in front of viewer *A*, who is in the proper location to view the film. Viewer *B*, on the other hand, is displaced well to the side. An interesting, perhaps counterintuitive, aspect of the cross ratio is that, for an object projected onto an imaginary plane in front of viewer *B*, the cross ratio is *exactly* the same as for

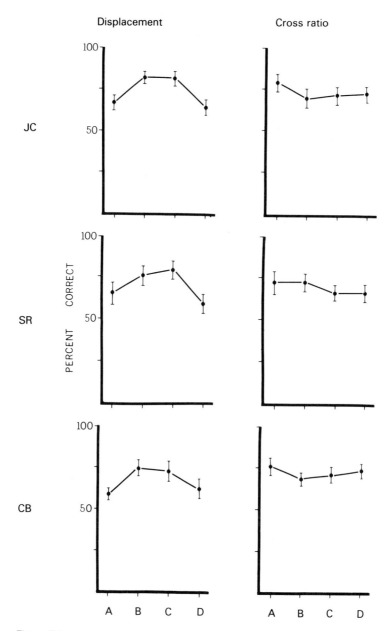

Figure 7.5
Results of experiment 3 for viewers JC, SR, and CB. The stimulus was a toppling object. Again, left- and right-hand panels are for conditions 1 and 2, respectively. The data shown are for all trials, because a rigid and a nonrigid stimulus were shown in every trial. As before, these results support the cross ratio hypothesis.

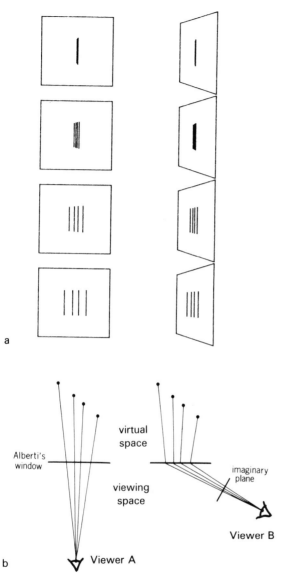

Figure 7.6
(a) The left-hand panels are static frames from a sequence showing a rigid, rotating planar object (like the objects in experiments 1 and 2) when viewed on a planar display (such as a film screen) at the correct station point. The right-hand panels show the analogous frames as seen from an incorrect station point. Cross ratios are preserved throughout object rotation in both cases, despite change in viewpoint and dynamic affine transformations of the stimulus in the right-hand panels. (b) The geometry of the planar projection for the two situations described in (a).

viewer A.[12] This is true not only of any particular static frame out of the rotational sequence but also for all frames taken out of that sequence. Thus, when the cross ratio of the object projected onto the image plane is preserved, it is also preserved at the viewer's eye, *regardless of where the viewer is located*. In addition, the amount of change in the cross ratio for nonrigid stimuli is the same regardless of viewpoint. Now, this is not to say that viewing a film from extreme angles does not yield perceptually noticeable distortions. I am stating only that, so long as the projection screen is planar, cross ratios are preserved. This means information is omnipresent, specifying planarity of the projected stimulus. Thus I would contend that, contrary to implications of Pirenne (1970), no cognitive process may be necessary to compensate for certain affine distortions in dynamic stimuli. Instead, the information in the array survives these distortions and can be picked up by the visual system in these circumstances. A fourth experiment was conducted to determine if the psychological utility of cross ratios remained when viewing from the side a projection of a rotating plane.

Experiment 4: Cross Ratios and La Gournerie's Paradox

Experiment 4 was exactly like experiment 2, except for the use of a double planar projection system, shown in the right-hand side of figure 7.6. Because Pirenne (1970) suggested that edges of the projection surface are used when looking at slanted photographs and because I am not interested in such contextual factors, these surfaces were removed from the display. This was done by exchanging imaginary for real projection surfaces in figure 7.6, as shown in figure 7.7. The angle between the two was changed to 45°. Thus, although the frame of the display scope was rectangular for the observer, the shapes of the rotating stimulus were like those in the right-hand panels of figure 7.6, with the right-hand elements slightly longer than they should be as a result of perspective transformation. Extending the rules of projection suggested by Alberti and following those of La Gournerie, I reconstructed the shape of the object in virtual space behind the image plane. If the lengths of the lines remain constant, the object itself must deform, collapsing and expanding like an accordion as it rotates in place. Such behavior is obviously not that of a rigid planar object. Can observers see the object as rigid, and can they detect nonrigidities resulting from displacements of single elements in the same way as in experiments 1 through 3? I was the only observer under conditions 1 and 2, where displacements and cross ratios were varied, respectively.

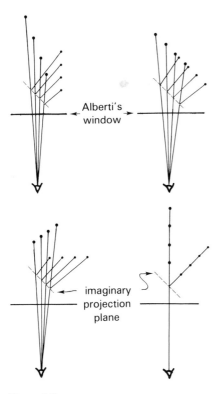

Alberti's window

imaginary projection plane

Figure 7.7
A top view of reconstructions in virtual space of the rotation of four coplanar lines, with an imaginary projection plane at a 45° angle to the primary projection surface. Notice that the reconstructions make the primary virtual object (shown in large dots) nonrigid, expanding and contracting as it turns. The secondary virtual object (shown in smaller dots) remains rigid throughout. These reconstructions show the affine distortions of the stimuli; perspective distortion is seen in the right-hand side of figure 7.6a.

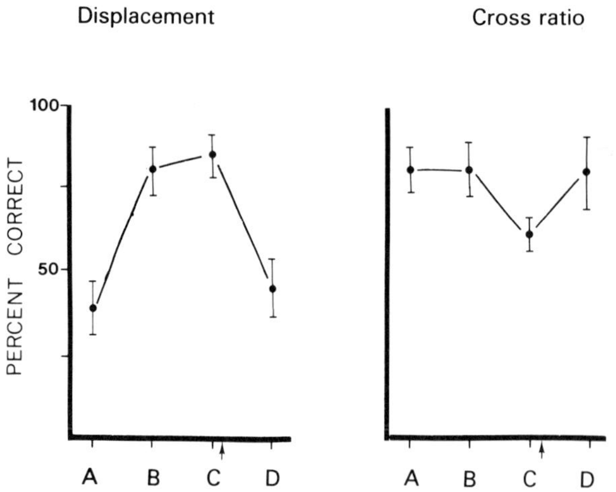

Figure 7.8
The results of experiment 4 for viewer JC. The data support the cross ratio as one answer to La Gournerie's paradox. The stimulus was a rotating object.

Results and Discussion
My data are shown in figure 7.8 and reveal the same patterns as before. Under condition 1, where displacement of a rigidity-violating element was held constant within a block, I performed much better on the central than peripheral members of the array; and under condition 2, where cross ratios were varied uniformly within a block, I performed almost uniformly throughout,[13] with a threshold at 0.025. Thus, not only is the cross ratio constant during any view of a planar projection of a rotating rigid object, but its utility appears general as well. The human visual system, then, may not be very sensitive to, or may easily filter out, certain affine and perspective transformations.

Affine distortions, although they preserve collinearity, do not preserve angular arrangements of three points other than 180°. Thus, when viewing a rotating three-dimensional object from the side, an observer may view the intersections of adjacent sides as acting like hinges. This creates some impression of nonrigidity because the surfaces remain rigidly flat but their dihedral intersections alter. A psychophysical study of the perception of dihedrals undergoing motion is needed. Unfortunately, such a study is beyond the scope of the present investigations. What is available, however, are studies by Perkins (1972) and Shepard (1981) on static trihedral intersections of planes and a study by Braunstein (1962) on coherence in three-dimensional arrays of moving dots.

Perkins (1972) and Shepard (1981) asked observers to discern whether or not the intersection of three lines could be a projection of the corner of a rectangular solid, what I call a *right corner*, and found great latitude in what observers would accept. We can interpret these results in several ways, but they may mean that observers are not very attuned to the distortions of right corners. That is, x, y, and z axes can undergo considerable shear against one another, and the observer will still see a right corner, provided that the configuration is a possible projection of one. This, of course, is exactly what happens when an observer views a rotating rectangular solid from the side of a movie screen. In a casual elaboration of his study, Perkins (1983, pp. 347–348) suggested:

> As we stroll down the street glancing about, it would seem that buildings do not appear to have the same proportions when we approach them as when we are opposite them. We live in a rubber world, but do not notice it, perhaps because intellectual assumptions about the stability of object shapes override the messages from our perceptual system per se.

Whether or not such intellectual elaborations are necessary, the relative insensitivity to distortions of right corners is clear. Thus, if we are relatively sensitive to cross ratios but relatively insensitive to affine and perspective transormations of right corners, then La Gournerie's paradox for film is explained.

Braunstein's (1962) results, however, place limitations on this view. He presented groups of dots rotating in virtual space seen in varying degrees of perspective. He noticed that increases in perspective (views from closer up) increased apparent depth but decreased coherence. That is, the array of dots did not seem to be part of a rigid system but instead deformed. If observers are generally insensitive to transformations under projection, no such effect ought to accrue. This effect, however, was not particularly large; a parallel projection of the moving dots was preferred over one of high perspectivity only about 30% of the time. Moreover, because the result was found for unconnected dots rather than for lines, it is not clear how effectively it should generalize to a richer cinematic situation.

Rephotography demonstrations by Pirenne (1970) and Gregory (1970), in which pictures of other pictures are taken from oblique angles, also pose a problem for my analysis. In these demonstrations the observer can discern that distortions have occurred. In particular, Pirenne juxtaposed faces in an affine-transformed (or slanted) format with normal faces. He suggested that information about orientation of the image surface is crucial to an explanation of the paradox. Of course, I would like to see these demonstrations repeated in cinematic format, like that of experiment 4. My suspicion, although uncorroborated at this time, is that rephotography transformations are most noticeable when a photograph contains both the distorted and undistorted figures. This dual representation forces the observer to discriminate, rather than merely identify, the contents of the pictures. Viewers are almost always good at discriminating, but whether or not they spontaneously notice transformations of what they identify is another matter.

Television and Curved Screens

Television, unlike film, uses curved projection surfaces. Most screens are convex, bowing outward in three dimensions toward the viewer, but many new sets have a cylindrical surface. Curvature in the screen is not used to normalize distances between cathode-ray gun and screen, as one might suspect, but to combat differential atmospheric pressure inside and outside the tube (Spooner 1969). Pincushion and barrel distortions are overcome by magnetic coils that alter the trajectories of electrons hitting the projection surface, and alignments are tuned for a viewer sitting directly in front of the screen along the surface normal to its center. Because adjustments can be made on most sets, the correct distance from the screen is variable, but a typical width is about 10° of visual angle.

When curvilinear surfaces are used for back projection, as they are in television, projective distortions will occur for any viewer not sitting directly in front of the set.[14] And strictly, the invariance of the cross ratio is broken *from all viewing positions* other than the position for which the set is adjusted. Television engineers have designed sets so that the curvature is as small as possible. I measured several different-sized standard televisions and monitors and found that the screen is a close approximation to a section of a sphere whose radius is about three times the screen width. If we assume that viewers can sit anywhere in front of the set, we can determine the locations where unsatisfactory distortions in the projected image will occur. In particular, if we imagine the stimuli used in experiments 1 through 3 projected onto a television screen (which in curvature is functionally equivalent to what they actually were projected onto), then we can determine isodeformation contours similar at least in spirit to those of Meister (1966). Experimental results suggest that changes in cross ratios of about 0.03 are at threshold for detecting nonrigidity. This value is based on stimuli whose cross ratio changed solely because of the movement of one line, but suppose that it generalizes to cases where more than one line has moved because of projection surface curvature.

Let me make the simplifying assumption that the rotating stimulus projected onto the middle half of a television screen consists of four equally spaced lines. The empirical question is: How much does its cross ratio change at any given viewpoint? Regions are delimited in

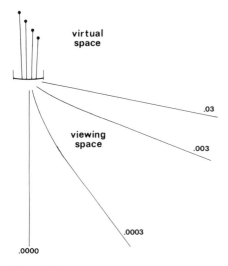

Figure 7.9
Iso–cross-ratio-change contours for a rigid stimulus with four equal-spaced elements projected onto a curved surface like that of a television set. The threshold for detecting nonrigidity through cross ratio change in experiments 1 through 3 is about 0.03, a value not reached until the station point is at an angle of 11° to the tangent to the center of the curved screen.

figure 7.9 for various viewing positions according to how much the cross ratio would change. What is remarkable is that for a rigid object the cross ratio changes little, regardless of where the viewer sits. In fact, the viewer would have to be located at an angle of 11° to the center of the screen (where 90° is looking head-on) in order for the cross ratio to change to the experimentally determined threshold value. Notice that these curves are unlike Meister's (1966) in figure 3.2; a viewer can sit far to the side, and information for rigidity remains satisfactory. At such extreme viewpoints the esthetic aspects of image distortion may be intolerable, as Meister suggested, but much structural information remains.

Overview

The results of four experiments suggest that perceivers use cross ratio information in making judgments about the rigid planarity of four parallel lines. These results indicate that invariants and projective geometry may be used in everyday perception.

If cross ratios are used in the perception of film and television, then La Gournerie's paradox can be explained. That is, the affine distortions in a virtual object resulting from a change in the station point do not alter cross ratios when the projection surface is flat. Experiment 4 demonstrated that the utility of the cross ratio holds under these conditions. Perhaps even more striking is that cross ratios change little, even when the projection surface is curved. If observers are relatively undisturbed by regular affine transformations of objects—transformations that change angles of intersection among surface planes but not local measures on any given plane—then La Gournerie's paradox completely disappears.[15]

This view is somewhat similar to that of the curved-world theorists discussed in chapter 4. That is, directly or indirectly, Watson (1978) and Indow and Watanabe (1984) suggested that we simply do not notice curvature of straight lines except under analytic conditions; here I suggest that we may not notice affine distortions except under similar conditions. The difference between their ideas and mine is that curved-world theorists suggest that the default state of visual space is curved; I suggest that it is not but that we are probably equally tolerant of all Riemannian curvatures near zero,[16] just as we are tolerant of affine transformations of Euclidean space.

8

Limitations and Extensions of Cross Ratios

The results of the experiments presented in chapter 7 indicate that the canonical cross ratio can serve as optic information on which rigidity of planar surfaces can be judged. Yet the cross ratio has serious limitations. One purpose of this chapter is to address some of these.

The first limitation is that the cross ratio is confined to collinear points or coplanar parallel lines. Such one-dimensional information may be reliable for the perception of certain flat surfaces but certainly cannot be for three-dimensional objects. What would the perceptual system do if no four elements were collinear? It seems unlikely to me that the perceptual system would be worse in judging rigidity when no collinearities existed, yet this is the prediction if changes in cross ratio were the only source of information used.

A second limitation is that the cross ratio is confined to *four* and only four elements; cross ratios cannot be calculated on three elements, and multiple cross ratios must be calculated on at least five. The three-element problem is a nagging limitation addressed directly by Simpson (1983) and indirectly by Lappin and Fuqua (1983). The latter study showed that viewers are extremely sensitive in determining equal virtual spacing of three collinear dots on an oscillating slanted line. The use of five elements yields computational inelegance. If there were five collinear elements to be considered and only one moved, an embarrassment of riches would follow as to how cross ratio information could be used. There are four cross ratios in flux. Perhaps it is the average change in these ratios that the perceptual system would pick up. The problem, however, is that the number of ratios burgeons exponentially as the number of elements increases linearly. Thus, for example, if there are 12 collinear elements and one of them moves, there are 165 ratios in flux. The utility of cross ratios seems diminished in such a situation. Parsimony suggests that some other information be used.

These two limitations would seem to make the perceptual utility of the cross ratio so small as to be freakish, but there is another possibility. Perhaps the canonical cross ratio is merely one of a class of measures that deals with distance relations among elements and of more general measures encompassing relations in two and three dimensions and among three or more elements. This possibility is attractive, particularly in view of the third limitation of the cross ratio as I have used it: That is, the canonical cross ratio is but one of six ratios, each having a different numerical value. Cross ratios 2 through 4 in table 6.1 have some of the same properties; namely, they change more with equal displacements of interior (B or C) rather than exterior (A or D) elements. But the magnitudes of the changes in cross ratios are not the same. For equally spaced elements the changes in interior versus exterior element shifts are about the same for cross ratios 2 and 4, differences of about 3:1. But for cross ratio 3 it is more than 4:1. And most striking is that for cross ratios 5 and 6 it is 1:1. If perception were deeply connected to the cross ratio, I assume that it would be connected to all of them, yet the results of experiments 1 through 4 do not support that view. To investigate this conundrum, reconsider certain properties of the canonical cross ratio.

Again, points A, B, C, and D are equally spaced; again their cross ratio is 0.750. If the locations of B, C, and D are fixed but A slides back and forth (near and far) from B, the cross ratio varies between 1.00 and some value asymptotically above 0.00. Similarly, if the locations of A, C, and D are fixed and B slides back and forth between A and C, the ratio varies between the same limits. Figure 8.1 shows the rates at which such changes occur. In the upper panel the vertical axis shows the absolute value of the cross ratio at every point through which A is moved, in the lower panel, the values for B. Notice three things: First, the closer A moves to B, the more rapidly the cross ratio changes. Second and similarly, the more B approaches C, the more rapidly it changes. But third, when point B is near to A and moves away from it, the cross ratio does not change much. I will return to this fact later, but it can be considered yet a fourth limitation of the cross ratio. In two cases out of three, however, the cross ratio changes faster when the displaced element is near to another. As should be clear, changes with movements of points C and D would be symmetric with B and A. The general pattern, then, is that cross ratio change is a function of proximity of a displaced element with others. Restated, cross ratios change more when a moving element is in a region that is more densely packed. Thus changes in cross ratio may have a systematic relation to various measures of density. The pursuit of this idea is the crux of this chapter.

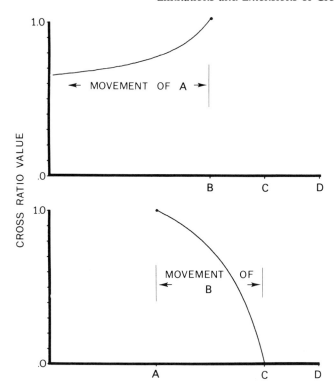

Figure 8.1
(Top) The changes in the cross ratio when element A is moved. (Bottom) The changes in the cross ratio when element B is moved. For both curves the elements are evenly spaced.

Cross Ratios and Density Indexes

Krumhansl (1978) proposed a distance-density model to account for spatial relations in similarity data. Although intended for psychological data, the model performs well in cases in which similarities are measured as physical distances (Appleman and Mayzner 1982, Krumhansl 1982). I measure similarity in this same way, using absolute distances among elements to determine the density at any given point. Krumhansl (1978) demonstrated many ways in which researchers might permute distance information in developing measures of density. I use four, three of which she discussed. Before specifying them, however, consider some criteria by which the different measures might be assessed.

Five Criteria for Density
1. *Applicability to Three or More Points.*   As mentioned earlier, one shortcoming of the cross ratio is that it applies to four and only four points. A general density measure should apply to all situations in which more than two elements are involved.

   2. *Applicability to Multidimensional Stimuli.*   Again, a second shortcoming of the cross ratio is that its measure demands collinearity. A more general measure ought to be applicable to two and more dimensions. For purposes of comparison with the experiments of chapter 7, however, I test potential measures in only one dimension.

   3. *Invariance under Transformation.*   The cross ratio contains its own scale factor. That is, it remains the same regardless of the general size or distance of the object measured. In addition, that object could be turned at various angles to the line of sight, introducing perspective distortions with no change in cross ratio. Insofar as possible, the density measure chosen might have these properties: invariance under reflection, translation, dilation, and rotation. The cross ratio is an invariant under polar projection, but unfortunately the density indexes discussed in what follows are not.[1] Thus I measure density in the two- or three-dimensional space of the object itself, not in the projection. For this reason I do not consider these measures to be invariants.

   4. *Continuity.*   Across the physical space of an object, density should be a continuous function, with no holes or gaps. Thus it ought to be measurable not only at the elements themselves but also at all places in between, generating density fields.

   5. *Continuous Variation.*   Not only should density functions have no holes, but also over scattered points they should have no large contiguous areas of the same density. In other words, the function ought to be smoothly varying.

Four Density Indexes
A variety of density indexes can be entertained. Index 1, the first and simplest, I call the *distance index*. The density ∂ at any given spatial location, i, is determined by

$$\partial(i) = \sum_i \sum_{j \neq i} d_{ij} \Big/ \sum_{j \neq i} d_{ij}, \tag{8.1}$$

where i and j are any two points in question and d_{ij} is the linear distance between them. The numerator is the sum of all distances between all points, and the denominator is the sum of all distances from a particular point i to all others.[2] The panels of figure 8.2a show the functions that this index generates. The top one shows the density function for four equally spaced points. To obtain it, a fifth point was moved throughout the space from left to right and density measured at each location. Dots mark locations of the four points in question. Below that panel is the function for seven equally spaced points, below that a function for four unequally spaced points, and finally a function for seven unequally spaced points. Values on the ordinate are arbitrary, but ratio is scaled. For this discussion only relative density is important.

Intuitively, the functions for evenly spaced points make a certain amount of sense: Points in the middle of the array are in denser regions than those at the periphery, and the even spacing yields symmetric functions. There is a small problem with four-point arrays. The area in the middle is flat, a violation of criterion 5. It turns out that for index 1 all even numbered arrays have a flat region between the two centermost points. This feature seems less than desirable. A larger problem is that with both odd and even numbered arrays the larger gaps between elements do not show decreases in density. This seems out of sorts with my intuitions of how a density function should look.

Another potential problem with the distance index is that the effect of distance between any two elements is linear. In fact, if there is anything like gravitational attraction between elements, we would assume that the distance would be represented nonlinearly. Rather than squaring distance, however, I chose to measure it reciprocally. Thus I call the second measure the *reciprocal distance index*. It is a small modification of Eq. (8.1), given as

$$\partial(i) = \sum_{j \neq i} 1/d_{ij} \Big/ \sum_{i} \sum_{j \neq i} 1/d_{ij}, \tag{8.2}$$

where the numerator is the sum of the reciprocal distances from point i to all others and the denominator is the sum between all pairs.

Density functions generated by index 2 are shown in figure 8.2b. These have the obvious flaw of being discontinuous, violating criterion 4. They approach infinity when density is measured at one of the points in question because $1/d_{ij}$ becomes undefined for zero distance. I would argue that density near a point ought to be quite high, though not infinitely so. Other than these infinite poles, however, the function seems fine. In particular, the gaps in uneven distributions generate low densities.

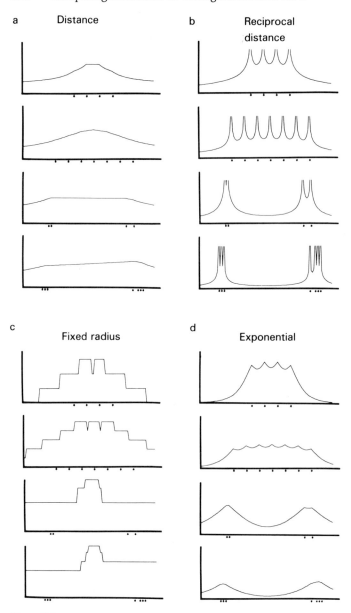

Figure 8.2
Four measures of relative density as applied to equally and unequally spaced distributions of four and seven points. (a) The functions for the distance metric (Eq. (8.1)). (b) The reciprocal distance metric (Eq. (8.2)). (c) The fixed radius metric (Eq.(8.3)). (d) The exponential metric (Eq.(8.4)).

Index 3 is a *fixed radius* measure. It simply counts the number of points along the axis that are within a fixed radius *r*:

$$\partial(i) = \sum k_{ij}, \tag{8.3}$$

where $k_{ij} = 1$ if $d_{ij} < r$, and 0 if $d_{ij} > r$. One possible radius is D, the mean of all distances between all possible points. The density functions generated from index 3 with $r = D$ are shown in figure 8.2c. Clearly, these are step functions without continuous variation. They also tend to have the same problem as index 1: When points are unevenly spaced with large gaps, density is highest in the middle of the gaps.

Finally, the fourth index is an *exponential index*:

$$\partial(i) = \sum_{j \neq i} e^{kd} \Big/ \sum_{i} \sum_{j \neq i} e^{kd}, \tag{8.4}$$

where $e = 2.718$, the base of natural logarithms; $d = d_{ij}/D$, the normalized distance between all points i and j; and k is an exponential constant. The constant I chose is 3.33, but a wide variety would do. The increased cumbersomeness of index 4 is compensated for by the features it possesses. Shown in the panels of figure 8.2d are the density functions for the same arrangements of points considered previously. There are no infinite poles, density is highest at the points themselves, and when gaps occur, density drops. All these features are desirable attributes, and as a cluster they are not shared by the other indexes.

Because perception seems coupled with changes in cross ratio, density should be highly correlated with them if they are to account for perception. Thus the density measures must now be compared with changes in the canonical cross ratio.

A Simulation Study

To assess the correlation between density and change in the canonical cross ratio, a simulation study was conducted. Nine conditions were tested, involving four to twelve points in one-dimensional, randomly generated arrays. Consider first the condition in which four points were used. The location of each element was determined by a random number between 1 and 1000, indicating the interval position along a line, say, from left to right. Points were then ordinally arrayed. As an example, consider points A, B, C, and D at positions 55, 406, 573, and 898, respectively. These are called the original positions and their cross ratio is 0.564. Manipulations of these points were as follows: Point A was moved five units to the left (to position 50), the cross ratio noted (0.562), then moved five units to the right of its original position (to position 60), and the ratio noted again (0.565). The difference between these

Table 8.1
Mean of Median Correlations of Density Measures with Mean Changes in
Cross Ratio

		Density Index			
Number of elements in array	Number of cross ratios involving each	1 (Distance)	2 (Reciprocal distance)	3 (Fixed radius)	4 (Exponential)
3	–	–	–	–	–
4	1	0.97	0.96	0.80	0.96
5	4	0.97	0.95	0.75	0.96
6	10	0.97	0.93	0.80	0.96
7	20	0.96	0.92	0.81	0.95
8	35	0.94	0.91	0.80	0.95
9	56	0.93	0.89	0.79	0.95
10	84	0.92	0.90	0.80	0.95
11	120	0.91	0.89	0.81	0.96
12	165	0.90	0.89	0.81	0.96

two was recorded (0.003), and the procedure repeated for points B, C, and D (cross ratio differences of 0.022, 0.023, and 0.003, respectively). Then the four changes in cross ratio were correlated with the density values of each of the four points at their original positions. Correlations were calculated for each of the four density measures and stored in computer memory. This procedure was then repeated 101 times within a block, and the median correlation was computed. Forty blocks were run. The mean of median correlations is shown in table 8.1.

All correlations were quite high. For four elements there were no essential differences among indexes 1, 2, and 4, with correlations very high, $r = 0.96$ or better. Index 3 was reliably lower. On the basis of these data alone there is little reason to choose among three contending indexes. In fact, correlations for indexes 1, 2, and 4 might have been even higher except for the one violation in the parallel between cross ratio change and density: When B moves and is near A (or C near D), the density is relatively high, but the change in cross ratio is relatively low. Indeed, inspection of individual simulated trials indicated that these yielded lowest correlations.

Consider next arrays of five and more points. In each case the points were randomly positioned from 1 to 1000 and ordinally arranged. In the five-point case consider elements A through E. When A is moved in the same manner as before, four cross ratios change, those involving $ABCD$, $ABCE$, $ABDE$, and $ACDE$. These were noted, averaged, and the procedure repeated for B, C, D, and E. Mean values at each point were then correlated with density indexes. Again 40 blocks of 101 arrays each were generated for arrays of size five through twelve, and the mean of median correlations are shown in the table.[3] With increase in array size, indexes 1 and 2 decreased in relation to the cross ratio, index 3 remained roughly the same but still below the other three, and index 4 remained high for all cases. Thus, not only does this index have intuitive appeal in the function shapes that it generates, but it also matches best the mean changes in cross ratios. Index 4 is used in experiments 5 and 6.

Other Cross Ratios

The results of the simulation study indicate that density is highly correlated with change in canonical cross ratio. What is not shown, however, is the correlation with the other five cross ratios. For completeness's sake, I must consider these. Although intensive simulations were not performed for the various density measures and other cross ratios, more limited ones were, and the results indicate that variations in cross ratios 2, 3, and 4 are about equally correlated with each density index, as is the canonical cross ratio. Cross ratios 5 and 6 are not.

I take these results to be salutary. It is something of an embarrassment to discover that the six classes of cross ratios have different numerical properties when the position of a single element is manipulated. That the perceptual system seems generally to follow the canonical cross ratio is fine, but no tests were provided for the others. I selected the canonical cross ratio because it has restricted range and most practically because it is the standard textbook form. That several of these cross ratios (1 through 4) are correlated with density provides some substance to a unifying theme. In particular, if density provides a framework for the detection of nonrigidity and if density is correlated with changes in many of the cross ratios, then we have some evidence that cross ratios 1 through 4 may have been equally sufficient in experiments 1 through 4. To be sure, cross ratios 5 and 6 remain outliers. The results of the simulation study are consistent with the idea that the cross ratio is part of a larger class of density measures. Experiments 5 and 6 use index 4 to determine if perception of nonrigidity follows density measures as well as it did changes in canonical cross ratio.

Experiment 5: Randomly Spaced Elements on Rotating Planes

Both experiments 5 and 6 had three conditions, which were designed to assess viewers' ability to judge rigidity in a rotating stimulus. Condition 1 involved a rotating plane with three parallel lines, condition 2 one with four lines (replicating experiments 1 and 4), and condition 3 with seven. The methods were essentially identical with those of experiments 1 through 3, and the stimulus situation—asymmetrically rotating planes—like that of experiment 2. The positions of the elements were randomly determined within spatial constraints. The three observers of experiment 2 participated, viewing about 40 hr distributed over a month's time. As before, each experiment consisted of many blocks. There were 12 trials per block under condition 1, 16 under condition 2, and 28 under condition 3. Again, half of all stimuli were nonrigid. Each session began with a block whose nonrigid trials were easily noticed. The total displacement of the rigidity-violating line was 10% of the mean width of the plane for the three- and four-element conditions and 5% for the seven-element condition.[4] Performance was always near perfect on this block, so displacements were halved for the next. If the modified staircase procedure was followed, then displacements varied around threshold for each participant.

Results
Analyses again concern the main effect—each observer's performance at detecting nonrigid trials as a function of the displaced element. Consider first the three-element data. As before, only those trials on which errors occurred are considered, and these are shown in the left-hand plots of figure 8.3. There was a clear and systematic relation between performance and ordinal position of the displaced element, corroborating the importance of density for perception. The four-element data are shown in the middle of the same figure and repeat the performance-density parallel. This result was expected because this condition most closely replicates experiment 2. And in the right-hand plots of figure 8.3 are the relations between performance and density for the seven-element stimuli. Again, the parallel recurs.[5]

The results are consistent with the idea that the local density of the rigidity-violating element is the major determinant of viewers' judgments of nonrigidity. In the manner of the previous studies, a complementary test was conducted: If a rigidity-violating element always appears in a region of the same density, it ought to be equally easy (or difficult) to detect, regardless of the ordinal position in which it appears and the number of elements.

Experiment 6: Equal-Density Elements on Rotating Planes

Again, rotating stimuli with three, four, and seven elements were used, and again they formed the basis of conditions 1 through 3. Initial positions were randomly generated, as in experiment 5 and previous studies. To achieve equal densities for the mean position of the rigidity-

Random spacing

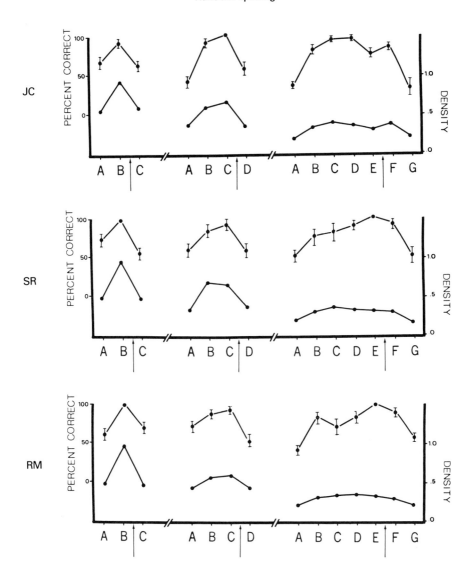

Figure 8.3
The results of experiment 5 for viewers JC, SR, and RM. The percent performance for
each viewer on each element in the nonrigid trials is plotted above the mean measured
density (index 4). The arrows indicate the axes of rotation. The stimulus was a rotating
object. The data in the center plots (axis of rotation between C and D) are a superset of
those in experiment 2 under condition 1.

violating element, however, the positions of the other elements were systematically manipulated. Generally, if an exterior element was to violate rigidity, other elements were moved toward it as a rigid unit in order to increase its density; on the other hand, if an interior element was to violate rigidity, elements on both sides were moved away from it as rigid units. All distances were then normalized so that the visual angle of stimuli was the same as that in experiment 5. The density values used were 0.86, 0.50, and 0.30 for conditions 1 through 3, respectively. Different values were chosen because no single value could be achieved across the three conditions; but this should not matter because the theory is that it is relative densities, not their absolute values, that are thought crucial to perception. Displacements within a block were modulated as before using a staircase procedure.

Results
Again, the effect of most interest is observers' performance at each ordinal position within a stimulus. The left-hand plots of figure 8.4 shows the three-element data for all three viewers. For two out of the three observers there were no reliable differences across element positions, as the density hypothesis would predict. In the middle plots of the same figure are the viewers' data for the four-element stimuli. For two out of the three observers flat functions were again found. And on the right-hand plots are the seven-element data, where for a third time two out of the three observers upheld the null prediction.[6] In general, then, as a superordinate to the cross ratio, density appears to be a potent perceptual property.

Density and Perception

In the first section of this chapter, I listed five criteria for density measures. Two were relatively unproblematic—that density functions for discrete points be continuous and continuously varying. These were met amply by index 4, the exponential index used in the present studies. The other criteria, however, raise deeper issues.

Applicability to More Than One Dimension
The data of the present studies do not speak to multidimensional separation. Parallel bars on a plane are two-dimensional stimuli with variation in only one dimension, and rotation in three dimensions does not increase the dimensionality of the stimulus variation per se. Thus there is the possibility of application of density to an object in more than one dimension, but there are no data as yet in its support.

Equal density

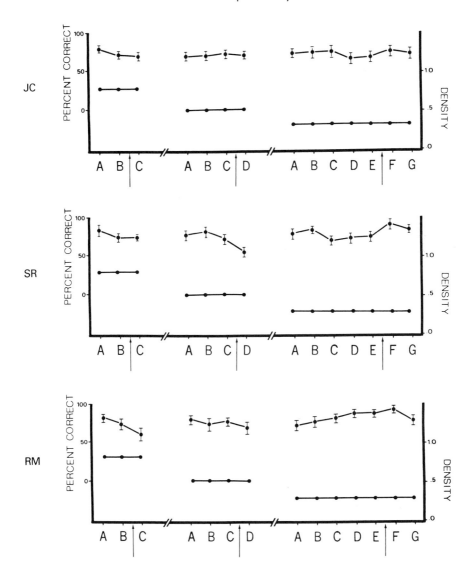

Figure 8.4
The results of experiment 6 for viewers JC, SR, and RM. The performance is plotted above the measured density. The arrows indicate the axes of rotation. The stimulus was a rotating object. The data in the center plots (axis of rotation between C and D) are a superset of those in experiment 2 under condition 2.

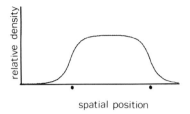

spatial position

Figure 8.5
The index 4 density distribution for 100 evenly spaced points on a line. The dots delimit the bounds of the array.

Invariance under Transformation

Any source of information that is to aid perception ought to, in its proximal properties, mimic the distal properties of the object under consideration. If the object moves closer to the observer, moves away from him or her, turns on any axis, or translates across the field of view, some sources of information ought to change in registration with the object. If the object itself does not change in shape, however, then some measure ought to remain constant, reflecting the object's constancy. The density measure used in the last two experiments is intended to be of the latter sort, but it is not an invariant. Density is simply a dimensionless number, measured at any location in the virtual space of the configuration but not on the projection surface.

Applicability to Points

Each density formulation is pointillistic, despite the fact that all generate fields of relative density. Most objects in our environment are not points at all but solid surfaces with measurable extent. Because a solid flat surface is a two-dimensional space of infinitely dense points, a question arises: What happens to density measures with increasingly dense points? An idea of this can be seen in the top panels of figure 8.2d. When four evenly spaced points are considered, the middle points occupy denser regions than peripheral points. When seven evenly spaced points are considered, however, the relative difference between interior and exterior points begins to disappear. A more extreme case is shown in figure 8.5, where 100 evenly spaced points are considered, bounded by markers shown on the x axis. By extension from this plot, we see that an infinitely dense array of points should yield a density distribution that is uniform throughout except near its edges. At the limit, the density field is probably little different from the shape of the object itself.

But in defense of pointillism, it is not clear what is really lost in points analysis. Despite the fact that objects are composed of infinitely dense points, it seems a strong assumption that all points are equally important to the visual system. Instead, points of high contrast or those created by intersecting lines ought to be more salient than others. Perhaps these could be weighted by contrast level or by illumination (Proffitt et al. 1983).

Overview

The results of the simulation study and experiments 5 and 6 corroborate what went before. The first four experiments suggested that perceivers use the cross ratio of four elements in making judgments about rigidity. In turn, the simulation showed a strong correlation between change in the canonical cross ratio and the density at a given point where rigidity violation may occur in an array. And experiments 5 and 6 showed that the perceptual system corroborates that correlation and treats the relations among coplanar parallel lines. Despite the shortcomings of the cross ratio, then, it still seems likely that the perceptual system uses information of this sort.

Let me clarify one point: I do *not* contend that index 4 is a computational algorithm used by the visual system. I suggest only that it captures constraints on the information used for making perceptual judgments. I assume that the visual system performs some structure-through-motion analysis, perhaps along the lines proposed by Ullman (1979). I assume further that densities at various points in the space around and on the object correspond to the sensitivities of the algorithms for determining a unique three-dimensional interpretation.[7] In regions of high density, the algorithm—whatever form it takes—should be sensitive to any point not in rigid relation to others, and in regions of low density it should be less sensitive. In other words, density measures predict the tolerance of the human visual system for small perturbations in the registration of the locations of particular points in the array.

9

Cross Ratios versus Flow Vectors

In chapter 7 I presented evidence that observers can pick up information from a moving display through the cross ratio of four coplanar elements. In chapter 8 I digressed to show that the cross ratio is limited in scope but that it might be considered a member of a broader class of density measures. In this chapter I reconsider the cross ratio. My goal here is to explicate cases 3 and 4 of figure 6.6, in which the cross ratio (or a density analog) can be used in two perceptual tasks but is not. The basis of the two experiments presented here is different from the previous six. In those experiments a global stimulus measure (cross ratio or density) was pitted against a local, nonrelational cue (secondary motion of a single line). In experiment 7, by contrast, two global measures (invariants) are put into competition. The first is the cross ratio, an invariant of configuration. The other is not specified in theorems of projective geometry; it is the uniform pattern of flow specifying the height of the observer's eye above a flat surface.

Eye height is the new term in this discussion, and it is central to what follows. The eye height for a person of average stature is about 1.5 m. If elements are seen from different altitudes—for example, three elements normalized to 1.0 eye height below the moving station point and one at 1.1 eye heights—then the relative motions of these points in optic flow reveal that one element is on a dip in the plane, at a lower elevation than the other three. If these elements are seen from the same height, on the other hand, their optic vectors specify coplanarity, or flatness.

Case 3: Specification of Coplanarity by Flow Vectors

Under ideal viewing conditions, which include standing on a perfectly flat terrain, the horizon is at eye height. If the angle from the eye to the horizon is set at 0°, the angle ϕ formed by the ray from the horizon to the eye to any element on the surface is (figure 9.1) given by

$$\phi = \arctan(y/z), \tag{9.1}$$

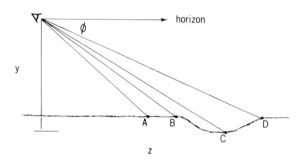

Figure 9.1
The geometry of case 3 (see figure 6.6) in which three elements have the same eye height and one has more; y is the eye height of the observer above a given element, and z is its distance from the point beneath the eye nearest to the plane of support.

where y is the eye height above the plane on which the object is found and z is the horizontal distance from the observer's feet to the object's base. But nothing about ϕ can specify the flatness of a surface unless the plane undergoes motion, usually caused by the movement of the observer. To discuss this flow we need calculus. The calculus is not difficult nor is its use intended to obfuscate. But it is needed as a tool to measure instantaneous changes that constitute a flow pattern.

When the observer moves along the z axis with his or her eye at a fixed height, angle ϕ for each texture changes. Measurement of the change in this angle entails taking the first derivative of Eq. (9.1) with respect to z:

$$d\phi/dz = v = -y/(y^2 + z^2).\tag{9.2}$$

For simplicity's sake, $d\phi/dz = v$, an instantaneous displacement. Notice that, as I did not calculate a time derivative, these are not relative velocity vectors. Instead, they are displacement vectors associated with movement along the z axis, regardless of the forward speed of the observer. Thus these relations hold equally for fast or slow locomotion. Because by rearranging Eq. (9.1), $z = y/\tan \phi$, Eq. (9.2) can be rearranged and rewritten as

$$y = -\tan^2 \phi/[v(1 + \tan^2 \phi)].\tag{9.3}$$

Relative eye height y thus becomes a somewhat cumbersome optic property of the viewing situation. Because $\tan^2 \phi$ is very small when objects are near the horizon (0.0003, 0.008, 0.03, and 0.07 for optic angles of 1, 5, 10, and 15°, respectively), Eq. (9.3) is approximated by

$$y \approx -\tan^2 \phi/v.\tag{9.4}$$

Here, we can more easily see that the displacement vector (v) and its location in the visual field (angle ϕ) determine eye height.

Three aspects of these calculations are important. First, Eq. (9.3) holds for all those points in the optic array along the line of movement of the observer, or more simply as measured vertically down the scope face. Points to the left and right near the line of movement have diagonal vectors of increased magnitude. Lee (1974), Koenderink and van Doorn (1981), and Longuet-Higgins and Prazdny (1980) presented different approaches to the same problem, as I will in chapters 12 and 13. But here, because the textures of flow in this study are lines orthogonal to movement and sight, the measures of Eq. (9.3) suffice. Second, this analysis is based on a mapping of proximal information (v and ϕ) onto distal information (y and z). Various other mathematical manipulations could be performed, but I have chosen this relation because of its similarity to those in the cross ratio. There, proximal relations among angles α, β, and γ were mapped onto distal relations among points A, B, C, and D. Third and most important, eye height as discussed thus far pertains to *each* element of the array. But this does not make it an invariant. When observers move over a plane, it is not the displacements and locations of single elements that are important but rather those of the whole set. Thus the concern of the moving observer is whether or not the right-hand side of Eq. (9.3) yields the same eye height for *all* elements. If it does, the plane is flat; if not, the plane is not.

Of central importance, then, is the relative ordering of the values of y for each element. If they have the same value, then the surface is smooth, even, and planar. If, on the other hand, they are unequal but appropriately ordered at all instants during movement, then the surface is not. Thus the perceptual invariant I propose is not the eye height of individual elements but their relative order as generated by optic flow. For simplicity's sake, however, I call it the *eye height invariant*.

Experiment 7: Cross Ratios, Flow Vectors, and a Surface of Support

Dynamic stimuli again consisted of four equal-length, generally coplanar parallel lines projected in depth.[1] These were orthogonal to the line of sight on the floor of a long hallway in the virtual space behind Alberti's window. At the beginning of the display sequence, the nearest line was at a mean distance of 13 eye heights from the viewer's feet (line A), and the farthest (line D) was 16 eye heights away. Stimulus motion consisted of these lines moving toward the observer (as if the viewer were moving through the environment) until the nearest line was at a mean distance of 4 eye heights and the farthest about 7. The lines then flowed backward to their original distances, as if the viewer backed

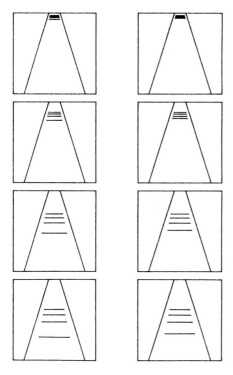

Figure 9.2
Four frames taken from each of two stimulus sequences from experiment 7. Those on the left-hand side correspond to a flat surface, and those on the right-hand side to a nonflat surface with line *B* (the second from the bottom) 0.05 eye heights below the plane of the others, a dip corresponding to about 8 cm (3 in). Such noncoplanarities are relatively easy to detect in the motion sequence.

up to the starting position. The cycle repeated three times within a trial to make stimuli comparable to those of the previous six experiments. Two image-plane factors changed during the course of a trial: Lines lengthened, and visual angles separating them increased in proportion to their proximity to the projected station point. To enhance the depth effect and to provide a reference to the horizon, converging lines were placed just beyond and parallel to the ends of the four lines. These mimicked the intersections of the floor with the walls. Thus all lines looked as if they were luminescent stripes painted on the floor of an otherwise dark hall. For an observer 1.83 m (6 ft) in height, this hallway would be 30 m long and about 3 m wide, with 2-m-wide lines painted across the width centered and orthogonal to the line of sight.[2] Figure 9.2 shows the arrangement of lines for four frames from each of two sample trials. Those on the left-hand side correspond to a flat plane, and those on the right-hand side to one not flat, with line B below the plane of the others by 0.1 eye height. In a continuous sequence the stimulus on the right is easily seen as nonplanar as a result of the motion parallax of the nonplanar element in rigid three-dimensional relations with the other three.

One stimulus was presented on every trial. In each block of trials, eight stimuli had four lines on a rigid flat surface and eight had three on the floor plane and one either *above* it (moving forward and backward faster than the other three) or *below* it (moving more slowly) by the same amount. All viewers—SR, CB, and me—found the rigid interpretations easy to see and for each trial indicated whether or not the hallway floor was flat.

Unlike the first six studies, condition 1 did not have equal displacements within a block. Instead, eye height differentials were held constant, one of the four lines being either above or below the plane of the others. Thus an eye height hypothesis is exchanged for the displacement hypothesis of figure 6.5. All viewers began sessions with eye height differentials of 0.10. Within the first block, eight trials presented stimuli with all lines at 1.0 eye height, four trials presented them with three lines at 1.0 and one at 1.1, and the other four with three lines at 1.0 and one at 0.9. For a viewer 1.83 m (6 ft) tall, these differentials correspond to bumps and dips of about 14 cm (5.5 in).

Under condition 2, as in previous experiments, the amount of change in cross ratio was held constant within a block. The secondary motion of the planarity-violating line was as before, completely in phase with the primary motion of the other lines. Thus across trials within a block the noncoplanar line was not at a constant eye height above or below the surface of the other three. All viewers began the first block of a session with cross ratio changes of 0.10.

Results

The data of condition 1, with equal within-block variations in eye height, are shown in the left-hand side of figure 9.3. These results suggest that the invariant of unordered eye heights was used by SR and me but not by CB. The data of condition 2, with equal within-block variations in cross ratio, are completely unlike those in any previous experiment, as seen in the right-hand side of figure 9.3. All viewers showed reliable main effects across the four line positions, and all these data are consistent with the idea that cross ratio is *not* an omnibus perceptual invariant.[3]

Overall, the results support the following scheme: First, the cross ratio is not generally used for the perception of planarity in optic flow

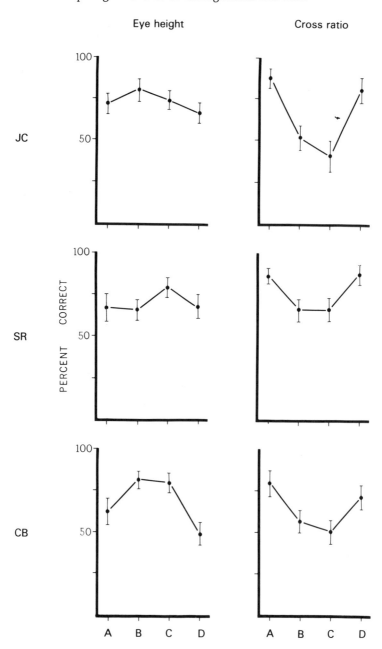

Figure 9.3
Results of both conditions of experiment 7 for viewers JC, SR, and CB. The stimulus was a flowing surface of support. The pattern shown here are unlike those of any of the previous experiments and in particular do not support the cross ratio hypothesis. Instead, an eye height hypothesis is better supported.

generated during locomotion. Second, uniform eye height receives support as a functional invariant from two of the three observers, SR and me. CB, on the other hand, presents a different pattern of data. His results from condition 1 are consistent with the idea that the cross ratio is used, but his results from condition 2 are consistent with eye height information. Because variations in eye height and cross ratio changes are always correlated, it is possible that CB used both. In fact, a detailed analysis of trial-by-trial data revealed just that. In summary, SR and I used only eye height information, and CB used both eye height and cross ratio data.[4]

Observers' sensitivities to deviations from coplanarity are shown in table 9.1. Normalized to the eye height of a 6-ft (1.83-m) person, all three could detect deviations slightly less than an inch (2 cm) above and below the hallway floor. The data of CB, of course, are confounded by his use of cross ratio, and his slightly worse performance at larger eye height differentials and slightly better performance at smaller ones indicate regression toward the mean, which might be expected. Nevertheless, such bumps and dips are detectable even in the impoverished displays used in this study. Of course, in real life we must be even more accurate—typically attuned to discontinuities of less than a half inch—to regulate footfall when walking or running. But rooms, fields, and roadways contain much more information than these displays. The differential richness of the real-world and laboratory situations, coupled with the comparability of the sensitivities, renders these results all the more impressive.

First Overview and a Conjecture

The results of experiment 7 sharply contrast with those of the four experiments reported in chapter 7 and, by extension, the two in chapter 8. In those studies there is strong evidence that cross ratio (or a density analog) is used for the perception of flat, rigid surfaces undergoing rotation. Here, in contrast, there is strong evidence from two observers that the cross ratio is of no use at all and from the third observer that it is useful only in conjunction with uniform eye height.[5] Perhaps cross ratios are perceptually important only when a planar object rotates. In experiments 1 and 2 (as well as experiments 4 and 5) the object plane rotated three times through 360°, and in experiment 3 it rotated through 90°. In experiment 7, by contrast, the plane rotated hardly at all.[6] Other factors, of course, separate the display of experiment 7 from those of the previous studies, and these could have affected the results as well. Nevertheless, experiment 8 was designed to test for rotation as the precondition for use of cross ratios. Perhaps under

Table 9.1
Signal Detection Analyses for Determining Nonflatness of Four Lines in Experiment 6

Viewer	Deviation from floor in eye heights	Deviation (in cm)[a]	Mean d'	Standard error
JC	0.050	8.4	2.82	0.12
	0.025	4.2	1.82	0.15
	0.013	2.1	0.98	0.21
	0.006	1.1	0.52	0.25
SR	0.100	16.8	2.47	0.63
	0.050	8.4	2.06	0.20
	0.025	4.2	0.60	0.29
	0.013	2.1	0.14	0.17
CB	0.100	16.8	2.52	0.36
	0.050	8.4	1.79	0.50
	0.025	4.2	1.01	0.26
	0.013	2.1	0.90	0.20

a. Normalized to the height of a person 1.83 m (6 ft) tall.

conditions in which the plane does not rotate, rigidity judgments are best done through analysis of displacement fields. Let me sketch how coplanarity might be specified in a circularly translating plane.

Case 4: Specification of Coplanarity by Flow Vectors

The viewing situation of case 4 is shown in figure 9.4. The plane moves in a circular path maintaining its face at right angles to the line of sight to the center of the display screen. Thus planar elements trace out in virtual space circles of the same size with common parallel tangents. For a noncoplanar stimulus, shown in figure 9.4, one element is advanced or recessed in virtual space but is held in rigid relation to the others. Its path does not share tangents with the others. From the viewer's perspective, consider the following set of relations:

$$\theta = \arctan[(r \sin \beta + x)/(z - r \cos \beta)], \tag{9.5}$$

where θ is the angle to the plane's midpoint, β is the angle through 360° that the object has traversed (with 0° the point closest to the observer), r is the radius of the circular path, z is the distance from the viewpoint to the center of the circular path, and x is the lateral distance outward of a particular element from the center of the plane.

As in case 3, this relation can be differentiated with respect to the motion in depth, which in this case is caused by changes in angle β.

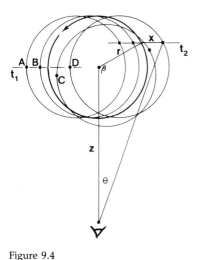

Figure 9.4
The geometry of case 4 (see figure 6.6), in which one element (C) is noncoplanar with the other three (A, B, and D), at two times, t_1 and t_2. The bold circle is the path of the middle of the stimulus plane, and the other circles are the paths of each element. z is the distance to the center of the circular path (underestimated for the purposes of this figure), θ is the angle between the line of sight to the center of the circular path (and the center of the screen) to the element in question (in this case D), β is the angle around the circular path, r is the radius of the circle, and x is the distance of the element from the center of the plane.

The relation $d\theta/d\beta$ can then be rearranged and a set of measures obtained that can be used in an invariant, just as with case 3. Here, rather than an ordering of eye heights constituting the invariant to be tested for perception, it is the ordering of elements in depth. If elements lie on the same plane, they are unordered and there is no motion parallax, but if one lies closer or farther, they are always ordered in the same way, yielding parallactic motions.[7] For simplicity's sake, I call this a planarity invariant.

Experiment 8: Cross Ratios, Flow Vectors, and Circularly Translating Planes

The purpose of this study was to explore case 4, where stimuli were as much like those of case 1 as possible but without rotation. Four frames from two such sequences of circularly translating stimuli are shown in figure 9.5, with those on the left-hand side depicting planar elements and those on the right-hand side, noncoplanar ones. Again, the right-hand stimulus is easily seen as noncoplanar because of motion parallax. Notice that elements are again end aligned, creating the strong

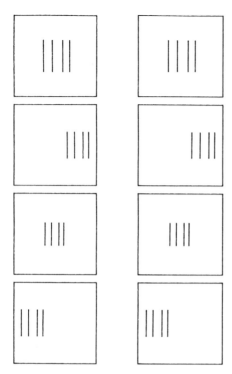

Figure 9.5
Four frames taken from two sample sequences from experiment 7. The panels on the left-hand side correspond to a rigid plane, and those on the right-hand side correspond to a rigid stimulus with one element, the second from the left, noncoplanar and closer to the observer in virtual space.

impression of nonrigidity in noncoplanar stimuli. Two observers participated—RM and me. In all other ways stimuli and procedures were identical with experiment 1:[8] Under condition 1, the distance in virtual space of the planarity-violating line was held constant within a block, and under condition 2 the change in cross ratios was held constant.

Results
By collapsing across blocks, we can see that the results shown in figure 9.6 are quite similar to those of the previous experiment. In particular, under condition 1 there is evidence, although not overwhelmingly strong, that the ordered pattern of displacements (motion parallax) is used in judgments of coplanarity, with both viewers yielding results like SR's and mine in experiment 7. Threshold performance for both observers occurred when the planarity-violating element was closer to

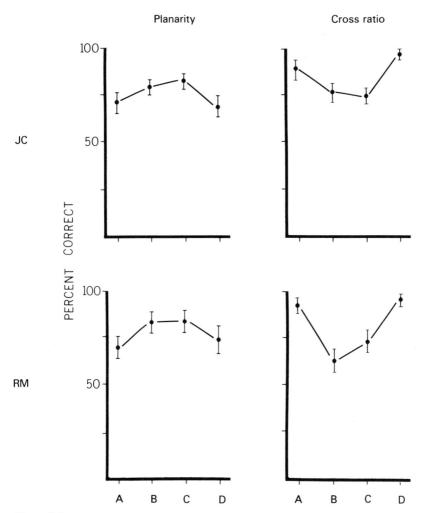

Figure 9.6
The results of both conditions in experiment 8, replicating those of experiment 7, for viewers JC and RM. Again the cross ratio hypothesis is disconfirmed, and a hypothesis concerning planarity and displacement vectors is generally supported. The stimulus was a circling object.

or farther from the others by 2% of the mean distance from the viewer. Under condition 2 there was no evidence for the efficacy of the cross ratio.[9] Such results reinforce the idea that cross ratios (or density analogs) may be useful for judgment of rigid coplanarity of rotating planes but not for those that translate and keep their faces in the same orientation toward the perceiver.

Perceptual Choice of Information

It is time to discuss the results of the first eight experiments, and to begin to place their results within a general theory of how information is used in perception. The latter part of this task is completed in chapter 15 for all studies but is broached here to introduce main points.

An Affirmation of Invariance in Perception

Gibson championed the idea that invariants under transformation are the key to understanding the perceived permanence of objects in the world. The results of studies presented in the last three chapters are entirely consistent with this idea. The cross ratio of four parallel, coplanar lines seems to be used by perceivers for judgment of rigid flatness in rotating and toppling objects, as shown in experiments 1 through 4. Not only is this invariant used, but also its use seems uncontaminated by other factors, such as the nonrelational cue of displacement in the rigidity-violating motion of one of the four lines. Moreover, the most elegant aspect of the cross ratio is that it stems from a theorem in mathematics.

A different invariant is used in the perception of the flow of a surface of support (case 3) and in nonrotating planes in general (case 4). These are not mathematical theorems, but they are equally well specified in the optic array as ordered displacement patterns. Uniformity of displacements is broken when a noncoplanar element is closer to the perceiver than the plane of the other elements, and it moves faster than those by a constant increment. If it is farther away from the perceiver, it moves more slowly. Two of the three observers in experiment 7 appeared to use eye height and no other information, not even the change in cross ratio. A third seemed to use both eye height and cross ratio. In experiment 8, both observers appeared to use vector displacements, specifying planarity with little support for cross ratios.

Thus under none of the conditions of these eight experiments is there strong evidence for the use of nonrelational cues, and in only one (CB in experiment 7) is there evidence that anything other than one source of information was used. Such results generally promote the straightforward nonelaborative view of perception that Gibson espoused.

An Affirmation of Projective Geometry in Perception
Johansson, following Russell and Poincaré, championed the idea that projective geometry is the key to understanding layout and its perception.[10] The results of the current set of studies are entirely consistent with this idea. The invariance of the cross ratio is derived from a theorem of projective geometry due to Pappas, and its apparent use by the observers in experiments 1 through 4 provides the strongest test of Johansson's idea to date. In these experiments I demonstrated that not only is projective geometry a good framework in which to consider the permanence of objects in optic flow but also one of its theorems is a perceptual "theorem," at least some of the time.

Eye height, and deviations from uniform eye height, can also be important to perception, particularly when observing the optic flow of a terrestrial surface. This idea finds support in the data of experiments 7 and 8, which in turn support the view that projective geometry is relevant to perception. The flow of a noncoplanar element against a nearby plane is entirely predictable from perspective transformations of projected displacements. These are not theorems of projective geometry because it is unlikely that they would be useful to mathematicians. But they reinforce Johansson's idea that optic flow is well captured by principles of station points and projective geometry. The similarity of results in the last two experiments support the idea that the nonrotational motion of a plane, regardless of its orientation to the observer, is perceived in the same manner. And projective geometry handily encompasses such results.

Underdetermination of Perceptual Process by Multiplicity of Invariants
Gibson consistently opposed the idea that information underdetermines perception. He believed that invariants negated the need to go beyond the information given to invoke some form of unconscious inference or representational mediation. He also opposed Johansson's decoding principles on the same grounds. In an open letter to him, Gibson (1970, p. 78) said:

> When you postulate rules for treating the stimulus data or principles for decoding the data you are taking it for granted that the data themselves are insufficient for perception.

But this statement misses the mark. Principles of decoding do not assume that stimulus data are insufficient, only that the grounds for deciding what information to use are insufficient. To understand the rationale for the differences between Gibson and Johansson, we must pursue the interplay between thresholds for information pickup and the multiplicity of invariant information.

In *The Senses Considered as Perceptual Systems*, Gibson (1966) discussed thresholds for registration of stimulus information. For him, however, true threshold situations were rare in the real world because an active explorer can always obtain more information by changing point of view or manipulating an object. But if invariants are revealed under transformation, then there is always the opportunity for some transformations to be too small to be revealed (discussed in chapter 5), for others to be at threshold, and for still others to be beyond it, revealing fully adequate information.

The present set of experiments manipulated this fact. At times displacements of a rigidity- or planarity-violating line were above threshold and easy to discern; at other times they were marginal and gave the observer a vague sense that something might be wrong, and at still other times they were so small as to promote sheer guessing. The procedure was designed to keep performance near threshold, prototypic of what Gibson discussed under the rubric of "causes of deficient perception." When the perceiver is presented with inadequate information, Gibson's (1966, pp. 303–304) most concrete suggestion was that

> the perceptual system *hunts*. It tries to find meaning, to make sense from what little information it can get. . . . The effort of apprehension may then be strenuous. With conflicting or contradictory information the overall perceptual system alternates or compromises . . . but in lifelike situations a search for *additional* information begins, information that will reinforce one or the other alternative. . . . If detection still fails, the system hunts more widely in space and longer in time. It tests for what remains invariant over time, trying out different perspectives. If the invariants still do not appear, a whole repertory of poorly understood processes variously called assumptions, inferences, or guesses come into play.

If the experimental displays discussed here bear no relation to reality, then it might easily be suggested that vacillating results from viewers are to be expected. I believe, however, that such a criticism cannot be levied. Experiment 7, in particular, was lifelike in that it presented optic information of the kind we need everyday. If we are not able to detect small, near-threshold deviations from flatness, we are likely to wind up on our faces, having tripped on a nail, a piece of gum, or a small hole in the floor. If the perceptual system must hunt in this lifelike situation—sometimes finding one invariant, sometimes another—then Gibson's scheme holds for search under conditions of inadequate information. Indeed, the data of CB in experiment 7 are consistent with this view. But the remaining data in experiments 7 and 8 present a more puzzling picture: RM, SR, and I hunted only in flow information.

Such a strategy does not stem from information inadequacy, because the experimental paradigms purposefully varied both sources of information over many blocks. Nor, moreover, does it stem from an inability to pick up cross ratios, because the results of experiments 1 through 4 indicate strong sensitivity to these changes within the ranges employed in experiments 7 and 8.

In terms that are quite foreign to this enterprise, CB appears to have followed a *satisficing* rule, whereas RM, SR, and I followed a *certainty* rule (Simon 1955). A satisficing rule suggests that the hunt for information continues until any adequate information is found, and the quote by Gibson (1966, p. 303) indicates that he thought the perceptual system would follow such a rule. A certainty rule, on the other hand, suggests that viewers should stick with one source of information.

Decoding Principles

I have chosen to talk about perceptual rules from a perspective far outside perception, so as to reintroduce *decoding principles* as proposed by Johansson (1970, p. 73) in a new light:

> I will stress that the visual system . . . contributes to the perceptual outcome from the proximal stimulus flow. . . . The efficiency of the system is given by a set of rules for stimulus data treatment (the programming of the visual computer, if you accept this metaphor), rules which work in an automatic way, but which result in veridicality when the proximal stimuli are projections from moving rigid objects and/or a rigid environment in motion relative to the eye. The principle of motion analysis . . . may be regarded as a general summarizing formulation of these decoding principles.
>
> Such rules have been shown experimentally to work in a blind, mechanical way and leave basically nothing for subjective choice. Therefore, I prefer to regard them as indicating a primary neurological "wiring." Their basic effect seems to be to filter out rigidity in space.

I contend that the use of ordered displacements rather than cross ratios in the last experiments is an example of strategic but unconscious choice of one decoding principle over another. Cross ratios filter out, in Johansson's sense, rigid flatness from nonflatness *or* nonrigidity, and displacement ordering filters out rigid flatness from nonflatness.

Invariants of Configuration and Flow

Why does the human visual system choose among equally available invariants? Any answer here must necessarily be premature, but let me offer a possibility. The cross ratio is an invariant of configuration.

That is, foremost in its calculation are the relative *positions* of elements on a plane, irrespective of planar motion. Measurement at any frozen instant in time suffices, so long as measures across time can be compared. Thus, in principle, no motion is essential to the display, only separate points of view. As discussed at the end of chapter 1, the cross ratio fits snugly within the computational approach of discrete points and views. The ordered displacements of eye height and planarity discussed in experiments 7 and 8, on the other hand, are invariants of flow. Here relative position is important, but most crucial is how that information combines with instantaneous displacements. This fact dovetails nicely with another approach in machine vision—that of discrete points and displacements.

Invariants of flow might seem inherently more complicated than those of configuration. We should not make the mistake, however, of assuming that what is simplest to express in equations is simplest for the visual system; Marr (1982), for example, suggested that computational theory ought to be independent of algorithm.

But why were cross ratios apparently used in the earlier experiments? Again, answers that can be offered at present are without any real force, but I suspect rigidity provides the key. In experiments 1 through 6 nonplanar stimuli could be seen only as nonrigid, whereas in experiments 7 and 8 nonplanar stimuli could always be seen as rigid. The particular style of nonrigidity employed broke up ordered displacement patterns. Perhaps it did so in such a way as to render them less useful than they might ordinarily have been. This view does not seem parsimonious because it suggests that the visual system uses different algorithms for assessments of rigidity and nonrigidity. Yet, at base, this may be what decoding principles are all about.

Second Overview

One explanation for the use of different invariants at different times stems from principles of decoding, and I believe that this concept has been misunderstood. In particular, I think that Gibson's view of decoding principles is incorrect: Johansson's decoding principles do not assume that information is insufficient in the optic array. Their necessity is due to quite the opposite state of affairs: Data in the optic array are too rich for the perceptual system to operate by invariant pickup alone. Invariants underdetermine perceptual process because, as demonstrated in the experiments of this chapter, there can be at least two, perhaps many more, invariants that specify the same thing. It would appear that invariants are relatively cheap in the optic array. They may be available in many forms, and some may be more informative than others at different times and in different places.

In the situations studied, the visual system appears to choose automatically which source of information, ordered displacements or cross ratio, to use. To me, the choice seems closed to introspection or conscious deliberation, and it is clear that individual differences occur. The necessity of choice implicates principles of decoding and in turn has ramifications for considerations of direct and indirect perception. But, again let me shy away from discussion of this topic until still more data are gathered. I return to classes of perceptual theories in chapters 14 and 15. What I discuss next is another type of flow, this time generated by a moving observer. Again, multiple sources of information are available, and again the visual system seems selective. Here, rather than an approach of discrete points and views or of discrete points and displacements, a third machine-vision approach is used—that of displacement fields.

III

Competing Invariants of Flow

The computation and interpretation of motions on a projection surface to arrive at a description of a 3D environment (exterospecific information) and/or observer motion relative to the environment (propriospecific information or egomotion) is one of the most challenging tasks . . . vision research is confronted with. . . . The fact is that the problem is very difficult indeed.

Prazdny (1983b, p. 239)

10
Ways of Wayfinding

In the previous chapter I began to discuss the optic flow generated by an observer moving through the environment. Here I expand this idea, addressing a fundamental problem for vision: Does dynamic information in the optic array specify the direction of an observer's movement? The answer, I suggest, is an unequivocal yes, but how we get there is a long and twisted tale, encompassing the next four chapters. Prazdny's admonition, given as the introduction to this part, applies equally to psychologists, philosophers, and computer scientists: We must proceed with care and not accept carte blanche any time-honored analyses.

My approach is three pronged. First, I briefly present facts on the accuracy needed to direct viewers' locomotion. I know of none presented previously in the perception literature, and my presentation provides a guideline for assessment of research done on wayfinding accuracy. Second, I look at various proposals for determining viewers' direction, starting with the focus of expansion and then considering several others. Data from all previous experiments seem to find all present concepts wanting. They typically do not show the accuracy needed for wayfinding without danger of personal injury. Third, I embark on a somewhat new path, direction finding based on motion parallax. This last enterprise is the most comprehensive and takes us through chapters 11, 12, and 13. But first, consider the accuracy needed for wayfinding.

Accuracy in Wayfinding

As pedestrians we would bump into many more stationary objects than we already do were we not able to judge our direction of locomotion within 5 to 10° of visual angle. Such a requirement, however, is not likely to strain the system. Instead of considering modal locomotion as dictating accuracy needs, we should probably consider needs more toward the limit of our ability to move through space. In particular, as runners we would be in grave danger were we not able to judge direction within 1° of visual angle. Such an estimate is based on the physics and geometry of turns, on footfall modulation time, and on reaction time.[1]

Interestingly, this same requirement is found in other settings. For example, safe driving at highway speeds entails judgments of about 1°; safe landing of conventional aircraft requires at least 1° accuracy, but here it is measured vertically so that the craft's wheels touch down at the correct point; and downhill skiing also needs an accuracy in this range. Assumptions underlying these estimates vary,[2] but it appears that technology, society, and recreation have converged with evolution toward the accuracy demanded in directional judgments. And this one-degree requirement is not likely the absolute limit: World-class sprinters, skiers, and race car drivers, as well as pilots landing on aircraft carriers, surely need even greater accuracy—at most half a degree and probably a lot less. In general, then, we should distrust any experimental evidence that does not indicate a wayfinding ability in the range of 1° or better. But how do we guide our movement with this accuracy? The first and most prominent proposal is the focus of expansion.

The Focus of Expansion

Independently, Gibson (1947, 1950) and Calvert (1950, 1954) proposed that we know our way from the location of a fixed point in the changing optic array. Early on, Gibson et al. (1955) called this fixed point the *focus of radial expansion*; later, he called it the *center of outflow* (Gibson 1979), and Calvert simply called it X. But most researchers use a version of the initial term—the *focus of expansion* (Gibson 1955)—and I follow this usage. The focus of expansion is shown schematically in the upper panel of figure 10.1. As indicated in the lower panel, this rendering is like Alberti's window, with the observer carrying the planar projection surface forward. According to both Calvert and Gibson, all motion *radiates* from this point. More concretely, this radiation occurs when changes in relative positions of objects in the world are projected to a moving point of observation and when the projectors are intersected by a surface. All changes on that surface can be described as vectors, or flow lines, and these purportedly point in a direction opposite the focus of expansion. Because analyses typically assume that the projection surface moves with the observer, I call it Alberti's windshield.

Calvert dubbed this general scheme for visual guidance the "parafoveal streamer theory"; Gibson (1979) later called it "streaming perspective." It should be clear, however, that such streamers may be equally if not more important in the peripheral visual field, beyond the parafovea. As I describe in chapters 11 and 12, the length of these streamers—or more properly vectors—is determined by three factors:

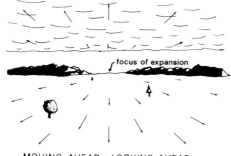

MOVING AHEAD, LOOKING AHEAD

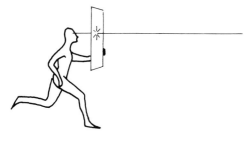

Figure 10.1
If a viewer is looking in the same direction as he or she is moving, as indicated in the upper panel, there is an optic focus of expansion. The lower panel shows that this representation is like Alberti's window, which moves with the observer. I call it Alberti's windshield.

the *instantaneous distance* of a given object from the viewer, its *instantaneous angle* from the direction of movement, and an underlying mapping assumption. But this gets us too far ahead of our story. Vector length is not critically important to either Calvert's or Gibson's thesis: We are told simply that all vectors, regardless of length, point away from the focus of expansion. And according to Gibson (1958, p. 188), "to aim locomotion is to keep the center of flow of the optic array as close as possible to the form which the object projects."

The great redundancy of information in this scheme is impressive. There are individual vectors associated with *every* part of *every* object in *every* location, and *all* of these, when extended backward, intersect at the same point. They make direction of movement, or so the theory goes, implicit, regardless of where an observer is looking. If an observer happens to be looking backward rather than ahead, it is claimed that the observer finds a complementary focus of contraction diametrically opposite the focus of expansion.

The simplicity of this proposal, especially as formulated by Gibson, attracted the attention of psychologists. General acceptance is indicated by the appearance of this scheme in many textbooks and articles on perception.[3] The extent of acceptance, however, is curious, given the lack of empirical support. In fact, if anything, almost all evidence is *against* the utility of the focus of expansion for visual guidance. The various studies, however, are not without their own problems. In several cases nearly unavoidable problems in experimental design or in the conceptualization of the optics of the situation have made the counter-evidence less impressive than it might have been. Because the difficulties with each experiment enlighten us to the problems in specifying optic flow and because their strengths denote problems with the focus of expansion, it is worth considering each in detail.

Utility of the Focus of Expansion: A First Pass

> When the focus of expansion is a spot on a vertical wall toward which a man walks, the flow is zero at that spot and increases symmetrically around it, if we disregard eye movements. When he approaches it at a slant, the flow is correspondingly asymmetrical, the velocity becoming greater on the near side.

With this statement Gibson (1950, p. 128) set the stage for more than three decades of research. And unfortunately, for reasons that will become clear, that stage was not in the theater of interest. The prototypic situation became that of an observer moving toward a (1) vertically oriented, (2) planar surface, (3) generally at right angles to a (4) linear path of movement. I enumerate these because all four have contributed substantially to the style of research done and all lead to oversimplifications and misunderstandings of the information available to a moving observer in a normal environment. One problem, oddly enough, is that it promotes an "air theory" rather than a "ground theory" approach to optic flow, as Gibson (1950) would have otherwise intended: Disembodied visual patterns are considered at an unknown depth rather than as interrelated and occluding patterns among objects along the ground plane.

Carel (1961)

Carel was among the first to conduct experiments on optic flow. In a technical report, he presented a series of experiments that employed a flight simulator of the kind used in flight training before the advent of computer-graphics technology. The apparatus simulated linear movement toward and impending collision with a surface oriented at various angles. Among other results, Carel found that the accuracy in locating the focus of expansion depends on two factors—observer speed and distance remaining to the point of impact. In general, the faster one travels and the nearer one is to impact, the better one's judgments are.

Consider an example. If a viewer is running at a velocity of 5 m/sec toward a wall visible from 100 m distant, Carel's results suggest that the viewer can correctly judge the point of impact within 4°, or about two thumb widths. Carel spoke of the distance/velocity ratio as being critical. Thus 100 m divided by 5 m/sec yields a distance/velocity ratio of 20 sec, the time until contact with the surface. Lee (1976, 1980b) later promoted this same information. Consider next some other accuracies at this same speed but different distances. With the plane of impact 50 m distant and a time to contact of 10 sec, the runner's accuracy increases to 2.5°, and at 10 m and 2 sec it further increases to 0.5°. These data suggest that runners are not very accurate in judging direction of movement unless objects along the path of movement are relatively near and collision imminent. Such accuracies seem barely sufficient for running and driving a car. Moreover, it is not even clear that the focus of expansion was being used by Carel's observers. Disappearance rates of textures off the edge of the display is another source of information available to them, but not necessarily to drivers and certainly not to runners.

Llewellyn (1971)
The first study of aim-point accuracy in mainstream psychology did not appear until a decade after Carel's study. Llewellyn conducted a series of experiments using velocities and distances consistent with the more distant (or slower) end of Carel's continuum. Llewellyn found that observers cannot determine their way better than to within 6° of visual angle. His apparatus was a shadow caster, much like that used by Gibson (1957a). With it Llewellyn back-projected arrays of lines and geometrical shapes onto a view screen. He generated flow by smoothly increasing the distance of the transparent textured surface from the image plane while leaving the image plane at a uniform distance from the observer and light source. The optics were generally correct for linear vection—the perception of self-movement through the environment along a straight line—properly mimicking the increased size of textures when an observer approaches them. Nevertheless, Llewellyn's observers were notably poor at pointing out their direction of movement.

One reason for their poor performance may have been that the stimulus array was a circular screen of only 15° radius. Although it is difficult to present wide-angle dynamic stimuli to a viewer without systematic distortion, we could argue that, because the optic array normally available to both eyes is an ellipsoidal cross section of a sphere about 180° wide by about 120° high, Llewellyn's exclusion of more than 95% of the visual field may have induced poor performance. Almost all peripheral "streamers" were excluded from his display. Moreover, narrow-field displays do not give an observer a good sense of being "in" the space depicted (Hatada et al. 1980). This criticism can be levied against almost all studies of optic flow. I return to the possible influence and impact of peripheral vision in chapter 11, where I consider detection thresholds for movement at various eccentricities.

Johnston et al. (1973)
In response to the problem of a narrow field of view, Johnston et al. presented their viewers with spherically projected dynamic images as large as 100° by 160°. Their displays simulated approach to a plane with final times to contact of 42.5, 21.5, 11, and 0.5 sec. All displays were computer generated on a flat screen, filmed frame by frame, and projected through a fish-eye lens into an amphitheater with a spherical screen, such as that found in a planetarium. Again, monocular optics were correct for an approach toward an extremely large and flat wall. Surprisingly, however, even in this full-field situation observers could not locate the focus of expansion better than to about 10°. Moreover, there was little effect of time to contact. Observers had a mean error of 11° for times to contact of 42.5 sec, and 8° for 0.5 sec—a scanty improvement out of scale with that predicted by Carel.

One reason for poor performance no doubt stems from the limited computer capacity then available to generate dynamic displays. Because it is more economical to draw points rather than lines and other shapes in a vector-graphics system, Johnston et al. generated dots that did not expand as the large plane loomed toward the viewer. Thus an important source of information for movement toward objects—increase in size—was absent. Perhaps the display looked less like the optic array during movement than like the explosion of elements at a fixed depth. If so, we would hardly expect the task to measure observers' ability to determine their way.

Regan and Beverley (1982)
More recently, Regan and Beverley found essentially the same result: Their viewers could not determine their direction better than to within 10°. They presented observers with vertical sine-wave gratings that

mimicked a line of fenceposts planted at right angles to the line of movement. These posts moved and expanded under computer control in simulation of linear vection. Like Llewellyn's display, Regan and Beverley's was relatively small, 16° by 20°, and insofar as this factor matters, its force is equally denigrating here. There are, however, many other important aspects of the Regan and Beverley study, so I return to it several times.[4]

Whatever the import of the size of the display and growth in size of textures, all three studies after Carel's used the type of experimental stimuli outlined by Gibson. The simulated environment consisted of a *vertical* textured *plane*, toward which one moved *orthogonally* along a *linear* path of movement. Such displays are not representative of what we see every day. Objects in the real world are not commonly coplanar, and if they are, that plane is rarely at right angles to the line of movement. In addition, our paths of movement are rarely linear. More often, we move in curved paths around corners and, even in those cases in which we intend to go straight, sideways and vertical oscillations during gait are unavoidable.[5] What follows, then, is a discussion of experiments that present observers with stimuli without the first and third of these limitations. They, like Carel, present *nonvertical* planes approached at *oblique angles*. I defer discussion of the second difference (*multiplanar* stimuli) until chapter 12 and of the fourth (*nonlinear* approaches) until chapter 13.

Kaufman (1968) and Ahumada (unpublished)

After Carel, a few studies did obtain direction-finding performance considerably better than 10°. Kaufman, for example, simulated landing on an aircraft carrier using a back-projection technique similar to Llewellyn's. Kaufman chose glide paths that were small and within a few degrees of being parallel to the surface, 3 to 6°, and in a range appropriate for landing on a carrier. He found that one observer yielded a 1.5° error in locating the point of impact. Simulated speed was quite high, about 60 m/sec, and the final distance to the carrier deck was about 90 m. With a time to contact of about 1.5 sec, the accuracy is about that predicted by Carel. However, Kaufman noted that, because of problems in the experimental design, this value is probably an overestimate. He also reported that even this is too poor for successful landing.

By far the most complete study of simulated aircraft landing is Ahumada's. His experimental situation is much like Kaufman's but with computer-generated graphics displays. These present a linear array of lights, such as pairs of landing lights on either side of a runway at night. The array filled 15° of visual angle measured vertically. Glide paths were varied from 2 to 12°, where the former is shallow and the latter much too steep for conventional landing. Trials simulated a 2-sec flight that ended at one of four times, from 30 to 3.75 sec before touchdown. Viewers indicated the location of their aim point—the point of impact with the runway—at the end of the trial by moving a cursor to the point on the screen where they thought they would touch down. During cursor placement, the last frame of the landing sequence remained on the screen. In general, the shallower the glide slope and the closer to touchdown the trial simulated, the more accurate observers were. Aim-point accuracy varied from 0.5 to 3.0°, depending on condition. Again, contrary to Carel, there was little effect of time to contact.[6]

What is not clear in Ahumada's study, as before, is whether or not viewers were using the focus of expansion. Although viewers sat in a darkened room, they probably could see the edges of the display. These would form a frame within which movement of the lights on the screen could be seen. Pilots often use such reference frames when landing, lining up a speck on the windshield with the aim point on the runway as they might use a gun sight (Langewiesche 1944, Hasbrook 1975). This idea of reference frames arises again in chapter 12 when motion parallax is discussed.

Warren (1976) and Riemersma (1981)
Not all wayfinding studies have used experimental situations of orthogonal or oblique approach to a plane. Warren, using a display of 53° width, explored a situation like that of driving a car, where an observer is not approaching the plane but moving over it. Viewing computer-generated displays, his observers could locate their direction of movement to within 5°. Because of problems in his response measure, he suggested that this is probably an underestimate of viewers' ability to judge direction of movement in his displays.[7]

Riemersma used a display more sophisticated than Warren's. Observers sat in a mock-up of a car and viewed a large screen. They determined whether or not a film clip of computer-generated edge lines or random dots simulated forward movement alone or forward movement with a slight turn. Using 2.5 sec as a standard driver response time (Road Research Laboratory 1963), Riemersma's participants yielded above-chance accuracies at about 1° of visual angle for speeds of 30 and 120 km/hr. This is the only result other than that of Ahumada that seems appropriate for the task of wayfinding. But again, it is not clear that the focus of expansion was used. Motion parallax through the windshield and, in the condition with road edge lines, linear perspective could easily have aided task performance.

First Overview

The focus of expansion appears to be difficult for perceivers to find. Most experimental results have failed to support the idea that viewers can accurately discern this information, as opposed to others, in optic flow.[8] By extension, it would appear that it is sometimes difficult to determine where one is going. But this is implausible: Runners, drivers, pilots, and skiers must direct their movement within 1° of visual angle. Another possibility is that the focus of expansion is not generally useful for directional guidance. This idea is supported indirectly by coarse-grained behavioral data showing that moving observers rarely even look in the direction they are going. Schiff (1980, pp. 254–255) noted:

> Studies performed on winding roads and utilizing head-mounted cameras have determined that the driver looks primarily at center lines and road edges while performing vehicle turns. All this suggests rather variable sampling of information regarding the environment and relation of the self-envelope to it, but indicates that flow information (optical motions and gradients) . . . and not the f.o.e. [focus of expansion] itself, are used for much vehicular guidance.

These results also suggest that important information for wayfinding lies off the path of movement. But the focus of expansion dies hard, and discussion has not ended with these experimental and behavioral data. Over the last few years new arguments and analyses have been presented. One such discussion is an exchange between Torrey (1985) and Regan (1985) over the distinction between optic and retinal motion.

Utility of Two Foci of Expansion: A Second Pass

Results like those cited so far led many of us to doubt the utility of the focus of expansion as information for directional guidance. Regan and Beverley (1982) offered a logical reason for its inadequacy: They demonstrated that during approach to a single plane, the situation chosen by Gibson to discuss, there is almost always a focus of expansion that corresponds to where we are *looking*, not where we are *going*. Because we always look at objects when we move, an object under scrutiny does not move from the fovea. The eye rotates to follow it during our movement. With this object fixed in position on the retina, all other textures necessarily flow away from it as we move forward. This pattern, demonstrated in figure 10.2a, occurs even if observers are not moving directly toward that object. What is important to remember, however, is that this representation of flow is two dimensional and measured on the retina.

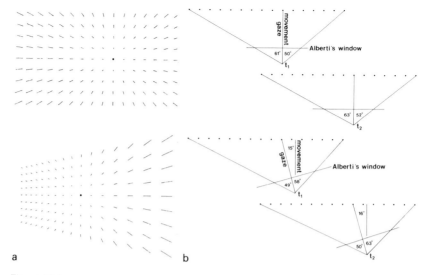

Figure 10.2
(a) Vector plots on Alberti's windshield of the optic displacements for an orthogonal
approach to a textured plane, with the dots representing fixation points. All vectors point
outward, away from the fixation, which serves as a focus of expansion. (b) Geometry
of the two situations at two times during approach to the plane, where at t_2 the observer
is 7% closer to the plane than at t_1. The top panels show vector plots and geometry for
an observer looking exactly in the direction of movement, and the bottom panels show
them for looking 15° off to the left-hand side of the path of movement at t_1 and holding
that fixation.

Regan and Beverley's analysis, as it turns out, is true only under
restricted conditions. Such retinal flow occurs only when the eye is
fixated on a spot on a textured plane, not in a cluttered environment.
Moreover, it occurs only when an observer approaches a plane at certain
angles and for certain lines of sight. For example, when an observer
is moving directly toward a plane, outflow occurs only when the observer is looking within 45° of the aim point. It does not occur, as
shown in figure 10.3, when the observer is looking farther outward at
steeper angles. There the flow develops the interesting characteristic
of having the fixation point become a focus of contraction.

Regan and Beverley's analysis, and my extension of it, is damaging
evidence against the efficacy of the focus of expansion. There is, however, a retort. The claim is that this analysis fails to distinguish retinal
flow from optic flow. The focus of expansion that Regan and Beverley
discuss is on the retina, dependent on where the eye is looking. On
the other hand, the focus of expansion of Calvert and Gibson is in the
optic array. Perhaps there is some way to disentangle the two and to

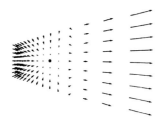

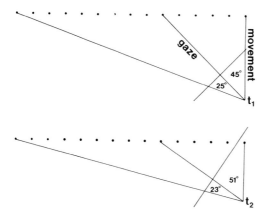

Figure 10.3
The top panel shows the vector plot on Alberti's windshield for an orthogonal approach
to a plane when looking at a spot that is initially 45° to the left. The middle and bottom
panels show the geometry of the situation. Notice that the fixation has become a local
focus of contraction. Although not shown, the vectors in the top panel should also be
slightly curved, a characteristic known as curl.

demonstrate that the *optic* focus of expansion is useful while acknowledging that the *retinal* focus is not. This is the view taken by Torrey (1985) and tacitly approved by Regan (1985). However, I do not agree. I contend that the focus of expansion in the optic array is a fiction of a particular choice of coordinate system for the spherical projection surface. I demonstrate in chapter 11 that Regan and Beverley were on the right track; they simply were not radical enough. But before beginning that discussion, the final section of this chapter outlines two other proposals for direction finding.

Alternatives to the Focus of Expansion

Ocular-Drift Cancellation

Llewellyn proposed a drift cancellation procedure for visual guidance. This drift parses two ways. The first is a drift of one object against another in the optic array, also known as motion parallax and discussed in the next chapters. The second, less important to Llewellyn's thesis but implicit in Calvert's thesis, is ocular drift. On this view, the observer moves through the environment and fixates various objects at varying locations. While locomoting forward and looking somewhat off to the side, the observer must rotate his or her eyes (or head) in order to maintain fixation on an object. If we assume that there is no head rotation, then only when an object is along the path of movement is there no ocular drift. This drift must be noticed through monitoring eye position dictated by efferent commands. Saccadic corrections are then made to a new object until no drifts are noticed. Once ocular movements have been canceled, the observer knows the direction of locomotion by his or her direction of gaze.

This is an eminently sensible proposal. Unfortunately, Llewellyn's data suggest that observers do not register either eye movements or eye position sufficiently well to perform this task. That is, observers cannot use it to determine direction to better than about 6°. Finally, a picky point: Ocular rotations are not *optic* information. Instead, eye movements are part of the effector system and are extraoptic. Thus, even if ocular-drift cancellation worked for direction finding, it would still not tell us what optic information specifies one's direction. Despite these criticisms, this scheme is similar to one I discuss in chapter 13.

Magnification in Retinal Flow

A completely different source of information was proposed by Regan and Beverley (1982)—the *point of maximum rate of magnification*. Their interest in it stems, in part, from their previous neurophysiological work. In general, the point lies between the aim point and the point on the plane nearest the observer.[9] Thus it does not specify the direction of movement; instead, it indicates only the direction that observers must shift their gaze to find it. Its location is schematically shown in figure 10.4. The top panel shows where the point would lie if the plane were approached at an oblique angle, fixating a point off the line of movement. The twelve functions in the lower panel correspond to the twelve locations along the path of approach.

Three problems make this formulation less than completely useful. First, from a distance the point of maximum rate of magnification is surrounded as broadly as 30° by other points with similar magnification rates. Thus it seems unlikely that the point could be discerned with accuracy until the observer is near impact. Second when moving parallel to a plane, as most terrestrial and airborne animals typically do, this point completely disappears because its equation of flow degenerates.[10] Third, Regan and Beverley generated optic flow by using an exponential algorithm to simulate the orthogonal approach of an observer toward a line of fenceposts. Two outcomes of such an algorithm are shown in the bottom panel of figure 10.4, where exponents of 1.0 and 0.7 for the velocity of elements are plotted against eccentricity in the optic array. Shown in the same panel as the dotted line is the true velocity of such fenceposts, revealing serious discrepancies in the periphery. Nevertheless, within 20° (the width of Regan and Beverley's display) the match is quite good, especially when the exponent is 1.0.

Putting this reanalysis aside, I also note a terminological problem—the use by Regan and Beverley and by Gibson of the term *magnification* in descriptions of optic flow. This term from telescopy does not generally apply to flow; it is almost always improperly used, and in its use are seeds for misunderstandings.

Against Magnification in Optic Flow

"Expansion" and "magnification" are kindred terms. "Expansion" denotes spreading out and "magnification" enlargement; "expansion" does not have the mixed blessing of connoting optic instruments, whereas "magnification" clearly does. Because the eye is an optic instrument, "magnification" would seem to be a word well suited to descriptions of optic flow. This fact has almost certainly promoted its use. For example, Gibson (1979, p. 227) said:

> An invariant feature of the ambient flow is that one hemisphere is centrifugal and the other centripetal. Outflow entails magnification, and inflow entails minification.

Gibson and many others[11] have used "magnification" to describe the effect when an observer moves toward an object. However, this choice

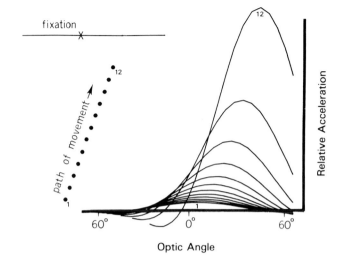

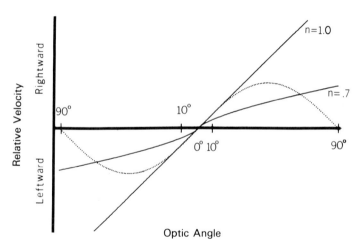

Figure 10.4
Examined in the top panel is Regan and Beverley's (1982) proposed method of direction
finding. The method locates the point of maximum rate of magnification in the vector
field during nonorthogonal approach to a plane, with maintained fixation point to the
left of the point of impact, yielding the relative magnification patterns shown. Peaks in
the functions correspond to points of maximum rate of change of magnification. In the
bottom panel are the relative velocities for two exponential flow patterns in their simulations
and the flow (dotted line) for actual orthogonal approach to a plane. After Priest and
Cutting (1985).

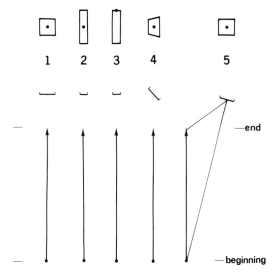

Figure 10.5

Five objects and paths of approach for consideration of magnification. The top panel shows the initial views of the objects and the fixation points; the bottom panel shows an aerial view of the geometry of the situations. Table 10.1 gives the visual angles involved at the beginning and end of observer movement.

of term, like those of "convention" and "cue" discussed in earlier chapters, is unfortunate. "Magnification" means to enlarge equally along x and y axes of the projection, and it is in this technical sense that a problem emerges. Magnification occurs with a zoom lens of a camera, but such optics are quite different from those for the approach to a plane (Hochberg 1978b).

True magnification in the optic array is extremely rare. Aside from looking through microscopes and telescopes, the only cases where it occurs are during the linear approach to the center of the equilateral face of an object that is orthogonally aligned to the path of movement and where that object is a perfect sphere, regardless of the path of locomotion, a situation considered by Regan et al. (1979). In all others, as the observer approaches an object, projective distortions increase the size of some dimensions more than others. This is a result of the spherical geometry and polar projection of the optic array.[12] To pursue the case against magnification, consider the angles subtended by objects aligned in different orientations from different paths of movement, as shown in figure 10.5. The particular angles involved are given in table 10.1. In each of the five cases, for simplicity's sake, I consider regular quadrilateral surfaces and how they project to the observer approaching them.

Table 10.1
Five Cases Demonstrating Increase in Optical Size (in Degrees) with an
Observer's Approach

Parameter	Case 1	Case 2	Case 3	Case 4	Case 5
Initial width	5.72	2.86	2.86	4.09	5.60
Final width	28.07	14.25	14.25	26.19	17.58
Initial height (left)	5.72	11.42	11.30	5.20	5.60
Final height (left)	28.07	53.13	45.00	18.44	24.71
Initial height (right)	5.72	11.42	11.30	6.35	5.60
Final height (right)	28.07	53.13	45.00	50.50	19.56
Initial height-to-width ratio	1:1	3.99:1	3.95:1	1.27:1[a] 1.55:1[b]	1:1[a] 1:1[b]
Final height-to-width ratio	1:1	3.73:1	3.16:1	0.70:1[a] 2.74:1[b]	1.41:1[a] 1.11:1[b]

a. left edge
b. right edge

Case 1 is a control, used for comparison purposes, in which true magnification occurs. The observer's eye moves toward the middle of the face of an object. If that object is 1 unit square and if the observer is initially 10 units away, both the horizontal and vertical visual angles are determined by Eq. (2.1): $\alpha = 2 \cdot \arctan(y/2z)$, where y is the projected extent of the object orthogonal to the line of sight and z is its distance from the observer. Initial visual angles are 5.72°. If the observer then moves forward by 8 units, the height and width of the object are 28.07°. Given that height and width are the same in initial and final positions, magnification has occurred.

But now consider the four cases in figure 10.5 in which enlargement is not uniform. Case 2 presents an object 2 units in height and 0.5 unit in width. Again, from a distance of 10 units the initial height is 11.42° of visual angle and the initial width, 2.86°. Although the real-world proportions of this figure are 4:1, the distortion of polar perspective reduces that ratio to 3.99:1. This is a small effect, at least for this case and this viewpoint. But when the observer moves forward 8 units, the height becomes 53.13°, the width 14.25°, and the ratio reduces to 3.73:1.

Case 3 is similar to case 2 but with the point toward which the observer's eye is moving displaced to the middle of the top edge of the object. Calculations differ from those using Eq. (2.1). The initial width of this object is, as it was before, 2.86°; its height has changed somewhat to 11.30°, and the height-to-width ratio is 3.95:1. When the observer moves to 2 units from the object, the width is again the same, 14.25°, but its height is now 45.0°, yielding a ratio of 3.16:1.

Case 4 presents a situation similar to that of case 1 but with the face of the object tilted at 45° to the line of movement, with the left edge farther to the right. The angular width of the object is uniform. From the center of the figure to the left edge is 1.84°, and from the center to the right edge is 2.25°, for a total width of 4.09°. The height of the left edge is 5.20°, and of the right edge 6.35°. The ratio of these two is 1.22:1, right edge to left. When the observer moves forward, these values increase. But as before, these values do *not* increase equally. The uniform width of the figure is now 6.72° from the center to the left edge and 19.47° from the center to the right edge, for a total of 26.19°. A dramatic change occurs in the relative heights for left and right edges. The left edge is now 18.44°, whereas the right edge is 50.50°, for a ratio of 2.74:1.

Case 5 employs an object of the same size as that in cases 1 and 4, but this time the movement path is off to the side so that the observer passes the object 2 units to the left of the object's left edge. Because the initial point in the path of movement is a little over 10 units away and because the object is oriented so as to be at a right angle to the line of sight, the initial proportions are similar to those of case 1—5.6° by 5.6°. When the observer moves forward the same distance as in previous cases, the projection changes considerably. The final width is 17.58°, the final height of the left edge (closest to the observer) is 24.71°, and that of the right edge is 19.56°. The height-to-width ratio for the left edge changes from 1:1 to 1.41:1, and that for the right edge from 1:1 to 1.11:1.

The purpose of this five-part exercise was to demonstrate that polar projections of objects near and far do not generally allow us to speak of magnifications.[13] To keep discussions of optic flow unclouded by error, we should not use the term.

Second Overview

After initial forays into the study of the focus of expansion, Regan and Beverley argued that it is not useful to visual guidance. They offered proof by demonstration, showing that the focus of expansion exists wherever one looks when approaching a plane. My own analyses placed further limitations on the concept. But Torrey countered by trying to distinguish retinal-image analysis, like Regan and Beverley's, from optic analysis. The hope was that the optic focus of expansion could still be saved. One of my purposes in chapter 11 is to show that it cannot.

Two other schemes for wayfinding were then discussed. The first was Llewellyn's ocular-drift cancellation theory. In it the observer scans objects in the real world, detects ocular rotations resulting from continued fixation on an object off the path of movement, and saccades in the reverse direction until ocular drift is canceled. Such a scheme has no evidence in its support, although it seems sensible and is related to an analysis of visual function that I discuss in chapter 13. The second scheme was proposed by Regan and Beverley and centered on locating the point of maximum rate of magnification in the optic array when approaching a planar surface. Several problems of locating this point were discussed, and it does not seem generally useful. And finally, the concept of magnification was examined, as it might reflect facts of optic flow, and found wanting. Magnification occurs with the use of extraoptic lenses but not without them, except in seriously circumscribed conditions. In summary, the proposed tools for wayfinding are inadequate. What is needed is a reanalysis of the changing optic array, which is the topic of chapter 11, and a new tool for wayfinding, the topic of chapters 12 and 13.

11

Multiple Representations of Optic Flow

Optic flow is the foundation of vision: Every time we move, the projections of the world change with us. Vision subserves our activity, telling us where we are (Lee 1980a). Such arguments, however, are often extended to state that the focus of expansion is the centerpiece of optic flow, and therein lie some difficult problems. Data reviewed in chapter 10 suggest, at best, that the focus of expansion is not always easy to find. Understanding its problems is contingent on understanding the plurality of representations for optic flow at a moving point. What follows in this chapter is an exploration of that plurality.[1]

Mapping Optic Flow

If the eye moves through the environment, the optic array changes. To study this change, we must consider displacement vectors that result from this movement. Helmholtz (1866, p. 295) provided a qualitative analysis of them:

> In walking along, the objects that are at rest by the wayside stay behind us; that is, they appear to glide past us in our field of view in the opposite direction to that in which we are advancing. More distant objects do the same way, only more slowly, while very remote bodies like the stars maintain their permanent positions in the field of view, provided the direction of the head and body keep their same directions. Evidently, under these circumstances, the apparent angular velocities of objects in the field of view will be inversely proportional to their real distances; and, consequently, safe conclusions can be drawn as to the real distance of the body from its apparent angular velocity.

The top panel of figure 11.1 shows one representation of flow. It is a familiar diagram from Gibson (1966, 1979). Unlike Alberti's windshield of figure 10.1, this projection surface completely surrounds the moving observer. The situation shown is complex: We must understand exactly

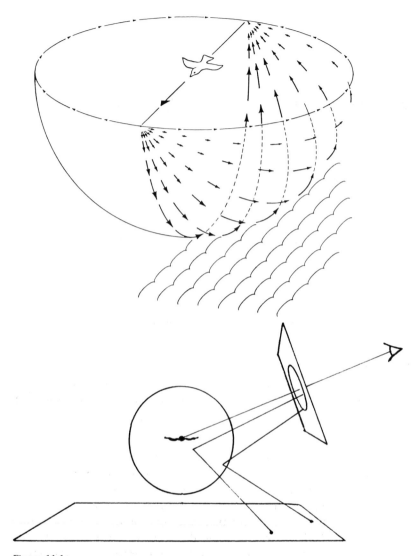

Figure 11.1
The top panel shows one mapping of the vector paths of objects and textures in the environment as an individual, in this case a bird, undergoes linear movement. This figure is from Gibson (1966, 1979), © Houghton Mifflin Company, reprinted by permission of Houghton Mifflin. The bottom panel shows how all surface information is projected onto an imaginary sphere in order to show the relative velocities of textures, then re-projected onto the picture plane.

what is depicted and why it is depicted that way to understand optic flow. The sphere (or hemisphere) around the bird is an imaginary projection surface, as suggested by Leonardo da Vinci and discussed in chapter 3, that allows the fewest distortions of natural perspective.

The arrows attempt to show unambiguous, instantaneous changes in optic angles corresponding to displacements of objects in the world as the bird flies. Textures on the planar terrain are mapped onto the sphere and marked by arrows. These are then mapped a second time onto the image plane, as shown in the bottom panel of figure 11.1. Vector lengths differ dramatically with two variables. One is the distance of objects from the projection sphere. Near objects move faster than far, and far objects project higher on the sphere. The second is the angle separating the line of sight to a particular texture from the path of movement. Instantaneous displacements are greatest at 90° from the path of movement and least at 0° and 180°, directly in front and behind. The combination of these two variables yields the largest vector traces directly beneath the bird.

The vector patterns are compelling; indeed, I have always found them elegant and beautiful. When extended backward, opposite the direction that they point, they denote the focus of expansion; and all traces, when extended around the surface of the sphere, point to a focus of contraction. There are, however, two problems with this figure, one computational and the other based on underlying assumptions. Consider the computational problem first. The length of the vectors shown in the top panel of figure 11.1, especially those nearest the foci of expansion and contraction, are too hopeful; they are exaggerated beyond actual flow. Figure 11.2 shows the vectors redrawn using a dynamic ray-tracing technique on a computer-driven plotter. Notice that those nearest the two foci have much shorter lengths, suggesting that a moving observer's ability to locate the focus of expansion would be diminished. The dynamic symmetry of this plot, however, is still salient. But consider next the assumption underlying it being drawn this way: This arrangement assumes a particular orientation of the coordinate system of the projection sphere at the beginning and end of the movement. In particular, it cannot rotate during the observer's locomotion. It is as if the moving observer must carry Leonardo's window—here perhaps best called Leonardo's windshield—and ensure that it maintains exact registration with the point toward which the observer is moving. Such a scheme is shown in figure 11.3.

What happens if the projection sphere cannot be held in place? In particular, suppose that the sphere rotates slightly during the forward movement. Consider three possible rotations, one each around the x, y, and z axes with a magnitude of 2°. The x axis runs 90° to the direction

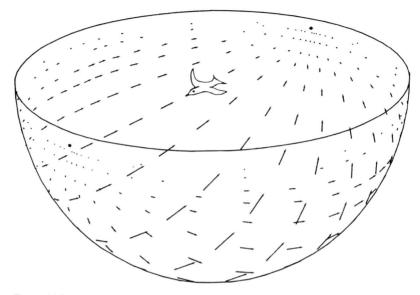

Figure 11.2
A computer-generated plot of the projection shown in figure 11.1. Notice that the vectors near the foci of expansion and contraction are smaller than in Gibson's figure.

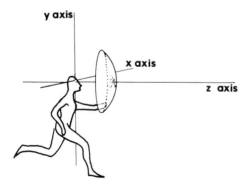

Figure 11.3
A representation of Leonardo's window, in which the moving observer carries the projection surface through the environment. In accordance with the lower panel of figure 10.1, I call this Leonardo's windshield. It is a section of the spherical projections shown in figures 11.1, 11.2, 11.4, and 11.5. Three axes of potential rotation are noted: x (which extends side to side across the observer), y (which runs vertically), and z (which extends along the linear path of movement). These axes of rotation are used in figure 11.4.

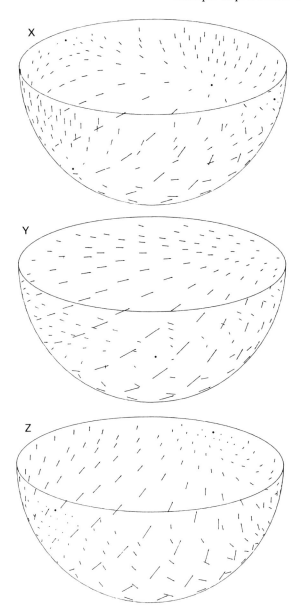

Figure 11.4
Alternative mappings of flow during forward linear locomotion. (Top) The spherical projection surface has been rotated around the x axis. Singularities are created where the x axis meets the horizon and beneath the observer. (Middle) Rotation around the y axis. Two new singularities are created to the left of the observer (one hidden at the edge of the drawing). (Bottom) Rotation around the z axis. The displays are valid representations of optic flow, as much so as those in figures 11.1 and 11.2.

of movement through the eye and meets the horizon on both sides. Such a rotation is seen in the top panel of figure 11.4 and might occur if the projection surface were tumbling during the observer's forward movement. In this vector field there are four singularities, indicated by dots, two at the horizon on either side of the observer and two beneath, one fore and one aft. None are extended out from the path of movement, and few vectors point in the direction of movement. Instead, the vector field has substantial curl, or curvature, in its vectors. A second rotation might occur around the y axis, or the vertical line running with gravity through the eye. Such a rotation, seen in the middle panel of figure 11.4, might occur if the projection sphere spins sideways as the observer moves forward. This mapping has two singularities and both happen to be below and to the left of the observer. Again few vectors point in the direction of movement, and the vector field is curled. The third rotation is around the z axis, or the path of movement. Such a rotation during the forward movement would yield an optic flow pattern like that shown in the bottom panel of figure 11.4. Two singularities exist, fore and aft, as before, but the horizon has shifted, as if the projection surface were executing a barrel roll. And against Calvert's and Gibson's theories, these vectors generally do not point in the direction of the singularities.

It is important to note that all three panels in figure 11.4 are legitimate representations of optic flow. These are not retinal projections; they are alternative optic projections. They capture equally well the displacement vectors of objects in the surround as an observer moves through the environment. These facts mean that something is odd about the flow in figures 11.1 and 11.2. Let us investigate this oddity in a more rigorous manner.

Flow patterns are mappings. To understand them, we must consider the spherical projections around the station point at a minimum of two times, t_1 and t_2, during which the observer has moved a fixed distance. And most important, we must consider the mapping between them. Let $h_1(p)$ be the spherical coordinates of a particular texture at time t_1, and $h_2(p)$ its coordinates at time t_2. Of most interest are textures for which $h_1(p) = h_2(p)$, the identity points. Figure 11.1 shows one possible mapping. But these patterns occur only under the conditions of flying over a flat terrain and, most important for this discussion, when the point on the horizon toward which the observer is moving is used as an identity point. The fundamental question, however, remains: How is its location fixed? Calvert, Gibson, and many others assumed that the location of the identity element should be directly along the line of movement, but it is crucial to understand that *any other point in the spherical projection could be used.*

All diagrams shown in figures 11.1 to 11.3 are *a*
from topology: Every point in the projection at
and only one point at t_2.[2] It is a nagging but un'
there is nothing in the mathematics of automorp'
requiring no occlusions, that dictates the loc
isfying the condition $h_1(p) = h_2(p)$. There is r
or fixed point, of the optic array at t_1, nor is the
no central point exists at any instant in time, none exists
without additional assumptions. Thus the idea of a uniquely spec
pattern of optic flow is incorrect—a given pattern is contingent on the
choice of identity point. Make no mistake, there must always be at
least one such point, or singularity, from which mappings are made;
Brouwer's theorem dictates this fact.[3] Moreover, the fixed point *is* a
topological invariant. But topology does not constrain locations such
that the fixed point's place in the mapping can be determined. It seems
to me that this is the most serious logical argument against the efficacy
of the focus of expansion. Nevertheless, we should remain wary; it is
possible that there may be some other way, using some other assumptions, for a moving observer to fix an identity point.

Five Problematic Assumptions Underlying a Fixed Identity Point

How might we choose an appropriate focus of expansion, registering
coordinates in the changing optic array? At least five different assumptions can be made, any one of which if true would do the trick.
The first assumes that the viewer's velocity through space does not
matter, the second fixes environmental information at the horizon, the
third fixes the orientation of the viewer's ocular system (registering the
optic and retinal arrays), the fourth considers the decomposition of
retinal motions resulting from observer translation and eye rotation,
and the fifth considers the interaction of acuity functions for motion
detection. All are interesting; all have problems.

Velocity-Independent Utility of Flow

When the velocity of the observer is sufficiently great, the problem of
flow mapping disappears. The spherical coordinates of flow simply do
not have an opportunity to change when the interval between t_1 and
t_2 becomes vanishingly small. The result is blurred flow radiating from
a focus of expansion, as portrayed by near warp-speed flight in science
fiction films, perhaps even in landing aircraft. Gibson, in assuming that
the focus of expansion is always useful, generalized from an unnatural
situation (landing a plane) with high-velocity flow to the natural one
of walking and running. With lower-velocity flow, the problems of

ation in Optic Array of Objects at Various Angles from the Direction of
otion before and after a Forward Linear Movement of 10 m

Distance from observer	Location off the line of movement			
	0°	5°	10°	20°
25 m	0.0 (0.0)[a]	8.3 (3.3)	16.5 (6.5)	32.4 (12.4)
50 m	0.0 (0.0)	6.3 (1.3)	12.5 (2.5)	24.8 (4.8)
100 m	0.0 (0.0)	5.6 (0.6)	11.1 (1.1)	22.2 (2.2)
200 m	0.0 (0.0)	5.3 (0.3)	10.5 (0.5)	21.0 (1.0)

a. Numbers in parentheses indicate the optical drift, or change in location, as a result of observer movement. All measures are in degrees.

stabilizing the coordinate system of the optic array become significantly greater because the interval between t_1 and t_2 is nontrivial.

Contrary to Gibson, Calvert (1954) and Hasbrook (1975) proposed velocity-*dependent* utility for the focus of expansion. They suggested that this dependence would be useful only when looking at near objects at high speeds. Such situations are typical of those for a pilot landing an airplane[4] and perhaps even for professional race car drivers and downhill skiers. Nevertheless, it is foreign to most everyday activity.

Fixed Horizon
A second assumption is that of a fixed horizon. Because all points on the horizon are at great distance—about 4 km for a person of normal height standing in Kansas in April—the optic flow of all points on the horizon is essentially nil. Even as one drives a car at 100 km/hr, the horizon is almost completely stable at all points, 360° around. Thus both retinal and optic flow of the horizon are negligible, regardless of where on the horizon one fixates—fore, aft, or to the side. This fact would minimize the *x* and *z* rotations seen in the top and bottom panels of figure 11.4 and ensure that fixation causes no ocular rotation. Thus a stable horizon could be used to fix the coordinate system within which to map flow.

This seems like an attractive solution. However, two problems arise. First, in cities and in tree-filled nonurban, nonmountainous environments, we typically cannot see into the distance. In fact, it is quite common for there to be no visible objects beyond a few hundred meters. Optic flow for these farthest-visible objects is nonnegligible even at pedestrian speeds. Unlike fixations on the horizon, those on near objects force ocular movement. Should some object off the line of movement be chosen as the identity point, serious misjudgments of movement direction could take place. Some of these are indicated in table 11.1.

Imagine a situation in which a runner is moving through a cluttered environment at 5 m/sec, the speed of a good run. Suppose that the runner is trying to take a linear path and looks out into the environment for some reference that can be used as an identity point to determine direction of movement and ensure a linear path. The best reference would be the visible object farthest away. If this object is at a functionally infinite distance, it can be used for direction finding quite well. But stars and the sun are typically well above the horizon, and gaze is usually just below it during locomotion. More convenient is some object near the horizon line and in the general direction that the runner is moving. If the horizon is assumed to be fixed, the object selected would best represent zero optic flow. After the runner has moved forward, say 10 m, how much have these objects moved in their angular projections with respect to the direction of movement? Values are given in table 11.1 for objects 0, 5, 10, and 20° off the path of movement at distances of 25, 50, 100, and 200 m. Notice that even relatively distant objects at small angles to the path of movement change their location. For an object 200 m in the distance at 5° from the path of movement, that change is about $\frac{1}{4}$° even when the runner has moved forward only 10 m. Objects at all other distances and all other angular discrepancies have larger changes in position. If any one of these is used as an identity point to map optic flow, the runner would turn rather than maintain linear trajectory. Given an unseen horizon, direction of movement might be more difficult to discern. We might then predict that individuals would be considerably worse at guiding their movements in relatively closed environments. Intuitively, such a finding seems unlikely. I know of no data that suggest people are poorer in knowing their heading in environments without horizons (say, inside buildings) than with them. In fact, it seems downright implausible.

A second problem with the fixed horizon assumption is that, when a viewer moves along a curved path, the horizon rotates with respect to the viewer. Optically, a rotational vector of constant size is added to vectors of all projections of objects in the ambient array. This is a considerable complication to the study of optic flow and forms the basis of chapter 13.

Gyroscopes

A third manner in which the registration of coordinate systems could be fixed is through a stabilizing system within the organism. We can imagine an internal gyroscope that maintains constant ocular orientation regardless of external affairs. That is, a person or any other creature with mobile eyes could register change in direction of gaze through registration of deflections in the gyroscope. This device would certainly facilitate choice of location of the identity point along the direction of movement because the orientation of the system would be constant in absolute coordinates. The individual need only locate any point that remains in fixed position as the gyroscope maintains its fixed orientation.

One problem with this idea, at least with respect to providing an *optic* solution to the problem of direction finding, is that the existence of a gyroscope is independent of flow: The gyroscope itself must be *in* the organism and cannot be *in* the optic array. A more pressing problem, however, is that the relevant human gyroscope, the vestibulo-ocular response system, is easily overridden by the field-holding reflex of the accessory optic system, of which the optokinetic response is a part (Simpson 1984). Because we look reflexively at things when we move, we rotate our eyes and continue to look at a stationary object while locomoting more often than we keep a steady gaze, letting objects flow by.

Decomposition of Motions

Longuet-Higgins and Prazdny (1980) and Koenderink and van Doorn (1981) claimed that instantaneous flow can always be parsed into two independent sets of motions. According to Longuet-Higgins and Prazdny, one set is *exterospecific* and dependent on the trajectory of the observer moving through the environment; the other set is *pro-priospecific* and dependent on where the observer is looking.[5] Koen-derink and van Doorn called the two sets of motions *lamellar* and *solenoidal* flow. The propriospecific component is thought to be under control in observer eye movements, the exterospecific in locomotion. As suggested in chapter 10, we might call the exterospecific component *optic* flow and the propriospecific component an addition of *retinal* flow. Both occur for any translating observer fixating an object in the environment off the path of movement. The claim is that, if the observer could tease these two flow fields apart, direction of movement could be discerned (Prazdny 1983a, 1983b).

Vector plots for composed and decomposed flows are shown in the panels of figure 11.5. The top panel shows that the flows result from forward movement and eye rotation to the right, as if the observer were looking at an object off to the right. This pattern is roughly a mirror image of the middle panel of figure 11.4, with a somewhat reduced y axis rotation. The middle panel shows the components stem-ing from Helmholtz's and Gibson's analyses of forward movement and the bottom from eye rotation in an otherwise still environment. The idea is that an observer can either add the two bottom patterns to achieve the top or subtract one of the bottom two from the top to achieve the other as residual. Direction finding could be aided, or so

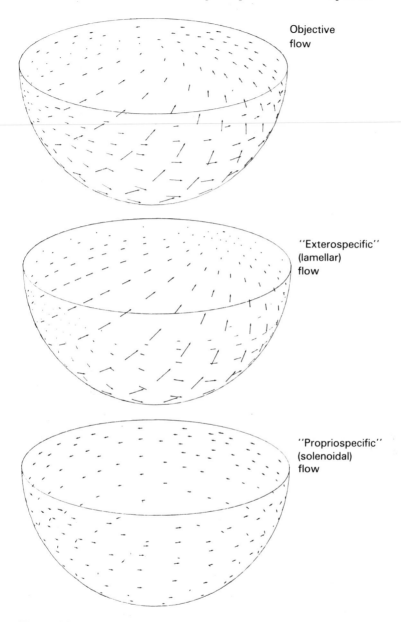

Objective flow

"Exterospecific" (lamellar) flow

"Propriospecific" (solenoidal) flow

Figure 11.5
Composition and decomposition of flow into two components, according to Longuet-Higgins and Prazdny (1980). (Top) The flow for a situation in which the observer moves linearly through the environment and rotates his or her eyes. (Middle) The optic flow putatively resulting from forward motion. (Bottom) The retinal flow resulting from eye rotation.

the theory goes, if the observer could retain eye rotation information and subtract out that vector to attain the flow pattern in the middle panel.

Two aspects of this analysis are absolutely correct, but a third is in error. It is unimpeachable that the addition of the vector fields in the middle and bottom panels yields the top. Moreover, it is unarguable that horizontal eye rotations yield vector displacements like those at the bottom. But that is where the good news ends. Longuet-Higgins and Prazdny claimed that the propriospecific component shown in the bottom panel is typical of retinal flow. This is true but not exclusively so. There is also a rotational component during curvilinear translation that is exterospecific. Curved paths without eye rotation generate flow like that in the top panel, a complication that I discuss in depth in chapter 13. But provisionally, imagine driving a car through a curve while looking at a fixed angle to the road surface, perhaps fixating on the smear of lines dividing one traffic lane from another. In doing this, the driver does not rotate his or her eyes, but the rotational component of flow is still present because the driver's head rotates in the environment. Thus the division of retinal flow into two components—which are mathematically and computationally sound—does not automatically separate flows of propriospecific from exterospecific perception. Thus feedback from eye muscles cannot generally be used as a basis for subtracting out the rotational vector field in the bottom panel.

Asymmetries of Retinal Flow

A final possibility concerns retinal flow asymmetries. These occur whenever the identity point is off the line of movement. As Richards (1975, p. 355) noted:

> If the observer is fixating off to one side away from his direction of movement, the asymmetric flow patterns on the retina will indicate that fixation is not in the primary direction . . . asymmetric flow patterns will result whenever the fixation point does not correspond to the vanishing point of flow set up by the body motion.

It seems possible, following Richards, that whenever the eye is focused on a point not along the direction of movement, asymmetries of flow might be detectable and usable. Two analyses are pertinent to this possibility, that of the sensitivity of the retina for detecting motion at varying eccentricities and that of relative flow at those same eccentricities from the direction of movement.

Figure 11.6 shows two functions. The first plots visual resolution against eccentricity, also known as the acuity gradient. Only one side

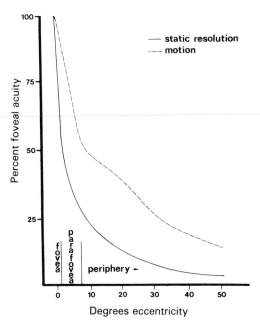

Figure 11.6
Two functions of acuity. Static resolution is based on detection of sinusoidal gratings as a proportion of performance at the fovea (about 45 sec of arc), adapted from Johnson and Leibowitz (1979). Motion detection for the movement of small squares is also plotted as a function of performance at the fovea (about 1.5 min of arc per sec), adapted from Leibowitz et al. (1972). Both data sets are uncorrected for refractive error in the periphery of the retina.

of the visual field is mapped, and the blind spot ignored (that region between 12 and 17° on the temporal side of the visual field of each eye, within which we have no sensitivity because of the disappearance of the optic nerve through the scleral wall). Plotted is the threshold for detection of high-contrast sinusoidal gratings.[6] The data are normalized to performance at the fovea, where gratings of about 45 sec of arc (0.0125°) are just detectable. Notice that acuity at 20° eccentricity is about 15% as good as at the fovea.

The second function plotted in figure 11.6 is more important to the analyses here. It maps detectability of a moving stimulus against retinal eccentricity. Again the data are normalized to performance at the fovea, where a small white square against a black background can be seen to move when it oscillates through 1.5 min of arc (0.025°) per second. Here, performance at 20° eccentricity is about 30% as good as that at the fovea. Three facts should be noted: First, the fovea is the most

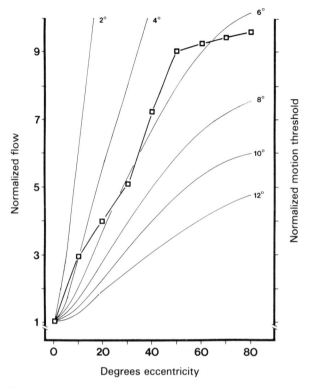

Figure 11.7
Relative retinal flow velocities at varying eccentricities. Gaze is at 0°, along the linear path of movement, and the instantaneous velocity of the point at fixation is set to 1.0. Relative flow is plotted for circular arcs at 2, 4, 6, 8, 10, and 12° below the horizon, corresponding to distances of 48, 24, 16, 12, 9.5, and 7.9 m from a moving observer whose eye height is 1.68 m. Also plotted is the normalized motion detection threshold (open squares) from Leibowitz et al. (1972), again uncorrected for refractory error in the periphery.

sensitive region of the retina for both resolution and motion detection; second, motion detection is more evenly distributed across the retina than is resolution; and third, both functions are asymptotic in an approximately exponential manner.

The family of curves shown in figure 11.7 are the absolute flow vectors plotted as a function of eccentricity. Measures were taken of instantaneous flow at various positions around the observer on meridians 2 to 12° below the horizon for linear movement, with gaze at the point below the horizon extended outward from the movement path. These values were then expressed as the absolute flow vector (that is, they ignore direction)[7] and normalized to that point on the meridian directly along the path. What is exciting about comparing motion sensitivity and flow is that their functions are nearly identical. This suggests that the thresholds for detection of motion resulting from linear movement over a plane are roughly the same across a horizontal meridian of the retina. If functions for suprathreshold sensitivity parallel these,[8] then large regions of the retina might be equally stimulated during linear movement of the observer, provided that the observer is looking along the path of movement and about 6° below the horizon. This coincidence suggests a method by which direction may be determined: The observer might locate the direction of movement by stimulating the motion detection system most uniformly across the retina, bringing into register the flow of the terrestrial plane and the sensory capabilities of the visual system.

Although this scheme seems attractive, particularly for pilots of low-flying aircraft, it has two serious difficulties. First, it assumes a flat plane and objects on it of equal height. In natural environments, however, we find things at many different heights—turf beneath our feet, other people, overhanging branches, buildings towering over us. This flow is not dictated primarily by the coordinates of objects in the optic array but by their distance from us. Thus, if we were running through a forest, the flow of objects at varying distances could not match the sensitivity function on the retina. Second, when observers locomote along a curved path, the pattern of optic flow is seriously distorted. These problems are considered in greater detail in later chapters.

Overview

To fix the location of the focus of expansion, assumptions about flow mapping must be made. Five proposals have been entertained. The first considered the possible velocity-independent utility of the focus of expansion as Gibson construed it. Unfortunately, pedestrian speeds are insufficient to guarantee the stability of the spherical coordinate system of the optic array. The second was that the stability of the horizon could provide anchors for mapping optic flow. But the horizon is often not visible during locomotion, and it moves in relation to the observer when the observer turns. Third, biological gyroscopes were considered but rejected on the grounds that they are not in the optic array and that much of the accessory optic system is devoted to overriding gyroscopic maintenance of eye direction. The fourth proposal, separating translational from rotational components of flow, is not supported by psychological evidence. Furthermore, it assumes that all rotations are due to the eyes in their sockets and is thus confined to linear observer movement. And the fifth proposal concerned matching flow and motion sensitivity functions. But this idea has difficulties with cluttered environments and with curvilinear movement.

Thus there remains no clear way to fix the identity point along the path of movement. Perhaps other assumptions can be made that I have not been clever enough to discover, but the outlook seems bleak. I suggest that an alternative method of wayfinding is needed. The next chapter presents a prime candidate—differential motion parallax.

12

Motion Parallax and Linear Movement

In chapter 10 I outlined the general failure of a series of information sources to specify the direction of observer movement—the focus of expansion, the point of maximum rate of magnification, and ocular drift cancellation. In chapter 11 I began formal reinvestigation of optic flow, with particular attention to multiple representation. In this chapter I present a different source of information for wayfinding that is generally available to the moving observer—*motion parallax*. Motion parallax, mentioned briefly in connection with experiments 7 and 8, is the relative displacement of objects caused by change in observer position. It was noted by Euclid and Helmholtz and has been studied by many others.[1] Graham et al. (1948), for example, showed that people can detect changes as small as half a minute of arc per second in the positions of two points. This is exquisite sensitivity.

Can this information be used for direction finding? In a commentary on Helmholtz's explanation of motion parallax, which I quoted in chapter 11, von Kries (1910, pp. 371–372) captured the tools for providing an affirmative answer:

> Helmholtz has described certain changes in the configuration of observed bodies due to motion on the part of the observer, and discussed the effect they had on perception of distance. The changes of which he speaks are such as the observer would notice if he advanced forward without changing attitude of his head or his eyes especially. In reality the phenomena are complicated by the fact that, supposing our attention is attracted, not by objects moving along with us, but by stationary external objects, we are invariably of the habit of keeping the eyes fastened for a brief space on some definite point, by turning them so as to counteract the effect of forward motion of the body. . . . What happens in this case is that for a brief space the image of the point of fixation for the time being remains stationary at the place where it is on the retina, while the images of objects that are nearer and farther than this point glide over the retina in opposite directions. And so the point

of fixation, being perceived as stationary, serves as a point of reference; and points which are farther away appear to be advancing in the same direction as the observer, while points which are nearer appear to be receding in the opposite direction.[2]

Here, von Kries laid much of the groundwork for what follows. Before expanding on his analysis, however, let me review some of the benefits of parallax descriptions of optic flow.

Benefits of Parallax

One of the good features of motion parallax is that large changes in the optic array occur even when measured locally. Thus, to study the efficacy of motion parallax, the researcher does not need large spherical projection surfaces. So long as the projected environment is rich enough, with numerous objects at different distances within a relatively small solid visual angle, motion parallax can be displayed accurately on a flat screen whose width and height are as small as a few degrees of visual angle.

More important, however, is that in motion parallax, as opposed to the descriptions of optic flow discussed in chapter 10, objects *must* be at different depths in three-dimensional space. In contrast, the discussions of the focus of expansion, asymmetries of flow, magnification maxima, and ocular drift assumed environments generally compressed along the z axis. In motion parallax, the objects interpose, passing through what I call the *plane of sight*—an imaginary vertically oriented plane intersecting both the eye and the object under scrutiny. When an observer locomotes with fixed gaze, it is the relative velocity with which objects pass through this plane that is of major interest, not occlusions generated by interposition. Thus parallax is discussed as instantaneous displacement differences, and no further mention is made of accretions and deletions of texture.

The optics of motion parallax generated from linear movement can be thought of in two ways: as translations in an affine approximation or as rotations and translations in Euclidean space. The first is conceptually easier and has been used for decades by psychologists and cartoon animators. But its ease is more than countered by the fact that it is geometrically incorrect. The second description is correct but conceptually more complex.

Translations in an Affine Approximation to Parallax Flow
Motion parallax is often discussed using a diagram similar to that shown in the top panel of figure 12.1. In such a situation, according to many

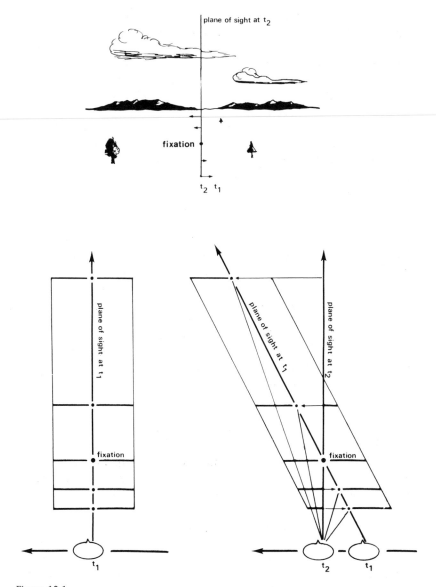

Figure 12.1
The upper panel shows a common but incorrect representation of motion parallax. A
new concept, the *plane of sight*, is introduced for all those objects on a vertical plane
that passes through the eye and the fixation point. The lower panels show the affine
space of motion parallax often used in cartoon animation and implied in most perception
textbooks. Motion is represented by shearing different parallel depth planes against one
another. This preserves collinearity of objects but not relative distances nor angles in
Euclidean space.

researchers, a viewer stares at an object in the mid-distance, 90° to the right of where the viewer is headed. Objects in front of fixation slide to the right and those in back slide to the left. This is a reasonably good approximation to optic flow, but it is true only for those motions of objects *exactly* at right angles to the direction of movement.

As indicated in the lower panels of figure 12.1, we might imagine objects laid out in depth as if they were on sliding vertical planes parallel to the path of movement. That is, within a small viewing angle, everything that is the same distance from the viewer is (roughly) on the same plane, and objects at different distances are on different parallel planes. Movement to the left is simulated by sliding these planes horizontally to differing degrees. Planes nearer than the object under scrutiny slide to the right, the plane of the fixated object remains stationary, and far planes slide to the left.

This conception is partly correct, but it is flawed because it does not compensate for changing distances among the observer and all objects off the plane of sight. Regardless, the phenomenal effect of affine shear is striking, and it demonstrates one of two major effects of motion parallax—the change in position of projected elements in the optic array against one another, shearing through the plane of sight.[3] Unfortunately, it dismisses the other important effect of parallax—rotation. And it is doubly unfortunate because this affine representation is precisely the one that appears most often in the literature.[4] It leads to mistaken ideas about the character of flow.

Rotations and Translations in Euclidean Parallax Flow
In the second, and geometrically correct, representation, the viewer must imagine that the object under scrutiny becomes the hub of a rotating and expanding (or contracting) array. Two manifolds of vectors are overlaid, as suggested in chapter 11. One is a set of expansions that accrue from moving closer to viewed objects (or contractions if the viewer is moving away), the other a set of rotations. When the viewer looks off to the right at some object, maintaining fixation on it while moving forward, the changing optic array is the same as if the ground and objects on it were rotating counterclockwise and expanding around a vertical axis through the fixation point. Similarly, when the viewer looks left, objects in the array rotate clockwise and expand around the fixated object. Because the world is seen in polar projection, these rotations generate important asymmetries of flow. Because this conception is undoubtedly difficult to grasp initially, this systematicness is the focus of the rest of the chapter.

As an introduction to the dynamic geometry of motion parallax, consider the panels of figure 12.2. On the left-hand side is a rendering

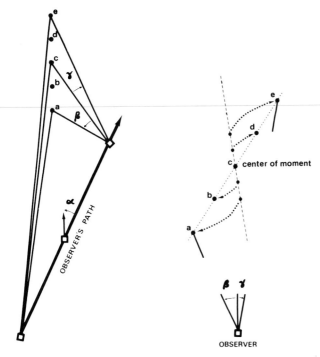

Figure 12.2
Representations of movement through space while observing a linear arrangement of fenceposts off to the left. The left-hand panel shows these relations in environmental coordinates with fencepost c the object under scrutiny. The right-hand panel shows the relations normalized to observer-object coordinates. Fenceposts a and e demonstrate the differential motion parallax. Angle α, that between directions of movement and gaze, is manipulated in three experiments in this and the next chapter. After Cutting (1983b).

of an observer traveling obliquely past a line of fenceposts, labeled *a* through *e*. Imagine that the observer continually fixates fencepost *c*. The turning of the square along the path indicates either head turning, ocular rotation, or their sum. This panel is drawn in environmental coordinates with the observer moving through a stationary environment. Such coordinates are object centered, following Marr (1982). The object of interest is fencepost *c*, which serves as the stationary origin in this coordinate system.[5]

The right-hand panel of figure 12.2 transforms the coordinate space according to the following scheme: Here, the two sets of vectors— rotations and expansions—are overlaid. If we measure the change in fencepost positions, normalizing the distance between and the positions of the observer and fencepost *c*, then the array of parallax motions (as if seen from above) is portrayed. Going beyond Marr, these parallax motions are in a hybrid of object- and viewer-centered coordinates. Notice that, because the direction of gaze is fixed in this coordinate system, the direction of movement must constantly change. Because the observer continually fixates fencepost *c*, it becomes the center of the flow pattern. Elsewhere, I have called this point a center of moment,[6] and here it is a fixed point (or identity point) in the retinal array.

Of current interest, however, is the flow pattern around the fixed point. Consider angle β as that between planes of sight to fenceposts *c* and *a*, and γ that between fenceposts *c* and *e*. While holding locations of the observer and *c* constant, the relative locations of *a* and *e* (as well as of *b* and *d*) must change. Thus β and γ must also change. In the right-hand panel of figure 12.2 is plotted the angular change from the starting point shown in the left-hand panel (denoted by the dashed line) to the last position (denoted by the dotted line). At the bottom of the right-hand panel the changes in β and γ are shown from the position of alignment of the fenceposts with the observer to the final position.

The crucial datum is that angle β grows faster than angle γ. Thus it can be seen that objects nearer to the observer than fixation generally shear faster than those farther away. Notice further that objects with greater motion move optically in the direction *opposite* the direction of movement. In other words, the faster-moving objects shear leftward through the plane of sight, and the direction of movement with respect to gaze is to the right.

A Note on Polar and Parallel Projection
The differential growths of β and γ are the centerpiece of my analysis: They are, quite simply, the reason we can determine direction of movement. They create what I call *differential motion parallax*, an invariant

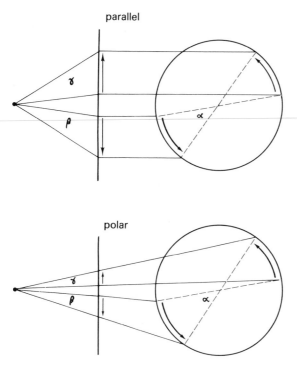

Figure 12.3
A rotating circle seen in polar and parallel projection as viewed from above. In both cases the angular rotation of the circles are equal to angle α. In parallel projection the vectors of projected motion are the same (angles β and α) on the back and front of the circle, whereas in polar projection they are different, with angle β larger than angle α. This is differential motion parallax, and it occurs only with polar projection.

ordering, an inequality, in optic flow. Such parallax is contingent on polar perspective. It is only under these conditions that things generally closer move more rapidly than and in the opposite direction to things farther away. Consider textures on the surface of a transparent sphere or cylinder, shown in figure 12.3.[7]

The bottom panel shows the top view of a rotating polar-projected cylinder. Note that the textures on the front and back surface move an equal amount in absolute coordinates (and thus have equal-sized absolute vectors) but that, when projected onto the screen, near textures move more than far ones. In parallel projection this is not true, as shown in the top panel. Because rays of projection are parallel, there is no diminution of projected size with distance. Thus textures on the back side move with the same velocities as those on the front. Parallel projection of textured, transparent rotating spheres and cylinders always yields ambiguity. The optics are equally correct (ignoring occlusions) for both clockwise and counterclockwise interpretations, and an observer is likely to shift back and forth between them (Braunstein et al. 1982). Ambiguity is due, in part, to lack of differential motion parallax in the stimulus. But, with respect to flow, the major analytic question remains: Under what conditions does differential motion parallax occur? More concretely, under what conditions of object spacing is the growth of β greater than that of γ?

Measuring Differential Motion Parallax

To measure motion with parallax, we need another digression into calculus. Two types of derivatives can be used—those of time and those of space. Again, I have chosen derivatives of space, incrementally small changes in the observer position along the z axis, to represent flow so that the patterns are not dependent on velocities, only on the extent of movement. In this manner, the patterns are as true for a pedestrian as they are for a pilot. To begin, it is easiest to consider functions generated with an identity point extended from the direction of movement. After that, I generalize flow patterns to cases in which a viewer is looking at an object off to the side.

Looking Directly Ahead

Let x be the axis running laterally along the frontal plane, y that running vertically along that plane, and z the dimension of depth along the path of movement. Now consider the case for all points on a second plane z units away from the observer and orthogonal to the line of movement and gaze. Measured horizontally along the planar surface, these points are x units from its origin, and measured vertically, they are y units from it. Converted to spherical coordinates, the angles are

$$\theta = \arctan(x/z), \tag{12.1}$$
$$\phi = \arctan[y/(x^2 + z^2)^{1/2}], \tag{12.2}$$

where θ is the horizontal angle (*yaw*) and ϕ is the vertical angle (*pitch*). Because I am interested in flow, it is the instantaneous changes in these angles that need to be considered as a function of the instantaneous change in z, forward linear movement. After differentiation, these relations are

$$d\theta/dz = -x/(x^2 + z^2), \tag{12.3}$$
$$d\phi/dz = -yz/[(x^2 + y^2 + z^2)(x^2 + z^2)^{1/2}]. \tag{12.4}$$

Equation (12.4) looks particularly formidable, but notice that, when $x = 0$, it reduces to

$$d\phi/dz = -y/(y^2 + z^2).\qquad(12.5)$$

The benefits of this reduction are that Eq. (12.5) has the same form as Eq. (12.3), and it is identical with Eq. (9.2). Analytically, the denominators of Eqs. (12.3) and (12.5) are formulas for circles, and in connection with their numerators these are displaced to each side by distances equal to their radii. Any point on these circles has an equal projected displacement vector away from the observer's heading. Those on circles to the right project with rightward motion, and those on the left move leftward. These are isoangular displacement contours, and they are shown in figure 12.4.

In absolute terms (ignoring direction of flow) all points on the figure eights in figure 12.4 project with equal instantaneous displacement. Moreover, because Eqs. (12.3) and (12.4) are for spherical coordinates, a figure eight can be rotated around the axis of movement in three dimensions, obtaining a toroid, or toruslike shape, as indicated in figure 12.5a.[8] Because these contours are associated with objects at different x and z coordinates, figure eights in two dimensions (and toroidal surfaces in three) are nested within one another, as shown in figure 12.4. They all share inner tangents at the location of the observer along the path of movement.

Looking Off to the Side
What has been presented thus far are the vector fields for when a viewer is already looking exactly in the direction of movement. The arguments presented previously suggest that this is the end result of direction finding, not the means by which it is accomplished. Thus we must complicate the vector fields by considering the more general case of looking off to the side. In such cases a viewer subtracts the particular vector for the fixated object from the fields in figure 12.4. Displacement contours remain circular, but matched pairs across the line of movement in the horizontal plane are of different sizes. In three dimensions the toroidal surface becomes asymmetric, resembling a lopsided bagel, as shown in figure 12.5b.

Consider again the two-step process needed to attain these shapes. First, the displacement field is generated as if the viewer is looking in the direction of movement. Next, the instantaneous displacement vector for the object actually at the fixation point is subtracted from the field. Its vector depends on its distance from the observer and on its angular departure from the line of movement. Thus *there is a different set of nested toroids for every fixated object at every instant around the line of*

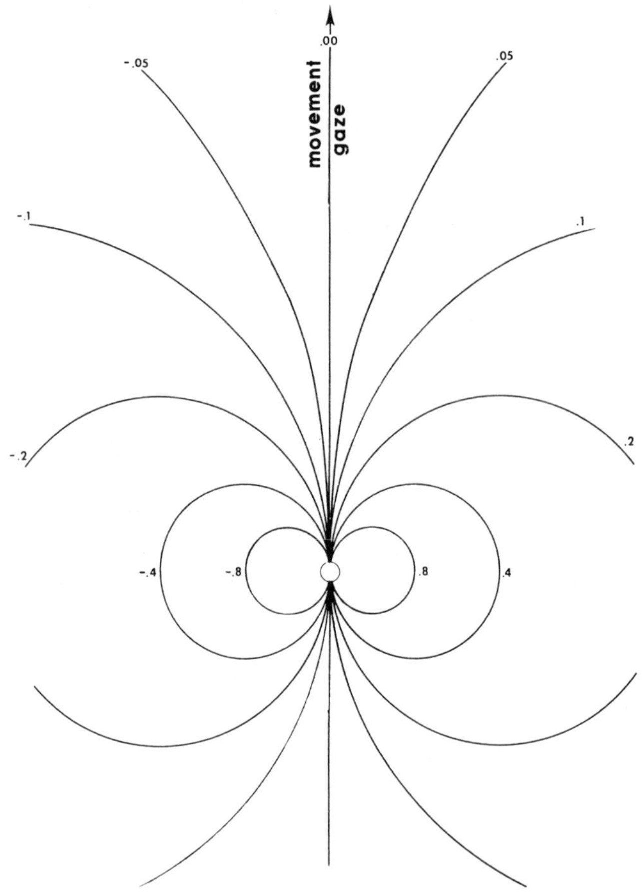

Figure 12.4
Isoangular displacement contours in the horizontal plane for linear movement under the condition of looking exactly in the direction of movement. Null velocity points are along the path of movement and gaze. All objects in the environment located on a given contour flow laterally with the same instantaneous displacement. Equation (12.3) specifies this flow. All contours are tangent to the line of movement at the location of the observer; the values of all contours at this point, however, are undefined (0/0).

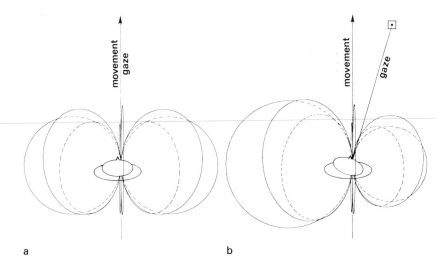

Figure 12.5
A three-dimensional instantaneous isoangular displacement contour for linear movement with gaze fixed along the movement path. This shape is a toroid, or figure eight rotated in the third dimension along the path of movement and gaze. Equations (12.3) and (12.4) specify this flow. (b) The same contours for an observer looking somewhat off to the side. The toroid has deformed into a shape more like a lopsided bagel.

sight, when the viewer is not looking in the direction of movement. This is simply another way of stating that there is a different set of parallaxes associated with every object that the viewer may choose to look at as he or she moves. In figure 12.6 are shown different cases in which a viewer is looking at objects at different locales and the resulting two-dimensional displacement fields. Of particular interest are the displacement contours across the line of sight.

Necessary Conditions for Differential Motion Parallax
One way to determine the limits of differential motion parallax is to explore the following situations: (1) Choose an object (object 1) at a given distance and angle and fixate it; (2) choose another (object 2) nearer than the fixated object; and (3) determine the locations of the class of entities (objects 3) farther away that moves with an instantaneous displacement *greater* than and in the direction opposite object 2. Reciprocally, if object 2 were farther away than object 1, we could determine the locations of a near class that moves *less* than and in the direction opposite object 2. Such demonstrations delimit regions in which differential motion parallax fails. Because of the general complexity of this formulation, it is prudent to consider objects only in the horizontal plane.

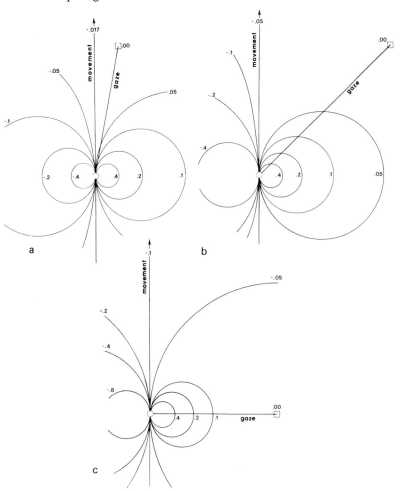

Figure 12.6
Isoangular displacement contours in the horizontal plane when an object off the line of sight is fixated. The velocity of the object under scrutiny has been subtracted from the motion of all other points. (a) The instantaneous contours when looking at an object at a fixed distance and 10° off to the right. (b) The same but at 45° off to the right. (c) The same but at 90°.

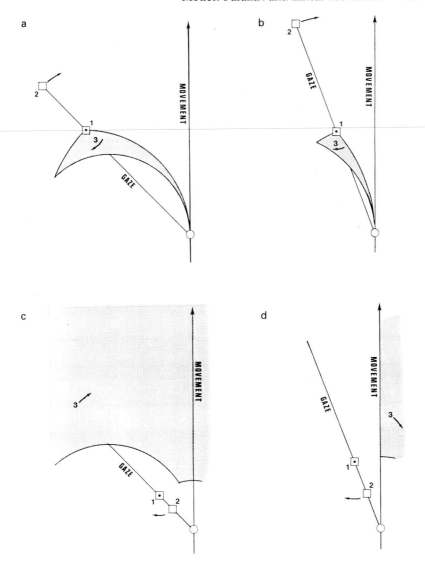

Figure 12.7
The conditions of differential motion parallax, considered only in the horizontal plane. Object 1 is fixated in all panels, object 2 is the reference object, and the shaded areas indicate possible locations of all objects 3 that *fail* to meet the conditions of differential motion parallax. (a, b) Cases in which nearer objects violate this parallax rule and all objects 3 shear leftward and more *slowly* than object 2 shears rightward. (c, d) Cases in which farther objects violate the parallax rule, shearing rightward faster than object 2 shears leftward. Most important is part (d): When object 2 is half the distance to object 1, no object out to infinity along or near the plane of sight moves with equal but opposite velocity.

Selected examples of this scheme are shown in figure 12.7. Object 1 is always the fixated object, bathing the fovea. Object 2 in figures 12.7a and 12.7b is nearer to the observer and in figures 12.7c and 12.7d it is farther away. All objects 3 that fall within the stippled areas *fail* as examples of differential motion parallax; nearer objects shear less rapidly than farther objects. Most important is figure 12.7d. When object 2 is only half the distance of object 1, *all farther objects near the plane of sight, no matter how distant, demonstrate differential motion parallax*. That is, no object, not even a star, would shear in the direction of movement as fast as object 2 shears the other way. Thus minimal and universal conditions for differential motion parallax have a reference object half the distance away from the fixated object. Having outlined the necessary conditions for differential motion parallax, in the next sections I formalize direction finding and present an experiment in support of this view.

Recursive Rules for Determining Direction of Movement

1. Determining the Direction of Gaze with Respect to Movement.   If, when looking at an object in the middle distance, a viewer sees that the class of objects shearing rightward through the plane of sight generally moves faster than that shearing left, then the viewer is looking to the right of the direction of movement. Contrariwise, if objects shear leftward generally faster, then the viewer is looking left.

2. Determining the Direction of Movement.   In order for a viewer to determine the direction of movement, he or she must shift gaze to a new object in the direction opposite the fastest motion in the retinal array. Rules 1 and 2 are repeated until no objects cross the plane of sight.

Constraints.   First, the local environment must be cluttered enough so that it contains a sufficient number of objects at various distances and directions. At a minimum there should be objects along or near the plane of sight that are both nearer and farther than an object under scrutiny. The real world usually satisfies this constraint. Second, the viewer must be looking far enough out into the world so that there is a sufficient number of objects closer than fixation. These objects will be positioned between the viewer and the viewed object, passing through the plane of sight. Near objects on the ground will pass through the lower part of the plane, and objects farther away through the higher part. This second constraint seems unproblematic because the viewer would not generally look nearby when wanting to know the direction of movement. Close work is stationary work. We do not want any movement when looking closely, say, at a newspaper, unless someone else, say, a bus driver, is responsible for locomotion. Looking at the opposite extreme, at the horizon, poses no problem because *all* moving objects, not simply the most rapid, shear through the plane of sight and in the direction opposite that of movement.

Experiment 9: Differential Motion Parallax and Linear Movement

Having formulated these rules, we need to see if they are used.[9] The basic technique is one from psychophysics and is like that used in experiments 1 through 8. In this experiment four observers participated individually: two graduate students, one undergraduate, and me. Participation entailed viewing dynamic computer-generated displays over the course of two 45-min experimental sessions. Stimuli were generated on the same apparatus as before and simulated linear movement through an environment. The environment itself was sparse, consisting of twelve vertical lines, four randomly placed on each of three parallel planes orthogonal to the line of movement. All lines extended the full vertical height of the scope face (about 8° of visual angle) so that no relative size information would be available to determine the distance to each plane.[10] The experimental situation is shown in figure 12.8.

Dynamic sequences were computed uniquely for each subject for each trial.[11] Simulated movement toward the planes was scaled to be about the same as that in Regan and Beverley's (1982) experiment, 58 km/hr. Movement began when the observer was, on this scale, 76 m distant from the middle plane and continued at constant velocity until he or she was 38 m distant. Each sequence of forward movement was repeated three times within a trial, with a 0.5-sec pause between presentations, yielding a trial duration of about 8 sec. Four viewing conditions were employed, each distinguished by the relative distances among the three planes. Each of these is indicated in figure 12.8, and four frames each of three trials under condition 1 are shown in figure 12.9.

Viewers were told to consider the dynamic displays as representing the movement through an environment with twelve vertical wires and that some trials simulated looking ahead, some looking left, some right. The task was to determine which of the three possibilities was shown on a given trial. Under each condition a viewer was presented with a random sequence of 15 trials per block—five for each direction of gaze. Viewers were given feedback after each trial. Within a block of trials the angle between the directions of gaze and movement (for left-looking

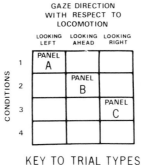

KEY TO TRIAL TYPES

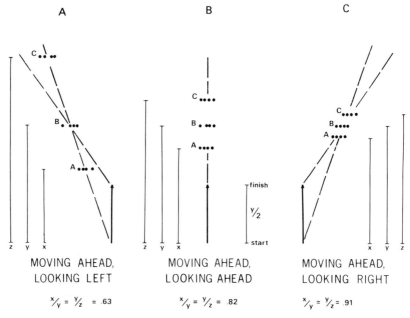

Figure 12.8
Stimulus conditions of experiment 9 in three different gaze-movement trials as might be viewed from the top. The conditions are distinguished by the distances among the planes, and the gaze-movement trials are distinguished by whether the simulations have the observer looking to the left, looking ahead, or looking to the right. As shown in the key, the trials in (A) correspond to condition 1, in (B) to condition 2, and in (C) to condition 3. A fourth condition (not shown) collapses all three planes together.

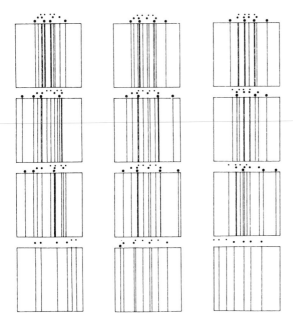

Figure 12.9
Four images taken out of each of three motion sequences used in experiment 9, corresponding to the 1st, 19th, 27th, and 55th (last) frames. Panels on the left-hand side are those for a trial that starts out looking 20° to the left, those in the middle for a trial looking directly ahead, and those on the right-hand side for a trial starting with a gaze-movement angle of 20° to the right. Above each panel are dots indicating to which plane each line belongs. Large dots at the bottom are those for plane A (the closest to the observer), small dots are for plane C, and medium dots are for plane B.

and right-looking trials) was fixed. I call this the *gaze-movement angle*. All viewers began their first block of trials under each condition with initial gaze-movement angles of 20°. That value was halved for each successive block until performance fell to chance. Figure 12.8 shows schematic renderings of the geometry of a left-looking trial under condition 1, an ahead-looking trial under condition 2, and a right-looking trial under condition 3. Before beginning, each viewer was given five practice trials from the first block under condition 1.

All planes were perpendicular to the direction of movement, and their centers were aligned with the line of sight when the trial began, as shown in figure 12.8. The locations of front and back planes (A and C, respectively) were chosen so that the absolute distance from A to B was less than that from B to C, providing a stronger test for differential motion parallax than shown in figure 12.2.[12] Because two-thirds of the trials began with an initial gaze-movement angle greater than zero and

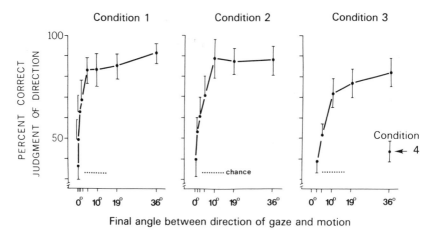

Figure 12.10
Results for all four conditions of experiment 9 (linear movement). Vertical bars indicate plus and minus one standard error of the mean.

because simulation mimicked continued fixation of a point in space (the center of plane *B*) as the viewer moved, subsequent gaze-movement angles systematically increased. Trials that began with angles of 20, 10, 5, 2.5, 1.25, and 0.625°, ended with ones of 36.05, 19.43, 9.93, 4.99, 2.50, and 1.25°, respectively. This latter set of values form the independent measures of the experiment. That is, if the observers started out on a trial looking 2.5° to the left, wound up looking 4.99° to the left, said that they were looking left on that trial, and were reliably correct for right-looking and ahead-looking trials within that block as well, then we can say that they were able to determine their heading within 5° of visual angle.

Results
Data for the four conditions are shown in figure 12.10. On the ordinate of each plot is the mean percentage correct. Chance performance is 1 trial correct out of 3, or 33%. On the abscissa is the final gaze-movement angle simulated by the left- and right-looking trials of each block. Under condition 1, where the planes were farthest apart, performance remained high (above 80%) for trials with final gaze-movement angles as small as 5°. More important, observer performance remained above chance for final gaze-movement angles as small as 37 min of arc. Under condition 2, with planes closer together, the same general pattern recurred but was attenuated somewhat. Performance remained high through trials, simulating final angles of 10°, and re-

mained above chance through 1.25 deg of arc. Under condition 3, with planes closer still, performance was decreased still further. It was never as high as under the other two conditions and was reliably above chance only through final angles of 5°. Finally, under condition 4, with all planes superimposed, performance was near chance, even at 36°. No further blocks were run because performance was so poor.

The results under condition 4 are a replication of Regan and Beverley's (1982): Observers really cannot discern their direction of movement for orthogonal approach to a single plane. The results under condition 1, on the other hand, exhibit exquisite observer sensitivity to differential motion parallax. Considering only the performance on the first five blocks under the first three conditions, the effect of changing the relative distances among planes was statistically reliable, as was the effect of reducing the final gaze-movement angles from 36° to 2.5°.[13] Phenomenal impressions of depth in general matched these results. Impression was strongest under the conditions with the largest gaze-movement angles and with the planes farthest apart. Condition 4 gave no impression of depth at all. Given the accuracy for judging gaze direction under condition 1—where left-, ahead-, and right-looking judgments could be made reliably for gaze-movement angles of less than 1° left, 0° ahead, and less than 1° right—we might conclude that viewers can accurately judge their direction of movement from the minimal displays used here.[14] Before drawing such a conclusion, however, reconsider what may seem to be a curious aspect of the stimuli.

On Simulated Fixation
Many readers may find odd the use here and by Regan and Beverley of a simulated fixation technique. The observer sees on the screen a stationary object that would be moving relative to him or her in the real world. Moreover, no matter how the observer's eyes move across the screen, that projection is unchanging—a situation completely unlike that of a real environment. How can such a situation be representative of the changing optic array?

The answer is twofold. First, when watching a film or television, the observer is often engaged in simulated fixation. The camera may pan around to follow something that is moving or the camera may be moving and focus on something that is not or both camera and object can be moving with focus on the object (see Gibson 1979, Hochberg 1978a). What is presented to the viewer on the stationary screen or monitor is a moving or changing world. The viewer may scan the film or television image, but he or she will not, even if a young child, find this situation difficult to apprehend.[15] It is a nontrivial question as to why it is not disruptive, but everyday experience says it is not. Part of the explanation must be that eye position and efferent commands are not potent sources of information when compared with motion in the optic array (Turvey 1977). Although this viewing situation is not ecologically valid in a biological sense, following Gibson (1966, 1979), it is very much so in a social sense, following Brunswik (1956) and Barker (1968): Television and film are deeply embedded in our culture.

The second part of the answer, and the part that provides theoretical justification, concerns the optics of polar projection. So long as the viewer's eyes are near the point of projection, the geometry will be correct regardless of where the viewer looks. If the simulated fixation point is at the center of the screen, the experimenter should probably assume that the statistical center of all fixations is there as well. The experimenter should also assume, however, that unless eye movements are monitored and provide evidence to the contrary, viewers will move their eyes about the screen as they would in any other everyday activity. What changes with these eye movements is the acuity gradient for the information seen, but the information itself is consistent and correct for the station point. The fact that the observer scans the scope face during the trial suggests a constraint on interpreting the data: Observers can make judgments about their direction of movement within 1° of visual angle, given a stimulus array size of about 4° radius. This is still a remarkable feat, especially given the minimality of these displays.

On Chance and Better Performance

One might, and indeed should, argue that the slightly-above-chance performance at a final gaze-movement angle of about 1° is not adequate. In chapter 10 I stated that runners, drivers, pilots, and skiers need to judge direction *accurately* at 1°; and surely we would not entrust our lives to a pilot or driver whose performance at avoiding obstacles was only slightly better than chance. One way to rectify these results with those demands is to consider an experiment that I performed that used regularly placed, rather than randomly placed, vertical lines on three planes. These stimuli looked like a march through a colonnade, and there I was able to judge direction within 6' of visual angle, almost an order of magnitude better. Another mechanism for improved performance would be to spread out the planes in depth to an even greater degree than under condition 1.

Overview

Differential motion parallax provides a plausible means for determining one's direction of movement. One need only pick out an object in the mid-distance of a cluttered environment and observe relative motions of other objects near it along the plane of sight. If the most rapidly moving objects shear to the right, one is almost surely looking to the right of one's direction of movement; and if the most rapidly moving objects shear left, one is almost surely looking left. The results of experiment 9 suggest that observers can use this information to discern their direction. Provided that objects are sufficiently far apart in depth, the observers were able to discern direction within a fraction of a degree of visual angle. Given that pilots appear to use vertical displacements of parallax information in visual landings of aircraft (Langewiesche 1944, Hasbrook 1975) to determine if they are too low in their approach and given that horizontal parallax displacements surround the terrestrial observer during all movements, it seems likely that differential motion parallax is used in everyday locomotion. Before concluding that, however, we need to consider the more general case—curvilinear translation through an environment.

13

Motion Parallax and Curvilinear Movement

In chapter 12 I presented the theory, mathematical formalisms, and data to support a method for determining heading during linear movement. It should be clear, however, that this is not the general case. More often, we move along a path that is at least slightly curved; we bob and weave when we walk or run, angling around corners, obstacles, and puddles. It would be much more convincing if differential motion parallax were useful for wayfinding along such paths. Thus in this chapter I extend the analysis to the curvilinear case.

There is an indefinite number of ways in which a path can be curved, but this should not detain us. For simplicity's sake it is easiest to start with paths that are an arc of a circle. The rationale was captured by Russell (1897, p. 17):

> Just as the notion of *length* was originally derived from the straight line, and extended to other curves by dividing them into infinitesimal straight lines, so the notion of *curvature* was derived from the circle, and extended to other curves by dividing them into infinitesimal circular arcs.

Again, it is easiest to consider flow in the horizontal plane. Thus the path of the observer is always along the perimeter of a circle, much as if the observer were on a merry-go-round, and the information considered is that at eye level. The generality of this analysis to other curved paths and to three dimensions is briefly considered later in this section.

For now, however, consider the situations shown in the upper panels of figure 13.1. Let r be the radius of the circle around which the observer moves, L the distance between the center of that circle and the object under scrutiny, and β the angle between lines from the circle's center to the observer and to the fixated object. The ultimate angle of interest, α, is that between the tangent to the circle and the line to the object at the point of the observer. Interest in α stems from the parallel that

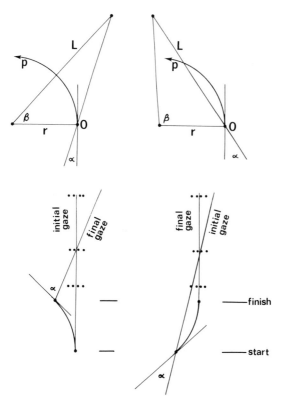

Figure 13.1
The geometry of curvilinear movement. O is the location of the observer, p is the perimeter of the circular path of movement, r is the radius of the circle, L is the distance (length) from the center of the circle to any particular object in the field of view, and α and β are two important angles for consideration. The left-hand panels show the situation of looking outward from the path of movement, and the right-hand panels for looking inward and across the path of movement. Angle α is the final gaze-movement angle during the simulated forward movement of an observer in experiment 10 and the initial angle in experiment 11. It is determined by the tangent to the movement path and the line of sight to the middle of the central plane.

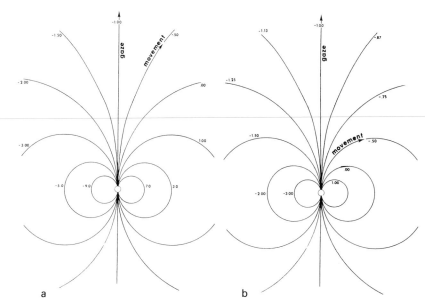

Figure 13.2
Isoangular displacement contours for curvilinear movement. Compare these to the contours in figure 12.4, noting not only the shapes but also the values of contours themselves. The circular path in (b) has a radius one-fourth that in (a). With tighter circles the differences in the vector fields get flatter and asympotically approach uniform flow when the observer simply twirls in place.

it sets up with the linear movement case (although spherical coordinates θ and ϕ are not used). For circular movement, α is determined by

$$\alpha = 90° - \arctan[L \sin \beta/(r - L \cos \beta)]. \tag{13.1}$$

If the observer moves around the circumference of the circle, then α changes as a function of β:

$$d\alpha/d\beta = L(r \cos \beta - L)/(r^2 - 2Lr \cos \beta + L^2). \tag{13.2}$$

The isoangular displacement contours, analogous to those in figure 12.4, are shown in figure 13.2a for the situation in which the radius is relatively large and in figure 13.2b, in which it is one-fourth the size. Notice that the two patterns differ only by a scale factor and that they are the same overall shape as those for linear movement. Notice further that the contour values are flatter for the tighter circle than for the larger. In the degenerate case, where $r = 0$, the entire optic field attains a uniform velocity of -1.00, signifying unit rotation.

Intuitively, the similarity of flow patterns for linear and curvilinear movement makes sense. After all, the special character of circular movement is in the derivatives of the displacements, which for convenience I simply call angular accelerations; instantaneous displacements (velocities) should not be affected.[1] The similarity also holds for generalization to other curved paths. That is, following Russell, we can always consider the movement along some suitably small section of a curved path as that along the arc of a circle. Regardless of how small this arc may be (unless curvilinear locomotion degenerates into pivoting in place), the contours are like those shown in figure 13.2. Only relative steepness is affected, and this is caused by the relative sharpness of the curve taken.

Differential motion parallax can be used in curvilinear movement as it is in linear movement. The contours in figure 13.2 are for reference, drawn by choosing the point projected outward from the instantaneous tangent to the circular path. If the observer happens not to be looking directly at that spot—a likely possibility—he or she will be looking at some object that has associated with it a particular instantaneous displacement with respect to this reference. That displacement can be nulled through vector subtraction. In other words, the same procedure as that in chapter 12 can be used. Of course, direction of movement is constantly changing, but changing (at least in this case) in the same manner at all instants. Differential motion parallax operates here because the pattern of motions along any line of sight is the same regardless of the shape of the curved path.

In three dimensions the isoangular displacements of figure 13.2 wrap around in the manner shown by comparing figures 12.5 and 12.6. That is, when a viewer is looking at some point along the contour with a value of 0.0, all those objects in the xz plane with a positive value of, say, 2.0 wrap around and meet those with values of -2.0. If, on the other hand, the viewer is looking at an object along the 1.0 contour, then those at 2.0 wrap around along three-dimensional figure eights and meet those on the 0.0 contour.

As would be expected, linear and circular movements differ in instantaneous acceleration contours. Figure 13.3a shows those movements for gaze directly along the path of linear movement, and figure 13.3b shows them for the tangent to a circular path.[2] Contours of other curved paths are variations on this theme. However, when the observer is not looking directly ahead along a straight path or along the tangent to a curved one, the situations are much more complicated for both linear and curvilinear movement. Luckily, because differential parallax concerns only relative displacements, not relative accelerations, no further use is made of acceleration analyses.[3]

If wayfinding is determined on the basis of instantaneous displacements, then we would expect the same pattern of results for curved

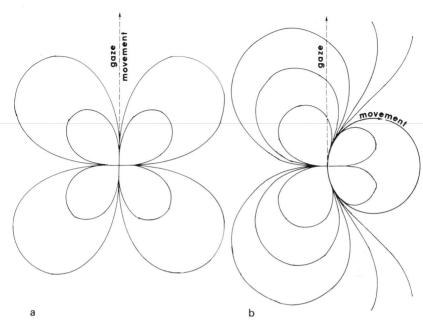

Figure 13.3
Isoangular acceleration contours for (a) linear and (b) curvilinear movement.

as for linear movement. Two situations are considered: moving along the path looking outward from the circle and looking inward and across it. The radius of the circle dictates relative sharpness of curvature and hence serves as an dependent measure. Ultimately, moving in circles with large radii approaches linear movement.

Experiment 10: Differential Motion Parallax and Looking out from a Curved Path

Four observers participated in this three-condition experiment: Three of us from experiment 9 and one naive observer.[4] In all respects but two, the procedures and stimuli were identical with those of the previous study: There was no condition 4 (under which three planes collapsed together), and the simulated path of movement, rather than being linear, followed the arc of a circle for those trials in which stimuli simulated looking off to the side. In one-third of the trials the path curved to the left, in one-third it was straight ahead, and in one-third it curved to the right.

Trials curving left and right began with paths orthogonal to the planes. As in experiment 9, the simulated fixation at the center of the

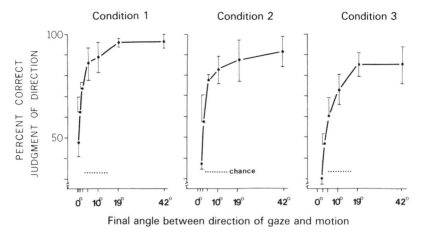

Figure 13.4
Results of the three conditions of experiment 10 according to final gaze-movement angles. All initial gaze-movement angles were 0°. The movement was curvilinear, and the direction of gaze was outward.

screen corresponded to the center of plane B. As before, the orthogonal distance traveled toward plane B was half the starting distance to it. Lateral distances varied according to curvature. Conditions began with blocks of trials whose path followed 0.50 rad of a circle (29° around the circumference). As before, successive blocks were increasingly difficult: 0.23 rad (13° of arc), 0.11 rad (6.4°), 0.06 rad (3.2°), 0.03 rad (1.6°), 0.014 rad (0.08°), and under condition 1, 0.007 rad (0.40°). Final gaze-movement angles were 42, 19.4, 9.6, 4.8, 2.4, 1.2, and 0.6°, respectively, and they serve as the independent measures. An overhead view of the geometry of a sample trial from block 1 of condition 1 is shown in the bottom left-hand panel of figure 13.1.

Results
The results are comparable with those of experiment 9, as shown in figure 13.4. Under conditions 1 and 2 performance remained high for trials simulating final gaze-movement angles as small as 5° and under condition 3 as small as 10°. Performance remained reliably above chance for angles as small as 0.6° under condition 1 and 2.4° under conditions 2 and 3. Significant differences were found across conditions and radii.[5] The comparability of results in experiments 9 and 10 corroborate the idea that the same information is available and used during linear and curvilinear movement. Before discussing this further, however, consider the remaining case.

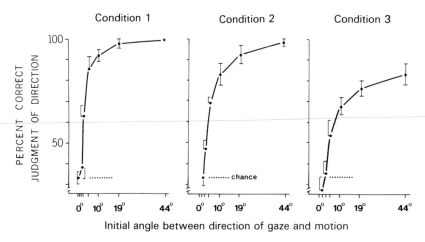

Figure 13.5
Results of the three conditions of experiment 11 according to initial gaze-movement angles. All final gaze-movement angles were 0°. The movement was curvilinear, and the direction of gaze was in and across.

Experiment 11: Differential Motion Parallax and Looking in and across a Curved Path

The four observers in experiment 10 participated here. The procedures were identical, and in all respects but one, the stimuli were identical as well. As shown in the bottom right-hand panel of figure 13.1, trials that did not simulate moving and looking straight ahead began along a curve and proceeded until the tangent to the path of movement was directly facing the center of all planes. Thus all curved trials began with the observer looking into the circle across the curved path of movement and cutting a chord across and beyond it. Because final gaze-movement angles were always zero, initial gaze-movement angles served as the independent measures. Successive blocks simulated the following paths around the circle: 0.88 rad (61° of arc), 0.38 rad (26°), 0.19 rad (12.7°), 0.90 rad (6.3°), 0.046 rad (3.2°), 0.023 rad (1.6°), and for condition 1 a final block of 0.010 rad (0.7°). Initial gaze-movement angles were 44, 19, 9.5, 4.7, 2.4, 1.2, and 0.6°, respectively, across blocks. Because all trials ended with a gaze-movement angle of 0°, viewers were asked to indicate which direction—left, ahead, or right— they had been looking during the course of the trial.

Results and Discussion

The results were comparable with those before, as shown in figure 13.5. Under condition 1 performance remained high for initial gaze-movement angles as small as 4.7°, and under the other two conditions it was only slightly worse. Under conditions 1 and 2 performance remained above chance for initial angles as small as 1.2° and under condition 3 as small as 2.4°.[6]

Differential motion parallax, then, appears suited to direction finding along both straight and curved movement paths. In fact, an oscillating path of gait—a slight waddling from side to side—may be beneficial. When a viewer is looking at an object generally in the direction of locomotion, other objects near and far oscillate back and forth through the plane of sight at rates dictated by differential motion parallax. Farther off the line of movement this oscillation ceases to be noticeable. Thus a crude measure of whether or not a viewer is looking in the direction of movement is to notice whether or not oscillatory motions occur. Finally, to round out the discussion, consider what other sources of information might do for curvilinear movement.

Curved Paths and Other Sources of Information

In chapter 10 I reviewed several schemes for direction finding other than differential motion parallax. Among them were the focus of expansion, which has the problem of specifying in a logically noncircular way an origin for a spherical coordinate system; asymmetries of retinal flow, which have the problem of assuming movement through a completely homogeneous environment; the point of maximum rate of magnification, which has the problem of disappearing when the observer moves parallel to a plane; and ocular-drift cancellation. This is the place to give them another airing.

Let me start with the focus of expansion, or center of outflow. During forward movement, Gibson (1979, p. 229) suggested:

> A shift of the center of outflow from one visual solid angle to another specifies a change in the direction of locomotion, a turn, and a remaining of the center within the same solid angle specifies no change in direction. The ambient optic array is here supposed to consist of nested solid angles, not of a bundle of lines. The direction of locomotion is thus anchored to the layout, not to a coordinate system. The flow of the ambient array can be *transposed over the invariant structure of the array*, so that where one is going is seen relative to the surrounding layout.

Gibson's concern with solid angles rather than with rays of lines stems from the necessity of representing continuous surfaces and occlusions in the optic array. The diagrams presented throughout chapters 10 through 13 show only edge information, but with some interpretive care the edges can be extended to represent the surface between them. Gibson's concern (see also Sedgwick 1983) with coordinate systems can be restated in the terms of figure 12.2, in which the coordinates important to him are those of the environment, not the retinal array (and observer). I have no qualms with preferring one over another, because I approach this analysis with the idea that coordinate systems are interconvertible. As stated in chapter 11, however, it is simply that the choice of an origin of the system at any point in time is always arbitrary and that there is a multitude of different possible mappings of optic flow.

But consider why Gibson's analysis is doubly flawed for curvilinear movement. A focus of expansion is thought to be a stable point. For linear movement figure 12.4 shows the focus of expansion as the point along the line of movement, which has null displacement. In figure 13.2, however, this point (and line) has unit negative displacement. Null instantaneous displacement occurs only for a circle that goes through the location of the observer, the center of the circle generating the circular path of movement, and two points half the radius to the right (for a rightward-going curve) along the x axis, with one forward along the z axis and the other back along it. When the path of movement curves to the left, the circle of null displacements would be in the mirror-image location. Properly, then, the points along this curve are the only ones that could serve as the focus of expansion for the optic array. Yet none has a location along the path of movement (except at the tangent to the circle at the location of the observer), nor does any indicate where the observer will soon be along the curved path. This curve simply floats off to the side.

Thus the focus of expansion during curved movement has two problems. The first, shared with the linear case, is that there is no apparent way to anchor the origin of the optic array's spherical coordinate system, and the second is that the focus of expansion is not a *point* along a curved trajectory but a *line* of no particular inherent importance except that it points in the direction of curvature. This latter fact is important to me because most rapid flow occurs in the direction opposite the turn.

The other three potential sources of information can be dealt with more succinctly. Going somewhat beyond the analysis of Richards (1975), when successive samples of the optic array are taken on a curved path, the vector paths of objects curve, like those shown in the top panel of figure 11.5. The asymmetry of these curved vectors indicates the direction the observer is turning, and its extent indicates the steepness of the curve. This analysis is fine as far as it goes, but it assumes that the eye maintains no fixation during the curved path. Instead, the observer stares blankly into space at a fixed angle from the curve's tangent. When the observer looks at any object during locomotion, the optics become much more complicated, and differential motion parallax is needed.

Setting aside terminological problems, consider next magnification, as proposed by Regan and Beverley (1982). Because the location of this point was worked out for only a single plane at a time, imagine a situation in which the observer takes a curved path toward that plane. If the observer is curving away from the plane, the point of maximum magnification becomes increasingly farther away from the point of impact, rendering it not very useful. If, on the other hand, the observer is curving into the plane, such a point might become useful, but the problems mentioned earlier still remain. In particular, the magnification function is not pronounced until quite close to impact. Thus it is not clear that this point could be located until the utility of the question about direction becomes moot.

Finally, Llewellyn's (1971) theory of ocular drift has particular difficulty when applied to curvilinear translation. If an observer fixates on an object, regardless of where it is in the optic array, the observer's eyes will rotate in their sockets. Thus drift occurs under all conditions, not simply those when the observer is not looking along the path of movement. Eye rotation cannot be particularly informative, except that saccades are most often made in the direction opposite movement. But there is a hint of truth here, and I return to it at the end of the chapter.

General Overview

The results of three experiments in the last two chapters and the analyses presented in the two preceding them suggest that differential motion parallax may be the only sufficient information for judging direction of movement in everyday settings. It seems useful for locomotion along straight and curved paths, and the accuracy with which direction can be judged is roughly the same—about half a degree of visual angle, given the range of spread between the near and far planes used in my experiments.

Other sources of information that have been proposed for direction finding have not generally produced results of such accuracy, or if they have, they were based on stylized and unnatural flow. Regan and Beverley (1982, 1983), for example, demonstrated that the point of maximum rate of magnification could be judged within fractions of a degree of visual angle, but their results are contingent on viewing the flow of a nonrigid world. When their display presented a rigid plane, the results suggested that their viewers were more than an order of magnitude worse. Llewellyn (1971) suggested that drift cancellation procedures could determine direction of movement. When that cancellation yielded motion parallax information, his results were roughly the same as reported here. When in his other experiments only ocular drift remained, his viewers also performed an order of magnitude worse.

Gibson proposed that the focus of expansion was sufficient to judge direction of movement under all conditions of forward velocity. Those under which it is an effective source, however, appear to be limited to those of high speed at low altitude—such as landing an airplane. Under more common conditions of movement, such as walking or running across a field, the focus of expansion is less implicit than previously suggested. But under precisely these conditions, motion parallax remains a rich source of information. The conditions simulated in my experiments are meant to be comparable with those of Regan and Beverley (1982)— with a forward speed of 58 km/hr moving toward a middle plane that is 76 m distant. Because this can be reduced by a scale factor, it also simulates movement at 5.8 km/hr (1.6 m/sec) toward objects that are 7.6 m distant, values like those for walking in cluttered environments.

On the Sufficiency but Nonnecessity of Motion Parallax
I make no claim that differential motion parallax is necessary to direction finding. Instead, I claim only that it is likely to be the best information for the task at normal speeds. It is easily supplemented by other information. When looking out at an object on a flat field, an observer not only has parallax but also information from relative size, height in the projection plane, and occlusions. In addition, stereoscopic differences in a nearby, rapidly moving object can be used to discriminate differences in direction of less than half a degree of visual angle (Regan and Beverley 1975). The first two factors, relative size and height in plane, may be responsible for the increased performance accuracy of the viewers of Kaufman, Warren, and Riemersma over those of Llewellyn, Johnston et al., and Regan and Beverley. With the addition of other information, it seems likely that accuracy of judging direction of movement in natural situations would be even greater than the half-degree value indicated here.

On the Natural Use of Optokinetic Nystagmus
Earlier I suggested that one aspect of Llewellyn's ocular drift cancellation theory might be on track. That aspect is its relation to the laboratory phenomenon of optokinetic nystagmus and how this reflex might function for an organism moving through its natural environment. Optokinetic nystagmus has two parts. If an individual is placed within a textured drum rotating around a vertical axis, his or her eyes first rotate

using pursuit vision to follow textures, then saccade rapidly back to (or beyond) their initial position to pick up the motion. This pattern of relatively slow pursuits and rapid saccadic flicks alternate so long as the drum rotates. The pursuit eye movements take advantage of the field-holding reflex of the accessory optic system (Simpson 1984), and the saccades occur often when no further mechanical rotation is possible. Such phasic responses occur involuntarily and have been found in every mobile-eyed vertebrate tested (Walls 1962).

How optokinetic nystagmus might serve directional guidance is as follows: The individual fixates an object in the environment off the path of forward movement. The eye rotates in its socket during the individual's locomotion, holding the object at the center of the field of view. The most rapid movement through the plane of sight is with the direction of eye rotation. When the eye rotates sufficiently or when other objects move through the plane of sight with sufficient velocity, the eye saccades quickly in the opposite direction. If the individual is on a linear path and if saccadic rotation is not quite extensive enough to align the eye with the path of movement, then the process repeats. If saccadic rotation overshoots the direction of movement, then the process reverses to the other side. Curvilinear locomotion complicates the situation not at all because the absolute direction of the line of sight at the end of the saccades is not pertinent to either the nystagmus of the differential motion parallax. In this manner, direction finding is well served by a well-understood eye-movement system. Moreover, the changes in the optic array pull the eyes of the observer in the direction of motion.

On Invariance
The first nine chapters of this book were chock-full of discussion about invariance. In these later chapters that discussion subsided somewhat, and it is time to reconsider the relation of invariance to descriptions of optic flow. Consider first the concentric toroids described in chapter 12. These toroids are oculocentric, wrapped in figure eights, and rotated around the path of the eye of the moving observer. They are observer-relative descriptions of *potential* optic motions. Any object or texture in three-dimensional space can be assigned an optic vector with one assumption and three variables. The assumption is that the objects in the world are not moving, and the variables are the object's instantaneous distance and direction from the observer and the observer's trajectory through the environment. These specify all flow. But these geometric formalisms yield variables, not invariants.

The toroidal description has the flavor of a medieval view of the universe. That is, it was thought that the solar system and the stars beyond it were placed on nested crystalline spherical shells that slid frictionlessly past one another. The sun, moon, planets, and stars were mounted on the separate shells, but viewers could see only the celestial bodies, not the shells themselves (Koyré 1957, Kuhn 1957). Similarly, in the parallax descriptions of flow that I have given, an observer can see only the objects and textures instantaneously "mounted" on the toroids; the observer cannot see the motion of the toroids themselves as they evert around the instantaneous axis of observer movement. Thus, in a manner that Plato might appreciate, the nested toroids are descriptions of the motions of abstract *space*, whereas optic flow is about the *place* of objects in a particular environment cluttered in a particular way. They generate ordered relations, but flow patterns are unique to each environment.

How can toroidal relations be converted into invariants to be used by the visual system? Given the descriptions above and a stable fixation point against which the relative motions of objects near and far can be compared, probabilism enters. That is, because a viewer cannot be assured of the relative instantaneous distances of objects while moving through the environment, the viewer must sample the optic array. Provided that a viewer is looking at an object, other objects that are half or less than half the instantaneous distance between the object and the observer will be moving at a retinal velocity that cannot be matched (in the opposite direction) by *any* object at *any* distance, no matter how far away. Thus the most rapidly moving objects in the retinal array will almost surely be moving more rapidly than and in the direction opposite the observer's movement. Expressed more formally,

$$N > -F,$$

where N is the velocity of near textures (and given positive value) and F that for far. Such a rule knows few bounds. It is true regardless of whether a viewer is on a straight or curved path; it is an inequality invariant in optic flow.

On Perceptual Choice of Invariants
An observer moving through an environment has a choice of invariants to use to guide his or her way. One, proposed by Calvert and Gibson, is the focus of expansion—a topological invariant and an instance of Brouwer's theorem. This theorem states that mappings of elements onto themselves (textures in the optic array projected from adjacent station points) have a fixed point whose coordinates have not changed. The other invariant is differential motion parallax. Given that there is some evidence that supports the focus of expansion for flying or, more

generally, for moving rapidly through environments but that the results of experiments 9–11 support differential motion parallax, observers again appear to have a choice among invariants in the task of wayfinding, in part depending on their speed. This is a situation like that described in chapter 9, where cross ratio and vector displacement patterns were contending invariants.

And most surely there are more cases than just these two in which multiple invariants have to be sorted out. It seems probable, in fact almost certain, that this may be the *general* perceptual situation, given a rich environment or even a rich experimental setup. If so, then this has serious implications for perceptual theories, particularly for those called direct and indirect. Consideration of them is the focus of chapter 14, untangling the problems of multiple invariants that of chapter 15.

IV
Classes of Perceptual Theories

A twentieth-century realist cannot *ignore the existence of equivalent descriptions: realism is not committed to there being one true description (and* only *one).*

Putnam (1978, p. 50)

14
Direct and Indirect Perception

It is time now to shift gears. Over the last eight chapters I have dealt with fairly hard-nosed computations and data. The brunt of all this was the discovery that there can be, and probably almost always are in suitably complex perceptual situations, multiple invariants in the optic array that specify the same object properties. What is left to my presentation is an application of this new fact to perceptual theory, which is my plan over the next two chapters. In this chapter I review classes of perceptual theories, and in the last I reformulate them and promote something new.

Two broad types of theory have been bruited about in the psychological and philosophical literature, most typically with respect to vision. These are the *direct* and *indirect* theories of perception, and they have generated a great deal of heat. My purpose in this chapter is to outline why I find both inadequate and why so much confusion surrounds them. The confusion is caused by the mismatch of attributes used to differentiate the two theories. Because definition and redefinition of terms have been rampant, I believe that the best approach to understanding the issues is historical. Through history we can see the terms appear, disappear, and reappear.

A Selective History

Most students of vision know direct perception as an epistemological position against a cognitive approach to perception. The cognitive approach typically employs the concept of inference or some cognate, such as problem solving or "taking into account." They know further that this position was held by Helmholtz, but it may be a surprise to many to find that the debate is much older. For example, Mill (1843, p. 420) addressed these same issues:

> In almost every act of our perceiving faculties, observation and inference are intimately blended. What we are said to observe is

usually a compound result, of which one-tenth may be observation, and the remaining nine-tenths inference.

I affirm, for example, that I hear a man's voice. This would pass, in common language, for a direct perception. All, however, which is really perception, is that I hear a sound. That the sound is a voice, and that voice the voice of a man, are not perceptions but inferences.

Mill was clearly not in favor of direct perception. Instead, he believed perception to be inferential, what we would now call indirect. But in Mill we find the same terms used in the same ways as we use them today. In fact, the use of these terms is even older. Helmholtz and Mill lie not at the beginning but in the latter half of the terms' chronology.

Nine Issues Concerning Direct Perception

How many ways might perception be direct? What follows is a brief presentation of nine issues relevant to analyses of direct perception,[1] after which I probe them in more depth. All were considered disqualifiers of directness and hence characteristics of indirect perception. I present them in chronological order as they appeared in the philosophical and psychological literature from the seventeenth century to the present.

1. Judgment and Inference. Direct perception has no thoughtlike processes that are part of it. This is perhaps the oldest and most important aspect of the traditional debate. In the English-language literature, Locke originated this view, believing that some (but not all) perception is judgmental. The nature of these judgments changed with Helmholtz, but inference did not. Inference continues to be important today (for example, Rock 1983 and Hoffman and Richards 1984).

2. Slowness. Direct perception is fast, not slow. Locke regarded rapid perception as a necessary but insufficient criterion for directness; Hochberg (1982) and Norman (1983) regarded slowness as a disqualifier.

3. Learning. Direct perception is innate, other perception the outcome of acquired associations. Early aspects of this issue appeared in Locke, but it did not come to the fore until Mill and Helmholtz.

4. Mediation. Direct perception is unmediated. After inference, perhaps the most important idea in the history of perceptual theories is mediation. The stages of description from physical object to visual percept, if perception is to be considered direct, cannot include intermediate steps involving other modalities or constructs. This crucial concept has at least four loosely allied meanings. One is the *tertium quid,* a Latin phrase meaning a third entity that stands between the physical object and perception of it. Many pre–twentieth-century philosophers employed a tertium quid—Locke's was in the form of ideas—and this view survives today in certain descriptions of mental representation. This notion might also be spoken of as *nonresonance* of the organism to certain aspects of the environment and as resonance only to representations, tertia quid, or the like.[2] The subdiscipline of information processing has recast this idea into a third form, the *plurality of stages* in perceptual process. Direct perception is typically thought to be single staged and indirect perception as multistaged. And this generalizes to a fourth idea, *computational difficulty*: Direct perception is considered computationally easy, indirect perception computationally difficult. Epstein (1981) has promoted plurality of stages and Ullman (1980) and McArthur (1982) have promoted computational difficulty.

5. *Suggestibility.* Direct percepts are irresistible; they run off automatically. Both Locke and Reid believed irresistibility to be a criterion for directness; Helmholtz also considered it. And automatic processing is a popular research issue today. Perception that is not direct, on the other hand, is suggestible and subject to the whims of intention. Berkeley originated this idea, Brown and Mill picked it up in the nineteenth century, and it continues today in cue theory—the idea, discussed in chapter 3, that proximal measures are probabilistically related to distal objects. But some positions against direct perception (Fodor 1983, Pylyshyn 1984) are also against suggestibility: Because of the alleged modularity of mind, some percepts are incorrigible and cannot be modified by thought processes—they are cognitively impenetrable.

6. *Awareness.* Direct perception occurs without awareness, indirect perception with it. Because we generally are not aware of processes, most perception must be direct. Reid and Bailey took this position; Helmholtz thought it irrelevant. Even Gibson discussed awareness.

7. *Physical Distance.* Direct perception occurs from stimulation contacting the individual. Indirect perception occurs when the sense organ is not in physical contact with a physical object. This idea may have first appeared in Brown (1820, p. 54):

> A distinction in this respect is very commonly made by philosophers, of external causes which act *directly*, as in smell, taste and touch, and others which act *through a medium*, as in hearing and vision.

In a modern interpretation of the issues at stake, this idea is confusing. It confounds mediation (a mental operation) with medium (physical stuff). This idea recurs periodically (see Heider 1926, 1958, and Fodor and Pylyshyn 1981), but I will not consider it in detail.

8. *Decomposition.* Direct percepts are of wholes. If a stimulus is decomposed into primitive units or features by a perceptual process, then perception is not direct. Decompositions reveal intermediate steps in the process. Ullman (1980) proposed this idea, although he cagily limited himself to *meaningful* decomposition. The idea is, in part, an affirmation of Titchener's (1906) atomistic approach to perception.

9. *Information Insufficiency.* Direct perception proceeds from adequate information. If necessary information is not present in the stimulus, perception is indirect. This is the *central idea* in Gibson's (1973a, 1979) theory. A corollary is that in indirect perception information is added during the perceptual process; it "goes beyond the information given" (Bruner 1957) or involves "taking into account" (Epstein 1973).

Other issues could be added to these nine,[3] and it should be clear that these are not independent. But I think that the cloudiness of current debate over these classes of theories is a result of the intermixing of these issues. Consider the literature in some detail.

Locke and Berkeley

Of the nine terms assaulting direct perception, Locke used the first five. In his *Essay Concerning Human Understanding* (1690, book II, chap. IX, para. 9), he discussed perception as a species of judgment. The issue was Molyneux's problem—a conjecture about the supposed inability of a blind person given sight to perceive shape.[4] According to Locke, shape "*judgment [is] apt to be mistaken for direct perception*" because it is "performed so constantly and so quick." But speed is not a sufficient criterion for directness. Locke reasoned that through habit (learning) our perceptions are unconsciously changed. Judgmental processes then entered Locke's discussion, summoned to reject direct perception of certain but not all things we perceive.

Also in Locke (1690, chap. VIII, para. 26) is mediation. He suggested that some qualities of objects are "immediately perceivable," others "mediately perceivable." He did not pursue this distinction in great detail, but in it are the seeds of all further debate. Locke suggested only that some qualities of objects appear to have the "power" to invoke immediate results in the mind, whereas others can work only indirectly. In several places he hinted that distance and shape in vision may be only mediately perceivable. Such tidbits aside, mediation as a tertium quid overrides his whole thesis. The central notion in Locke's theory of mind is the *idea*: "*External objects* furnish the mind with the ideas of sensible qualities, which are all those different perceptions they produce in us" (1690, chap. I, para. 5). Sensation is thus "the great source of most of the ideas we have" (1690, chap. I, para. 3). In anticipation of much twentieth-century debate, Locke suggested that sensation stands as a third entity between reality and the mind; sensory ideas bridge the Cartesian gap between physical essence (qualities) and mental essence (percepts).

Finally, Locke (1690, chap. IX, para. 1) reasoned that "in bare naked perception, the mind is, for the most part, only passive; and what it perceives, it cannot avoid perceiving." Bare naked perception is not suggestible and therefore, by association with the rest of his theory, must be direct.

Locke presented a complex view. He used five criteria—judgment, speed, learning, mediation, and suggestibility—to reject the notion that *all* perception is direct; some perception is not direct. Berkeley agreed on the split between direct and indirect perception, but he adopted only Locke's ideas of mediation and suggestibility in his *Essay towards a New Theory of Vision* (Berkeley 1709). Satisfied with Locke's notion of primary and secondary qualities but dissatisfied with the clarity of his distinction between mediate and immediate, Berkeley reasoned (1709, para. 50):

> In order, therefore, to treat accurately and unconfusedly of vision, we must bear in mind that there are two sorts of objects apprehended by the eye—the one primarily and immediately, the other secondarily and by intervention of the former. Those of the first sort neither are nor appear to be without the mind, or at any distance off. They may, indeed, grow greater or smaller, more confused, or more clear, or more faint. But they do not, cannot approach or recede from us. Whenever we say an object is at a distance, whenever we say it draws near or goes farther off, we must always mean it of the latter sort, which properly belong to touch, and are not so truly perceived as suggested by the eye.

Thus, to be more concrete, color is immediately perceived, according to Berkeley, but distance and figure are not. Instead, the last two are mediated through touch and kinesthesis.[5] In a later essay, *The Theory of Vision, or Visual Language, Vindicated and Explained* (1733, para. 42), Berkeley elaborated the theme of mediacy and immediacy, but clearly separated Locke's ideas of judgment and inference from his own. In place of inference, suggestibility was substituted:

> To perceive is one thing; to judge another. So likewise to be suggested is one thing, and to be inferred another. Things are suggested

and perceived by sense. We make judgments and inferences by the understanding. What we immediately and properly perceive by sight is its primary object—light and colours. What is suggested, or perceived by mediation thereof, are tangible ideas—which may be considered as secondary or improper objects of sight. We infer causes from effects, effects from causes, and properties from one another, where the connexion is necessary.

Two points are critical. First, Berkeley's theme, that kinesthesis and touch carry much of the burden for vision, is at the base of mediation. For him, the tangible ideas of space and form (those through the sense of touch) mediate visual perception of figure and distance; Berkeleyan mediation goes through another modality. Second, perception is *not* a judgmental process. Instead, we either perceive immediately (as with color) or other senses "suggest" and we perceive mediately (as with distance and form); but only the mind infers. In this manner, Berkeley proposed a mediated but noninferential theory of visual perception. Inference was a faculty of understanding, which he saw as flawless and independent of potentially unruly associations; suggestions of the secondary objects of vision (figure and space) are fraught with flaws.

Neither speed nor learning were important in Berkeley's theory, but ideas were at least as important as they were to Locke. For Berkeley, visible ideas and visible appearances were the same (Pastore 1971). But because nature and all physical things are but a reflection of the ideas of the mind (Berkeley 1713), there is no need for a tertium quid. Ideas exist everywhere.

Porterfield, Reid, and Bailey
Mediated perception and hence indirect perception have dominated Western European thought from Locke, Molyneux, and Berkeley through to the present day. But dissidents from a received view are never hard to find. Among the first to dissent was Porterfield in his *Treatise on the Eye, the Manner and Phenomena of Vision* (1759). Porterfield said (p. 299), in a partial anticipation of Kant:

The judgments we form of the situation and distance of visual objects, depend not on custom and experience, but on original, connate, and immutable law, to which our minds have been subjected from the time they were at first united to their bodies.

For Porterfield, visual perception of distance and form were uninferred, unlearned, unmediated, unsuggested. He disbelieved Berkeley's views on the inapplicability of geometry to visual perception, and he was nonplussed by Descartes's separation of mind and body. If the

Cartesian distinction were true, the soul could "never perceive the external bodies themselves" (1759, p. 356), making perception forever impossible.

Reid was more tentative than Porterfield but elaborated the idea of immediacy of perception in his *Essays on the Intellectual Powers of Man* (1785, p. 57). Ideas and suggestibility remained important, awareness entered as a concern, and speed reappeared in the discussion:

> If, therefore, we attend to that act of our mind which we call perception of an external object of sense, we shall find in it these three things: *First*, Some conception or notion of the object perceived. *Secondly*, A strong and irresistible conviction and belief of its present existence. And, *thirdly*, that this conviction and belief are *immediate*, and not the effect of reasoning.

Arguing against judgment and inference in perception, Reid stated (1785, p. 61) that believing what one perceives "is *equally immediate* and *equally irresistible.* . . . No man thinks of seeking a reason for believing what he sees; and before we are capable of reasoning, we put no less confidence in our senses than after." Lack of awareness of intervening stages was paramount to Reid. But notice that the force of the argument is directed against Locke and judgment, not Berkeley and suggestibility. Associations could still make percepts irresistible, even though they might mediate them. Moreover, Reid's use of "immediate" appears to implicate only speed.

The idea of speedy, irresistible, but mediated perception emerged when Reid (1785, p. 151) discussed Locke's distinction between primary and secondary qualities:

> There appears to me to be a real foundation for the distinction, and it is this: that our senses give us a *direct* and *distinct* notion of the primary qualities, and inform us what they are in themselves; but of the secondary qualities, our senses give us only a *relative* and *obscure* notion.

Because Reid counted extension, figure, motion, solidity, and softness among the primary qualities and sound, color, taste, and smell among the secondary, he proposed something quite different from Berkeley. For Berkeley, perception of figure and extension were mediate and that of color was immediate; for Reid, figure and extension were direct and immediate and color immediate but not direct.

Reid's position confounded many. Brown (1820), Hamilton (1858), and Bailey (1855) all tried to make sense of what he said, and Mill (1842, 1865) and Bailey (1855, 1858) quibbled over interpretations. The median position is that of Hamilton (1859, p. 80):

I beg you to keep in mind the necessary contrasts by which an immediate or intuitive is opposed to a mediate and representative cognition. The question to be solved is,—Does Reid hold that in perception we immediately know external reality, in its own qualities, as existing; or only mediately know them, through a representative modification of the mind itself?

Hamilton answered that Reid held both positions, straddling the direct/mediated issue. But more interesting is that in Hamilton we find a new distinction: *Intuition* is associated with the immediate, direct view of perception and *representation* with the mediate, indirect view. Reference to the former is found in Helmholtz's later work and to the latter in Gibson's work.

The most forthright of dissidents, however, was Samuel Bailey. Bailey was vehemently against all extant theories of perception: "I contend for the direct perception of external objects against Hobbes, Locke, Berkeley, Hume and others" (Bailey 1858, p. 10). He also suggested that Reid's advocacy of direct perception had not gone far enough (1858, p. 11):

> You will particularly observe, on a close inspection, that I maintain the direct perception of external objects in a much more rigorous sense than many or most of the philosophers of the Scottish school. They, amongst other things, contend for an irresistible belief in the existence of the external world; I, on the contrary, for a direct knowledge of it.

Bailey allowed no tertium quid because our awareness allows for none. He also pointed out, foreshadowing the work of Walk and E. Gibson (1961), that many young animals move about without prior tactile experience with surfaces in the world. Thus in these creatures there is no chance of touch mediating vision, in Berkeley's or any other sense. Bailey was perhaps more eloquent in his attacks on others than in expounding how perception actually occurred. In Bailey, however, we find a spirit close to Gibson. Bailey's position was simple and clean and a deceptively easy mark.

Mill and Helmholtz
Mill criticized Bailey, especially in the latter's critique of Berkeley. Mill (1842, p. 251) was well aware of the problems of oversimplifying issues and accused Bailey of slipperiness in the use of the term "Perception, a word which has wrought almost as notable mischief in metaphysics as the word Idea."[6] Mill was particularly alert to the use of awareness as a criterion for discussing perceptual process. Arguing for Berkeley's

theory of visual signs (later cues) that *suggest* what we perceive, Mill dismissed awareness (1842, pp. 254, 259):

> The distance of an object is not "perceived" directly, but by means of intermediate signs; not seen by the eye, but inferred by the mind . . . [and] when the suggesting power of the sign has been often exercised, our consciousness not only of the sign itself, but of much of what is signified by the sign, becomes much less acute.

With increase in associative strength, awareness declines and suggestibility increases. Mill took seriously Bailey's arguments concerning early behavior of young animals but argued that there was no evidence that animals used "sight itself" (1842, p. 261) rather than signs or that human infants behave like young animals even when their "organs have attained sufficient maturity" (1842, p. 263). In general, Mill's theory of perception was almost identical with Berkeley's, except for the reinjection of inference into perception and for a quibble over Molyneux's premise (Pastore 1971).

Next and central to any discussion of indirect perception is, of course, Helmholtz. Like Locke and Berkeley, Helmholtz had a place for direct perception. But unlike Berkeley, he (1868, p. 200) thought objects in depth were directly perceived: "It is important to remember that this perception of depth is fully as vivid, direct, and exact as that of the plane dimensions of the field of vision." The issues of directness for Helmholtz concerned at least four factors: suggestibility, learning, and a compound of judgment and lack of awareness, usually translated as "unconscious inference."

Consider suggestibility and learning. With regard to the first Helmholtz (1868, p. 219) claimed:

> Conclusions in the domain of our sense perception appear as inevitable as one of the forces of nature, and their results seem to be directly perceived without any effort on our part.

But lack of suggestibility did not mean that perception was immutable to experience. In fact, on the contrary, learning became a central attribute in the debate over direct and mediated perception. Helmholtz (1868, pp. 213–214) took a strong position against the intuitive (or direct) theories of Porterfield and Bailey:

> It follows that the hypotheses which have been successively framed by the various supporters of intuitive theories of vision, in order to suit one phenomenon after another, are really quite unnecessary. No fact has yet been discovered inconsistent with the empirical theory . . . and . . . every form of the intuitive theory has been

obliged to revert to [experience] when all other explanations failed. . . .

It is impossible to draw any line in the study of our perception of space that will sharply divide those which belong to immediate awareness from those which are the result of extended experience. If we attempt to set such a boundary, we find that experience proves more exact, more direct, and more specific than immediate awareness and, in fact, proves its superiority by overcoming the latter.

Two things stand out in this discussion. First and oddly, perception is more direct through experience than through immediate awareness. Second, Helmholtz attacked a straw man. He regarded intuitive (direct, innate) theories as unable to account for all aspects of perception and as having to resort to learning but regarded empirical (associative, learning) theories as accountable for everything. Yet this is no reason not to accept an intermediate view allowing for both innate and learned attributes. Moreover, the omnipotence of the empirical theory as Helmholtz presented it is not desirable in a psychological theory today.[7]

The centerpiece of his views on perception is the much-discussed concept of unconscious inference. Helmholtz (1868, p. 217) was aware that inference is usually reserved for the "highest of the conscious operations of the mind." That is why he prefixed it with "unconscious."[8] But he then stated:

There appears to me in reality only a superficial difference between the inferences of logicians and those inductive inferences whose results we recognize in the conceptions we gain of the outer world through our sensations. The chief difference is that the former inferences are capable of expression in words, while the latter are not.

As in logic, if the grounds of visual perception are sure, perception will be veridical; if they are not sure, perception will be faulty. The feature of unconscious inference that allows separation from direct perception as Gibson used the term is that some grounds for perceiving may not be in the optic array or in the biological design of the visual system. Memory and reasoning can be invoked. But if all grounds are in the stimulus and system design, then unconscious inference and Gibson's direct perception are the same. I will not address further the *unconscious*, or nonawareness, issue in perception. Instead, consider inference. From Helmholtz and Mill we get the idea of perception as *inductive*, and it is worth investigating this idea further.

For our purposes logic divides into *deductive* and *inductive* branches. Despite common usage, deduction and induction have nothing inherently to do with the particular, the general, and the manner of going between them (see, for example, Skyrms 1975). Instead, the key difference is in probability. Deductive inferences are like proofs in mathematics; they are either valid or invalid, with no room for chance. Inductive inferences, on the other hand, vary from strong to weak, depending on epistemic probability; essentially, they are our prediction about what will happen based on our knowledge at a given time. In part because of Hume (1739) and Popper (1962), induction has fallen on hard times as an example of logic, at least as defined in common parlance; we barely know how it works at all. Baldly put, induction is simply guessing. Some of it is good guessing, but it is guessing nonetheless.

For perception to be inductive it has to be a chancy business; percepts are thought not assured on the basis of information given.[9] Sense data talk and the arguments from illusion are thought to reinforce this idea. My point in this book, however, is that not all of perception has to work this way. Some perception might even be called deductive. This is an idea I pursue in chapter 15.

Helmholtz, like all his predecessors, allowed for direct perception but did not allow for clear demarcation between what is and what is not. The implication was that most perception by adults is inferential. But both direct and inferential perception imply a real world, and this was not an accepted theme in many philosophies, particularly that of the English at the end of the nineteeth century. The English, in a unique departure from empiricism, were dominated by the idealism of Hegel.

Moore, Russell, Ayer, and Austin
The first break with idealism was Moore's, followed quickly by Russell's at the turn of the twentieth century. Together they established the analytic school of philosophy and also generated the concept of sense data, discussed in the first chapter. Sense data are at the heart of the "causal theory of perception," an attempt at the synthesis of common sense, analysis, and the older British tradition of Mill. The causal theory also possessed rudiments of an information-processing account of perception. Its basics were expounded by Russell (1927, p. 197):

> Common sense holds—though not very explicitly—that perception reveals external objects to us directly: when we "see the sun," it is the sun that we see. Science has adopted a different view, though without always realizing its implications. Science holds that, when we "see the sun," there is a process, starting from the sun, traversing the space between the sun and the eye, changing its character when it reaches the eye, changing its character again in the optic

nerve and the brain, and finally producing the event which we call "seeing the sun." Our knowledge of the sun thus becomes inferential; our direct knowledge is of an event which is, in some sense, "in us." This theory has two parts. First, there is the rejection of the view that perception gives direct knowledge of external objects; secondly, there is the assertion that it has external causes as to which something can be inferred from it. The first of these tends towards skepticism; the second tends in the opposite direction. The first appears as certain as anything in science can hope to be; the second, on the contrary, depends upon postulates which have little more than a pragmatic justification.

Again, direct and inferential perception co-occur, but this time as part of the same process. According to causal theory, we directly perceive sense data, but we do not directly perceive objects; those are known only through inference. The major issue that dominated the philosophy of perception for fifty years thereafter was justification of inference. Ayer (1940, 1956) played a particularly dominant role.

Austin (1962) was among the first to question causal theory. In keeping with the analytic tradition, his critique of Ayer and of causal theory was more about words than perception. Driven by common sense, Austin chose to analyze the terms "direct" and "indirect"—the latter had made its belated appearance in Ayer (1956). Ignoring 250 years of tradition, Austin suggested that "direct" implies "direction" and line of sight and that "indirect" implies binoculars or periscopes that bounce light rays around in several directions. In fact, "indirect" is not at home in discussion of the other senses, of television, of cloud chambers, or of much else. Austin (1962, p. 19) thus rejected Russell's "scientific" analysis and concluded:

> It is quite plain that the philosophers' use of "directly perceive," whatever it may be, is not the ordinary, or any familiar, use; for in *that* use it is not only false but simply absurd to say that such objects as pens or cigarettes are never directly perceived.

I dislike this style of argument. It has the two prongs of appealing to the commonsense use of words and of shaming those who do not use them that way, however consistent that use may be. Such arguments do not help an understanding of perception at all. Careful use of words is a laudatory goal in this case, but it elucidates the issues little more than does enunciation, cleanliness, or any other personal habit.

Of all philosophers supporting direct perception, however, Austin appears to have influenced Gibson most.[10] And because Austin's analysis was linguistic rather than logical and historical, Gibson could use the terms "direct" and "indirect" as he chose. Two things became important to Gibson's theoretical analysis: Against Berkeley and Helmholtz, Gibson denied any form of mediation, judgment, or inference in normal perception, where normality conditions exclude mirrors, telescopes, Ames rooms, and pictures; and he declared that information in the optic array was sufficient for normal perception.[11] The latter is the only positive suggestion new to Gibson. Its central concern is a mapping between proximal and distal stimuli, a topic at the core of the next chapter. Before considering mappings, however, let me make a final assessment of the other issues surrounding direct perception with an eye to this final one—information adequacy.

An Assessment of Eight Disqualifiers of Directness

It is convenient to divide the issues into two groups of four. The first group contains those issues I believe not relevant to the current debate over direct and indirect perception: slowness, learning, awareness, and physical contact. The second group consists of suggestibility, decomposition, mediation, and inference, which I try to relate to information sufficiency.

Irrelevant Issues

Let me start by justifying dismissal of the first set. Locke (1690) was first to suggest that *slowness* implied indirect perception, and Hochberg (1982) and Norman (1983) were among the first to explore this idea experimentally. But speed of perception can be a difficult thing to measure. Reaction-time experiments assume some point in time from which perceptions start and a point from which all stimulus information is present. This latter assumption is inappropriate for a moving stimulus. Reaction time is an almost completely useless dependent measure for studies of motion and change because the visual system continues to accrue information over time.

Learning is next. Helmholtz (1868) was first to juxtapose learning and direct perception. He contended that "intuitive" theories relied on innate predispositions of vision. Although this criticism can be leveled at Porterfield and Bailey, it is not relevant to twentieth-century discussions. Eleanor Gibson (1967) and James Gibson (1979) redefined the issues of perceptual learning as the acquisition of new abilities to pick up information through differentiation. To be sure, Walk and Gibson (1961) denied learning in the perception of objects laid out in depth: They demonstrated what Bailey (1855) discussed, that infants and young animals can perceive objects in depth with no previous coordinated visual and tactile experience. But this research effort falsified ideas from

Locke and Berkeley. Walk and Gibson suggested that not all of what is seen is learned; they did not suggest that all of what is seen is innate. Third, there is *awareness*, a central issue to much of psychology, but I do not believe it relevant here. We may or may not be aware of perceptual processes, pancreatic processes, or pulmonary processes. But because we may be aware of stomach growls or wheezes does not make these indirect digestion or indirect respiration. Why should awareness make perception indirect? Moreover, information is not a term comfortable with the idea of awareness. In the experiments reported here, for example, percipients were aware of rigid and nonrigid planes and of three-dimensional environments. But it seems inappropriate to me to suggest that they were either aware or unconscious of the cross ratio, the index 4 measure of density, or differential motion parallax. As abstract formalisms that reflect regularities in the world, these do not seem to be the stuff that can fill or not fill awareness.

And finally, it is not relevant that there is *physical distance* between objects and eyes or a medium through which information is presented. Indeed, vision and audition are distal senses; taste, touch, and kinesthesis proximal (and smell dependent on definition). But a medium is not a mediator; it is a transducer. The transduction of information through air and space makes perception no more indirect than the transduction of information through peripheral nerves.

Relevant but Tangential Issues
Four issues of some import to direct and indirect perception are suggestibility, decomposition, mediation, and inference. Consider first *suggestibility*. From Locke (1690) we get the idea that direct visual perception is not suggestible, it is an automatic process that runs off without check or modification; and from Berkeley (1733) we get the idea that mediate perception is suggestible, proceeding on the grounds of information from sources other than the optic array. But this clean pairing is muddied by Reid (1785), Mill (1842), and Helmholtz (1868). All considered some perception to be both inferential and nonsuggestible. For Mill, inferences are built up through associations that have become so strong that there are no alternatives. The effects of the Ames room and the trapezoidal window are cases in point: Inferences might be made about the geometry of the setting that are difficult to contravene.

There is, however, something cogent about the idea that suggestibility should have a place within a theory of direct perception: If information *specifies*—a term much stronger than *suggests*—something about a particular object that is useful to an individual, then that individual ought to use that information in actions with it. I claim that the individual may choose other information that specifies the same property, but as

I discuss in the final chapter, this is not entirely consistent with direct perception.

Decomposition is another relevant, but I think tangential, aspect of the direct/indirect debate. Ullman (1980) proposed that information for perception, if it is direct, cannot be "meaningfully" decomposed into more elementary primitives. And Michaels and Carello (1981) claimed that direct perception is the study of higher-order invariants, which are presumably those not decomposed into primitives useful to the individual. I would claim, however, that the level of order is not so important as the demonstration of perceptual utility; thus one need and need only attain a level at which relational information is perceptually useful, be it variant or invariant. Direct perception does not claim that variable information, even a variable within an invariant, is unregistered by the perceptual system. Instead, it claims only that information is adequate for perception without cognition.

Decomposition also has stage-theoretic implications: It is often said that direct perception is a one-stage process and that indirect perception is multistaged. Although defenders of direct perception have stated this point of view (Runeson 1977, Michaels and Carello 1981), it seems to me that there are too many unexamined assumptions about what constitutes a separate *stage* in a perceptual *process* to make a meaningful statement about it. Physiology bats last in determining stages; but because it is equally foolish to deny visual physiology or to claim that it is sufficiently known in complex perceptual acts, this appeal carries no weight.

Mediation is a third relevant issue, but none in the whole set is trickier; it can have myriad sources. Consider three. First, for Berkeley, mediation occurs when kinesthesis and convergence educate us about depth when we normally and improperly impute it to vision. This leads us back to the issue of suggestion, which has already been considered and rejected. Second, mediation can come from memory and learning. In Mill and Helmholtz we find that learned associations among attributes of objects affect perception. But again, both Eleanor and James Gibson construed learning such that mediations from stored patterns do not enter the process; instead the ability to differentiate information in the optic array gets better. Given that learning can be construed favorably on behalf of both sides of the debate, it cannot distinguish between them. And third, Gibson (1979) stated that perception is not mediated by representations (or pictures) external or internal; there is no tertium quid between perceiver and object. But Gibson's idea of representation, as a re-presentation of object attributes, is at such variance with the rest of cognitive science that little light is thrown on the debate, unless the issue of inference is considered, which I discuss in what follows.

Thus it seems to me that, because mediation can have so many meanings, little is gained by its use. As suggestibility, it comes closest to bearing on issues of current import.

Finally, consider *inference*. From Locke, Mill, and Helmholtz came the idea that perception is an inferential process. But if all premises of the inference are either sources of information in the optic array or derived from the way that the visual system is built, then this type of inference is no different from Gibson's direct perception. Thus using the formalisms of inference as a tool for understanding perception may be fine, but it is the premises that determine whether perception is direct or indirect. Given the entanglements of premises involving the design of the visual system, I believe that we can prove indirect perception only by disproving the *possibility* of direct perception. And we can prove direct perception impossible only by proving that information is *inadequate* in the stimulus to specify the perceived. This is a formidable task in everyday situations. The laboratory is by tradition impoverished, and it heavily burdens the experimental situation with outcomes consistent with indirect perception. Given that most visual stimuli in experiments are pictures (virtual rather than real objects) and that Gibson stated that picture perception is indirect, most psychological experiments have never been relevant to the direct/indirect distinction as he construed it. Moreover, I have doubts as to whether the distinction between theoretical positions *can* be litigated. It has basically been a debate over how to use words. I believe that the only arena of possible utility is to reconsider the issue of information efficacy.

Overview

A history of the issues involved in debates over direct and indirect perception was pursued from Locke through Austin and relates to the recent psychological literature. Nine issues were discussed in some detail. Of the eight that appeared earliest, four are without consequence—slowness, learning, awareness, and the medium through which information reaches the senses. The other four, however, have some systematic if tangential import. Suggestibility bears on the selectivity of the visual system for information available—a topic I consider in the next chapter. Decomposition concerns the level of analysis at which information *informs* the perceiver but typically addresses receptors rather than the system as a whole. It also addresses the side issue of stages, which in the broader scheme of perception I regard as a tangled nest of ideas that we have little prospect of unraveling. Mediation is ill suited to differentiating the two kinds of perception unless it is construed as inference. And inference is the same as direct perception if all premises for it are based on information in the optic array or in the visual system's structure. The remaining issue, adequacy of that information, is the topic of the final chapter.

15
Directed Perception

At the beginning of chapter 1 I posed a series of questions: How is it that we make sense of the visual patterns that surround us? Why does everyday perception work so well? And what is the nature of information in our environment such that it has meaning for us? I have answered only the third of these, emphasizing the importance of structural relations among elements projected to the eye over space and time. In particular, I pursued two instances of flow—one for a moving object and a generally stationary observer and the other for a stationary environment and a moving observer. Cross ratios, density, ordered displacement vectors, and differential motion parallax by no means exhaust the information that we might look at, but at least they are examples not typically pursued by vision researchers. They are also examples in which motion yields trustworthy grounds for perception.

It is time now to consider briefly the first two questions. The first is a general question about process—*How* is sense made of what is projected in the optic array? The second is about the surety of perception. Both can be considered subspecies of perhaps the most important question asked about visual perception (Koffka 1935): Why do things look as they do? The seeming simplicity of this query masks its depth. All theories of perception must address the issue of *information* in light of *phenomenology*. In the previous chapter I presented a historical outline of two classes of perception—direct and indirect—but I did not relate them to Koffka's query or to issues about process and surety. Those are dealt with here, alas in an all-too-sketchy manner. But the larger goal of this chapter is to present a third class of perceptual theory and the necessity for it. I also compare it with the direct and indirect theories on the basis of information available in the optic array. This new class has so far gone unnamed, but it is implicit in various works. I call it *directed perception*, focusing on the idea that observers are directed at and select among multiple sources of information that may specify a given stimulus. Attributes of both direct and indirect approaches can be found in directed perception, but the most important attribute is quite different from both. After treating this, I relate all three classes to Koffka's query and related questions.

Meaningful comparison of the three theory classes can take place most satisfactorily, and perhaps only, within the framework of one of the nine issues broached in the previous chapter—information sufficiency for perception. None of the other eight, it seems to me, provide well-defined grounds for separating them: Slowness, learning, awareness, media, suggestibility, decomposition, mediation, and inference, in my view, simply do not get at the guts of why we perceive the way we do. Only the discussion of mappings between information and object properties in the environment approaches this goal.

Information-to-Object Mapping

At the core of modern versions of perceptual theory—direct, indirect, or directed—are assumptions about the way information is mapped onto object properties. This core constrains many, if not all, other attributes in theories of vision. Whether discussed explicitly or not, each mapping proceeds backward from proximal image (optic array) to distal stimulus (environmental object or event). Now, this appears to be an odd way for theories of perception to differ. In particular, mapping is not at all about process; nor does it even deal with the perceiver. Instead, it is concerned solely with an attitude toward a given object or event and more broadly toward our visual environment. Thus these mappings do not address issues of psychophysical relations between stimulus and percept; nor do they easily submit to behavioristic versus rationalistic analysis. Instead, they address only surety of information. Consider each theory class in turn.

Direct Perception

In direct perception, theorists have generally assumed a one-to-one mapping between information and the object properties associated with it.[1] Some of the statements supporting this characterization were outlined in chapters 5 and 9, so much of it need not be repeated here. But to refresh this idea, consider the following (Gibson 1965, p. 68):

> The specific hypothesis is that the invariant component in a transformation carries information about an object and that the variant component carries other information entirely, for example, about the relation of the perceiver to the object.

Again, the use of "invariant" and "object" as singular nouns makes it difficult not to read this statement except as a one-to-one mapping, shown schematically in figure 15.1. Connectivity is clean, clear, and

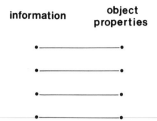

information   object
              properties

Figure 15.1
One-to-one information-to-object mapping in direct perception.

unambiguous: It assumes that, for each meaningful aspect of the environment around us, there is one and only one invariant associated with it. The elegance of such a system is patent: Perception begins as the match of information to objects, which is unproblematic and uncomplicated by unruly networks of mapping relations.

One problem with this formulation is that perceptual scientists have not found and specified many invariants. Thus, although objects and object properties on the right-hand side of this mapping diagram (figure 15.1) are plainly and generally known, the invariants on the left-hand side are not. Neisser (1977) claimed that this is the outstanding problem for direct perception. Unfortunately, there is no recourse other than to discover invariants one by one. It is a plodding, empirical endeavor, and if all research efforts are gauged collectively, the invariants appear to be somewhat recalcitrant to discovery. Gibson turned his later efforts away from this type of empiricism toward explicating the notion of *affordances*. But to emphasize the mapping structure in much of Gibson's thought, the same one-to-one relations hold in this new domain as well. For each potential action we can take with an object, there is one affordance, and for every affordance, one action. There is a mutuality (Gibson 1979) between perception and action that can occur only if mappings are bijectional (one to one). Unfortunately, the relation between invariants and affordances is not well explicated beyond the notion that invariants are structural relations geared to the perceiver and that affordances are functional ones corresponding to them.[2]

Indirect Perception
Indirect theorists, by contrast, have generally assumed a one-to-many mapping from information to object properties. Cue theory, for example, implies exactly this mapping, as shown in figure 15.2.[3] Notice that this mapping leaves information nonspecific: No source on the left-hand side of the figure is associated uniquely with any object property on

information   **object properties**

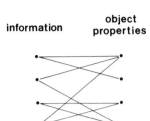

Figure 15.2
One-to-many information-to-object mapping in indirect perception. This mapping could just as easily be called many to many.

the right-hand side. The mapping does not preserve structure across domains. More simply, it is unruly.

Such a situation presents the perceptual system, and the perceptual theorist, with a serious problem. Without information specification, considerable conceptual or computational force must be brought to bear on the problem of untangling information as it represents real and false targets. How might the perceptual system work from nonspecific sources of information to correct perceptual interpretations at a given place and time? Rightward branching trees of information-to-object mappings must be severely pruned, eliminating fruitless alternatives, lest all possible objects be considered as potential percepts, thereby leaving the mind forever lost in thought, unable to plug itself into any reality. It is often suggested that a certain amount of perceptual hypothesis testing proceeds in such situations of ambiguity. The problem for perceptual theory is that we do not know the number of simultaneous hypotheses that might be tested at any given time.

Typically in indirect theory, however, only a small number of information-to-object mappings are entertained for any given percept. If every source of information were associated with, say, between two and eight objects or classes of objects, then the perceptual system might be able to deal with the large number of possibilities in every natural scene, perhaps by some Brunswikian scheme of assessing cue validity. But computation and storage requirements are still too vast to align information with objects properly. Many researchers regard this situation as tractable, but it seems so only if constraints on the number of branches from each information source are severe enough. Without such a priori knowledge it is not clear how the second question asked in chapter 1— Why is it that perception is correct most of the time?—can be answered satisfactorily. Constraining information to represent one and only one object or event, as Gibson did, seems principled, but constraining it to

information   **object
properties**

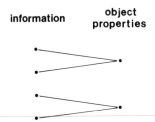

Figure 15.3
Many-to-one information-to-object mapping proposed for directed perception.

between, say, two and eight seems ad hoc. Open the gates to more than one object and it seems difficult not to let everything flood in.[4]

Directed Perception

The class of theory that I wish to promote is *directed perception*, which makes a different assumption about the mapping between information and environmental objects. As shown in figure 15.3, the mapping is many to one. That is, any single source of information maps backward onto one and only one class of object properties, but many different sources of information can map onto each class. Thus, once a source of information is selected for use, the rest of the perceptual act is as clean and elegant as in direct perception. But information must be selected by the perceiver, although it is not open to conscious deliberation. This view brings new meaning to Putnam's statement at the beginning of this section: We cannot ignore equivalent descriptions of—or, in my terms, different information about—any object or event in the real world.

Directed perception is a necessary perspective on information-to-object mapping if we are to account for the results of research reported in earlier chapters. In experiments 1 through 6 the cross ratio (or density analog) appeared to be used by perceivers. In experiments 7 and 8, however, the perceptual system generally chose other information, another invariant (the ordered relations among displacements), even though cross ratios and density measures were still available. No single invariant yet found can account for results in both settings, and given the incommensurability of the results, such an invariant seems unlikely. In experiments 9 through 11, taken in conjunction with data and theory from elsewhere, a similar pattern emerges. Calvert, Gibson, and others proposed the utility of the focus of expansion for wayfinding. Although there has been little experimental evidence in its support, flying an aircraft at low altitude, driving a race car, sailing an iceboat, running a bobsled, or downhill skiing lend credence to this idea. In such situations the geometric constraints on the location of a fixed point may be much greater than during pedestrian locomotion. However, in the latter situation and in experiments that mimic it, there is strong support only for the utility of differential motion parallax. Both invariants may be present, but one is useful under one set of circumstances and the other under another.

These two data sets are not alone. Cutting and Millard (1984), for example, demonstrated that different sources of information were used for the perception of flat versus curved surfaces. The perspective gradient (or the invariant that underlies it) is based on an assumption about the uniform absolute size of objects and accounted for most of the variance in the perception of flat surfaces. On the other hand, the compression gradient is based on the assumption that textures lie flat, and it accounts for almost all variance in the perception of curved surfaces. But in our experiment both perspective and compression, as well as a third gradient (density), were present in all displays. Yet choices were made, presumably because some information is more efficacious for some decisions than others.

In all three situations, the two reported here and that of Cutting and Millard (1984), more than one source of information specified what was to be perceived, and data support the idea that the perceptual system selects among these sources. We might regard this, and properly so, as a slim base on which to propose a general class of theories for visual perception, but neither of the other two—direct and indirect perception—appear to have any real means for beginning an account. Moreover, it is my assumption, albeit a strong one, that, when looked at closely, most rich perceptual situations are like those discussed here: Invariants and variants abound, and choices must be made even when an observer regards a single aspect of a single object.

Initial Comparison of Theory Classes
Consider the set of relations among the approaches to perception that I have outlined. First, the only serious distinction between direct and indirect perception, I claim, is the mapping between information and object. One way to construe the mappings is as a correlation: In direct perception emphasis is placed on correlations that are 1.00; indeed perhaps all are unity and all perception deductive. In indirect perception, however, emphasis is placed on correlations that are less, and indeed perhaps all are less, making all perception inductive. Second, I claim that the difference between direct and directed perception is the normally tacit but sometimes explicit assumption underlying direct perception— that information is only as rich as the number of objects in the envi-

ronment. Directed perception, on the other hand, allows for more than one perfect information-to-object cross-situational correlation. There may be more than one deductive path. And finally, the main difference between directed and indirect perception is the reversal of bifurcation. Both require statements about process, but different pluralities of nodes breed different accounts.

Consider the three classes of theory in light of process and outcome for each by an attending perceiver. In direct perception, information *specifies* process (the individual picks up what is there, one source of information) and *specifies* outcome (the object or event is perceived as it is). In indirect perception, information *underspecifies* process (the perceiver does his or her damnedest to make do with what is there) and *underspecifies* outcome (internal sources of information may be brought to bear on what is seen). In directed perception, on the other hand, information *underspecifies* process (there is enough different information such that the scientist cannot know a priori what algorithm might be used) and *overspecifies* outcome (whatever source is used, the percept would be the same). I will return to other questions about how directed perception is different from the others. Next, however, consider more implications of these views of information-to-object mappings.

On Why Things Look As They Do

Koffka's question can be divided many ways. Part of the answer is determined by our orientation toward contexts for information and part by an orientation toward process. These in turn affect assessments of causes for appearances.

Contexts for Information

Direct perception assumes that the richness of the optic array just matches the richness of the world. To guarantee sufficient richness, however, this approach has always looked to the natural environment, eschewing laboratory situations with their picturelike stimuli. In such impoverished situations, according to this view, the perceptual systems are apt to do as best as they can, performing all sorts of feats that may look like, and may actually be, conceptual elaborations. But these are said to be outside the province of normal perception and outside the scope to which perceptual theories ought to aspire. From this perspective, vision researchers start with the goal of understanding perception in the context of information within which perceptual systems evolved, only to consider special cases later.

Indirect perception generally assumes that the optic array is impoverished. And indeed, few experimental situations can provide sufficient information for perception to pursue an unambiguous course. But indirect theorists, or so it often appears, tacitly extrapolate from the laboratory setting to all others when describing perception as a taking-into-account procedure. An assumption is made that the world is like the laboratory, sufficiently impoverished to make perception a guessing game. That perceptual systems can guess should be no surprise, but that they guess all the time seems an unwarranted inference. Of course, it would be odd for me to indict laboratory studies, and I certainly do not. The issue is not about the ecological validity of experimentation but about the representativeness of stimuli used in experiments, an issue that both Brunswik and Gibson well appreciated. To feel comfortable in extrapolating from the laboratory to the world, stimuli should look at least somewhat like objects in the real world and have as many of their attributes as possible while still allowing control. The closer the appearance, the more assured we can be when making generalizations about perception. I believe that motion is the key to producing lifelike stimuli. Computer control over graphics displays has removed forever the necessity of using static picture perception as the laboratory model for real-world perception.

Directed perception assumes that the optic array is unknowably rich, far outstripping the number of objects in the real world.[5] This over-determination can even occur within laboratory settings. Thus directed perception places at least two humbling demands on the perceptual theorist: The theorist must be aware of the potential richness of information available in the everyday optic array, and he or she must stand ready to recognize that human perceptual systems, like all complex biological systems, are eclectic and do their best in different ways under different circumstances. In perception this means that perceptual systems may use different sources of information at different times, even when performing the same apparent task and when all sources equally specify the object or event perceived.

Implications for Process
The mapping relations shown in figures 15.1 through 15.3 also have implications for perceptual process. Direct perception makes the outline of process relatively straightforward (Ullman 1980, Pylyshyn 1984, Runeson 1977): The perceptual system consists of some special purpose devices that extract information matched to the properties of the world. Attend to an object or event, register its information, and perception will follow; it cannot go astray. There are, in general, no particular computational burdens on the system; it is designed to work in the way that it does. Such statements are truisms, but we learn little from them. Many of us would like to know how perceptual systems work

in a nuts and bolts manner. To say that the perceptual system works effortlessly does not make a positive contribution.

Indirect perception, on the other hand, places rather rigorous requirements on perceptual process. The weeding out of false targets connected with the given information is a task of highest priority. Much computational power must be directed at relatively early levels of visual analysis to select among, for example, possible depth arrangements. It is difficult to know how this power will play itself out. It might manifest itself in the number of processing stages, increased time at a given stage, or simply as the number of neurons engaged simultaneously. There is at the present time no appropriate measure of such power. There are only the assumptions that the need is there and that they must be met. What is clear to me, however, is that the use of the term *computation* in explaining perception is a poor choice: The Latin root *computare* means "with thinking," and although I do not wish to isolate perception from cognition, it seems clear to me that most perception is not done with thinking; it is done on its own terms.

Directed perception, however, has the noncomputare ease of direct perception coupled with the underdetermination of instantiated algorithms of indirect perception. Perceptual systems are attuned to sources of information and use different ones according to the task at hand. Effort is not in computation but in the search for appropriate information. The algorithms, or special purpose devices, stand ready for use and run off automatically when triggered by the appropriate information in the appropriate task.[6] Which process is used, however, is not predetermined.

Causes for Appearances

How we get from information to subjective experience is almost a complete mystery, regardless of the approach that is taken. But because of the different attitudes of these approaches toward contexts and process, it is not difficult to generate three different, albeit sketchy answers to Koffka's query. A theory of direct perception responds, in essence, by stating that things look as they do because information in the optic array specifies that appearance to our visual system, which has evolved to pick up that information and see things in given ways (Gibson 1971b, but also see Kolers 1978). Construing in this manner, direct theorists take most seriously the idea that, once the individual has chosen to attend to a particular aspect of the environment, perception is driven from the bottom up, with evolutionary constraints guiding all outcomes. Information and evolution shape appearances.

A theory of indirect perception, on the other hand, would suggest that the appearance of things is due, in part, to downward cognitive processes, computations, and algorithms.[7] Without these, things would not *appear* at all. Evolution plays a role only in providing a backdrop for more-general-purpose computation. Cognition and computation have the heavy hand in shaping appearances.

Directed perception negates neither of these ideas:[8] Perception is driven from bottom up but constrained from the top down according to the task at hand. Downward constraints are necessary, insofar as any of the data that I have presented force this conclusion, because we now know that the perceptual system selects among multiple sources of information that specify the same thing. This is a new reason for interest in process and algorithms, because the perceiver often has several information sources to bring to bear on a given solution.

Implications for Research and Theory

If directed perception is a reasonable approach, what kinds of questions for research does it foster? It seems to me that three emerge. It is instructive to consider how these questions and their answers differ from those ordinarily found in direct and indirect perception. Overlaps and disjunctions prove interesting.

1. What information is available? The researcher must look throughout arrays presented to each sense modality for possible sources of information. Relational information, in particular, should be sought as appropriate for a given perceptual task. Invariants may be important, variants may also be. It is too early to make even a preliminary tally. Concentration on information, of course, has been a hallmark of direct perception; indirect theorists ought to take notice. The obvious problem, however, is that there are no a priori guidelines available for framing the forms that information might take. Projective geometry has face validity for vision, but no corresponding bodies of formalism seem to have the same relation to other modalities. Moreover, it may be too hopeful even to expect that projective geometry will prove more useful to the vision researcher. The problems of the perceptual system and the problems of the mathematician, as suggested in chapter 5, are different enough so that we might easily expect no overlap at all. Ultimately, only the ingenuity of the researcher can be of aid: Information is where the researcher can find it. And it is hard work, intermittently rewarding.

2. What information is used? This is the easiest question to answer. Given that we have discovered potentially useful sources of information, they can be tested through normal experimental, typically psychophysical, procedures. Because both direct and indirect approaches regard experimentation as important, there is nothing new to directed perception here. Nonetheless, two hints are worth mentioning. First, paradigms should be varied enough so that when an information source is found, the boundary conditions on its use can also be explored, with the hope of stumbling across other possible sources. Second, stimuli and contexts presented to observers should be rich enough to allow use of alternative information.

3. *Why is information intermittently useful?*   This is the most difficult question of the set. It is unasked by direct perception because it is defined outside the realm of possibility, but it is asked in a slightly different way all the time in indirect theory: What is the value of a particular "cue"?

It seems to me that there are two possible approaches here, one information driven and the other, task driven. The first is to look at the nature of specification, which might be called the *quality of the information*. In the example of cross ratios versus displacement patterns, a violation of the invariance of cross ratio simply indicated that the surface was not planar, whereas violation of uniform displacement indicated the locus of the noncoplanar element. Thus an unvarying cross ratio is a global specifier; displacement nonuniformity is both a global and a local specifier. In the case of wayfinding by optic flow, differential motion parallax may be high-quality information at relatively low forward velocities, but the focus of expansion is a high-quality source at higher velocities.

A second possibility is that the task guides the search. In the case of experiments 7 and 8, cross ratios may not generally have been considered at any putative stage of the perceptual process. Moving over terrains may be sufficiently important to demand and activate special procedures for picking up information. It is not clear to me, however, how task differences would affect choices between the focus of expansion and differential motion parallax. Ultimately, however, it seems likely that these two approaches are not really different; it is just that the first clearly throws its lot in the direction of the stimulus (and direct perception) and the second toward the observer (and indirect perception).

Some Final Thoughts

Directed perception does not emerge here full blown. Roots are never hard to find. Some expressions of the mapping ideas that I have presented can be found in Helmholtz (1866, 1894), Heider (1958), and

Hochberg (1979, 1981), and more explicitly in Johansson (1970, 1977) and Marr (1982). More than anyone else, however, it was Gibson who forced the hand. By relentlessly sticking by the notion of invariants, Gibson and others discovered some. It now appears that there are even more than he thought. I contend that this is embarrassing for direct perception.

Embarrassing for me is that nowhere in my discussion of directed perception, or in my discussion of direct or indirect perception for that matter, is the concept of meaning. This omission was intended; I frankly have not the vaguest idea how to deal with it. Tacit, or sometimes explicit, in some presentations of indirect perception is that meaning is contributed by the perceiver; in direct perception, on the other hand, meaning occasionally appears to be in the stimulus. Both these ideas must be wrong. Gibson was more careful than this caricature of direct perception and gave us *affordances* as a hopelessly tangled but important attempt to account for meaning in the mutuality of the perceiver and environment. Something similar to the idea of affordances is likely to be right, but its current formulation so sticks in my craw that anything I might add here would contribute nothing.

Finally, with regard to information for perception, specification versus underspecification is no longer the only issue to consider; specification versus overspecification must join the debate. Of course, Gibson allowed perceivers to search out invariants, but he was never clear about what would happen if perceivers found more than one: Would they satisfice or would they optimize? This question demands an answer informed by process and context. It seems that the following generalization is almost certainly true: The more impoverished the perceptual situation, the more demands are made on the cognitive system to make sense of what is presented. And if so, indirect perception occurs. On the other hand, the richer the perceptual situation, the more the individual can choose among specifying sources of information. If only one invariant is present and if perception follows suit, direct perception occurs; if several invariants are present and perception follows only one, or even some combination of those present, then directed perception occurs. In other words, underdetermination and overdetermination are part of a continuous theoretical fabric according to the contexts in which perception is found. Because our normal surrounds are rich, our normal perception must be directed.

Notes

Chapter 1   Information

1. The temporary fall of perception from a central place in philosophy occurred in the middle of this century. It was due to drab discussions by sense data theorists, ill-providing assurance for the existence of physical objects in the real world. Even philosophers who purported to be discussing perception at that time (Austin 1962, Chisholm 1957) were really discussing words, in the tradition of analytic and linguistic philosophy. There were, of course, exceptions, Ayer (1940, 1956, 1973) being the most obvious (and the most drab). Since 1960, however, perception has regained respect, and this is a development which should please psychologists. Armstrong (1961), Hamlyn (1961, 1983), Pitcher (1971), Dretske (1969, 1981), and Fodor (1983) are but a few of the philosophers who have taken the problems of perception seriously again, and there are even those, for example, Heil (1983), who start with the conceptions of Gibson.

2. Interestingly, the connection of the term *metaphysics* to philosophy is accidental. Aristotle called his philosophical works "ta meta ta physika biblia" ("the books after the books on nature"). They were called *Metaphysics* because they followed his *Physics*, bound together in the same volume.

3. Recently, there was an interesting interchange on this matter. Wilcox and Edwards (1982) suggested that physics has played an all too intrusive role in perceptual psychology and that psychologists have too readily adopted the ontology (the physical measures) of physics. Three replies ensued. Haber (1983b, p. 158) stated that

> Fechner did not tell us what physical units to use; nowhere did he say light must be measured as quanta, quanta per unit time, quanta per unit area, patterns of discontinuities of quanta over time and space, Fourier transforms of the above, texture gradients, or any of many other possible units. His demand was that it be in some physical unit, independent of the resultant appearance to any potential or real perceiver. When we move away from adherence to this strict demand, lawfulness eludes us.

I wholeheartedly agree. Hudson (1983), in a second reply, suggested that the physical terms adopted for perception must be satisfactorily constrained; otherwise perceptual theory becomes tautological. He suggested that classical optics provides such constraints. I agree and explore these ideas in chapters 2 through 4 (see also Cutting 1982b). On the other hand, de Wit and de Swart (1983, p. 173) suggested that "as psychologists we do not need to look for some solid basis of physical description." The question here, it seems to me, is: What constitutes a physical description? Photons are not needed, but relations among objects most certainly are. Which relations are appropriate out of the universe available is an empirical question.

4. Although epistemology has traditionally been a part of metaphysics, the philosophy of this century has denied it a place within that area. The reason is that epistemology, but not metaphysics, is thought to be susceptible to philosophical analysis. For purposes of my discussion, however, placing epistemology under metaphysics causes no harm. In fact, in modern philosophy, epistemology and metaphysics may eventually show rapprochement.

5. See Garner (1966) and Gibson (1979). A handy way to discuss this idea is to use the phrase "epistemic perception" (Heil 1983, Shaw and Bransford 1977).

6. This solipsism is a prospect that is not abhorred by all those interested in cognitive science (Fodor 1980).

7. See, for example, Moore and Stout (1913–1914) and Schilpp (1942).

8. Following Gibson (1954a) I use the term *movement* to signify changes in observer position relative to environmental coordinates and *motion* to indicate changes in object position relative to an observer. Thus I speak of the observer's movement but of object, retinal, and optic motion. This distinction, however, can be confusing and difficult to maintain. For example, it makes little sense to speak of *locomovement*, and the verb underlying motion and movement is the same, *move*.

9. A common argument is heard in this connection: If there is an indefinite number of environments that could lie behind any given two-dimensional projection, then there is an indefinite number that could lie behind each frame in a sequence of projections. Thus going from a static to a dynamic situation would appear to gain nothing in surety. The problem with this idea, I believe, is that a dynamic projection of a rich environment is typically consistent for one and only one *rigid* arrangement of objects. To be sure, there are an indefinite number of plastic environments that the projection sequence could represent, but the philosopher must then argue why each of those should have a status equal to a rigid one. It is true that not all things around us are rigid, nor do they always remain in rigid relation to one another, but for those cases in which rigidity holds, elegant algorithms are available to determine the three-dimensional structure of a scene.

10. See, for example, Attneave (1954, 1955), Broadbent (1958), and Garner (1962, 1970, 1974).

Hochberg and McAlister (1953) conjoined the ideas of amount of information and simplicity in an analysis of figural goodness and started a long tradition of the measurement of information in stimuli. See Hatfield and Epstein (1985) for a review. In this tradition, Leeuwenberg and colleagues have promoted what is now called structural information theory (see, for example, Leeuwenberg 1971, Buffart et al. 1983, and Restle 1979). Although I respect many of the ideas in this approach (see Cutting 1981a), in my view it is a forced march through the analog spatial world around us on the legs of a propositional network. It seems hampered by ad hoc assumptions about the primitives used in the information scheme and confined to less interesting paths of two-dimensional, simplistically shaded drawings.

Finally, Dretske (1981, p. 142) tried to recast information theory in terms he thought appropriate for perception, but he redefined perception in an old way, similar to that of Locke:

> Perception is a process by means of which information is delivered within a richer matrix of information (hence in *analog* form) *to* the cognitive centers for their selective use.

On this view, perception stands between sensation and cognition and has nothing to do with the external world. Perception is thus a process between two states, an arrow between two boxes. I like this idea no more than did Gibson (1979).

11. Chomsky (1965), for example, considered pragmatics a side issue to a formal analysis of language.

12. See, for example, Rosch and Lloyd (1978), Smith and Medin (1981), and Zadeh (1969, 1983).

13. Roth and Shoben (1983) demonstrated that the structure of conceptual categories depends on context, and Barsalou (1983) showed that ad hoc categories that have the same structure as natural ones can be constructed on the spot.

14. The issue of sets is raised again in chapter 5 under the idea of groups. There, like here, I take a negative view of them for perception. My qualms notwithstanding, there have been some interesting applications of sets to perception (see Alexander and Carey 1968, Garner 1974, and Palmer 1983), in which information in sets (or groups of rotations and translations) is combined with geometrized information. Groups have been long discussed in relation to perceptual constancies (Cassirer 1944, 1945; Poincaré 1907, Russell 1927).

15. From my view it seems that many relations may be best expressed in a propositional (more languagelike) format and others best expressed in an analog (more spatial) format. Because visual perception is largely concerned with the layout of objects in space, I find it easier to speak of relations in spatial terms. See Anderson (1983) for a propositional view of the mind and Shepard and Cooper (1982) for analog constraints. In a precomputational tradition, Paivio (1970) promoted a hybrid view. Jackendoff (1983) tried to come to grips with meshing propositional information from language with analog information from vision.

Despite the ink spilt over this debate, I see little problem with a hybrid view: discussing language in propositional terms, the optic array in spatial terms, and the area of intersection in either set, whichever is more convenient. Differences over which format human minds might use can be litigated at some point when domains, theories, and data are sufficiently sharp to warrant it.

16. To be sure, light rays can be bent by gravity; by passing them through different media, such as air, water, and glass; by passing them through different temperatures in the same medium, yielding mirages; and by diffraction, or curving around edges. But these are special cases. The rectilinearity of rays is sufficiently true for human-scale observations so that treating them as straight loses nothing essential.

17. The assumption here is, following Roger Bacon, that structures of the real world can be known through principles of geometry, particularly those of Euclid. This is an assumption worth investigating, and I pursue it in chapter 4. I assume that the foundations problem in perception is no worse than in Euclidean geometry. Some, of course, regard foundation efforts in geometry (and mathematics, generally) as demonstrating the sand-castle nature of the mathematical constructs (for an overview, see Davis and Hersh 1981), but for a psychologist they seem pretty firm.

18. Berkeley (1709) was first to suggest that distance was not visually perceptible, and his view became so firmly held that Mill (1842, p. 249) could state:

> The doctrine concerning the original and derivative functions of the sense of sight, which, from the name of its author, is known as "Berkeley's Theory of Vision," has remained, almost from its first promulgation, one of the least disputed doctrines in the most disputed and most disputable of all sciences, the Science of Man.

19. Invariance cannot dissolve the skeptical problem of perception of the physical world, but it can provide an answer to the content problem.

20. Restricted motions are those for which additional assumptions are made. For biological motions, like those of human gait (Johansson 1973b; Cutting et al. 1978; Cutting 1978, 1981a), Hoffman and Flinchbaugh (1982) included a planarity assumption

about the motion of limbs that sufficiently restricts the universe of solutions so that the structure of a person can be recovered. See Ballard and Brown (1982) for an overview of computation approaches to the visual perception of motion.

21. Lappin et al. (1980) have shown that many points on a transparent sphere can yield a coherent percept in two views, and Lappin and Fuqua (1983) have shown that a continuous presentation of three moving points on a line can easily be discerned as being rigid.

22. Horn and Schunk (1981), Prazdny (1981), and Rieger and Lawton (1983), among others, have used this type of analysis in the study of optic flow for a moving viewer.

23. Ballard and Kimball (1983), Clocksin (1980), Hildreth (1984), Longuet-Higgins and Prazdny (1980), Koenderink and van Doorn (1976a, 1981), among many others, have used this approach.

Chapter 2   Projections, Optics, and the Optic Array

1. See, for example, Boynton (1974), Braunstein (1976), Gibson (1966), and Johansson (1975).

2. Agatharchus is credited with the initial discovery and use of perspective twenty-five centuries ago. He wrote what is almost surely the first book on natural depiction, which influenced both Democritus and Anaxagoras, who also wrote on perspective and in turn influenced Euclid.

3. It may seem odd that discussion of the camera obscura, which dates from Alhazen (Polyak 1957), preceded discussions of eyes as cameras, but there was resistance to inversion of retinal image. Because it was known that the image in the camera obscura was inverted, the analogy could not be put forth until this reticence was overcome.

4. Kepler's title, *Ad Vitellionem Paralipomena*, translates humbly as "A Supplement to Witelo," but the work was a counter to Alhazen. Witelo's optics was bound to Alhazen's *Perspectiva*, and together they formed the most important compendium at that time. Kepler's optics demonstrated that the lens of the eye is not the sense organ itself but merely a conduit that sends the pyramid of light to the retina in inverted form.

   Molyneux (1690, p. 105) was first to give the correct answer to the retinal-inversion paradox:

   > The eye or visive faculty takes no notice of the internal posture of its own parts, but uses them as an instrument only, contrived by nature for the exercise of such a faculty.

5. Pinhole projection has many interesting properties. One is that there is infinite depth of focus. Because of diffraction, the focus is nowhere sharp, but objects nearby are registered as clearly as those far away, a situation quite unlike a normal camera or human eye. The pinhole's image is normally dim. Thus sensitive film or long exposure times are needed to record the projection. And of course there is no analog to exposure time for a biological eye, other than perhaps the much discussed icon (Haber 1983a, Loftus 1985). In a camera, long exposure times mean insensitivity to motion; moving objects leave blurred trails across the film during the duration of the exposure.

   The biological and photographic solution to dimness is dioptric pupils—large apertures with refracting lenses. These lenses bend light so that more rays emitted or reflected from an object pass through the pupil and converge to the same point on the projection surface. Because the range of pupil size for the human eye is about 2–8 mm, the human eye allows much more light to strike the retina. Calculation would suggest that the eye should be about 400 times as sensitive as a pinhole camera. In fact, however, light passing through different parts of the pupil is not equally effective in producing a sensory response. This phenomenon, known as the

Stiles-Crawford effect (Bartley 1951), is due to the alignment and shape of the cones (but not the rods) on the retina. In general, light entering at the edge of a dilated pupil is only one-fifth as effective as light entering at the center; light entering halfway out from the center is about two-thirds as effective. Such an effect for photopic (day) vision would limit refractive error while at the same time boosting the luminance of the input over what could be had with a pinhole instead. In general, during maximum dilation of the pupil, the human retina receives about 100 times as much light as a pinhole camera.

The cost of a dioptric system is limited focal depth: Neither a perceiver nor a photographic camera can focus both near and far at the same time. Many biological eyes overcome this problem through accommodation (control over the shape of the lens), focusing at different depths at different times. But despite the complication of dioptrics over pinhole cameras, we can consider the optics of projection to be essentially the same. This similarity is known as the *Gaussian approximation* (Pirenne 1970).

6. Naimark (1981) composed striking examples of the third type. He photographed a still-life scene of household objects, spray painted everything white, and then projected a photographic slide of the original scene onto the white environment, recreating the colored scene. The impression can be so realistic that registration of projecting contours and real object contours must be broken in order for anything unusual to be seen. The white objects could be called a *reality-shaped projection surface*.

7. See Leeman et al. (1976) and Battisti et al. (1981) for discussions of anamorphic art.

8. Ptolemy's work, entering Florence about 1400, was at least as influential in the development of perspective drawing and painting as the medieval texts on optics (Edgerton 1975). Of course, maps date from well before Ptolemy, at least to Babylon, but these make no pretense of being true projections.

9. In cartography, "polar projection" is a term used in reference to regions of the globe. Thus a polar map is one that shows the North or South Pole. When I use the term, however, I refer to the method of projection, not the subject matter projected.

10. For mapmakers, the major difference between Mercator and Lambert projections is that the former is *orthomorphic* (or conformal) and the latter is *authalic*. An orthomorphic projection preserves relative north-south and east-west distances at any point, an authalic the area of any projected region. Both are distinguished from *aphylactic* projections, which preserve neither (Steers 1927).

11. Other mapping principles have been employed to reduce distortions (Steers 1927, Fisher and Miller 1944). One has been to use polyhedra, particularly the icosahedron, with its twenty equilateral triangles as faces, devised by Fuller (1963). In maps this icosahedral projection reduces local distortions between points on the globe and points within all triangles. It is polar, using the center of the earth as the pole. But this kind of map suffers significant topological breakage: It unfolds horribly into a latticework of triangles connected on one side, and it creates problems in distance estimation along geodesics between points on nonadjacent faces of the map.

12. In science, for example, parallel projection has often been used by the artificial intelligence community (Marr 1982; Ullman 1979, 1983) because of its relative simplicity for computational approaches to object recognition.

13. In fact, light fans out from points on an object and enters the pupil, in some sense reversing the pyramid. Boynton (1974) chastised Gibson for missing this fact, but more facts were on Gibson's side. The Gaussian approximation, discussed in note 5 to this chapter, states that nothing essential is lost by assuming that the eye is like a pinhole camera and that the pyramid of sight is like that suggested by Euclid, Ptolemy, and Gibson.

14. Five variables determine a polar projection (Carlbom and Paciorek 1978): (1) orientation of the projection plane with respect to the principal face of the object, which separates

one- from two- and three-point perspectives; (2) height of the center of projection with respect to the object (or the height of the horizon); (3) distance of the center of projection from the object, often measured in stimulus diameters; (4) distance of the projection plane from the object, which affects only the *size* of the projection; and (5) orientation of the centric ray with respect to the image plane, relevant to anamorphic art. Carlbom and Paciorek suggested that a good naturalistic three-point perspective should have the walls of a rectilinear object appear at angles to the projection plane, have the horizon such that it intersects the object at the eye height of the observer, and have the viewpoint be from at least two stimulus diameters so that the object does not occupy more than about 45° of visual angle.

15. Binocularity is ignored, in part, because the consequences to vision in stepping from no eyes to one are vastly greater than from one to two. A one-eyed individual can drive a car legally and can fly an airplane as well as a person with two eyes (Grosslight et al. 1978); a no-eyed individual should attempt neither. Nevertheless, perhaps the most charming counter to my claim that cyclopean considerations are sufficient for vision was given by Molyneux (1690, pp. 294–295) at the very end of *Dioptrica Nova*:

> And as a conclusion to the whole I shall only add one Experiment that demonstrates we see with both eyes at once; and 'tis, that which is commonly known and practiced in all tennis-courts, that the best player in the world hoodwinking one eye shall be beaten by the greatest bungler that ever handled a racket; unless he be used to the trick, and then by custom he gets an habit of using one eye only.

But I am not even sure that this would be true.

16. Evidence by Williams and Collier (1983) and Yellott (1983) suggests that image degradation serves the purpose of keeping acuity below the Nyquist limit of sampling frequency. In essence, if we could see any better, our visual images would suffer aliasing problems just like those seen on raster-scan displays. Our visual world, then, would suffer the "jaggies," just like the images of curved objects on poor quality video games.

17. Because the center of rotation of the eye and the nodal point of the projection are not the same, the optic array changes somewhat with ocular rotation (see Gulick and Lawson 1976). The amount it changes, however, is not likely to be psychologically relevant.

18. Todd (1984) suggested that there is an inherent incompatibility of this assumption with the first. Because information in the optic array is not punctate—rays are infinitely dense, and information is spread over them—it is difficult to locate particular points as discrete from their neighbors. Todd's solution was to consider visual solid angles rather than points. But regress shows that solid angles project from perimeters, which are lines, which in turn are made up of points. Regardless, what follows throughout these chapters is an analysis of points. From points I derive angles, lines, and surfaces, and although it is certain that the perceptual system does not perform this same operation, an analysis of points provides a more than useful beginning. Just as astronomy and physics were advanced through the useful fiction of point masses, the study of visual perception can be advanced through consideration of point elements in the optic array.

19. For example, if an observer marks a point on the horizon, then moves the eye horizontally 90°, marks that point, and moves vertically 90°, the observer is still only 90° from the starting point. If such measures were taken on a plane, we would expect Pythagoras to rule, and the distance covered by these orthogonal moves to be about 127°. But this is incorrect. A triangle on a sphere can be drawn with three right angles, or three of any size so long as their sum is at least 180° and less than

540°. One with three right angles takes up one-eighth the surface of a sphere. Such a section cannot be measured in degrees *squared* because squaring is not the proper algorithmic process.

20. The word *subtend* means "stretch beneath"; so to subtend an angle is to stretch an arc or a line from one side of an angle to the other. For example, the hypotenuse of a triangle subtends its right angle.

21. Direction of rays also concerned Euclid. Like many before him, he proposed an extromissionistic theory (in which the eye emits rays of light that bathe objects) rather than an intromissionistic one (in which the eye receives reflected light). Aristotle opposed the former view, but Alhazen was the first to present convincing evidence against it (Lindberg 1967): The eye could be injured when it looked at something very bright, such as the sun, and it was difficult to imagine how or why an organ would thus injure itself. See Grant (1974) for later, medieval arguments by Robert Grosseteste, Roger Bacon, John Pecham, and Witelo.

22. Five centuries later, Ptolemy realized the limitations of delimiting areas by conic sections and first spoke of the "pyramid of sight," with the eye at the apex and with the base a perimeter of any possible shape. Euclid did not state exactly where within the eye the true apex appeared. Following his lead, Galen, in the second century, assumed that, because the lens was at the apex, it was the receptor surface of the eye. This idea persisted in many forms until Kepler. Heliocloris of Larissa realized the problem of considering the eye as a point and appears to have been the first to propose that the pupil is wide enough for the apex to lie within the eye (Ronchi 1970). For the Gaussian approximation, we now know that the apex lies at the front of the lens in the cornea-lens dioptric system (Pirenne 1970).

At the other end of the pyramid, of course, was the object. In Euclid's analysis the rays from the eye simply fanned out, but Ptolemy added the notion that (when an object's flank is orthogonal to the line of sight) the line of sight to the object's center, the centric ray, is the shortest. He believed that this ray carried the truest information about the object. In a similar vein, Alberti later called this the "prince of rays" (Edgerton 1975), and this ray eventually became that from the eye to the vanishing point in a one-point perspective drawing.

23. Different translations of *Optics* include more definitions at the end of the list, some of which are never used in the body of the work. One is that all light rays travel at the same speed, a view that reinforces Ptolemy's idea that the centric ray has pre-eminence and that it provides "clearer" information about the object. A second is that all objects subtend only certain angles, suggesting that small angles do not reveal visible objects (Ronchi 1970).

24. Ronchi (1970) thought Euclid may have been talking not only about distant objects but also about near ones. If this is true, Euclid was the first to discuss the near point of accommodation, the point closest to the lens on which the eye can focus.

25. See, in particular, Ronchi (1957, 1970, 1974). Ronchi had clear influence on Gibson, although Gibson chastised him for his dualistic view of perception and for his belief that the mind perceives off the retina. To Ronchi (1957, p. 288), nerve impulses in the visual system are

> turned over in the mind which studies their characteristics and compares them with the mass of information in its files. In conclusion it creates a luminous and colored figure which it places where it believes the initial group of atoms to be.

26. The shift from psychology to physiology was subtle but almost inevitable with Alhazen's proof that the eye receives rather than emits light. All students of optics turned toward reception and eventually to receptors. Psychological issues, such as constancy, were generally lost. To be sure, the subdiscipline of physiological optics

often contained treatments of perception, and Helmholtz's (1866) treatise is the out-
standingly comprehensive example.

Chapter 3   Pictures

1. Picasso could not have espoused a belief about perspective as extreme as this appears.
   Flanner (1956, p. 84), in an essay on Georges Braque and cubism, discussed an
   interaction between Stein and Picasso that promotes a different impression:

   > Miss Stein, with her hearty curiousity for explanations, asked Picasso to put
   > Cubism into words, to which he replied, "You paint not what you see but what
   > you know is there."

   Others who have espoused a conventionalist approach to perspective are Steinberg
   (1953) and Arnheim (1954).
2. For a detailed discussion of contracts and contractualism as a psychological and
   philosophical approach, see Proffitt (1976) and Proffitt and Halwes (1982).
3. See, for example, Gibson (1954b, 1971b), Gombrich (1960, 1982), and Hochberg
   (1978a).
4. See Gibson (1954b) and Hochberg (1962) for discussions of fidelity. The closest
   nonphotographic approximations to the optic array are works of *trompe l'oeil*, paintings
   that "fool the eye." Perhaps the grandest trompe l'oeil is the Pozzo ceiling, painted
   in the late seventeenth century in the church of St. Ignazio in Rome and particularly
   studied by Pirenne (1970, 1975). Painted on this ceiling are images of columns adorned
   with angels that, when viewed from the center of the floor beneath it, look like a
   continuation of the real columns and space below. Because the artwork is on a high
   ceiling, binocular disparities are diminished, enhancing the effect. Trompe l'oeil has
   been relatively rare in art since the development of photography.

   Back to surrogates, Gibson later dropped the term from his discussions of picture
   perception (Gibson 1960b) because it had no further role in his evolving theory. He
   first adhered to a fairly strict perspectivist view (Gibson 1954b), suggesting that
   pictures are essentially copies of the optic array at a particular place and time; he
   next rejected that idea (Gibson 1966), suggesting that pictures are stationary structures
   of gradients, discontinuities, and textures; and ultimately, he (Gibson 1979) proposed
   that a picture is an arrangement of persisting invariants of structure. This is a curious
   idea that I return to in chapter 5.
5. See Hagen (1979, 1980) and Kennedy (1974) for reviews of the various positions.
6. The other important school of picture perception is the *gestalt* approach, best represented by Arnheim (1954, 1969), who said little about surrogates per se. Instead,
   he demonstrated that gestalt principles—such as those of figure and ground, good
   continuation, and pragnanz—have felicitous application in the domain of art. In fact,
   because most of the principles were first developed and demonstrated with line
   drawings, it is no surprise that gestalt properties might have great explanatory value
   in picture perception.
7. Strictly, the surfaces of picture and mirror need not be parallel in Brunelleschi's
   experiment. When not parallel, the image in the mirror undergoes perspective transformation, a tapering in one direction that preserves betweenness, but for either a
   "narrower" or a "flattened" environment. See also Arnheim (1977).
8. For a photograph, the location of the proper station point is along the perpendicular
   from the center of the picture. The distance along that line is the focal length of the
   lens times the enlargement of the picture.
9. This is done by drawing projectors from the eye to each point in the picture and
   beyond it into virtual space. The projector is truncated when the ratio of its distance

beyond the image plane divided by the total distance to the station point attains the same ratio as that from the correct station point in the scene when the picture was originally taken, scaled up or down by any enlargement or diminution of the picture.

10. See, for example, Anstis et al. (1969), Pirenne (1970), and Wallach (1976a). Goldstein (1979) also discusses the phenomenon in an altered experimental context.

11. This idea was suggested to Pirenne in a letter from Einstein in 1955 just before Einstein's death. Pirenne also felt that La Gournerie's paradox was related to mathematical homology. Here, I think, he was on the right track. Images of a photograph seen from right and wrong station points have identical topologies.

12. See Shepard and Cooper (1982) and Cooper and Shepard (1984) for summaries of mental rotation phenomena. In this vein, Kubovy (1986) assumed that some form of mental rectification brings the image in register with the eye so that the picture is "seen" from a view orthogonal to the image plane. That is, it is as if the observer undergoes a mental out-of-body experience and is placed directly in front of the picture. Greene (1983) is less clear but presents a system not unlike Kubovy's for reconstructing the preferred viewpoint. Moreover, like Pirenne, Greene (1983, p. 102) seemed to think that his rectification is a cognitive process:

> The extent to which different people can ignore whatever extra mental effort is required to reject these improbable (though optically consistent) subjects is shown by their degrees of tolerance of seats to either side of center at the cinema. This extra effort would also explain why the 'illusion of depth' is . . . stronger the closer we are to the preferred viewpoint.

One problem for such accounts is anamorphic art, where the appropriate point of view is *not* at right angles to the image plane, but at very sharp angles, often 15° or less. Anamorphic art demonstrates that the mental rectification of the proximal image in La Gournerie's paradox is not compulsory.

Whatever the process, there is little question that the slant of the picture, derived from cropping or from graded binocular disparities, can be important to perception. Pirenne (1970) and Gregory (1970) amply demonstrated that pictures taken of other pictures at a slant can reveal large distortions in the original. It remains possible, however, that the accounts of Pirenne, Greene, and Kubovy apply to static images but that a different kind of analysis applies to moving images, particularly cinema. The rationale for this is that in cinema invariants under transformation can be studied, whereas in static images (at least in my view) there are no transformations to reveal the invariants.

13. See, for example, Kubovy (1986). With him, I concur that Hagen and Elliott's stimulus selection was odd. More important, however, is that the preferences demonstrated do not indicate the limits of the visual system in resolving distortions. Several other studies have investigated the relation between perception of space and effects of foreshortening caused by looking through a telephoto lens, a situation that creates similar affine distortions. Purdy (1960), Farber and Rosinski (1978), Rosinski and Farber (1980), and Lumsden (1980) have shown that observers can be reasonably accurate in determining the slant of a depicted surface.

14. Hagen and Jones (1978) demonstrated further that, when the same situation is used to judge the shape of objects, adults can match the pictured objects with the three-dimensional shapes quite well but children cannot.

15. The cue concept began with what Berkeley (1733) called *signs* to the perception of objects in depth. Signs are surrogates that stand in the place of what they signify. Mill (1843) followed Berkeley's use. James (1890, p. 518) may have been the first to use *cue*. He discussed it as an impetus to action:

It will be remembered that we distinguish two orders of kinaesthetic impression, the *remote* ones, made by the movement on the eye or ear or distant skin, etc., and the *resident* ones, made on the moving parts themselves, muscles, joints, etc. Now do resident images, exclusively, form what I have called the mental cue, or will remote ones equally suffice?

There can be no doubt whatever that the mental cue may be either an image of the resident or of the remote kind.

Thus external and internal information can cue action. It is a small step to consider these cuing perceptions as well, as Titchener (1909, p. 314) used the concept:

In monocular vision the sensations of accommodation, and in binocular vision the sensations of convergence, give fairly accurate cues to the position of objects in external space.

Harper and Boring (1948) discussed the history of the word *cue* within psychology but seemed to have missed James. They also did not find the analog of the theatrical word for cue, *Stichwort*, in German psychological texts. They traced the use of the German for sign, *Zeichen*, to Lotze. But again, overlooking some English-language tradition, they missed Mill's and Berkeley's use of it. Harper and Boring also argued for switching to the term *clue*. But in either case, cues and clues are prompts for perception, not sources of information that specify an object.

Enumeration of cuelike sources of information about depth began with Porterfield (1759) and Reid (1764). Reid, following Berkeley (1733), called these "signs by which we learn to perceive distance." In modern garb, those listed by Reid were accommodation, convergence, aerial perspective, and familiar size.

16. For an observer 1.83 m tall, his or her eyes will be about 1.68 m above the ground and the horizon (assuming that the earth is a perfectly smooth sphere) is at about 4.72 km (see also Warren 1976). But since the arctangent of 1.68/4720 is 89.98°, the line from the eye to the horizon is virtually parallel to the ground.

Chapter 4   Space

1. Wiggins (1968) noted that different kinds of things can be in the same place at the same time. Thus one's brain and one's mind, universities and certain buildings, and cathode-ray excited phosphor and prose on a text editor occupy the same place, respectively.

2. Some deny the existence of perceptual error (Shaw and Bransford 1977, Michaels and Carello 1981), regarding the term as a category mistake, whereas others regard this idea as difficult to maintain (Cutting 1982b), in part because discussion of perceptual error dates back continuously at least to Malebranche (1674) and is attuned to common usage.

3. The clearest presentations of this idea are in Shepard (1981, 1984) and Shepard and Cooper (1982).

4. Some claim that natural geometry is an explanatory device at variance with Descartes's rationalistic approach to perception (Pastore 1971), whereas others regard it as central to Cartesian thought (Maull 1980). Regardless, the concept speciated and proved central to many accounts of perception. For example, Malebranche (1674) altered it to *natural judgment*. Consider his strikingly modern account of the moon illusion (p. 35):

For our imagination does not represent great distance between objects unless it is aided by the sight of other objects between them, beyond which it can imagine more objects.

This is why we see the moon much larger when it is rising or setting than when it is well above the horizon; for when the moon is high, we see no objects between us and it whose size we might know in order to judge the size of the moon by comparison. But when it has just risen or is about to set, we see between us and the countryside, whose approximate size we know, and thus we judge it to be farther away and as a result we see it larger.

It should be noted that when the moon has risen above our heads, although we might know for certain through reason that it is at a great distance, we cannot help but see it as quite near and small, because these natural judgments of vision occur in us, independently of us, and even in spite of us.

5. Actually, the thrust of Berkeley's theory is to separate geometry from vision but not from touch. The latter section of that work (1709, para. 149–160) attempts to establish geometry as the proper object of tactile impression.

6. Non-Euclidean geometries have a history before the nineteenth century. Torretti (1978), Davis and Hersh (1981), and particularly Kline (1980) provide overviews. Perhaps the most interesting sidelight is that Reid (1764) provided some bases for what was later to become Riemann's double elliptic geometry (Daniels 1974, Angell 1974).

7. Gauss was not alone in his warnings. Bolyai, codiscoverer with Lobachevski of the first non-Euclidean geometry, had letters from his father urging him to stop tinkering (Davis and Hersh 1981, pp. 220–221):

> For God's sake, please give it up. Fear it no less than the sensual passions because it, too, may take up all your time and deprive you of your health, peace of mind and happiness in life.

8. Helmholtz (1868) recognized that his notion of intuition was not that held by an older tradition. He argued that by working on abstract problems, these entities take on a rich and real existence. It is not one that comes instantly; they do not have "the effortlessness, speed, or immediate clarity of our perceptions, say, of a room which we enter for the first time" (p. 380), but they can be imagined.

9. In his *Treatise on Human Nature*, Hume (1739, book I, part III, sect. I) felt ambivalent about the purity of geometry in relation to the rest of mathematics:

> 'Tis for want of such a standard of equality in extension, that geometry can scarce be esteem'd a perfect and infallible science.
>
> But here it may not be amiss to obviate a difficulty, which may arise from my asserting, that tho' geometry falls short of that perfect precision and certainty, which are peculiar to arithmetic and algebra, yet it excels the imperfect judgments of our senses and imagination. The reason I impute any defect to geometry, is, because its original and fundamental principles are deriv'd merely from appearances; and it may perhaps be imagin'd, that this defect must always attend it, and keep it from ever reaching a greater exactness in the comparison of objects or ideas, than what our eye or imagination alone is able to attain.

10. Mill also thought that the foundations of all branches of mathematics, not just geometry, were empirical.

11. Many disagreed with Poincaré. For example, Hempel (1945) presented a set of arguments like mine against conventionalism of linear perspective: Conventions are contracts, and it is not clear that the parties involved have the authority to determine the nature of the contractual form. In science, the simplicity of Euclidean geometry as a descriptive system for the physical world cannot be explained away by convention.

12. This last view presents a conundrum of two spaces (Strawson 1966): The phenomenal space of appearances in which we live is Euclidean, and the physical space of the universe is not. Although this view may seem inconsistent, practically it is not.

Hopkins (1973), for example, suggested that the degree of curvature in physical space is so small that, on a local level, it cannot be decided whether phenomenal space is Euclidean or only an extremely good approximation thereof. The differences are so small as to render the question moot.

The philosophy of geometry is still much debated. See, for example, Grünbaum (1969, 1973) and Putnam (1963). And the form of physical versus visual geometry is also of much interest to philosophers. See, for example, Angell (1974), Daniels (1974), Roberts and Suppes (1967), and Suppes (1977).

13. This is the treatment that Gibson (1976b) gave in his reply to Berkeley.

14. See also Kenyon (1898), Pierce (1898), and Miles (1931).

15. See Ames (1951, 1960), Ittelson and Kilpatrick (1951), Ittelson (1952), and Kilpatrick (1961).

16. Gehringer and Engel (to be published) have shown that distortions of size and depth in the Ames room are reduced by almost an order of magnitude with stereoscopic vision and observer movement.

17. Despite his interest, however, Gibson performed few formal analyses of vision. His most quantitative effort was a collaboration (Gibson et al. 1955).

18. See, for example, Hardy et al. (1953), Blank (1978), and Indow and Watanabe (1984); Suppes (1977) provides a philosophical overview.

19. Riemann proposed a system of geometries with different curvatures: positive (elliptic), zero (Euclidean), and negative (hyperbolic). Traditionally, the positive-curvature geometries are called Riemannian and the negative-curvature ones Lobachevskian (see Davis and Hersh 1981). The entire descriptive system, however, is called Riemannian, easily creating confusion. In general, the literature on non-Euclidean visual space deals with empirical investigation into Riemannian curvature, and the particular geometry supported is usually Lobachevskian.

20. More recently, Indow and Watanabe (1984) have used moving lights and found essentially the same results as Luneburg (1947) and Blank (1978). The displays, however, are still impoverished, consisting only of a pair of lights moving along the z axis. Moreover, it should be noted that not all those who have reviewed the results of the alley experiments regard them as evidence for a non-Euclidean space (see, for example, Fry 1950, Grünbaum 1973, chap. 5).

21. Indow (1982) is an exception. He ran observers in horopter and alley experiments in both darkened and illuminated conditions and found curvature results for both.

I also realize that I am skating on fairly thin ice here. Much of my own research has dealt with a small number of lights seen in a dark surround (see, for example, Cutting 1981a, 1982a; Cutting and Proffitt 1982; and Cutting et al. 1978). The differences, I hope, are important. Although my stimuli were points of light that appeared on a dark field, they moved in a coherent and mechanically reasonable fashion, providing rich structural relations among parts. The crux of these demonstrations is that a relatively small number of lights can reveal rich spatial relations, all of which are mathematically specified when a few assumptions, such as rigidity and planarity (Hoffman and Flinchbaugh 1982), are made. The normal environment is richer still.

22. Indow (1982) has adopted Poincaré's (1905) position in this regard: All measurements are interconvertible between Riemannian and Euclidean spaces. But there remains the problem of measurement under impoverished conditions, which in the Luneburg tradition yields a Riemannian space, and measurement under normal conditions, which yields a Euclidean space.

23. A third group interested in curved geometries consists of graphic engineers, photographers, and other artists. Rudiments began with Leonardo (Richter 1883), who was dissatisfied with strictures of perspective. Among modern writers, Reggini (1975)

noted that the eye is naturally presented with a curved geometry when exposed to large visual angles. There are several problems, however, with this kind of analysis. One is that we do not perceive our proximal images; we perceive distal stimuli. There is no need for a Cartesian natural geometry of cultural convention, suggested by Hansen (1973), to straighten out the hyperbolic curves on the proximal image. We simply do not see them except perhaps as part of an introspectionistic exercise like that of Helmholtz (1866).

Both Helmholtz and Hansen reported that, when an observer fixates with one eye some location near a straight edge, he or she can see that edge as curved. Consider the vertical edge of a door, where the top and bottom project to the extreme periphery and the middle of the door to a region just outside the parafovea. It is said that this edge will look like it arcs overhead and beneath the observer's feet. It doesn't look this way to me, but I do not deny that with glasses there is an apparent curvature to some straight lines at the corners of rooms and ceilings. Within moments, these curvatures are adapted to and are no longer apparent. This fact might be modeled with hyperbolic geometry. But with different glasses, the edges of rooms may bow in the opposite direction, consistent with an elliptic geometry. Rather than say that the visual system is tailored to one non-Euclidean geometry or another, I suggest that it is simply not hypersensitive to curvature, with a reasonable region of tolerance centered around Euclidean geometry.

It is clear, however, that we see the curvature of straight lines in panoramic photographs (see Malde 1983). These lines actually *are* curved in the plane of the image itself. But this fact is an artifact, an extension of Panofsky's account of convention in depiction. The photograph is a proximal image from within the camera. When we look at the picture, we see this image rather than the distal array of objects. The curved lines in the panoramic photograph are the result of taking a curved projection of the real world through a particular camera lens and flattening that image out onto a plane.

Chapter 5   Invariants

1. The first half of this chapter is reworked from the *Journal of Experimental Psychology: Human Perception and Performance*, 1983, 9:310–317.
2. There are, of course, many candidates for the fundamental problem of perception. Consider four. First, Titchener (1906, p. 15) suggested that we must analyze "mental experience into its simplest components" and "discover how those elements combine." But the centrality of this idea should be questioned; the decomposition and recomposition of percepts assumes a kind of mental process that may never occur. Mill (1865) debated Hamilton (1858) over this same issue.

Second, Hayek (1952, pp. 7–8) proposed that we must "start from stimuli defined in physical terms and proceed to show why and how the senses classify physical stimuli sometimes as alike and sometimes as different, and why different physical stimuli will sometimes appear as similar and sometimes as different." But the physical dimensions most appropriate to the observer may not be those that would ordinarily occur to the psychophysicist.

A third approach is to focus on processes and mechanisms. Lindsay and Norman (1972, p. 1), for example, proposed that "the task before us is to discover the psychological processes that are operating and as much as possible of the wiring diagram of the neural networks that are involved." But such a view presupposes knowledge about *what* is processed and what the perceptual systems need to do, a set of issues that can no longer be ignored (Marr 1982).

A fourth approach is that of Shepard (1981, p. 283), who claimed that "the problem of internal representation looms as *the* central problem of perception." But the focus on internality (or mental events), like that on process, assumes too readily that external sources of representation are well described and well established, a view with which I cannot agree.

3. The appearance of the term *invariant* here is due, in part, to translation. The same phrase appeared in Cohen and Wartofsky (1977, p. 136) as "lawlike behavior." Similarly, Cassirer (1944, p. 10; translated by Gurwitch) quoted Katz as follows: "The idea of invariance, which is an epistemological problem of validity of the foremost importance, has one of its roots, and perhaps the most nutritive one, in the psychology of perception." But in a different translation of Katz (1935, p. 185, by MacLeod and Fox) the same statement appeared as: "The concept of 'constancy,' which involves an epistemological problem of the greatest importance, has perhaps its most important root in the psychology of perception."

4. See, for example, Baird (1970), Cassirer (1944, 1945), Hochberg (1974, 1979).

5. Meanwhile, the concept of invariance cropped up in the perception literature independent of Gibson. See, for example, Allport (1955), Heider (1958), Luchins and Luchins (1964), and Platt (1970).

6. Luchins and Luchins (1954, p. 315) expressed exactly this concern over the importation of mathematical terms into psychology:

   Psychologists use . . . mathematical terms . . . . But they often fail to specify whether or not these terms and symbols have the same meanings as in mathematics, and thereby, it seems to us, pave the path for confusion.

7. See Bell (1945) and Klein (1908).

8. See, for example, Julesz (1971), Michaels and Carello (1981), Piaget (1970), Shaw et al. (1974), and Shaw and Pittenger (1977).

9. Cutting (1981b, 1982b) and Cutting and Proffitt (1981).

10. This asymmetry is to be contrasted with structural invariants and structural variants, as both would seem to exist. Thus the term *structural invariant* seems better than *transformational invariant*, although without the benefit of its paired member, the former term may be redundant. Its use (see, for example, Shaw and Pittenger 1977) also seems not far removed from *structure invariance* as used in measurement theory (Luce and Krumhansl 1986).

11. This point was made by Hochberg and Smith (1955), Epstein and Park (1964), Freeman (1965, 1966), and more recently by Rock (1983).

12. See also Topper (1977, 1979).

13. See Russell (1927), Balzano (1980), Palmer (1983), and Warren and Shaw (1984) for opposing views.

14. There are, of course, a number of exceptions, among them Cutting et al. (1978) for the perception of gait and Proffitt and Cutting (1980) for the perception of rolling objects, neither of which was discussed as projective invariants; Todd (1981) for the perception of moving objects; and, more generally, Ullman (1979, 1981) for the perception of rigid objects. See also Clocksin (1980), Koenderink and van Doorn (1975, 1981), Longuet-Higgins and Prazdny (1980), Lee (1980a), Nakayama and Loomis (1974), and Prazdny (1983b) for optic flow; the ideas discussed in these papers are considered in more detail in chapters 10 through 13.

15. Some have suggested that Gibson gave up one-to-one mappings. But as Ullman (1980) noted, there are two mappings to consider: that from the distal object to the proximal image and that between image and percept. The only mapping that I am concerned with here is the first, which concerned Gibson throughout his career.

16. To be sure, Gibson (1954b, 1966) talked about equivalent sources of information,

and hence perhaps equivalent invariants, but he did so only in the context of the relation between pictures and what they represent or in the context of different sensory modalities. Gibson (1972, p. 226) also said:

> If unequivocal stimulus information is made available to an observer in an experiment, his perception will be determined by it and by nothing else. When *ambient* stimulus information is available to an observer outside the laboratory he can *select* the information that interests him; he can give attention to one part instead of another, but his perception will be determined by the information he attends to.

In the latter part of this passage, Gibson speaks of an observer attending to different *parts* of what he or she sees, surely picking up different invariants. That process, however, is not relevant. My claim is that the *whole* of an object, under some circumstances, is specified by *at least two different* sources of information (invariants). These sources are not equivalent, despite the fact that they specify the same thing. In the earlier part of the quotation, Gibson suggested that if unequivocal information is given to the observer, his or her perception will follow. But in the experiments in later chapters two sources of unequivocal information are displayed and the observers generally use but one.

17. See, for example, Cutting and Millard (1984), Epstein (1981), Flock (1965), and Rosinski and Levine (1976).
18. See, for example, Goldstein (1981) and Cutting (1985).
19. My definition of an invariant differs from that typically given in the ecological approach (Gibson 1979, Michaels and Carello 1981) in my rather ardent demand for a particular kind of mathematical specificity. Generally, I claim that if the invariant exists, it can be measured, with a numerical value or a relation among numerical values placed on it. In fact, with Lappin (1984) I like to think of perceptual process, in part, as the measurement of this information. I may be overly strict, but this constraint serves as a check on invariance. I suggest that if someone proposes an invariant but cannot measure it by determining its numerical value on the scale of real numbers, then we should be wary. I mistrust discussions of topological invariants (such as number of edges, surfaces, and holes) that allow no measure except the cardinal numbers. Although Chen (1982) reported that topology influences the discrimination of briefly presented displays, Rubin and Kanwisher (1985) reported that his results are probably an artifact of luminance differences. It is possible, of course, that we might yet find topological invariants that are perceptually useful. The focus of expansion might be one, but in chapters 10 through 13 I find no real evidence for its use.

Chapter 6   Cross Ratios

1. See, for example, Hochberg (1978a) and Rock (1983).
2. Pylyshyn (1984) argued that the only psychophysical experiments worth doing are those requiring no cognitive intervention or, better yet, those that are impervious to cognitive intervention. None of the tasks employed in this work are of this kind, but this does not dismay me at all. Although I am sensitive to concerns of demand character by stimulus selection, the designs I employ in chapters 7 through 9 allow alternative response patterns. It is those alternatives that interest me, and the paradigms bias the participant in neither direction.
3. Experiments 1, 3, and 7 were first reported at the 15th Annual Meeting of the Society for Mathematical Psychology, Princeton, New Jersey, in August 1982, and at the 23rd Annual Meeting of the Psychonomic Society, Minneapolis, Minnesota, in November 1982. Experiments 5 and 6 were reported at the 8th Annual Interdisciplinary Conference, Steamboat Springs, Colorado, in January 1983.

For those not familiar with experimental procedures, a statistical note is in order. Data are almost always contaminated by "noise," or random error. This noise may result from the improper presentation of a stimulus (computers are not always smoothly performing), inattention on the part of the perceiver, spontaneous neural activity in the visual system, shifts in criterion for initiating a particular type of response, poor coordination of action, poor motor performance, or any number of other causes. At all points in the information-delivery and information-processing systems, small perturbations can occur that result in less than perfectly clean data. No amount of tidying up of the experimental situation or of training participants can ever wholly get rid of noise. Thus a perceptual psychologist must assume that responses are probabilistic; they are more or less randomly sampled from distributions of possible responses that a systematic observer might make. The larger the number of responses, the more secure the performance estimate. We can consider the sample of estimates as having some modal (or mean or median) value as its central tendency. Of course, many of these estimates are lower than this central estimate, and others are higher. The central limit theorem, however, suggests that the sample mean converges to the population mean.

Statistics are invoked when this mean is compared with performance expected by chance. The burden of chance is great in psychological methodology, and it takes the form of a null hypothesis, a theoretical prediction that there is nothing but random error in the data. We assess the plausibility of the null hypothesis (we can never prove it wrong). Its rejection is based on the likelihood ratio, or probability value (p value), that a given outcome could occur by chance. The standard criterion for rejecting the null hypothesis, and going on to consider other more interesting hypotheses, is that the probability must be less than 0.05 (an occurrence by chance of 1 in 20).

The statistical techniques that I report—F tests, t tests, and χ^2 tests—are all part of the standard armamentarium of experimental psychology. Each of these symbols—F, t, or χ^2—is followed by a number or numbers in parentheses, an equal sign, and another number before the p value. These values allow the statistically more sophisticated reader to assess the manner in which I make my conclusions.

4. Stimuli were generated on-line by FORTRAN programs on a Hewlett-Packard (HP) 1000L Series computer and displayed on an HP 1350S vector-plotting display system with a P31 phosphor. This phosphor is one with relatively rapid decay when seen in room light and allows presentation of smoothly moving green elements on a black background. Resolution on this 40-cm display (measured diagonally) is 1024 by 1024 programmable locations.

I participated in all experiments; one undergraduate student (SR) participated in experiments 1–3 and 5–7; one graduate student (CB) participated in experiments 1, 3, and 7, and a second graduate student (RM) participated in experiments 2, 5, 6, and 8. Each experiment involved many sessions, and sessions were generally distributed over several months' time.

Each experiment consisted of many *blocks*, each a complete replication of all possible types of trials (usually 16), randomly ordered before the block begins. A *trial* consists of a fixed sequence of events. It begins with a warning tone, alerting the viewer to the presentation of the stimulus. Simultaneous with the tone is presentation of the within-block trial number at the center of the display screen. One second later the stimulus begins and cycles through its motion three times. Durations varied from 5.3 to 13.3 sec, depending on the case studied. The viewer was prompted at the end of stimulus presentation by another tone and asked to make a judgment indicating whether the stimulus was rigid or nonrigid (or flat or not flat in experiment 7). The viewer responded on a console keyboard and was given immediate feedback. No reaction time was measured, and nothing other than accuracy was stressed. Then followed an intertrial interval of 5.5 to 20 sec, again depending on the case studied, during which the next trial's stimulus was computed. This sequence of events repeated until the end of the last trial of a block. The viewer was then informed on the console screen how many responses were correct and given the opportunity either to quit or to go on to the next block. Responses and stimulus conditions were stored in a computer file when the viewer ended the session. Each block duration was 6–18 min long, according to the experiment.

Before the first block of each session, the participant entered a starting value indicating the degree of change in either displacement or cross ratio. If the viewer got more than 75% of the trials correct within the first block, that value was quartered for the next block; if the viewer got less than 75% correct, that value was doubled; otherwise it was unchanged. In this manner, so long as the viewer ran through a substantial number of blocks within a session, performance across blocks stabilized near 75% correct.

Chapter 7   Cross Ratios and Motion Perception

1. Consider a plane one arbitrary unit across, rotating around a central vertical axis. If all lines are equally spaced throughout that plane, they appear on it (moving from left to right) at equal intervals of 0.333 unit: line A at -0.500 unit from the central axis, B at -0.167 unit, C at $+0.167$ unit, and D at $+0.500$ unit. However, each line was randomly placed within a region that centers on these values, with a width of 0.267 unit. Thus line A appeared anywhere between -0.633 and -0.367 unit, B between -0.300 and -0.033, and so forth. In this manner, adjacent lines could be as close as 0.067 unit and as far apart as 0.600 unit, and the lines farthest apart (A and D) could be separated as little as 0.733 unit or by as much as 1.267 units. No pairwise or higher constraints were placed on the positions of the lines. Cross ratios varied randomly within a skewed distribution from 0.191 to 0.988, with a mode of 0.830.

Rotation of these four-line objects through 360° was accomplished in 72 frames, 5° per frame and successively presented. Each frame was displayed for 47 msec, with no interval between frames. In this manner, one rotation of the object took 3.4 sec, and because the stimulus rotated three times within a trial, recycling the 72 frames twice more, the total trial duration was 10.2 sec. Starting and ending positions for every stimulus were generated such that the plane of the four lines was nearly parallel to the line of sight. The first frame began with the plane 2.5° out of parallel to the right (line D slightly to the right of the viewing axis) and the 72d frame ended with the plane 2.5° out of parallel to the left. Perfect alignment was avoided because the overlap of the four lines caused a striking increase in momentary brightness of the display.

2. The rate of the secondary motion followed a cosinusoid $(1 - \cos \alpha)$. Let 0° represent frame 1 (nearly aligned with the line of sight); 90°, frame 19 (nearly orthogonal to the line of sight); 180°, frame 37 (again, nearly parallel); and 270°, frame 55 (again, nearly orthogonal). At frame 1 the rigidity-violating line was the original position. By frame 19 the line had moved to half its maximum displacement, by frame 37 to its maximal displacement, and by frame 55 back to half. From frame 72 and back to frame 1, the line returned to its initial position. Phenomenally, it was at least as compelling to see this line leaving the plane of the others, even though all elements remained end aligned, as it was to see it move laterally within the plane.

3. Initial values for CB and me were 0.10 unit, and those for SR 0.15 unit. Consider two factors about these initial displacements. First, their value is 10% (or 15%) of

the width of the spinning plane, and second, given that the two lines could be as close as 0.067 unit (or 6.7%), an occasional trial had the ordinal positions of the two lines exchanged. This, of course, was an obvious sign of nonrigidity and made for an easy trial. Over all blocks, however, such an exchange happened only once or twice for each subject.

4. My initial values were 0.10 and those for CB and SR, 0.15. As for condition 1, there was an occasional trial that transposed ordinal positions of moving lines with a static line. This occurred because the initial ratios could be generated to be as high as 0.988 and because any cross ratio greater than 1.0 has transposed elements, A with B or C with D. Because no cross ratio less than 0.191 could be generated, given the constraints, decreases in the cross ratio of 0.15 and 0.10 never involved transposition (B with C).

5. Across the 28 blocks of my data, the main effect of performance for motions of lines A through D was highly reliable, $F(3, 81) = 8.14$, $p < 0.0001$. Across 16 blocks SR's data showed essentially the same pattern, $F(3, 45) = 5.27$, $p < 0.005$; as did CB's across 20 blocks, $F(3, 57) = 9.76$, $p < 0.0001$. Quadratic trend tests were all reliable, with accuracy of detecting motions of lines B and C significantly higher than those for A and D: For me, $F(1, 81) = 19.5$; for SR, $F(1, 45) = 13.1$; and for CB, $F(1, 57) = 20.43$; all of us had $p < 0.001$.

6. Across 39 blocks of trials there was no regular variation in my data, $F(3, 144) = 1.03$, $p = 0.38$; none in those of SR over 28 blocks, $F(3, 81) = 0.81$, $p = 0.49$; and none for CB over 26, $F(3, 75) = 0.63$, $p = 0.60$. These results are further supported by trend analyses. The displacement hypothesis predicts an upwardly turned parabola. Although all three participants appear to show a weak trend in this direction, none was reliable at the usual statistical criterion of 0.05: For me, $F(1, 114) = 3.35$, $p = 0.07$; for SR, $F(1, 81) = 0.99$, $p = 0.35$; and for CB, $F(1, 75) = 0.83$, $p = 0.37$.

Secondary analyses support these findings. Consider first the data from condition 1. Although displacement was the primary experimental variable, change in the cross ratio was recorded for each trial in each block. For each observer, then, we can pool within a block all nonrigid trials in which the observer incorrectly reported the trial as rigid and compare these values with those for nonrigid trials correctly reported as rigid. My mean of median cross ratio change values for incorrect and correct trials was 0.034 and 0.052, $t(23) = 4.49$, $p < 0.001$; those for SR were 0.061 and 0.121, $t(14) = 3.37$, $p < 0.01$; and those for CB, 0.042 and 0.103, $t(14) = 2.63$, $p < 0.05$.

Finally, consider d' analyses, which measure observer sensitivity independent of response bias. As expected, all viewers showed monotonically decreasing performance with decrease in the within-block cross ratio variation. At cross ratio changes of 0.100, 0.050, 0.025, and 0.013, my d' scores were 2.90, 2.17, 1.19, and 0.03, respectively. Values for SR at cross ratio changes of 0.150, 0.075, 0.038, and 0.019 were 2.42, 1.54, 0.67, and 0.27, respectively; and corresponding values for CB, 2.87, 1.94, 0.71, and 0.00. My sensitivity remained above chance at changes of 0.025, and for SR and CB at 0.038.

7. Under condition 1 all viewers participated in 15 blocks. I demonstrated the same main effect as before, $F(3, 42) = 23.6$, $p < 0.001$, with a reliable quadratic trend, $F(1, 42) = 65.2$, $p < 0.001$. SR showed the same pattern, $F(3, 42) = 5.01$, $p < 0.005$, and $F(1, 42) = 14.67$, $p < 0.001$ for main effect and quadratic trend, respectively; as did RM, $F(3, 42) = 7.11$, $p < 0.001$, and $F(1, 42) = 16.3$, $p < 0.001$.

Under condition 2 all viewers participated in 20 blocks. There were no reliable main effects at an alpha level of 0.05: $F(3, 57) = 2.26$, 1.38, and 1.36 for SR, RM, and me, respectively. Trend analyses were computed by using the mean distances of each element to the axis of rotation (minus the average distance of all elements from that axis) as trend weights. For example, the mean distance of lines A through D from the axis of rotation for me were 7.46, 3.80, 0.94, and 2.28 arbitrary units, respectively. The grand mean of these values is 3.62. Thus the trend weights used in analysis of variance are 3.84, 0.18, -2.68, and -1.34, respectively, for A through D. For none of the observers were these trend tests reliable: For me, $F(1, 57) = 0.30$; for SR, $F(1, 57) = 1.10$; and for RM, $F(1, 57) = 1.69$.

To test the Weber fraction hypothesis, a series of partial correlations were calculated from the trial-by-trial data of condition 1. Let $r_{jc.w}$ stand for the partial correlation between the judgments of nonrigidity (with 1 the code for a correct judgment and 0 for an incorrect judgment) and the amount of change in the cross ratio with the Weber fraction of secondary to primary motion removed. Similarly, let $r_{jw.c}$ stand for the partial correlation between judgment and the Weber fraction with the change in cross ratio removed. The data of all three observers showed larger values for $r_{jc.w}$ than for $r_{jw.c}$: Those for me were 0.50 and 0.25; for SR, 0.25 and 0.18; and for RM, 0.36 and 0.03. Values were reliably larger for RM and me, $\chi^2 = 6.88$ and 5.78, $p < 0.05$, respectively, but not for SR. These data are consistent with the idea that change in cross ratio, and not a Weber fraction, is the primary cause of the results. Correlations for the results of condition 2 corroborate this view. For SR, RM, and me, $r = 0.07, 0.13$, and -0.04, respectively, offering no support for the Weber fraction.

8. Line A, the highest rung, was placed at an average height of 1.0 unit, B at a height of 0.70 unit, and C at 0.40 unit. Line D was always at 0.00 and stayed in place as if firmly on the ground. It, like A, bounded the length of the ladder. Lines A, B, and C could vary in height in their placement, up or down by as much as 0.09 unit. Thus A was randomly placed between 1.09 and 0.91 units above the base (line D) and so forth. This generated a somewhat different population of cross ratios, with fewer as low or as high as in experiments 1 and 2. The modal cross ratio for these stimuli was 0.780, with a minimum and maximum of 0.390 and 0.921, respectively.

Toppling was through a projected path of 90°, from fully erect to prone on the plane of support. The movement was accomplished linearly, through successive presentation of 31 frames, with a stimulus rotation of 3° per frame. Each frame was presented for 57 msec, for a cycle duration of 1.77 sec. To make stimuli more comparable with those in the previous study, the toppling cycle was repeated three times, giving the observer three opportunities to view the stimulus over 5.3 sec.

9. The rate of motion of the rigidity-violating line(s), again, was a cosinusoid $(1 - \cos \alpha)$. Unlike experiments 1 and 2, however, the motion was only from 0° to 90° of that function. That is, each toppling cycle began with the two stimuli identical, ended with the rigidity-violating element most out of alignment, and at 45° (frame 16) that element was 29% through its displacement. Phenomenally, this motion appeared as accelerated lengthening or shortening of the end segment when lines A or ABC moved, and it appeared as the sliding of one element when it involved B or C. Unlike those in experiment 1, the lines of the stimuli in this study were nearly always seen as coplanar.

10. I began a session by specifying changes of 0.10, and SR and CB began with 0.15, as before. These values correspond to 11.4 and 17% of the ladder height. Because stimuli were generated with cross ratios no higher than 0.93, few trials presented transpositions, and these occurred only for CB and SR at the change value of 0.15.

11. In my condition 1 data, across 57 blocks, the main effect was highly reliable, $F(3, 168) = 10.47$, $p < 0.0001$, as it was for SR across 27 blocks, $F(3, 78) = 5.01$, $p < 0.005$, and CB across 25, $F(3, 72) = 3.96, p < 0.05$. Quadratic trends for all three viewers were reliable: For me, $F(1, 168) = 24.23, p < 0.0001$; for SR, $F(1, 78) = 7.64$, $p < 0.01$; and for CB, $F(1, 72) = 11.27, p < 0.005$. The Weber fraction hypothesis

would predict that motion of line C should be easier to detect than motion of line B,which in turn would be easier than that of A. Results show detection of motions in line A inferior to the others, with no difference between B and C. The real test, however, concerns lines A, B, and C. A hypothesis that predicts detectability of secondary radial motion to be a function of the length of the radial arm finds no support in the fact that trials with A, B, and C in motion are among the most difficult to detect.

Under condition 2, across my 43 blocks there was no reliable main effect, $F(3, 126) = 1.31$, $p = 0.27$; across 26 blocks none for SR, $F(3, 75) = 0.87$, $p = 0.46$; and across 33 blocks none for CB, $F(3, 96) = 1.12$, $p = 0.34$. No significant quadratic trends were found either: For me, $F(1, 126) = 0.60$, $p = 0.44$; for SR, $F(1, 75) = 0.00$; and for CB, $F(1, 96) = 2.46$, $p = 0.12$. A Weber fraction hypothesis would predict performance for detecting motions of line B to be worse than that for C, which clearly did not occur in any of the three sets of data. It would also predict that the conjoined motions of lines A, B, and C would be most easily detected, and this did not occur either.

Secondary analyses support the primary results. Under condition 1 nonrigid stimuli incorrectly reported as rigid had reliably smaller changes in cross ratio than did those correctly reported as nonrigid: Means of medians were 0.037 for incorrect and 0.050 for correct trials for me, $t(13) = 2.5$, $p < 0.05$; 0.039 and 0.069 for SR, $t(18) = 2.46$, $p < 0.05$; and 0.033 and 0.049 for CB, $t(23) = 3.38$, $p < 0.01$.

Signal detection analyses of the condition 2 data were calculated from the tables of Hacker and Ratcliff (1979). At changes in cross ratio of 0.100, 0.050, 0.025, and 0.013, I yielded d' scores of 2.52, 1.10, 0.78, and 0.15, respectively; for changes of 0.150, 0.075, 0.038, and 0.019, SR yielded scores of 2.20, 1.86, 0.63, and 0.15; and CB, scores of 1.91, 1.67, 0.55, and 0.10. SR's sensitivity in this experiment was almost identical with her sensitivity in experiment 1; whereas the sensitivites for CB and me were somewhat less.

12. As a proof of cross ratio invariance at nonpreferred viewpoints, consider the following: Imagine a static frame of one of my stimuli on a film screen. If the observer moves around the theater at different distances and angles from the center of the screen, this situation is logically identical with the screen rotating and dilating with a fixed image on it. The cross ratio of angles projected from that image will remain constant regardless of where the observer moves, according to the projected-angles proof of chapter 6. Now, when the next frame of the stimulus sequence is displayed, the cross ratio has not changed when measured at the preferred viewpoint, nor has it changed measured elsewhere. And the same will be true for all subsequent frames.

13. The main effect of stimulus position was reliable under condition 1, $F(3, 57) = 13.36$, $p < 0.0001$, as was the quadratic trend, $F(1, 57) = 39.4$, $p < 0.0001$. Under condition 2, the main effect just missed statistical significance, $F(3, 57) = 2.66$, $p = 0.056$, but the quadratic trend was not close, $F(1, 57) = 2.19$, $p = 0.145$.

14. Video projection systems use a front-projection technique, and the projection surface on inexpensive models is concave, rather than convex, with respect to the viewer. More expensive models have flat screens. The reason for the curvature appears to be for ease of focus and uniformity of brightness and because it was thought that people like curved screens. As in standard television, these curved projection systems create distortions for all viewers not sitting directly in line with the projectors and the projection surface.

15. Hochberg (1971), in his review of Pirenne (1970), makes a similar point. Also Kanade and Kender (1983) discussed skewed symmetries in affine-transformable figures that lend some substance to this conjecture.

16. This idea is supported by results of Hay and Pick (1966). Under a control condition of a prismatic adaptation study, they found that the observers could not discern curvature in straight lines subtending 45° of ±0.6 diopters. In addition, a curvature resulting from a lens of 3 diopters can appear straight after a few minutes of adaptation (Rock 1984).

Chapter 8   Limitations and Extensions of Cross Ratios

1. To make the difference between cross ratio and density clearer, consider again figure 7.1. The cross ratio can be measured on line L_1 and on L_2, projecting from one to the other or onto any other line. I am measuring density, however, only on L_1, the distal object in the world. To be sure, density could be measured at the projective surface, L_2, but problems arise that I wish to avoid. With polar projection, as used in these experiments, the density of a point with a *rigid* object measured on the projection plane *changes* during rotation. For example, the density at point B is lower than at B' because A is relatively farther away from B than A' is from B'. And if L_1 continues to rotate clockwise, the density at B' continues to rise until the plane is aligned with the line of sight.

For a planar array of lines, the density indexes used in this chapter are invariant under reflection, dilation, translation, and parallel-projected rotation—but for me this is not good enough.

2. Murdock (1960) used distinctiveness, the inverse of this formulation, in an account of memory for a list of items. Distance for him was the ordinal place difference among items.

3. The entire set of calculations took one CPU week on a Hewlett-Packard 1000L Series computer.

4. Block duration was 4–15 min according to condition; sessions varied from 30 min to 2 hr at the discretion of the viewer. Short breaks were taken frequently. When performance was better than 75% on a block, displacements were halved; when it was 75%, they remained the same, and when it was less than 75%, displacements were doubled.

For stimuli with three parallel lines, imagine lines A and C fixed on the surface of a plane 1 unit apart. Line B appears randomly in a position between 0.1 (near A) and 0.9. Index 4 density was noted for each element. The transparent plane rotated around a point three-quarters the distance from A to C. For stimuli with four elements, lines A through D were at mean positions of 0.00, 0.33, 0.67, and 1.00 along the plane. Each, however, could occur randomly within an area that was 0.30 unit wide centered on these values. Again, density at each point was noted. The axis of rotation was at 0.80 unit, typically between lines C and D. And for stimuli with seven elements, lines A through G appeared at mean positions of 0.00, 0.17, 0.33, 0.50, 0.67, 0.83, and 1.00 unit, within a range of 0.15. Density values were again recorded, and the axis of rotation was always between E and F, at 0.75 unit.

5. Condition 1: I participated in 15 blocks, and the main effect of ordinal position was reliable, $F(2, 28) = 5.82$, $p < 0.01$. Index 4 densities were recorded on each trial for the rigidity-violating line at the middle point in its excursion (on frames 1 or 37). Values for lines A, B, and C for me were 0.556, 0.848, and 0.588, respectively, as shown in figure 8.3. By normalizing these values around their grand mean, we can use the density values as trend weights in an analysis of variance. Because the mean of these values is 0.664, this value can be subtracted from each mean to yield trend weights of -0.108, 0.184, and -0.076 for A, B, and C, respectively. The density trend was highly reliable, $F(1, 28) = 10.18$, $p < 0.005$, indicating strong correlation

between the two data sets. The same patterns were found for SR across 15 blocks: There was a main effect of ordinal position of rigidity-violating element, $F(2, 28) = 14.69$, $p < 0.0001$, and a reliable trend for density as a predictor of performance, $F(1, 28) = 25.07$, $p < 0.001$. The pattern repeated for RM across 20 blocks: $F(2, 38) = 11.58$, $p < 0.001$ for the main effect, and $F(1, 38) = 21.89$, $p < 0.001$ for density. Signal detection analyses revealed the same patterns. Concerning the Weber fraction hypothesis, no reliable effects were found: For me, $F(1, 28) = 0.02$, $p = 0.89$; for SR, $F(1, 28) = 0.006$, $p = 0.94$; and for RM, $F(1, 38) = 0.82$, $p = 0.37$.

Condition 2: My main effect and density trend were reliable, $F(3, 42) = 23.7$, and $F(1, 42) = 65.2$; as they were for SR, $F(3, 42) = 14.7$ and $F(1, 42) = 13.9$; and for RM, $F(3, 57) = 11.2$ and $F(1, 57) = 27.6$; all of us had $p < 0.001$. No Weber fraction trends were reliable: For me, $F(1, 42) = 2.15$, $p = 0.15$; for SR, $F(1, 42) = 0.62$, $p = 0.44$; and for RM, $F(1, 57) = 0.06$, $p = 0.81$.

Condition 3: My main effect was reliable, $F(6, 84) = 16.9$, as was the density trend, $F(1, 84) = 96.0$; for both, $p < 0.0001$. And the pattern repeats again for both SR, $F(6, 84) = 7.8$ and $F(1, 84) = 77.9$; and for RM, $F(6, 114) = 14.6$, and $F(1, 114) = 61.1$, all $p < 0.0001$. Unlike the previous two conditions, however, there was some relation between Weber fraction and performance. There was no reliable trend for me, $F(1, 84) = 1.89$, $p = 0.17$, but there was for both SR, $F(1, 84) = 4.66$, $p < 0.05$, and for RM, $F(1, 114) = 6.0$, $p < 0.02$. These effects are not simply due to increased correlation between Weber fraction and density (which did indeed occur). But to test for this, I analyzed the data on a trial-by-trial basis. Point biserial partial correlations were performed, and both density and Weber fraction emerged as reliable correlates of performance. For density the partial correlations were, for me, $r = 0.38$, $t(207) = 5.82$; for SR, $r = 0.36$, $t(207) = 5.50$; and for RM, $r = 0.28$, $t(287) = 4.91$, all $p < 0.0001$. For Weber fractions, correlations were somewhat, but not reliably, smaller: For me, $r = -0.14$, $t(207) = -2.08$, $p < 0.05$; for SR, $r = -0.12$, $t(207) = -3.07$, $p < 0.005$; and for RM, $r = -0.19$, $t(287) = -3.17$, $p < 0.005$. One explanation for this effect is that the farther an element is from the axis, the more difficult it is to discern nonrigidity in the plane as a whole. The reason for this may be due to display factors. At 21.3 frames/sec, each stimulus rotated once in 3.38 sec. Lines near the axis of rotation have small displacements across consecutive frames. Those farthest away, however, have large displacements, as much as 23 min of arc per frame. Phenomenally, these lines appeared more blurred or subject to motion aliasing.

6. Generally, more data were needed than in experiment 5. Given that the null hypothesis can never be proven, ample opportunity must be given for it to be falsified. Toward this end, I participated in 73 blocks under condition 1, 40 under condition 2, and 26 under condition 3; SR participated in 50, 50, and 30 blocks under the three conditions, respectively; and RM participated in 30, 20, and 20.

Condition 1: My main effect was not reliable at an alpha level of 0.05, $F(2, 144) = 2.74$, $p = 0.068$. No density trend can be predicted because equal density across all positions is, literally, no trend. The Weber fraction showed no reliable trend, $F(1, 44) = 0.09$, $p = 0.76$. For SR neither the main effect nor the Weber fraction trend was reliable, $F(2, 98) = 1.94$, $p = 0.15$, and $F(1, 98) = 0.10$, $p = 0.90$. For RM, the main effect was significant, $F(2, 58) = 6.74$, $p < 0.003$, but the Weber fraction trend was not, $F(1, 58) = 0.53$, $p = 0.47$.

Condition 2: My main effect was vanishingly small, $F(3, 117) = 0.05$, $p = 0.98$, and there was no Weber fraction trend. For SR, on the other hand, there was a reliable main effect resulting almost entirely from her difficulty in discerning motions of line D, $F(3, 147) = 6.3$, $p < 0.0005$. This effect, however, cannot be attributed to a

Weber fraction, $F(1, 147) = 0.58$, $p = 0.45$. RM, like me, showed neither a main effect, $F(3, 57) = 1.09$, $p = 0.36$, nor a Weber fraction trend, $F(1, 57) = 1.92$, $p = 0.28$. Condition 3: I showed neither a main effect nor trend, $F(6, 150) = 0.28$, $p = 0.95$ and $F(1, 150) = 0.03$, $p = 0.86$. There was, however, a main effect for SR, $F(6, 174) = 3.60$, $p < 0.002$, but no Weber fraction trend, $F(1, 174) = 0.24$, $p = 0.63$. And there were marginal effects of both for RM: $F(6, 114) = 1.823$, $p = 0.10$ and $F(1, 114) = 3.48$, $p = 0.065$, respectively. RM did not repeat a reliable Weber fraction trend for experiment 5 under condition 3. The nonuniformities in data sets, although relatively modest, are somewhat peculiar. For RM under the three-element condition and for SR under the four-element condition, the line that was by itself on one side of the axis of rotation was relatively difficult to discern when moving in a rigidity-violating manner. These results are clearly not effects of proximity to the axis of rotation because the Weber fraction hypothesis predicts that performance ought to be *better* the closer the rigidity-violating line is to the axis.

One possibility for the reliable effects of SR and RM is that different exponential constants, k, may be used by different observers. The lower the value, the more the central elements of the display will generally have higher denisties, compared with peripheral ones. Thus the top two panels of figure 8.2d would show higher central peaks for B and C of the four-element array and C, D, and E for the seven-element array. Conversely, the higher the k, the more the peripheral elements show peaks. Given that throughout the experiment the exponential constant was fixed at 3.33, the nonrigid trials involving central elements might be relatively harder for a viewer who is modeled better with a lower constant and relatively easier for those modeled better by a higher constant. To assess this possibility, quadratic trend tests were performed on the data of SR and RM under condition 3. Both were reliable; for SR it was a concave parabolic function, $F(1, 174) = 2.96$, $p < 0.05$, and for RM a convex function, $F(1, 114) = 8.09$, $p < 0.005$. Systematically retransforming the data by the differential weights obtained from the different exponential constants, I estimated the best-fitting exponential constant for the data of SR to be 1.6 and that for RM to be 6.7. It should come as no surprise that the constant of 3.33 fit my own data best, as extensive pilot testing indicated a value in that range to yield the flattest functions across ordinal positions for me. Unfortunately, the patterns of results from conditions 1 and 2 do not lend themselves to an assessment of the parameter values of the exponential constants.

7. Ullman (1984) proposed an incremental model for rigidity detection like the spring-dipole model of Julesz (1971). Each pair of points in an array can be connected by a spring with a spring constant associated with it. Ullman assumed that lower constants could be used for longer springs (corresponding to less dense regions in an array) or that long distances between points could be ignored altogether.

Chapter 9   Cross Ratios versus Flow Vectors

1. In experiment 7 the secondary motion of one element was uniform with respect to the primary motion of the other three—its instantaneous displacement is simply more or less by a constant, the difference in its value of y. Thus, unlike the displays of previous experiments, these allowed perception of the fourth element in rigid configuration with the others, but not on the same plane.

2. Placement of the four parallel lines was again random within certain regions. The modal spacing was uniform, just as in experiments 1, 2, 4, and 5. Displacements within these regions were also the same. The course of optic flow of all elements was cosinusoidal. The stimuli started at a mean distance of 14.5 eye heights (for all

four lines), came as close as 5.5 eye heights, receded to 14.5 again, and repeated this cycle two more times. A cycle consisted of 120 frames, each presented for 37 msec, for a cycle duration of 4.44 sec and a trial duration of 13.3 sec.

3. Under condition 1, across 40 blocks I showed no main effect, $F(3, 117) = 2.02, p = 0.11$; nor did SR across 30 blocks, $F(3, 87) = 1.46, p = 0.23$. On the other hand, CB showed a strong main effect across 30 blocks, $F(3, 87) = 10.0, p < 0.001$. Essentially the same pattern accrued for tests of quadratic trend: My trend was only marginal, $F(1, 117) = 3.33, p = 0.07$; for SR it was essentially nil, $F(1, 87) = 0.82, p = 0.41$; but for CB it was as prominent as any in this set of studies, $F(1, 87) = 71.6, p < 0.0001$.

Under condition 2, all effects were reliable: Across my 14 blocks, $F(3, 39) = 12.66$, $p < 0.001$; 36 blocks for SR, $F(3, 105) = 5.68, p < 0.002$; and 28 blocks for CB, $F(3, 89) = 5.02, p < 0.01$. All viewers showed reliable quadratic trends: For me, $F(1, 39) = 37.9$; for SR, $F(1, 105) = 17.02$; and for CB, $F(1, 81) = 15.99$; all $p < 0.001$.

4. Across blocks and trials of condition 1, the correlation between eye height and cross ratio change was high: $r = 0.43, 0.28$, and 0.53; and under condition 2, $r = 0.42$, 0.51, and 0.62, for SR, CB, and me, respectively; all $p < 0.0001$.

As before, changes in cross ratio were recorded for condition 1 and differential eye heights for condition 2. Under condition 1, any support for cross ratio should be found in the means of median changes in cross ratio for incorrect and correct trials. For me, they were 0.037 and 0.046, respectively, $t(29) = 1.15, p = 0.15$; for SR they were 0.083 and 0.087, $t(29) = 0.42, p = 0.51$. Thus the secondary data of neither viewer support the idea that cross ratio is perceived in these displays. CB, on the other hand, showed a marked difference: 0.039 and 0.119, $t(23) = 6.57$, $p < 0.0001$. Thus cross ratio did seem to play a role in his perception. Under condition 2, eye height differentials for incorrect and correct trials were recorded. My means of medians were 0.012 and 0.035 eye height, $t(18) = 6.09, p < 0.001$; for SR they were 0.032 and 0.052, $t(27) = 4.04, p < 0.001$; and for CB they were 0.016 and 0.029, $t(22) = 4.29, p < 0.001$. Thus information about differential eye heights appeared to be used by all three participants.

5. Simpson (1983) also showed that cross ratios are not always useful. His purpose, however, was to demonstrate that cross ratios are not necessary for the perception of rigidity, but because he never measured nor varied them to test the sensitivity of the perceptual system, he did not address the sufficiency of cross ratios for the perception.

6. The displays of experiment 7 actually rotated a small amount. When the front element (line A) of the stimulus was at a projected distance of 13 eye heights, the stimulus plane was nearly parallel to the line of sight (176°), but when it was at a projected distance of 4 eye heights, it was more out of parallel (166°), yielding 10° rotation.

7. The instantaneous change in θ with respect to β is given by

$$d\theta/d\beta = \frac{r(z \cos \beta - x \sin \beta) - r^2}{x^2 + z^2 + r^2 - 2r(z \cos \beta - x \sin \beta)}.$$

This relation does not simplify as handsomely as Eqs. (9.2)–(9.4), but we should be wary of criteria that assume perceptual, and mathematical algorithms should both strive for simplicity. Cumbersomeness of expression does not, by itself, lend force against perceptual utility (Marr 1982).

It also happens that the motion of the planarity-violating line is similar to the nonrelational cue used in experiments 1 through 6—its lateral displacement without respect to the positions of the other elements. Here, however, the displacements are greater for elements farther away from the center of the circling plane, whereas with the nonrelational cue, secondary displacements would be uniform regardless of position.

8. The random placement of elements within the plane was identical with experiment 1. The center of the object plane's path was six times the width of the mean stimulus, and the radius of that path was equal to the mean stimulus width. Circulation time was 3.4 sec, equal to the rotation times of experiments 1, 2, 4, 5, and 6. Again, 72 frames of the stimulus were shown for 47 msec each. Frame 1 showed the stimulus closest to the observer, frame 37 farthest away, frame 19 rightmost, and frame 55 leftmost. Each trial presented three circulations. The secondary motion of the planarity-violating line followed a cosinusoid. As before, the movement of this line could be seen as nonrigid lateral motion within the object plane or as circular motion out of the plane. It was most readily seen as the latter by both viewers.

9. Under condition 1, my data across 40 blocks showed no reliable main effect, $F(3, 117) = 1.76$, $p = 0.16$, but there was a small parabolic trend, $F(1, 117) = 4.89$, $p < 0.03$. RM's data showed a similar pattern across 40 blocks: No main effect, $F(3, 117) = 1.89$, $p = 0.135$, but a small parabolic trend, $F(1, 117) = 5.44$, $p < 0.025$. These trends are not consistent with the idea that displacement patterns are the only information used in the perception of these displays. But trial-by-trial analyses show that cross ratios seem not to be involved in these trends. Median values of cross ratio change were recorded for correct and incorrect trials, but neither participant showed a difference. For me, the cross ratio change values for incorrect and correct trials were 0.037 and 0.033, respectively, $t(32) = -0.46$, $p = 0.64$; and for RM they were 0.023 and 0.028, $t(28) = 1.02$, $p = 0.32$. Thus these analyses provide no support for the cross ratio.

   Under condition 2, I showed a large main effect and parabolic trend, $F(3, 87) = 5.97$ and $F(1, 87) = 16.6$, $p < 0.001$; as did RM, $F(3, 87) = 9.56$ and $F(1, 87) = 25.47$, $p < 0.001$.

10. It is interesting that, whereas Gibson's position on invariants and Johansson's on projective geometry are closely allied, the two were never merged. The lack of synthesis may have been due to an overriding conflict. Gibson, while espousing invariants, could not fully acknowledge the importance of projective geometry because it has no concept of occlusion. On the other hand, Johansson, while espousing projective geometry, doubted the complete utility of invariants to perception because so much of his work relies on decoding principles. This work clearly sides with Johansson.

Chapter 10   Ways of Wayfinding

1. Consider an individual running through light brush, fleeing from danger and trying to avoid running into branches and trees. Judging the direction of movement is couched as the angle between the current linear path and that needed to be taken in order to avoid the object, usually specified as a continuous uniform turn. The solution to this problem, and others to follow, is an application of a standard physics problem (see, for example, Sears et al. 1980) with the addition of some psychological assumptions. We start with the equation: $F_0 = mv^2/r$, where F_0 is the centrifugal, or outward, force on the object in question, m is its mass in kilograms, v its velocity in meters per second during linear movement, and r the radius of the circle whose perimeter forms the path of avoidance. This radius must be small enough to permit the runner to skirt around the tree. For a circular path, the outward force exerted is specified in the given equation. This force must be counteracted by an equal centrifugal (inward) force. Human beings accomplish this by leaning into the direction that they turn. This lean cannot be too extreme, given a flat terrain, otherwise slips will occur as a result of inadequate friction between foot and ground. Given soft, flat turf, a person can probably lean as much as $25°$.

A normal runner should be able to maintain a velocity of 5 m/sec (about 11 mph) for a moderate distance. If the individual weighs 65 kg (about 143 lbs), then the following relation holds: $F_0 = 1625/r$. If the runner leans inward by 25°, then $F_i = \sin \alpha \, mg$, where α is the angle of lean, m is the person's mass, and g is the force of gravity (9.80 m/sec²). Substituting these values, $F_i = 292.2$ kg·m/sec². Because F_0 and F_i must be equal, $292.2 = 1625/r$. By rearranging terms, we obtain $r = 5.56$ m. Thus, given the assumptions above, the radius of curvature that can be undertaken in a path of avoidance is 5.56 m.

Next we must determine how wide a clearance the runner needs to give the tree. If we assume that its trunk is vertical and has minimal thickness, the clearance is the sine of 25° (0.4226), the angle of lean, times the runner's height. If the runner is 1.75 m tall (about 5'8"), then the clearance needed is 0.74 m. Because a runner's foot is not infinitesimally narrow, we should probably increase this value to about 1.0 m. The end result is equivalent to a situation in which there is no inertia and the runner is moved laterally about a half-body width, or about 0.25 m, enough to just clear the object along the linear path of motion. The most important number to fall out of this analysis is the distance from the tangent of the circle to the potential object of impact, 3.48 m.

Consider next reaction time. Let us assume that it takes 0.75 sec for the runner to recognize the presence of the tree, yielding an additional 3.75 m traveled during the interval. And finally, we cannot guarantee that the runner's footfall will be appropriate for turning. In particular, one cannot turn unless a foot is on the ground, and one cannot usually turn well unless one is pivoting on the foot opposite the direction of the turn. Given that a step cycle (two full strides) takes about 700 msec when running at 5 m/sec (Carlsöö 1972; but for higher speeds, see Lee et al. 1982), an average of 350 msec must pass before the runner will be in a good position to initiate a turn in a given direction. Assuming further that the footfall modulation time is independent of the reaction time, an additional 1.75 m is traveled.

Thus, in order to veer 0.25 m (a half-body width) away from impending collision along a linear course of movement, a runner needs to be 8.98 m away from the object, and arctan (0.25/8.98) = 1.6°, the *maximum* angle through which the runner can correct the course of locomotion under the assumptions stated. Different estimates of the runner's height and weight, of reaction time, and of running speed alter this assessment little. Reworking the analyses for walking indicates a need of about 5 to 10°.

2. Consider first driving a car in two situations: (1) braking for a pedestrian or animal and (2) swerving to avoid a stationary object while maintaining speed. Because vastly different estimates can be obtained for different vehicular speeds, two will be considered: velocities of 13.2 and 26.4 m/sec (30 and 60 mph). All estimates are made for conditions involving a dry road with good tires, allowing standard traction.

(1) Braking distances vary, but the Road Research Laboratory (1963, p. 378) suggested that they can be fit by the function: $D = 0.053v^2$, where D is braking distance in feet and v is the car's velocity in miles per hour. Converting to metric units: $D = 0.084v^2$. At 26.4 m/sec, then, the braking distance is 58.5 m, but at 13.2 m/sec, it is only 14.6 m. The Laboratory (p. 350) reported that reaction times of 2.0 and 3.0 sec are common under normal driving conditions at speeds of 30 and 60 mph; Probst et al. (1984) gave somewhat lower values. If we use the lower value from the Road Research Laboratory, the distances traveled before initiating braking are 52.8 m when driving at 26.4 m/sec, and 26.4 m for 13.2 m/sec. Summing the distances traveled during reaction time and braking yields distances of 111.3 m and 41.0 m for the faster and slower speeds, respectively. If we consider the crucial width of concern to be one

traffic lane wide, typically about 6 m, then the distance from the middle of the lane, where the driver is traveling, to the outermost boundary of this path is about 3 m: arctan(3/111.3) and arctan(3/41) equal 1.5° and 4.2°, respectively, for the two velocities.

(2) Swerving assumes a curved path and, as with the runner, the curved path is circular. If the car has a mass of 1000 kg and is traveling at a velocity of 26.4 m/sec, then $F_0 = 697,000/r$. For a speed of 13.2 m/sec, $F_0 = 174,000/r$. Unlike the runner, the car cannot lean. Instead, the driver must count on friction between tires and road surface. The Road Research Laboratory estimated the coefficient of friction μ_s between a good tire and a good road surface under dry-weather conditions to be about 0.80. This means that the normal force sustainable without the car skidding sideways during a turn is $F_i = \mu_s mg$, or $F_i = 7840$ kg·m/sec². Because F_0 must equal F_i, $r = 89$ m for the faster speed and $r = 22$ m for the slower. If the distance from the center of the front bumper to safely clear an object is about 2 m, the forward distance traveled during the swerve is 18.8 m and 9.2 m for two speeds, respectively. Add to these the reaction-time-interval distances of 52.8 m and 26.4 m; then the summed distance to correct the direction of motion so as to just miss the object is 71 m and 35.6 m: arctan(1/71) = 50 min of arc, and arctan(1/35.6) = 1.6 deg of arc.

Consider next pilots. The data estimating landing accuracy for a commercial aircraft are given in Hasbrook (1975). A 3° glide slope is standard for approach. Assume that the plane requires 4000 ft of contact with the runway during landing, that the runway is 8000 ft long, that the pilot should land the plane at the 1000-ft mark from the beginning of the runway, and that the current position of the plane is 2 miles out at an altitude of 600 ft. A 3° approach will land the craft safely, a 2.35° glide slope will run the plane off the end of the runway, and a 3.3° glide slope will land the plane too short. Thus, ignoring the asymmetry around 3°, the pilot must be able to judge the point of impact within 30 min of arc. Pilots of smaller planes need less accuracy.

Finally, consider a downhill skier. If the skier's mass is 70 kg (about 150 lb) and the velocity is 13.5 m/sec (about 30 mph), a 45° lean into the hill generates a force of 485 kg·m/sec², with a turn radius of 26.5 m, ignoring slippage across the snow. If the coefficient of friction between the skis and snow is 0.1, the instantaneous radius becomes 265 m. To avoid an obstacle (like a small rock), the skier would traverse 5 deg of arc along the circular path, or move forward about 23 m. If reaction time is 1.0 sec, an additional 13.5 m will be traversed, yielding a total distance of 36.5 m; and arctan(0.5/36.5) = 0.78°.

3. For textbooks, see Ballard and Brown (1982), Bartley (1969), Brown and Deffenbacher (1979), Bruce and Green (1985), Coren et al. (1984), Dember and Warm (1979), Goldstein (1984), Haber and Hershenson (1973), Hochberg (1978b), Michaels and Carello (1981), and Schiff (1980); and for articles of expository or technical content, see Cutting (1981b), Cutting and Proffitt (1981), Hochberg and Smith (1955), and Neisser (1977).

4. Regan and Beverley's (1982) study had one important difference from the others. In addition to forward linear movement, they introduced lateral motion in the display that mimicked looking off to the side at an object. I call this simulated fixation, and I use it in the experiments discussed in chapters 12 and 13. The merits of simulated fixation are discussed at the end of chapter 12.

5. See Murray (1967) and Carlsöö (1972) for an analysis of lateral oscillations in gait. I would argue, and later do, that these may actually help direction finding.

6. Ahumada also found that observers overestimated the aim point when trials ended nearest the runway and underestimated it when they ended farther way. Such results are consistent with night landing accidents.

7. Warren coined the term *egomotion* for the sensation of moving through an environment. Vection is another term for the same thing. I have used neither. "Vection" is arcane, and "egomotion," I believe, is apt to confuse, because with Gibson (1954a) I reserve the term "motion" for the change in position of objects and "movement" for the change in position of an observer (or observer parts, as in eye movements). Thus I suggest that the term "egomotion" is not needed, and that its extension, *egomovement*, is redundant.

8. Neither Ahumada (unpublished) nor Riemersma (1981) claimed that their observers used the focus of expansion for visual guidance.

9. The equations that determine the point of maximum magnification rate are derived as follows: Consider the gerneral case in which an observer is approaching a plane at any angle. The optic angle θ between the line of sight to any point on the plane and the line of movement is

$$\theta = \arctan[x \sin \beta/(D - x \cos \beta)],$$

where β is the angle of incidence between the line of movement and the plane, D is the distance from the current location to the plane along the path of movement, and x is the horizontal distance along the plane to the point under consideration. If the observer moves forward,

$$d\theta/dD = -x \sin \beta/(D^2 - 2Dx \cos \beta + x^2).$$

This equation yields the velocity function of all points on the plane with respect to the fixed point along the path of movement. To obtain the function for magnifications, we must take the second derivative with respect to x:

$$d^2\theta/dDdx = -\sin \beta \cdot (x^2 - D^2)/(D^2 + 2Dx \cos \beta + x^2)^2.$$

The minima and the maximum of this function occur where the third derivative is zero. But the point of maximum rate of magnification is not along the direction of movement except when the approach to the plane is orthogonal (at 90°). Regan and Beverley (1982) claimed that the point of maximum rate of change in magnification lies at the point halfway between the point of impact and the point directly beneath the observer at any one time. My formulation differs from theirs, but they misspecify their optics.

10. Notice that in the last equation in note 9 when β is 0°, or parallel to the plane, the numerator goes to zero.

11. See, for example, Eriksson (1974b), Hay (1966), and Regan and Beverley (1979, 1982).

12. Following La Gournerie, many have noted problems of magnification in pictures, among them Purdy (1960), Hochberg (1978a, 1978b), Lumsden (1980), and Rosinski and Farber (1980). Also, there is a deeper confusion in the literature here than may be apparent. We can talk about magnification measured on the projection plane and speak correctly if that plane is orthogonal to the line of sight. But, as discussed in earlier chapters, planar projections distort proper measurement; measures are to be taken in the spherical coordinates of the optic array. Thus, although magnification can occur on the projection plane (occurring when the direction of motion is directly toward the center of an object), magnification does not occur where it counts—in the optic array.

13. It is true that near-uniform magnifications occur when we approach objects that are relatively distant from us. Noticeable distortions typically occur only when objects are fairly close, presenting their largest projected face to be as much as 15°. Because most objects that we look at and that are important to us are considerably smaller

than this, projective distortions resulting from approach or recession from an object are probably not crucial. Much more serious, however, is the distortion resulting from movement paths that are *not* directly toward objects under scrutiny, and it is always the case that more objects lie off our path of movement than on it. For these objects, planar projections of surfaces distort, and magnification is not the rule.

Chapter 11   Multiple Representations of Optic Flow

1. In some regards, this analysis is an extension of the logic and discussions of Koenderink and van Doorn (1976a, 1976b, 1981), Longuet-Higgins and Prazdny (1980), Prazdny (1981a, 1983a, 1983b), and Regan and Beverley (1982); but most of what I present is my own.
2. Clocksin (1980), Hasbrook (1975), Lee (1974), and Nakayama and Loomis (1974) assumed automorphic mappings around the point extended out from the direction of movement. Lee, unlike the others, used a set of cylindrical coordinates to map flow. This has several advantages over a spherical system, but the choice of an identity point on the cylinder must still be made.

   In spherical mappings there is always at least one fixed point, sometimes more. Brouwer's theorem (see Gellert et al. 1977) in topology states that if *f* is a continuous mapping of an *n*-dimensional ball into itself, then *f* has a fixed point. Occlusions keep most optic array mappings from being automorphic.
3. Some caution must be exercised here. If the optic array is considered a complete sphere, then by Brouwer's theorem it must have at least one fixed point. If, on the other hand, only the truncated section of an optic array projected to one eye is considered, then it need not. Brouwer's theorem holds only for a continuous closed surface, not a bounded surface (such as the optic array clipped by brow ridges, eye lashes, and lids).
4. Harrington et al. (1980) and Harrington and Harrington (1981) studied blur patterns as sources of information for directional guidance and looked for the efficacy of divergence in flow. The focus of expansion would be the source of such divergence. See also Whiteside and Samuel (1970).
5. Lee and Lishman (1977) simply combined them and called the motion *expropriospecific*.
6. Sinusoidal gratings are a standard psychophysical stimulus for the measurement of visual sensitivity. They are called gratings because they look like fuzzy parallel bars. They are sinusoidal in that the luminance profile follows a sine wave. One measure of sinusoidal gratings is cycles per degree of visual angle.
7. Data were computed using the equations given in chapter 12. See also Gordon (1965).
8. Stoffregen (1985) reported that adjustments in stance resulting from optic flow are made to motions that are everywhere below threshold for detection of single moving points of light. Thus motion effects sum over large visual angles.

Chapter 12   Motion Parallax and Linear Movement

1. See, for example, Eriksson (1974a), Gibson (1950), Gogel (1977), Gogel and Tietz (1973), Graham (1951), Hershberger and Urban (1970), Hershberger et al. (1974), Hershberger and Starzec (1974), Johansson (1973a), Rogers and Graham (1979), and Zegers (1948). Motion parallax was formalized by Gibson et al. (1955) and more recently by Koenderink and van Doorn (1975, 1976a, 1981).

   Motion parallax has not met with universal approval as a trustworthy source of information in optic flow. The reasons for this are not entirely clear. Gibson et al.

(1955, p. 373), for example, denied the general utility of motion parallax when looking in the direction of movement. Their comment was terse and unmollified: "In short, motion parallax does not occur . . . for objects ahead during forward locomotion." Strictly this is true, but conceptually this analysis has the same difficulty as Molyneux's premise. Gibson (1976b) realized this flaw but apparently failed to note it in his earlier statement about motion parallax: Although looking exactly in the direction of movement yields no parallax, looking a degree or two off to the side does. Gibson et al. (1955) went on to define and use concepts of motion perspective and focus of expansion because of the difficulties they thought existed in motion parallax. Because the older term, "motion parallax," is perfectly descriptive of the situations I wish to explore, I use it instead.

E. Gibson et al. (1959) also discussed ambiguity in motion parallax. They distinguished two-velocity parallax from flow-velocity parallax, where the former concerns the relative motion of two elements in the visual field and the latter concerns many more. Their qualms were of relativity in motion, noting that two-element parallax does not determine which element is moving against the other or whether both are in motion. The differential motion parallax discussed here is more like the flow-velocity concept and might be called three-velocity or three-element parallax, where an object is fixated and used as a fixed point against which the relative velocities of other objects are compared.

Gordon (1965), citing Helmholtz's description of motion parallax, also suggested that "safe conclusions" concerning real distance as a function of optic flow are not so safe. In particular, he demonstrated that when the observer is undergoing curvilinear translation, Helmholtz's rule does not generally hold: Projections of more distant objects do not necessarily move more slowly in the optic array then nearer ones. But Gordon's is not the only way to construe this situation. In terms of *differential* motion parallax, the curved-path movement case does not present problems.

Finally, consider a terminological point. In note 8 of chapter 1 (and note 7 of chapter 10) I said that, following Gibson (1954a), I would use the term *motion* for displacement of objects in space and *movement* for observer displacement. In studies of optic flow, several authors have discussed *movement parallax* (Eriksson 1974a, Johansson 1973a) resulting from the observer's movement through space, rather than *motion parallax*, which might implicate the motions of objects. Because I discuss parallax as it refers to retinal motions, I have decided to stick with the more traditional term. Gibson (1954a, p. 305) also took this position: "The visual component of stimulation [during locomotion] results from the fact of motion parallax, and consists of differential motions of different parts of the image."

2. Von Kries (1910, p. 372) deferred to Helmholtz when he closed out this passage:

Now these apparent motions are just as useful as those described by Helmholtz for forming estimates of distance; and the probability is that both of them generally contribute to the result in some way, although it would be hard to say exactly how.

The point of chapters 10 through 13 is to show that one aspect of von Kries's analysis relates to differential motion parallax and is much more helpful to direction finding than Helmholtz's analysis (which is also Gibson's) and that these effects can be empirically separated.

In addition to my analysis, Rieger and Lawton (1983) in machine vision have found differential parallax information more useful than other analyses for direction finding.

3. I use the term *shear* for two reasons. First, its common usage implies rips or breakage. As objects undergo motion parallax, their ordinal arrangement in the optic array

often changes. Betweenness is then violated and the projected topology is broken. Second, in affine geometry shear is the movement of one parallel line or plane of affinity against another. This would change a square, for example, into a parallelogram. Gibson (1966) used the term in a different way.

The affine transformations here are similar to the analyses of pictures viewed from the sides, shown in figure 3.1, but without perspective transformation.

4. See, for example, Gibson (1950), Haber and Hershenson (1973), and Schiff (1980).

5. Sedgwick (1983) discussed this type of coordinate system as "environment centered." Although I sympathize with this idea, the environment has no center. Marr's object-centered coordinates suffice.

6. Cutting (1981b), Cutting and Proffitt (1981), and Cutting et al. (1978) defined a center of moment as that point within a coherent structure around which all other points have simplest systematic reference. For a rolling wheel this point would be the axle, but if lights are mounted asymmetrically on that wheel and the surround darkened, the center of moment is typically seen as the centroid (center of gravity) of the configuration of lights. For a human being walking, the center of moment is between the shoulders and hips, those four points considered as the corners of a twisting flat spring. The intersection of stress lines across that spring occur at the center of moment, typically near the navel. From displays of a few lights mounted on joints (Johansson 1973b), viewers can tell the sex of a walker at greater-than-chance accuracy. The information appears to be in the relative motions of the shoulders and hips, dictating the center of moment for that individual. Other structures, such as trees and bushes, also have nested centers of moment. These are similar to the singularities discussed by Koenderink and van Doorn (1976b).

7. Lappin et al. (1980) and Petersik (1979) explored situations like this.

8. See also Gordon (1965) and Whiteside and Samuel (1970).

9. Experiment 9 was first reported at the 4th Meeting of the International Society for Ecological Psychology, Hartford, Connecticut, October 1982.

10. Optic density of the lines corresponded to the distance to each plane, but viewers could not segregate planes until motion began.

11. Computation time for each trial was about 15 sec, a period during which the participant simply waited. Each trial presented a dynamic sequence by rapid successive presentation of 50 static frames, much like a movie projection. These frames were presented at 47 msec each, for a sequence duration of 2.35 sec.

12. If we consider x to be the initial distance from the station point to plane A (the plane closest to the observer), y that to plane B, and z that to C, then the various conditions are determined by ratios of these distances (where $x/y = y/z$). Under condition 1 the planes were far apart, with both ratios equal to 0.63; under condition 2 they were relatively closer, with ratios of 0.82; under condition 3 they were closer still, with ratios of 0.91; and under condition 4 the distance degenerated such that all twelve lines were on the same plane, $x/y = y/z = 1.0$.

13. $F(2, 6) = 6.8$, $p < 0.03$, and $F(4, 12) = 22.8$, $p < 0.0001$, respectively, for the effects of spacing and gaze-movement angle. When viewers were wrong in their judgments, there was no systematic pattern of errors. That is, if the trial displayed the optics of looking to the left, viewers were no more prone to make incorrect responses saying that they were looking right than looking straight ahead. Moreover, viewers were not systematically more correct for left- and right-looking trials than for straight-ahead trials.

14. We might also conclude that the results of this experiment do not show that observers can judge direction of gaze with respect to movement. Instead, they may show that observers can learn to judge proximal flow on the display scope. On this view, the

task was simply one of perceptual learning in which three classes of nonsense stimuli were assigned three labels. There are four responses to this possibility.

First, the proximal stimuli on the display scope had complete correspondence, through Alberti's window, to the distal stimuli described. Except for binocular non-disparities, surface information of the display face, and minor phosphor persistence, these stimuli were optically identical with the distal stimuli simulated. Thus these were not nonsense stimuli; they were accurate computer simulations.

Second, Regan and Beverley (1982) also used feedback. They found that observers could *not* learn the location of a focus of expansion for orthogonal approach to a single plane. Experiment 9 used feedback and found that observers *could* learn about flow patterns that simulate parallax shifts. Even if proximal flow were all that was being judged, the experiment demonstrates that flow corresponding to parallax motion is learnable and that which corresponds to radial patterns from a focus of expansion (without parallax) is not. Learnability constraints play an important role in theoretical discussions of language acquisition (Wexler and Culicover 1981); they should play no less a role in theoretical discussions of the acquisition of perceptual skills.

Third, all observers reported that the stimuli phenomenally mimicked movement through a twelve-line environment. Moreover, phenomenal impression of depth generally followed observers' ability to make accurate judgments. Basically, I take the verbal reports to mean two things: the simulations were successful in mimicking most aspects of linear vection and the stimuli had the phenomenal appearance of objects moving in depth.

Fourth, excluding the Regan and Beverley study with plastic deforming worlds, only three experiments have shown accuracy of direction finding equal to that found in experiment 9. All were conducted without feedback. Llewellyn (1971, experiment 9) demonstrated that observers, when given other visual information in the background, could alter that background; this observation is consistent with the idea that the observers could make judgments of where they were going during linear movement to within 37 min of arc. This altered-background information was the drift of the looming target against a stable aperture, a situation analogous to having a gunsight or window frame through which to aim at a target. The motion of the target is nulled by keeping it within the limits of a gunsight. This target/gunsight relative motion is motion parallax. Riemersma (1981) and Ahumada (unpublished) also found a 1° accuracy in aim-point estimation, but their viewers may have used the relative motions in the stimulus against the edges of the screen. This too is motion parallax.

The important difference between the current study and these three is that their observers needed a prosthetic referent (like a gunsight) with which to measure change in the visual field. Without it, Llewellyn's observers were an order of magnitude worse. In this experiment, on the other hand, objects in the array moved with respect to one another; these objects were interreferential, and their differential parallax specified the direction of movement of the observer. The case considered here is much more like the conditions under which we evolved—gunsights and window frames are artifacts of recent vintage, but objects arrayed in depth have always been with us.

15. See Hochberg and Brooks (1978) for a discussion of moving camera techniques. Historically, the effects of pans were rather momentous in film. The first were used at the beginning of the twentieth century, and perhaps the first well-known pan appeared in the Porter and Edison film "The Great Train Robbery," released about 1903. This pan was only through about 45°, starting with a view of a train and ending with a campsite. The effect apparently stunned the audience, creating dizziness in many.

Chapter 13   Motion Parallax and Curvilinear Movement

1. Analytically, this result also makes sense. If we convert coordinates between Eq. (12.3) for linear movement and Eq. (13.2) for curvilinear movement, $x = L \cos \beta - r$ and $z = L \sin \beta$. Once converted, the two equations differ only by a constant and a scale factor. The scale factor is due to the size of r, as it affects the size of $d\beta$, and the constant -1.0 is due to the fact that when β is 45°, the value of $d\alpha/d\beta$ is -1.0.

2. Instantaneous acceleration functions for linear and curvilinear movement are generated by the following equations, respectively:

$$d^2\theta/dz^2 = 2xz/(x^2 + z^2)^2,$$
$$d^2\alpha/d\beta^2 = rL \sin \beta \cdot (L^2 - r^2)/(r^2 - 2rL \cos \beta + L^2)^2,$$

where z is the dimension of distance along the instantaneous path of linear motion, x is the lateral displacement of the object from the path, r is the radius of the circle, and L is the distance between the center of the circle and the object under scrutiny. Angles θ and α are the angles of gaze from the instantaneous path of motion and β is the angle through which the path of motion has moved along the circular path.

3. For linear movement, acceleration contours in three dimensions are generated simply by rotating the two-dimensional contours around the z axis, accommodating left-side/right-side differences (if they exist). For curvilinear movement, the three-dimensional acceleration contours are *much* more complex and can be approximated by imagining figure 13.3b as the projection in the xz plane, figure 13.3a as the yz plane, and intermediate projections for rotations around the z axis. All such displays and analyses are not needed here. But I would not say that acceleration information is uninformative to the moving observer, only that instantaneous displacements may be sufficient for wayfinding.

4. Experiments 10 and 11 were first reported, along with experiment 9 at the 25th Annual Meeting of the Psychonomic Society, San Antonio, Texas, November 1984, and at the 10th Annual Interdisciplinary Conference, Jackson, Wyoming, January 1985.

5. $F(2, 6) = 9.52, p < 0.015$, and $F(5, 15) = 87.3, p < 0.0001$, respectively, for effects of spacing and final gaze-movement angle.

6. As before, there was a reliable mean effect of the size of initial gaze-movement angle, $F(5, 15) = 144.2, p < 0.0001$; and a main effect of spacing, $F(2, 6) = 23.4, p < 0.01$.

Chapter 14   Direct and Indirect Perception

1. A certain amount of care is necessary when interpreting what seventeenth- and eighteenth-century philosophers meant by the term *perception*. Locke did not really distinguish it from thinking, and it was only with Reid (1764) that a distinction between sensation and perception was made. Also, the term *direct* has appeared in other similar contexts that I do not take the space to discuss, for example, in Condillac's (1780) discussion of *direct sensation*.

2. See Gibson (1966), Heider (1926), Natsoulas (1984), and Shepard (1984) for discussions of resonance.

3. Michaels and Carello (1981) discussed other attributes of Gibson's direct perception, but they conflate direct theory and ecological theory, a distinction that I would like to maintain. Brunswik (1956), for example, presented an ecological indirect theory.

4. Early evidence on recovery from cataract operations, such as the Cheselden case (Pastore 1971), appeared to support Locke's and Molyneux's view—shape was difficult

for newly sighted people to comprehend. But more recent evidence (Gregory 1974) suggests that this is not always the case.

5. The idealist, or immaterialistic, aspect of Berkeley's theory is ignored here. Obviously, if the world is simply a figment of one's imagination, one would hardly be concerned about being in direct contact with it through perception.

6. Bailey (1855) was later quite careful in stating what he meant by perception, delimiting it from conception.

7. Even von Kries, in his first appendix to Helmholtz (1866), felt that Helmholtz's views on the empirical theory were out of line and that certain physiological (innate) bases were needed for all learning.

8. Helmholtz (1878a, p. 381) later regretted the use of the term "unconscious inference" because it was easily confused with a concept of Schopenhauer's with the same name. Southard's translation of Helmholtz (1866) always uses the term "unconscious conclusions." Many, however, currently embrace the original term. Rock (1983, p. 272) is one:

> By unconsious inference I mean that the process of arriving at the percept is one much like reasoning in which conclusions are drawn from premises, except that in perception the process is not conscious and the outcome is a percept rather than a conclusion. I do *not* argue as Helmholtz did that such a process is necessarily a direct result of experience. That is a separate question.

Because Rock dismisses experience as a necessary input to perception, his idea of inference is little different than Gibson's direct perception. Rock's (1984, p. 234) overall view is:

> Although perception is autonomous with respect to such higher mental faculties as are exhibited in conscious thought and in the use of conscious knowledge, I would still argue that it is intelligent. By calling perception "intelligent," I mean to say that it is based upon such thoughtlike mental processes as description, inference, and problem solving, although these processes are rapid-fire, unconscious, and nonverbal.

Descriptions, for Rock, are abstract geometrical analyses, with which Gibson would be comfortable. Inference is largely a red herring unless premises come from experience, which Rock allowed but did not consider necessary. And problem solving is typically demonstrated with impoverished picturelike stimuli, which Gibson thought were always perceived indirectly.

9. Hoffman and Richards (1984) presented the clearest exposition I have seen of inferential processes as they might work in perception. They conclude that a percept is never guaranteed and can often be falsified. As they put it (p. 86): "This is not good news." I, on the other hand, think that no theory of perception can be both ineliminably inductive and true.

10. See, for example, Gibson (1976a) and his discussion of Austin. The next strongest candidate is Malcolm (1963), who wrote about direct perception while at Cornell.

11. Interpreting Gibson has taken on a Talmudic, hermeneutic air, to which I have done more than my fair share of contributing (Cutting 1982b, 1985). Because of this state of affairs, it becomes important to assess what others have said with regard to Gibson. In the context of explicating direct theory, Reed (1983) concurred that nonmediation and information specificity are the core concepts. Katz (1984) then raised the issue of processing, to which Reed (1984) replied that Gibson said lots about processing. Reed (1984) also raised the issue of awareness of external objects as central to Gibson's theory, with "internal" awareness as incidental.

Chapter 15   Directed Perception

1. Again, the one-to-one mapping that I discuss is *not* that between stimulus and percept. Instead, it is only half the mapping, that between available information in the optic array and the distal object in the environment. But, I would claim, the brunt of Gibson's (1959, p. 465) *psychophysical hypothesis* is close to what I present here as the mapping function for direct perception:

> The explicit hypothesis is that *for every aspect or property of the phenomenal world of an individual in contact with his environment; however subtle, there is a variable of the energy flux at his receptors, however complex, with which the phenomenal property would correspond if a psychophysical experiment could be performed.*

By 1970, Gibson (Reed and Jones 1982, pp. 90–105) rejected at least two parts of this description, one major and one minor. The minor aspect is that he meant invariants rather than variables, and the major one is the worry of behavioristic mapping of stimuli onto responses. But notice that the quotation emphasizes the phenomenal world of the individual *in contact* with the world. Thus, if perception *is* occurring and the individual *is* attending to the proper attributes of the optic array, then the mapping from stimulus to percept is correct. The problem is that we cannot guarantee that the information is picked up at any given point in time. The individual may not yet have learned to differentiate it. Thus Gibson was forced to decouple the percept as a necessary function of the stimulus. But he did not decouple the information in the optic array from the real-world objects.

Curiously, he expressed rather strong reservations about mappings. In his last statement on invariants, for example, Gibson (1979, p. 310) stated:

> It would simplify matters if all these kinds of change in the optic array could be understood as transformations in the sense of *mappings*, borrowing the term from projective geometry and topology. The invariants under transformation have been worked out. Moreover it is easy to visualize a form being transposed, inverted, reversed, enlarged, reduced, or foreshortened by slant, and we can imagine it being deformed in various ways. But, unhappily, some of these changes *cannot* be understood as one-to-one mappings, either projective or topological.

This might appear to be damaging evidence against my assertion, but Gibson's thoughts on mappings are confined to projections and topology, not to logic. In his appendix he refered to an earlier section (1979, p. 108) that makes this clearer:

> Foreshortening or compression of texture preserves one-to-one mapping only until it reaches its limit, after which texture is lost. The emergence of new texture with rupturing of a surface, the nullification of texture with dissipation of a surface, and the substitution of new texture for old are still other cases of the failure of one-to-one mapping, or projective correspondence. In all these cases it is not the fact that each unit of the ambient array at one time goes into a corresponding unit of the array at a later time.

The mappings discussed by Gibson are element-to-element matches across time slices of the optic array. The foreshortening of a flat surface as it rotates and eventually becomes parallel to the line of sight is indeed a case in which each element in the optic array corresponding to a particular point on the surface becomes smaller and eventually disappears. Thus over time many elements are lost. But the information about the surface (perhaps cross ratios for its flatness) is in the array at all times until the surface is aligned to the eye—and then the cross ratio disappears at exactly the same moment that the textures on which it is computed can no longer be seen. It seems to me that this is one-to-one mapping with a vengeance.

2. See Cutting (1982b) for a critique of the concept of affordances. Also, although Gibson claimed the concept to be new, the notions of grasp-ableness, pick-up-ableness, and throw-ableness can be found in Tolman (1933) as part of his notion of sign gestalt.

3. The mapping shown in figure 15.1 could also be called many-to-many, but because I am emphasizing the direction of the mapping process—from information to object properties—I consider one source of information at a time. Many-to-many and one-to-many mappings are equally illegitimate as functions.

4. Here, I may seem to be negating the idea of parallel computation in visual perception, but I am not. Indirect perception, in my view, demands a parallel computation in *cognition*—matching cues with their probabilistic referents in the world and using a vast covariation matrix of cue-object relations. It is this to which I object. Parallel computation in *vision* (see, for example, Ballard et al. 1983) seems not only necessary but wonderfully efficient.

5. Barwise and Perry (1983) take a similar view to this in their situational semantics: More information is present than is used. In their terms interpretation underdetermines information.

6. Cooper (1983) has also expressed the necessity of multiple approaches to the same problem, entailing multiple representations. My representations are external, hers internal, but task specificity is inherent in both.

7. Rock (1984, p. 231) straddled the issue, acknowledging the import of information but more heavily emphasizing cognition:

> My answer to Koffka's query—Why do things look as they do?—would be: because of the cognitive operations performed on the information contained within the stimulus.

8. In fact, we may have begun to worry that directed perception comes dangerously close to an eclecticism that tries to please all, but in fact pleases none.

References

Adams, K. R. (1972). Perspective and the viewpoint. *Leonardo* 5:209–217.

Ahumada, A. J. (unpublished). Bias and discriminability in aimpoint estimation. *Journal of Experimental Psychology: Human Perception and Performance.*

Alexander, C., and Carey, S. (1968). Subsymmetries. *Perception & Psychophysics* 4:73–77.

Allport, F. H. (1955). *Theories of Perception and the Concept of Structure.* New York: Wiley.

Ames, A. (1951). Visual perception and the rotating trapezoidal window. *Psychological Monographs* 65, no. 7.

Ames, A. (1960). *Morning Notes.* H. Cantril (ed.). New Brunswick, N.J.: Rutgers University Press.

Anderson, J. R. (1983). *The Architecture of Cognition.* Cambridge, Mass.: Harvard University Press.

Angell, R. B. (1974) The geometry of the visibles. *Noûs* 8:87–117.

Anscombe, E., and Geach, P. T. (eds. and trans.) (1954). *Descartes. Philosophical Writings.* London: Thomas Nelson and Sons.

Anstis, S. M., Mayhew, J. W., and Morley, T. (1969). The perception of where a face or television "portrait" is looking. *American Journal of Psychology* 82:474–489.

Appleman, I. B., and Mayzner, M. S. (1982). Application of geometric models to letter recognition: Distance and density. *Journal of Experimental Psychology: General* 111:60–100.

Armstrong, D. M. (1961). *Perception and the Physical World.* New York: The Humanities Press.

Arnheim, R. (1954). *Art and Visual Perception.* Berkeley: University of California Press.

Arnheim, R. (1969). *Toward a Psychology of Art.* Berkeley: University of California Press.

Arnheim, R. (1977). Perception of perspective pictorial space from different viewing points. *Leonardo* 10:283–288.

Arnheim, R. (1979). Some comments on J. J. Gibson's approach to picture perception. *Leonardo* 12:121–122.

Attneave, F. (1954). Some information aspects of visual perception. *Psychological Review* 61:183–193.

Attneave, F. (1955). Symmetry, information, and memory for patterns. *American Journal of Psychology* 68:209–222.

Austin, J. L. (1962). *Sense and Sensibilia.* Oxford: Oxford University Press.

Ayer, A. J. (1940). *Foundations of Empirical Knowledge.* London: Macmillan.

Ayer, A. J. (1956). *The Problem of Knowledge.* London: Macmillan.

Ayer, A. J. (1973). *The Central Questions of Philosophy.* London: Weidenfeld and Nicolson.

Ayres, F. (1967). *Theory and Problems in Projective Geometry,* Schaum's Outline Series. New York: McGraw-Hill.

Bailey, S. (1855). *Letters on the Philosophy of the Human Mind,* vol. 1. London: Longman, Brown, Green, and Longmans.

Bailey, S. (1858). *Letters on the Philosophy of the Human Mind*, vol. 2. London: Longman, Brown, Green, Longmans, and Roberts.

Baird, J. C. (1970). *Psychophysical Analysis of Visual Space*. New York: Pergamon Press.

Ballard, D. H., and Brown, C. M. (1982). *Computer Vision*. Englewood Cliffs, N.J.: Prentice-Hall.

Ballard, D. H., and Kimball, O. A. (1983). Rigid body motion from depth and optical flow. *Computer Vision, Graphics, and Image Processing* 22:95–115.

Ballard, D. H., Hinton, G. E., and Sejnowski, T. J. (1983). Parallel visual computation. *Nature* 306:21–26.

Balzano, G. J. (1980). The group-theoretic description of 12-fold and microtonal pitch systems. *Computer Music Journal* 4:66–84.

Barker, R. G. (1968). *Ecological Psychology*. Stanford: Stanford University Press.

Barsalou, L. (1983). Ad hoc categories. *Memory & Cognition* 11:211–227.

Bartley, S. H. (1951). The psychophysiology of vision. In *Handbook of Experimental Psychology*, S. S. Stevens (ed.). New York: Wiley, 921–984.

Bartley, S. H. (1969). *Principles of Perception*, second edition. New York: Harper and Row.

Barwise, J., and Perry, J. (1983). *Situations and Attitudes*. Cambridge, Mass.: The MIT Press, A Bradford Book.

Battisti, E., Carnemolla, A., Masters, R. J., and Menna, F. (1981). *Anamorphosis: Evasion and Return*. Rome: Officina Edizioni.

Bell, E. T. (1945). *The Development of Mathematics*. New York: McGraw-Hill.

Berkeley, G. (1709). An essay towards a new theory of vision. Reprinted in *The Works of George Berkeley* (1837). London: Thomas Tegg and Son, 86–116.

Berkeley, G. (1713). Three dialogues between Hylas and Philonius. Reprinted in *The Works of George Berkeley* (1871). Oxford: Clarendon Press, 255–360.

Berkeley, G. (1733). The theory of vision, or visual language, vindicated and explained. Reprinted in *The Works of George Berkeley* (1871). Oxford: Clarendon Press, 369–400.

Blank, A. A. (1978). Metric geometry in human binocular perception: Theory and fact. In *Formal Theories of Visual Perception*, E. L. J. Leeuwenberg and H. F. J. M. Buffart (eds.). Chichester, England: Wiley, 82–102.

Boring, E. G. (1952). Visual perception as invariance. *Psychological Review* 59:141–148.

Boynton, R. (1974). The visual system: Environmental information. In *Handbook of Perception*, E. Carterette and M. Friedman (eds.). New York: Academic Press, vol. 1, 286–308.

Braunstein, M. (1962). Depth perception in rotating dot patterns: Effects of numerosity and perspective. *Journal of Experimental Psychology* 64:415–420.

Braunstein, M. (1976). *Depth Perception through Motion*. New York: Academic Press.

Braunstein, M., Andersen, G. J., and Riefer, D. M. (1982). The use of occlusion to resolve ambiguity in parallel projections. *Perception & Psychophysics* 31:261–267.

Broadbent, D. E. (1958). *Perception and Communication*. London: Pergamon.

Brown, E. L., and Deffenbacher, K. (1979). *Perception and the Senses*. New York: Oxford.

Brown, T. (1820). *Sketch of a System of Philosophy of the Human Mind*. Reprinted 1977. Washington, D.C.: University Publications of America.

Bruce, V., and Green, P. (1985). *Visual Perception: Physiology, Psychology, and Ecology*. London: Erlbaum Associates.

Bruner, J. S. (1957). Going beyond the information given. In *Contemporary Approaches to Cognition: The Colorado Symposium*, J. S. Bruner et al. (eds.). Cambridge, Mass.: Harvard University Press.

Brunswik, E. (1956). *Perception and the Representative Design of Psychological Experiments*. Berkeley: University of California Press.

Buffart, H., Leeuwenberg, E., and Restle, F. (1983). Analysis of ambiguity in visual pattern completion. *Journal of Experimental Psychology: Human Perception and Performance* 9:980–1000.

Burke, R. B. (trans.) (1928). *The Opus Majus of Roger Bacon*, vol 1. Philadelphia: University of Pennsylvania Press.

Burton, H. E. (trans.) (1945). The optics of Euclid. *Journal of the Optical Society of America* 35:357–372.

Calvert, E. S. (1950). Visual aids for landing in bad visibility with particular reference to the transition from instrument to visual flight. *Transactions of the Illuminating Engineering Society, London* 15:183–219.

Calvert, E. S. (1954). Visual judgments in motion. *Journal of the Institute of Navigation* 7:233–251, 398–402.

Carel, W. L. (1961). *Visual Factors in the Contact Analog*. Ithaca, N.Y.: General Electric Advanced Electronics Center Publication R61 ELC60, 1–65.

Carlbom, I., and Paciorek, J. (1978). Planar geometric projections and viewing transformations. *Computing Surveys* 10:465–502.

Carlsöö, S. (1972). *How Man Moves*. London: Heinemann.

Carrier, D. (1980). Perspective as convention: On the views of Nelson Goodman and Ernst Gombrich. *Leonardo* 13:283–287.

Cassirer, E. (1944). The concept of group and the theory of perception. *Philosophy and Phenomenological Research* 5:1–35.

Cassirer, E. (1945). Reflections on the concept of group and the theory of perception. In *Symbol, Myth, and Culture*, D. Verene (ed.). New Haven: Yale University Press, 1979, 271–291.

Chen, L. (1982). Topological structure in visual perception. *Science* 218:699–700.

Chisholm, R. M. (1957). *Perceiving: A Philosophical Study*. Ithaca, N.Y.: Cornell University Press.

Chomsky, N. (1965). *Aspects of the Theory of Syntax*. Cambridge, Mass.: MIT Press.

Clocksin, W. F. (1980). Perception of surface slant and edge labels from optic flow: A computational approach. *Perception* 9:253–270.

Cohen, R. S., and Wartofsky, M. W. (eds.) (1977). Hermann von Helmholtz: Epistemological Writings. *Boston Studies in the Philosophy of Science* 37.

Condillac, E. (1780). *Logic* (J. Neef, trans., 1809). Reprinted 1977. Washington, D.C.: University Publications of America.

Cooper, L. A. (1983). Flexibility in representational systems. In *Human and Machine Vision*, F. Beck, B. Hope, and A. Rosenfeld (eds.). New York: Academic Press, 97–106.

Cooper, L. A., and Shepard, R. N. (1984). Turning something over in the mind. *Scientific American* 251(6):106–114.

Coren, S., Porac, C., and Ward, L. M. (1984). *Sensation and Perception*, second edition. New York: Academic Press.

Cornsweet, T. N. (1962). The staircase-method in psychophysics. *American Journal of Psychology* 75:485–491.

Cornsweet, T. N. (1970). *Visual Perception*. New York: Academic Press.

Cutting, J. E. (1978). Generation of synthetic male and female walkers through manipulation of a biomechanical invariant. *Perception* 7:393–405.

Cutting, J. E. (1981a). Coding theory adapted to gait perception. *Journal of Experimental Psychology: Human Perception and Performance* 7:71–87.

Cutting, J. E. (1981b). Six tenets for event perception. *Cognition* 10:71–78.

Cutting, J. E. (1982a). Blowing in the wind: Perceiving structure in trees and bushes. *Cognition* 12:25–44.

Cutting, J. E. (1982b). Two ecological perspectives: Gibson versus Shaw and Turvey. *American Journal of Psychology* 95:199–222.

Cutting, J. E. (1983a). Four assumptions about invariance in perception. *Journal of Experimental Psychology: Human Perception and Performance* 9:310–317.

Cutting, J. E. (1983b). Perceiving and recovering structure from events. In *Motion: Representation and Perception,* ACM SIGGRAPH/SIGART Interdisiplinary Workshop. New York: Association for Computing Machinery, 141–147.

Cutting, J. E. (1985). Gibson, representation, and belief. *Contemporary Psychology* 30:186–188.

Cutting, J. E., and Millard, R. T. (1984). Three gradients and perception of flat and curved surfaces. *Journal of Experimental Psychology: General* 113:198–216.

Cutting, J. E., and Proffitt, D. R. (1981). Gait perception as an example of how we may perceive events. In *Intersensory Perception and Sensory Integration,* R. Walk and H. L. Pick, Jr. (eds.). New York: Plenum, 249–273.

Cutting, J. E., and Proffitt, D. R. (1982). The minimum principle and the perception of absolute, common, and relative motions. *Cognitive Psychology* 14:211–246.

Cutting, J. E., Proffitt, D. R., and Kozlowski, L. T. (1978). A biomechanical invariant for gait perception. *Journal of Experimental Psychology: Human Perception and Performance* 4:357–372.

Daniels, N. (1974). *Thomas Reid's Inquiry.* New York: Burt Franklin.

Davis, P. J., and Hersh, R. (1981). *The Mathematical Experience.* Boston: Houghton Mifflin.

Dember, W. N., and Warm, J. S. (1979). *Psychology of Perception,* second edition. New York: Holt, Rinehart, and Winston.

de Wit, H. F., and de Swart, J. H. (1983). Some perspectives on the way that psychologists use "ecological physics." *Acta Psychologica* 53:171–176.

Dretske, F. I. (1969). *Seeing and Knowing.* Chicago: University of Chicago Press.

Dretske, F. I. (1981). *Knowledge and the Flow of Information.* Cambridge, Mass.: The MIT Press, A Bradford Book.

Dunn, B. E., Gray, G. C., and Thompson, D. (1965). Relative height on the picture-plane and depth perception. *Perceptual and Motor Skills* 21:227–236.

Eckoff, W. J. (trans.) (1970). *Kant's Inaugural Dissertation of 1770.* New York: AMS Press. Originally published in 1894.

Edgerton, S. Y. (1975). *The Renaissance Rediscovery of Linear Perspective.* New York: Basic Books.

Einstein, A. (1922). *Sidelights on Relativity.* Reprinted 1983. New York: Dover.

Epstein, W. (1973). The process of "taking-into-account" in visual perception. *Perception* 2:267–285.

Epstein, W. (1977). Historical introduction to the constancies. In *Stability and Constancy in Visual Perception,* W. Epstein (ed.). New York: Wiley.

Epstein, W. (1981). The relation between texture gradient and perceived slant-in-depth: Direct or mediated? *Perception* 10:695–702.

Epstein, W., and Park, J. (1964). Examination of Gibson's psychophysical hypothesis. *Psychological Bulletin* 62:180–196.

Eriksson, E. S. (1974a). Movement parallax during locomotion. *Perception & Psychophysics* 16:197–200.

Eriksson, E. S. (1974b). A theory of veridical space perception. *Scandinavian Journal of Psychology* 15:225–235.

Farber, J., and Rosinski, R. R. (1978). Geometric transformations of pictured space. *Perception* 7:269–282.

Fisher, I., and Miller, O. M. (1944). *World Maps and Globes.* New York: Essential Books.

Flanner, J. (1956). Profiles: Master-I. *The New Yorker,* October 6, 49ff.

Flock, H. R. (1965). Optical texture and linear perspective as stimuli for slant perception. *Psychological Review* 72:180–196.

Fodor, J. A. (1980). Methodological solipsism as a research strategy for cognitive psychology. *The Behavioral and Brain Sciences* 3:63–109.

Fodor, J. A. (1983). *The Modularity of Mind*. Cambridge, Mass.: The MIT Press, A Bradford Book.

Fodor, J. A., and Pylyshyn, Z. (1981). How direct is perception? Some reflections on Gibson's "ecological approach." *Cognition* 9:139–196.

Foley, J. M. (1964). Desarguesian property in visual space. *Journal of the Optical Society of America* 54:684–692.

Foley, J. M. (1966). Locus of perceived equidistance as a function of viewing distance. *Journal of the Optical Society of America* 56:822–827.

Freeman, R. B. (1965). Ecological optics and visual slant. *Psychological Review* 72:501–504.

Freeman, R. B. (1966). Optical texture versus retinal perspective: A reply to Flock. *Psychological Review* 73:365–371.

Frege, G. (1884). *The Foundations of Arithmetic* (J. L. Austin, trans.). Oxford: Oxford University Press, 1950.

Fry, E. F. (1966). *Cubism*. London: Thames and Hudson, Ltd.

Fry, G. A. (1950). Visual perception of space. *American Journal of Optometry* 27:531–553.

Fuller, B. (1963). *Ideas and Integrities*. New York: Prentice-Hall.

Garner, W. R. (1962). *Uncertainty and Structure as Psychological Concepts*. New York: Wiley.

Garner, W. R. (1966). To perceive is to know. *American Psychologist* 21:11–19.

Garner, W. R. (1970). Good patterns have few alternatives. *American Scientist* 58:34–42.

Garner, W. R. (1974). *The Processing of Information and Structure*. Hillsdale, N.J.: Erlbaum Associates.

Gehringer, W. L., and Engel, E. (to be published). The effect of ecological viewing conditions on the Ames distorted room illusion. *Journal of Experimental Psychology: Human Perception and Performance*.

Gellert, W., Küstner, H., Hellwich, M., and Kästner, H. (1977). *The VNR Concise Encyclopedia of Mathematics*. New York: Van Nostrand Reinhold.

Gibson, E. J. (1967). *Perceptual Learning and Development*. New York: Appleton-Century-Crofts.

Gibson, E. J., Owsley, C. J., and Johnston, J. (1978). Perception of invariants by five-month-old infants: Differentiation of two types of motion. *Developmental Psychology* 14:407–415.

Gibson, E. J., Gibson, J. J., Smith, O. W., and Flock, H. (1959). Motion parallax as a determinant of perceived depth. *Journal of Experimental Psychology* 58:40–51.

Gibson, J. J. (ed.) (1947). *Motion Picture Testing and Research*. Army Air Forces Aviation Psychology Research Reports, no. 7. Washington, D.C.: U.S. Government Printing Office.

Gibson, J. J. (1950). *The Perception of the Visual World*. Boston: Houghton Mifflin.

Gibson, J. J. (1954a). The visual perception of objective motion and subjective movement. *Psychological Review* 61:304–314.

Gibson, J. J. (1954b). A theory of pictorial perception. *Audio-Visual Communications Review* 1:3–23.

Gibson, J. J. (1955). The optical expansion pattern in aerial locomotion. *American Journal of Psychology* 68:480–484.

Gibson, J. J. (1957a). Optical motions and transformations as stimuli for visual perception. *Psychological Review* 64:288–295.

Gibson, J. J. (1957b). Survival in a world of probable objects. *Contemporary Psychology* 2:33–35.

Gibson, J. J. (1958). Visually controlled locomotion and visual orientation in animals. *British Journal of Psychology* 49:182–192.

Gibson, J. J. (1959). Perception as a function of stimulation. In *Psychology: A Study of a Science*, S. Koch (ed.). New York: McGraw-Hill, vol. 1, 456–501.

Gibson, J. J. (1960a). Information contained in light. *Acta Psychologica* 17:23–30.

Gibson, J. J. (1960b). Pictures, perspective, and perception. *Daedalus* 89:216–227.

Gibson, J. J. (1961). Ecological optics. *Vision Research* 1:253–262.

Gibson, J. J. (1965). Constancy and invariance in perception. In *The Nature and Art of Motion*, G. Kepes (ed.). New York: George Brazilier, 60–70.

Gibson, J. J. (1966). *The Senses Considered as Perceptual Systems*. Boston: Houghton Mifflin.

Gibson, J. J. (1967). New reasons for realism. *Synthese* 17:162–172.

Gibson, J. J. (1970). On theories for visual space perception: A reply to Johansson. *Scandinavian Journal of Psychology* 11:75–79.

Gibson, J. J. (1971a). The information available in pictures. *Leonardo* 4:27–35.

Gibson, J. J. (1971b). The legacies of Koffka's *Principles. Journal for the History of the Behavioral Sciences* 7:3–9.

Gibson, J. J. (1972). A theory of direct visual perception. In *The Psychology of Knowing*, J. R. Royce and W. W. Rozeboom (eds.). New York: Gordon and Breach, 215–240.

Gibson, J. J. (1973a). Direct visual perception: A reply to Gyr. *Psychological Bulletin* 79:396–397.

Gibson, J. J. (1973b). On the concept of formless invariants in visual perception. *Leonardo* 6:43–45.

Gibson, J. J. (1974). A note on ecological optics. In *Handbook of Perception*, E. Carterette and M. Friedman (eds.). New York: Academic Press, vol. 1, 309–311.

Gibson, J. J. (1976a). The myth of passive perception: A reply to Richards. *Philosophy and Phenomenological Research* 37:234–238.

Gibson, J. J. (1976b). Three kinds of distance that can be seen, or how Bishop Berkeley went wrong. In *Studies in Perception: Festschrift for Fabio Metelli*, G. B. Flores D'Arcais (ed.). Milan: Giunte Editore, 83–87.

Gibson, J. J. (1979). *The Ecological Approach to Visual Perception*. Boston: Houghton Mifflin.

Gibson, J. J., Olum, P., and Rosenblatt, F. (1955). Parallax and perspective during aircraft landings. *American Journal of Psychology* 68:372–385.

Gibson, J. J., Gibson, E. J., Flock, H., and Smith, O. (1959). Motion parallax as a determinant of perceived depth. *Journal of Experimental Psychology* 58:40–51.

Gogel, W. C. (1977). The metric of visual space. In *Stability and Constancy in Visual Perception*, W. Epstein (ed.). New York: Wiley, 129–181.

Gogel, W. C., and Tietz, J. D. (1973). Absolute motion parallax and the specific distance tendency. *Perception & Psychophysics* 13:284–292.

Goldstein, E. B. (1979). Rotation of objects in pictures viewed at an angle: Evidence for different properties of two types of pictorial space. *Journal of Experimental Psychology: Human Perception and Performance* 5:78–87.

Goldstein, E. B. (1981). The ecology of J. J. Gibson's perception. *Leonardo* 14:191–195.

Goldstein, E. B. (1984). *Sensation and Perception*, second edition. Belmont, Calif.: Wadsworth.

Gombrich, E. H. (1960). *Art and Illusion: A Study of the Psychology of Pictorial Representation*. Princeton, N.J.: Princeton University Press.

Gombrich, E. H. (1982). Image and code: Scope and limits of conventionalism in pictorial representation. In his *The Image and The Eye*. Ithaca, N.Y.: Cornell University Press, 278–297.

Goodman, N. (1968). *Language of Art*. Indianapolis: Bobbs-Merrill.

Gordon, D. A. (1965). Static and dynamic fields in human space perception. *Journal of the Optical Society of America* 55:1296–1303.

Graham, C. H. (1951). Visual perception. In *Handbook of Experimental Psychology*, S. S. Stevens (ed.). New York: Wiley, 868–920.

Graham, C. H., Baker, K. E., Hecht, M., and Lloyd, V. V. (1948). Factors influencing thresholds for monocular movement parallax. *Journal of Experimental Psychology* 38:205–223.

Grant, E. (ed.) (1974). *A Source Book in Medieval Science*. Cambridge, Mass.: Harvard University Press.

Greene, R. (1983). Determining the preferred viewpoint in linear perspective. *Leonardo* 16:97–102.

Gregory, R. H. (1970). *The Intelligent Eye*. New York: McGraw-Hill.

Gregory, R. H. (1974). Recovery from early blindness. In his *Concepts and Mechanisms in Perception*. New York: Scribners, 65–129.

Grosslight, J. H., Fletcher, H. J., Masterton, R. B., and Hagen, R. (1978). Monocular vision and landing performance in general aviation pilots: Cyclops revisited. *Human Factors* 201:27–33.

Grünbaum, A. (1969). Reply to Hilary Putnam's "An examination of Grünbaum's philosophy of geometry." *Boston Studies in the Philosophy of Science* 5:1–150.

Grünbaum, A. (1973). *Philosophical Problems of Space and Time*, second edition. Boston: Reidel.

Gulick, W. L., and Lawson, R. B. (1976). *Human Stereopsis*. New York: Oxford University Press.

Haber, R. N. (1979). Perceiving the layout of space in pictures: A perspective theory based upon Leonardo da Vinci. In *Perception and Pictorial Representation*, C. F. Nodine and D. F. Fisher (eds.). New York: Praeger, 84–99.

Haber, R. N. (1980). Perceiving space from pictures: A theoretical analysis. In *The Perception of Pictures*, M. A. Hagen (ed.). New York: Academic Press, vol. 1, 3–31.

Haber, R. N. (1983a). The impending demise of the icon: A critique of the concept of iconic storage. *The Behavioral and Brain Sciences* 6:1–54.

Haber, R. N. (1983b). Psychology cannot blame its theoretical mistakes on physics. *Acta Psychologica* 53:155–162.

Haber, R. N. (1983c). Stimulus information and processing mechanisms in visual space perception. In *Human and Machine Vision*, J. Beck, B. Hope, and A. Rosenfeld (eds.). New York: Academic Press, 157–235.

Haber, R. N., and Hershenson, M. (1973). *The Psychology of Visual Perception*. New York: Holt, Rinehart, and Winston.

Hacker, M. J., and Ratcliff, R. (1979). A revised table of *d'* for *M*-alternative force choice. *Perception & Psychophysics* 26:168–170.

Hagen, M. A. (1976). Influence of picture surface and station point on the ability to compensate for oblique view in pictorial perception. *Developmental Psychology* 12:57–63.

Hagen, M. A. (1979). A new theory of the psychology of representational art. In *Perception and Pictorial Representation*, C. F. Nodine and D. F. Fisher (eds.). New York: Praeger, 196–212.

Hagen, M. A. (1980). Generative theory: A perceptual theory of pictorial representation. In *the Perception of Pictures*, M. A. Hagen (ed.). New York: Academic Press, vol. 2, 3–46.

Hagen, M. A., and Elliott, H. B. (1976). An investigation of the relationship between viewing condition and preference for true and modified linear perspective with adults. *Journal of Experimental Psychology: Human Perception and Performance* 2:479–490.

Hagen, M. A., and Jones, R. K. (1978). Differential patterns of preference for modified linear perspective in children and adults. *Journal of Experimental Child Psychology* 26:205–215.

Hamilton, W. (1859). *Lectures on Metaphysics*, vol. II. Edinburgh: William Blackwood and Sons.

Hamlyn, D. W. (1961). *Sensation and Perception*. London: Routledge and Kegan Paul.

Hamlyn, D. W. (1983). *Perception, Learning, and the Self*. London: Routledge and Kegan Paul.

Hansen, R. (1973). This curving world: Hyperbolic linear perspective. *Journal of Aesthetics and Art Criticism* 32:147–161.

Hardy, L. G., Rand, G., Rittler, M. C., Blank, A. A., and Boeder, P. (1953). *The Geometry of Binocular Space*. Elizabeth, N.J.: Schiller.

Harper, R. S., and Boring, E. G. (1948). Cues. *American Journal of Psychology* 61:119–123.

Harrington, T. L., and Harrington, M. K. (1981). Perception of motion using blur pattern information in the moderate and high-velocity domains of vision. *Acta Psychologica* 48:227–237.

Harrington, T. L., Harrington, M. K., Wilkins, C. A., and Koh, Y. O. (1980). Visual orientation by motion produced blur-patterns: Detection of divergence. *Perception & Psychophysics* 28:293–305.

Hasbrook, A. H. (1975). The approach and landing. *Business and Commercial Aviation* November, 39–43.

Hatada, T., Sakata, H., and Kusaka, H. (1980). Psychophysical analysis of the "sensation of reality" induced by a visual wide-field display. *Journal of the Society for Motion Picture and Television Engineers* 89:560–569.

Hatfield, G., and Epstein, W. (1985). The status of the minimum principle in the theoretical analysis of visual perception. *Psychological Bulletin* 97:155–186.

Hay, J. C. (1966). Optical motions and space perception: An extension of Gibson's analysis. *Psychological Review* 73:550–565.

Hay, J. C., and Pick, H. L., Jr. (1966). Gaze-contingent prism adaptation: Optical and motor factors. *Journal of Experimental Psychology* 72:640–648.

Hayek, F. A. (1952). *The Sensory Order*. Chicago: University of Chicago Press.

Hecht, E., and Zajac, A. (1974). *Optics*. Menlo Park, Calif.: Addison-Wesley.

Heider, F. (1926). Thing and medium. Trans. in *Psychological Issues*, 1959, 1(3):1–35.

Heider, F. (1958). *The Psychology of Interpersonal Relations*. New York: Wiley.

Heider, F., and Simmel, M. (1944). A study of apparent behavior. *American Journal of Psychology* 57:243–259.

Heil, J. (1983). *Perception and Cognition*. Berkeley: University of California Press.

Helmholtz, H. von (1866). *Physiological Optics*, vol. 3 (third edition, J. P. C. Southall, trans., 1925). Menasha, Wisc.: The Optical Society of America.

Helmholtz, H. von (1868). Recent progress in the theory of vision. In *Selected Writings of Hermann von Helmholtz*, R. Kahl (ed.). Middletown, Conn.: Wesleyan University Press, 1971, 144–222.

Helmholtz, H. von (1870). The origin and meaning of geometric axioms I. In *Selected Writings of Hermann von Helmholtz*, R. Kahl (ed.). Middletown, Conn.: Wesleyan University Press, 1971, 246–265.

Helmholtz, H. von (1871). The relation of optics to painting. In *Selected Writings of Hermann von Helmholtz*, R. Kahl (ed.). Middletown, Conn.: Wesleyan University Press, 1971, 297–329.

Helmholtz, H. von (1878a). The facts of perception. In *Selected Writings of Hermann von Helmholtz*, R. Kahl (ed.). Middletown, Conn.: Wesleyan University Press, 1971, 366–407.

Helmholtz, H. von (1878b). The origin and meaning of geometric axioms II. In *Selected Writings of Hermann von Helmholtz*, R. Kahl (ed.). Middletown, Conn.: Wesleyan University Press, 1971, 360–365.

Helmholtz, H. von (1894). The origin and correct interpretation of our sense impression. In *Selected Writings of Hermann von Helmholtz*, R. Kahl (ed.). Middletown, Conn.: Wesleyan University Press, 1971, 501–512.

Hempel, C. G. (1945). Geometry and empirical science. *American Mathematical Monthly* 52:7–17.

Hershberger, W. A., and Starzec, J. J. (1974). Motion-parallax cues in one-dimensional polar and parallel projections: Differential velocity and acceleration/displacement change. *Journal of Experimental Psychology* 103:717–723.

Hershberger, W. A., and Urban, D. (1970). Three motion-parallax cues in one-dimensional polar projections of rotation in depth. *Journal of Experimental Psychology* 86:380–383.

Hershberger, W. A., Carpenter, D. L., Starzec, J., and Laughlin, N. K. (1974). Stimulation of an object rotating in depth: Constant and reversed projection ratios. *Journal of Experimental Psychology* 103:844–853.

Hildreth, E. C. (1984). *The Measurement of Visual Motion*. Cambridge, Mass.: MIT Press.

Hochberg, J. (1962). The psychophysics of pictorial perception. *Audio-Visual Communication Review* 10:22–54.

Hochberg, J. (1971). Perception and depiction. *Science* 172:685–686.

Hochberg, J. (1974). Higher-order stimuli and interresponse coupling in the perception of the visual world. In *Perception: Essays in Honor of James J. Gibson*, R. B. MacLeod and H. L. Pick (eds.). Ithaca, N.Y.: Cornell University Press, 17–39.

Hochberg, J. (1978a). Art and perception. In *Handbook of Perception*, E. C. Carterette and M. P. Friedman (eds.). New York: Academic Press, vol. 10, 225–259.

Hochberg, J. (1978b). *Perception*, second edition. Englewood Cliffs, N.J.: Prentice Hall.

Hochberg, J. (1979). Sensation and perception. In *The First Century of Experimental Psychology*, E. Hearst (ed.). Hillsdale, N.J.: Erlbaum Associates, 89–142.

Hochberg, J. (1981). Levels of perceptual organization. In *Perception Organization*, M. Kubovy and J. R. Pomerantz (eds.). Hillsdale, N.J.: Erlbaum Associates, 255–278.

Hochberg, J. (1982). How big is a stimulus? In *Organization and Representation in Perception*, J. Beck (ed.). Hillsdale, N.J.: Erlbaum Associates, 191–217.

Hochberg, J., and Brooks, V. (1978). The perception of motion pictures. In *Handbook of Perception*, E. Carterette and M. Friedman (eds.). New York: Academic Press, vol. 10, 257–304.

Hochberg, J., and McAlister, E. (1953). A quantitative approach to figural "goodness." *Journal of Experimental Psychology* 46:361–364.

Hochberg, J., and Smith, O. (1955). Landing strip markings and the "expansion pattern" I. Program, preliminary analysis, and apparatus. *Perceptual and Motor Skills* 5:81–92.

Hoffman, D. D., and Flinchbaugh, B. E. (1982). The interpretation of biological motion. *Biological Cybernetics* 42:195–204.

Hoffman, D. D., and Richards, W. A. (1984). Parts of recognition. *Cognition* 18:65–96.

Hopkins, J. (1973). Visual geometry. *Philosophical Review* 82:3–34.

Horn, B. K. P., and Schunk, B. G. (1981). Determining optic flow. *Artificial Intelligence* 17:184–204.

Hudson, P. T. W. (1983). A rose is a rose is a rose: Minimalism in perception. *Acta Psychologica* 53:163–169.

Hume, D. (1739). *A Treatise on Human Nature*. London: John Noon.

Indow, T. (1982). An approach to geometry of visual space with no a priori mapping functions: Multidimensional mapping according to Riemannian metrics. *Journal of Mathematical Psychology* 26:205–236.

Indow, T., and Watanabe, T. (1984). Parallel- and distance-alleys with moving points in the horizontal plane. *Perception & Psychophysics* 35:144–154.

Ittelson, W. H. (1952). *The Ames Demonstrations in Perception*. Princeton, N.J.: Princeton University Press.

Ittelson, W. H., and Kilpatrick, F. P. (1951). Experiments in perception. *Scientific American* 185(2):50–55.

Jackendoff, R. (1983). *Semantics and Cognition*. Cambridge, Mass.: The MIT Press, A Bradford Book.

James, W. (1890). *The Principles of Psychology*, vol. 2. New York: Henry Holt.

Johansson, G. (1970). On theories for visual space perception: A letter to Gibson. *Scandinavian Journal of Psychology* 11:67–74.

Johansson, G. (1973a). Monocular movement parallax and near-space perception. *Perception* 2:135–146.

Johansson, G. (1973b). Visual perception of biological motion and a model for its analysis. *Perception & Psychophysics* 14:201–211.

Johansson, G. (1974). Projective transformations as determining visual space perception. In *Perception: Essays in Honor of James J. Gibson*, R. B. MacLeod and H. L. Pick (eds.). Ithaca, N.Y.: Cornell University Press, 117–138.

Johansson, G. (1975). Visual motion perception. *Scientific American* 232(6):76–88.

Johansson, G. (1977). Spatial constancy and motion in visual perception. In *Stability and Constancy in Visual Perception*, W. Epstein (ed.). New York: Wiley, 375–419.

Johansson, G. (1978). About the geometry underlying spontaneous visual decoding of the optical message. In *Formal Theories of Visual Perception*, E. L. J. Leeuwenberg and H. F. J. M. Buffart (eds.). Chichester, England: Wiley, 265–276.

Johansson, G., von Hofsten, C., and Jansson, G. (1980). Event perception. *Annual Review of Psychology* 31:27–66.

Johnson, C. A., and Leibowitz, H. L. (1979). Practice effects for visual resolution in the periphery. *Perception & Psychophysics* 25:439–442.

Johnston, I. R., White, G. R., and Cumming, R. W. (1973). The role of optical expansion patterns in locomotor control. *American Journal of Psychology* 86:311–324.

Jowett, B. (trans.) (1952). *The Dialogues of Plato*. Chicago: Encyclopedia Britannica.

Julesz, B. (1971). *Foundations of Cyclopean Perception*. Chicago: University of Chicago Press.

Kanade, T., and Kender, J. (1983). Mapping image properties into shape constraints: Skewed symmetry, affine-transformable patterns, and the shape-from-texture paradigm. In *Human and Machine Vision*, J. Beck, B. Hope, and A. Rosenfeld (eds.). New York: Academic Press, 237–257.

Katz, D. (1935). *The World of Color* (R. B. MacLeod and C. W. Fox, trans.). London: Kegan Paul, Trench and Trubner.

Katz, S. (1984). A reply to Reed's note: "What is direct perception?" *International Society for Ecological Psychology Newsletter* 1(3):4–5.

Kaufman, L. (1968). *Research in Visual Perception for Carrier Landing*, suppl. 2. Great Neck, N.Y.: Sperry Rand Research Center.

Kennedy, J. M. (1974). *A Psychology of Picture Perception*. San Francisco: Jossey-Bass.

Kenyon, F. C. (1898). A curious optical illusion connected with an electric fan. *Science* 8:371–372.

Kilpatrick, F. P. (ed.) (1961). *Explorations in Transactional Psychology*. New York: New York University Press.

Klein, F. (1908). *Elementary Mathematics from an Advanced Standpoint*. Reprinted 1939. New York: Macmillan.

Kline, M. (1959). *Mathematics and the Physical World*. New York: Dover.

Kline, M. (1980). *Mathematics: The Loss of Certainty*. New York: Harcourt, Brace.

Koenderink, J. J., and van Doorn, A. J. (1975). Invariant properties of the motion parallax field due to the movement of rigid bodies relative to an observer. *Optica Acta* 22:773–791.

Koenderink, J. J., and van Doorn, A. J. (1976a). Local structure of the motion parallax field. *Journal of the Optical Society of America* 66:717–723.

Koenderink, J. J., and van Doorn, A. J. (1976b). The singularities of visual mapping. *Biological Cybernetics* 24:51–59.

Koenderink, J. J., and van Doorn, A. J. (1981). Exterospecific component for the detection of structure and motion in three dimensions. *Journal of the Optical Society of America* 71:953–957.

Koffka, K. (1935). *Principles of Gestalt Psychology.* New York: Harcourt.

Kolers, P. A. (1978). Light waves. *Contemporary Psychology* 23:227–228.

Koyré, A. (1957). *From the Closed World to the Infinite Universe.* Baltimore, Md.: Johns Hopkins University Press.

Kries, J. von (1910). Notes on the perception of depth. In *Physiological Optics,* H. von Helmholtz (J. P. C. Southall, trans., 1925). Menasha, Wisc.: Optical Society of America, third edition, 369–400.

Krumhansl, C. L. (1978). Concerning the applicability of geometric models to similarity data: The interrelationship between similarity and spatial density. *Psychological Review* 85:445–463.

Krumhansl, C. L. (1982). Density feature weights as predictors of visual identifications: Comment on Appleman and Mayzner. *Journal of Experimental Psychology: General* 111:101–108.

Kubovy, M. (1986). *The Arrow in the Eye.* London: Cambridge University Press.

Kuhn, T. S. (1957). *The Copernican Revolution.* Cambridge, Mass.: Harvard University Press.

Langewiesche, W. (1944). *Stick and Rudder.* New York: McGraw-Hill.

Lappin, J. S. (1984). Reflections on Gunnar Johansson's perspective on the visual measurement of space and time. In *Persistence and Change,* W. H. Warren, Jr., and R. E. Shaw (eds.). Hillsdale, N.J.: Erlbaum Associates, 67–86.

Lappin, J. S., and Fuqua, M. A. (1983). Accurate visual measurement of three-dimensional moving patterns. *Science* 221:480–482.

Lappin, J. S., Doner, J. F., and Kottas, B. L. (1980). Minimal conditions for the detection of structure and motion in three dimensions. *Science* 209:717–719.

Le, D. N. (1974). Visual information about locomotion. In *Perception: Essays in Honor of James J. Gibson,* R. B. MacLeod and H. L. Pick, Jr. (eds.). Ithaca, N.Y.: Cornell University Press, 250–267.

Lee, D. N. (1976). A theory of visual control of braking based on information about time to collision. *Perception* 5:437–459.

Lee, D. N. (1980a). The optic flow field: The foundation of vision. *Philosophical Transactions of the Royal Society, London B* 280:169–179.

Lee, D. N. (1980b). Visuo-motor coordination in space-time. In *Tutorials in Motor Behavior,* G. E. Stelmach and J. Requin (eds.). Amsterdam: North-Holland, 281–295.

Lee, D. N., and Lishman, R. (1977). Visual control of locomotion. *Scandinavian Journal of Psychology* 18:224–230.

Lee, D. N., Lishman, R., and Thomson, J. A. (1982). Regulation of gait in long jumping. *Journal of Experimental Psychology: Human Perception and Performance* 8:448–459.

Leeman, F., Elffers, J., and Schuyt, M. (1976). *Hidden Images.* New York: Harry N. Abrams.

Leeuwenberg, E. (1971). A perceptual coding language for visual and auditory patterns. *American Journal of Psychology* 84:307–347.

Leibowitz, H. W., Johnson, C. A., and Isabelle, E. (1972). Peripheral motion detection and refractive error. *Science* 177:1207–1208.

Lewin, K. (1943). Defining the "field at a given time." *Psychological Review* 50:292–310.

Lindberg, D. C. (1967). Alhazen's theory of vision and its reception in the west. *Isis* 58:321–341.

Lindsay, P. H., and Norman, D. A. (1972). *Human Information Processing.* New York: Academic Press.

Llewellyn, K. R. (1971). Visual guidance of locomotion. *Journal of Experimental Psychology* 91:245–261.

Locke, J. (1690). *An Essay Concerning Human Understanding.* Reprinted 1952. Chicago: Encyclopedia Britannica.

Loftus, G. (1985). On worthwhile icons: Reply to Di Lollo and Haber. *Journal of Experimental Psychology: Human Perception and Performance* 11:384–388.

Longuet-Higgins, H. C., and Prazdny, K. (1980). The interpretation of moving retinal images. *Proceedings of the Royal Society, London B* 208:385–397.

Lotze, H. (1878). *Metaphysic,* vol. 1 (B. Bosanquet, trans., 1887). Oxford: Clarendon Press.

Luce, R. D., and Krumhansl, C. L. (1986). Measurement, scaling, and psychophysics. In *Handbook of Experimental Psychology,* R. C. Atkinson, R. J. Herrnstein, G. Lindzey, and R. D. Luce (eds.). New York: Wiley, second edition.

Luchins, A. S., and Luchins, E. H. (1954). Variables and functions. *Psychological Review* 61:315–322.

Luchins, A. S., and Luchins, E. H. (1964). On the study of invariants. *Journal of General Psychology* 70:265–277.

Lumsden, E. A. (1980). Problems of magnification and minification: An explanation of the distortions of distance, slant, shape, and velocity. In *The Perception of Pictures,* M. A. Hagen (ed.). New York: Academic Press, vol. 1, 91–135.

Luneburg, R. K. (1947). *Mathematical Analysis of Binocular Vision.* Princeton, N.J.: Princeton University Press.

Mach, E. (1906). *Space and Geometry.* Chicago: Open Court.

Malcolm, N. (1963). *Knowledge and Certainty.* Englewood Cliffs, N.J.: Prentice-Hall.

Malde, H. E. (1983). Panoramic photographs. *American Scientist* 71:132–141.

Malebranche, N. (1674). *The Search after Truth* (T. M. Lennon and P. J. Olscamp, trans., 1980). Columbus: Ohio State University Press.

Marr, D. (1982). *Vision.* San Francisco: Freeman.

Maull, N. L. (1980). Cartesian optics and the geometrization of nature. In *Descartes: Philosophy, Mathematics, and Physics,* S. Gaukroger (ed.). Sussex, England: Harvester Press, 23–40.

McArthur, D. J. (1982). Computer vision and perceptual psychology. *Psychological Bulletin* 92:283–309.

Meister, R. (1966). The iso-deformation of images and the criterion for delimitation of the usable areas in cine-auditoriums. *Journal of the Society for Motion Picture and Television Engineers* 75:179–182.

Michaels, C. F., and Carello, C. (1981). *Direct Perception.* Englewood Cliffs, N.J.: Prentice-Hall.

Miles, W. R. (1929). Figure for the "windmill illusion." *Journal of General Psychology* 2:143–145.

Miles, W. R. (1931). Movement interpretations of the silhouette of a revolving fan. *American Journal of Psychology* 43:392–405.

Mill, J. S. (1842). Bailey on Berkeley's theory of vision. In *Essays on Philosophy and the Classics by John Stuart Mill,* J. M. Robson and F. E. Sparshott (eds.). Toronto: University of Toronto Press, 1978, 245–270.

Mill, J. S. (1843) *System of Logic,* eighth edition, 1889. London: Longmans, Green.

Mill, J. S. (1865). *An Examination of Sir William Hamilton's Philosophy.* London: Longmans, Green, Reader, and Dyer.

Miller, G. A. (1956). The magical number seven, plus or minus two. *Psychological Review* 63:81–97.

Miller, G. A., and Frick, F. C. (1949). Statistical behavioristics and sequences of responses. *Psychological Review* 56:311–324.

Molyneux, W. (1690). *Dioptrica Nova*. London: Benjamin Tooke.

Moore, G. E. (1905–1906). The nature and reality of objects of perception. *Proceedings of the Aristotelian Society* 6:68–127.

Moore, G. E., and Stout, G. F. (1913–1914). Symposium—The status of sense-data. *Proceedings of the Aristotelian Society* 14:355–406.

Murdock, B. B. (1960). The distinctiveness of stimuli. *Psychological Review* 67:16–31.

Murray, M. P. (1967). Gait as a total pattern of movement. *American Journal of Physical Medicine* 46:290–333.

Naimark, M. (Fall 1981). Some notes on movies and form. *Video* 80:21.

Nakayama, K., and Loomis, J. M. (1974). Optical velocity patterns, velocity-sensitive neurons, and space perception. *Perception* 3:63–80.

Natsoulas, T. (1984). Towards the improvement of Gibsonian perception theory. *Journal for the Theory of Social Behavior* 14:231–258.

Neisser, U. (1977). Gibson's ecological optics: Consequences of a different stimulus description. *Journal for the Theory of Social Behavior* 7:17–28.

Norman, J. (1983). Are the direct and indirect theories of perception incompatible? *The Behavioral and Brain Sciences* 6:729–749.

Paivio, A. (1970). *Imagery and Verbal Processes*. New York: Holt, Rinehart, and Winston.

Palmer, S. E. (1978). Fundamental aspects of cognitive representation. In *Cognition and categorization*, E. Rosch and B. B. Lloyd (eds.). Hillsdale, N.J.: Erlbaum Associates, 259–303.

Palmer, S. E. (1983). The psychology of perceptual organization: A transformational approach. In *Human and Machine Vision*, J. Beck, B. Hope, and A. Rosenfeld (eds.). New York: Academic Press, 269–339.

Pastore, N. (1971). *Selective History of Theories of Visual Perception: 1650–1950*. New York: Oxford University Press.

Perkins, D. N. (1972). Visual discrimination between rectangular and nonrectangular parallelopipeds. *Perception & Psychophysics* 12:396–400.

Perkins, D. N. (1973). Compensating for distortion in viewing pictures obliquely. *Perception & Psychophysics* 14:13–18.

Perkins, D. N. (1982). The perceiver as organizer and geometer. In *Organization and Representation in Perception*, J. Beck (ed.). Hillsdale, N.J.: Erlbaum Associates, 73–93.

Perkins, D. N. (1983). Why the human perceiver is a bad machine. In *Human and Machine Vision*, J. Beck, B. Hope, and A. Rosenfeld (eds.). New York: Academic Press, 341–364.

Petersik, J. T. (1979). Three-dimensional object constancy: Coherence of a simulated rotating sphere in noise. *Perception & Psychophysics* 25:328–335.

Piaget, J. (1970). *Structuralism*. New York: Basic Books.

Pierce, A. H. (1898). The windmill illusion. *Science* 8:479–480.

Pirenne, M. H. (1970). *Optics, Painting, and Photography*. Cambridge, England: Cambridge University Press.

Pirenne, M. H. (1975). Vision and art. In *Handbook of Perception*, E. Carterette and M. Friedman (eds.). New York: Academic Press, vol. 5, 434–490.

Pitcher, G. (1971). *A Theory of Perception*. Princeton, N.J.: Princeton University Press.

Platt, J. (1970). *Perception and Change*. Ann Arbor: University of Michigan Press.

Poincaré, H. (1905). *Science and Hypothesis*. Reprinted 1952. New York: Dover.

Poincaré, H. (1907). *The Value of Science* (G. B. Halsted, trans.). Reprinted 1958. New York: Dover.

Polyak, S. (1957). *The Vertebrate Visual System*. Chicago: Chicago University Press.

Popper, K. R. (1962). *Conjectures and Refutations*. London: Routledge and Kegan Paul.

Porterfield, W. A. (1759). *Treatise on the Eye, the Manner and Phenomena of Vision*, vol. II. Edinburgh.

Prazdny, K. (1981a). Determining the instantaneous direction of motion from optical flow generated by a curvilinearly moving observer. *Computer Graphics and Image Processing* 17:238–248.

Prazdny, S. K. (1981b). A note on "Perception of surface slant and edge labels from optic flow." *Perception* 10:579–582.

Prazdny, K. (1983a). A sketch of a (computational) theory of visual kinesthesis. In *Human and Machine Vision*, J. Beck, B. Hope, and A. Rosenfeld (eds). New York: Academic Press, 413–423.

Prazdny, K. (1983b). On the information in optic flows. *Computer Vision, Graphics, and Image Processing* 22:235–259.

Price, H. H. (1932). *Perception*. London: Methuen.

Priest, H. F., and Cutting, J. E. (1985). Visual flow and direction of locomotion. *Science* 227:1063–1064.

Probst, T., Krafczyk, S., Brandt, T., and Wist, E. R. (1984). Interaction between perceived self-motion and object-motion impairs vehicle guidance. *Science* 225:536–538.

Proffitt, D. R. (1976). Demonstrations to investigate the meaning of everyday experience. Ph.D. dissertation, The Pennsylvania State University. *Dissertation Abstracts International*, 1977, 37:3653B (University Microfilms 76–29,667).

Proffitt, D. R., and Cutting, J. E. (1980). An invariant for wheel-generated motions and the logic of its determination. *Perception* 9:435–449.

Proffitt, D. R., and Halwes, T. (1982). Categorical perception: A contractual approach. In *Cognition and the Symbolic Processes*, W. B. Weimer and D. S. Palermo (eds.). Hillsdale, N.J.: Erlbaum Associates, vol. 2, 295–319.

Proffitt, D. R., Thomas, A. M., and O'Brien, R. G. (1983). The roles of contour and luminance distribution in determining perceived centers of objects. *Perception & Psychophysics* 33:63–71.

Purdy, W. C. (1960). *The Hypothesis of Psychophysical Correspondence in Space Perception*. Ithaca, N.Y.: General Electric Advanced Electronics Center Publication R60 ELC56, 1–62.

Putnam, H. (1963). An examination of Grünbaum's philosophy of geometry. In *Philosophy of Science*, B. Baumrin (ed.). New York: Interscience, 205–255.

Putnam, H. (1978). *Meaning and the Moral Sciences*. London: Routledge and Kegan Paul.

Pylyshyn, Z. (1972). Competence and psychological reality. *American Psychologist* 27:546–552.

Pylyshyn, Z. (1984). *Computation and Cognition*. Cambridge, Mass.: The MIT Press, A Bradford Book.

Quastler, H. (ed.) (1955). *Information Theory in Psychology*. Glencoe, Ill.: Free Press.

Reed, E. S. (1983). What is direct perception? *International Society for Ecological Psychology Newsletter* 1(2):7.

Reed, E. S. (1984). Information pickup and direct perception. *International Society for Ecological Psychology Newsletter* 1(3):5–6.

Reed, E. S., and Jones, R. (1982). *Reasons for Realism*. Hillsdale, N.J.: Erlbaum Associates.

Regan, D. M. (1985). Visual flow and direction of locomotion. *Science* 223:1064–1065.

Regan, D. M., and Beverley, K. I. (1975). The relation between discrimination and sensitivity in the perception of motion in depth. *Journal of Physiology* 249:387–398.

Regan, D. M., and Beverley, K. I. (1979). Visually guided locomotion: Psychophysical evidence for a neural mechanism sensitive to flow patterns. *Science* 205:311–313.

Regan, D. M., and Beverley, K. I. (1982). How do we avoid confounding the direction we are looking and the direction we are moving? *Science* 215:194–196.

Regan, D. M., and Beverley, K. I. (1983). Psychophysics of visual flow patterns and motion in depth. In *Sensory Experience, Adaptation, and Perception*, L. Spillman and B. R. Wooten (eds.). Hillsdale, N.J.: Erlbaum Associates, 215–240.

Regan, D. M., Beverley, K. I., and Cynader, M. (1979). The visual perception of motion in depth. *Scientific American* 241(1):2–13.

Reggini, H. C. (1975). Perspective using curved projection rays and its computer application. *Leonardo* 8:307–312.

Reid, T. (1764). *Inquiry into the Human Mind*. Reprinted 1970. Chicago: University of Chicago Press.

Reid, T. (1785). *Essays on the Intellectual Powers of Man* (J. Walker, ed., 1864). Philadelphia: E. H. Butler.

Restle, F. (1979). Coding theory of the perception of motion configurations. *Psychological Review* 86:1–24.

Richards, W. (1975). Visual space perception. In *Handbook of Perception*, E. C. Carterette and M. P. Friedman (eds.). New York: Academic Press, vol. 5, 351–386.

Richter, J. P. (1883). *The Notebooks of Leonardo da Vinci*. Reprinted 1970. New York: Dover.

Rieger, J. H., and Lawton, D. T. (1983). Determining the instantaneous axis of translation from optic flow generated by arbitrary sensory motion. In *Motion: Representation and Perception*, ACM SIGGRAPH/SIGART Interdisciplinary Workshop. New York: Association for Computing Machinery, 33–41.

Riemersma, J. B. J. (1981). Visual control during straight road driving. *Acta Psychologica* 48:214–225.

Road Research Laboratory (1963). *Research on Road Safety*. London: Her Majesty's Stationery Office.

Roberts, F. S., and Suppes, P. (1967). Some problems in the geometry of visual perception. *Synthese* 17:173–201.

Rock, I. (1983). *The Logic of Perception*. Cambridge, Mass.:The MIT Press, A Bradford Book.

Rock, I. (1984). *Perception*. New York: Scientific American Books.

Rogers, B., and Graham, M. (1979). Motion parallax as an independent cue for depth. *Perception* 8:125–134.

Ronchi, V. (1957). *Optics: The Science of Vision* (E. Rosen, trans.). New York: New York University Press.

Ronchi, V. (1958). Twenty embarrassing questions (E. Rosen, trans.) *Atti della Foundazione Georgio Ronchi* 13:173–190.

Ronchi, V. (1970). *The Nature of Light*. London: Heinemann.

Ronchi, V. (1974). Perspective based on new optics. *Leonardo* 7:219–225.

Rosch, E. H. (1973). On the internal structure of perceptual and semantic categories. In *Cognition and the Acquisition of Language*, T. E. Moore (ed.). New York: Academic Press, 111–144.

Rosch, E. H. (1975). Cognitive reference points. *Cognitive Psychology* 7:532–547.

Rosch, E. H., and Lloyd, B. B. (eds.) (1978). *Cognition and Categorization*. Hillsdale, N.J.: Erlbaum Associates.

Rosinski, R. R., and Farber, J. (1980). Compensation for viewing point in the perception of pictured space. In *The Perception of Pictures*, M. A. Hagen (ed.). New York: Academic Press, vol. 1, 137–176.

Rosinski, R. R., and Levine, N. P. (1976). Texture gradient effectiveness in the perception of surface slant. *Journal of Experimental Child Psychology* 22:261–271.

Roth, E. M., and Shoben, E. J. (1983). The effect of context on the structure of categories. *Cognitive Psychology* 15:346–378.

Rubin, J. M., and Kanwisher, N. (1985). Topological perception: Holes in an experiment. *Perception & Psychophysics* 37:179–180.

Runeson, S. (1977). On the possibility of "smart" perceptual mechanisms. *Scandinavian Journal of Psychology* 18:172–179.

Russell, B. A. (1897). *Essay on the Foundations of Geometry.* Cambridge, England: Cambridge University Press.

Russell, B. A. (1914). *Our Knowledge of the External World.* Chicago: Open Court.

Russell, B. A. (1927). *The Analysis of Matter.* London: Kegan Paul, Trench, Trubner.

Schiff, W. (1980). *Perception: An Applied Approach.* Boston: Houghton Mifflin.

Schilpp, P. A. (ed.) (1942). *The Philosophy of G. E. Moore.* Evanston, Ill.: Northwestern University Press.

Sears, F. W., Zemansky, M. W., and Young, H. D. (1980). *College Physics,* fifth edition. Reading, Mass.: Addison-Wesley.

Sedgwick, H. (1973). The Visible Horizon. Ph.D. dissertation, Cornell University. *Dissertation Abstracts International,* 1973–1974, 34:1301–1302B (University Microfilms 73–22, 530).

Sedgwick, H. (1983). Environment-centered representation of spatial layout: Available visual information from texture and perspective. In *Human and Machine Vision,* J. Beck, B. Hope, and A. Rosenfeld (eds.). New York: Academic Press, 425–458.

Seidenberg, A. (1962). *Lectures in Projective Geometry.* Princeton, N.J.: Van Nostrand.

Shannon, C. E., and Weaver, W. (1949). *The Mathematical Theory of Communication.* Urbana: University of Illinois Press.

Shaw, R. E., and Bransford, J. (1977). Introduction: Psychological approaches to the problem of knowledge. In *Perceiving, Acting, and Knowing,* R. E. Shaw and J. Bransford (eds.). Hillsdale, N.J.: Erlbaum Associates, 1–39.

Shaw, R. E., and Pittenger, J. B. (1977). Perceiving the face of change in changing faces: Implications for a theory of object perception. In *Perceiving, Acting, and Knowing,* R. E. Shaw and J. Bransford (eds.). Hillsdale, N.J.: Erlbaum Associates, 103–132.

Shaw, R. E., McIntyre, M., and Mace, W. (1974). The role of symmetry in event perception. In *Perception: Essays in Honor or James J. Gibson,* R. B. MacLeod and H. L. Pick (eds.). Ithaca, N.Y.: Cornell University Press, 279–310.

Shepard, R. N. (1981). Psychophysical complementarity. In *Perceptual Organization,* M. Kubovy and J. R. Pomerantz (eds.). Hillsdale, N.J.: Erlbaum Associates, 279–341.

Shepard, R. N. (1984). Ecological constraints on internal representation: Resonant kinematics of perceiving, imagining, thinking, and dreaming. *Psychological Review* 91:417–447.

Shepard, R. N., and Cooper, L. A. (1982). *Mental Images and Their Transformation.* Cambridge, Mass.: The MIT Press, A Bradford Book.

Simon, H. A. (1955). A behavior model of rational choice. *Quarterly Journal of Economics* 69:99–118.

Simpson, J. I. (1984). The accesory optic system. *Annual Review of Neuroscience* 7:13–41.

Simpson, W. A. (1983). The cross-ratio and the perception of motion and structure. *Motion: Representation and Perception,* ACM SIGGRAPH/SIGART Interdisciplinary Workshop. New York: Association for Computing Machinery, 125–129.

Skyrms, B. (1975). *Choice and Chance,* second edition. Belmont, Calif.: Wadsworth.

Smith, E. E., and Medin, D. L. (1981). *Categories and Concepts.* Cambridge, Mass.: Harvard University Press.

Smith, R. (1738). *A Compleat System of Opticks,* vol. 2. Cambridge, England: Cornelius Crownfield.

Spooner, A. M. (1969). Telerecording. In *The Focal Encyclopedia of Film and Telvision Techniques*. London: Focal Press, 846–859.

Steers, J. A. (1927). *An Introduction to the Study of Map Projections*. London: University of London Press.

Steinberg, L. (1953). The eye is a part of the mind. *Partisan Review* 20:194–212.

Stevens, S. S. (1951). Mathematics, measurement, and psychophysics. In *Handbook of Experimental Psychology*, S. S. Stevens (ed.). New York: Wiley, 1–49.

Stoffregen, T. (1985). Flow structure versus retinal location in the optical contral of stance. *Journal of Experimental Psychology: Human Perception and Performance* 11:554–565.

Strawson, P. F. (1966). *The Bounds of Sense*. London: Methuen.

Suppes, P. (1977). Is visual space Euclidean? *Synthese* 35:397–421.

Thomas, T. (1944). *The Concept of Invariance in Mathematics*. Berkeley: University of California Press.

Titchener, E. B. (1906). *An Outline of Psychology*. New York: Macmillan.

Titchener, E. B. (1909). *A Text-Book of Psychology*. New York: Macmillan.

Todd, J. T. (1981). Visual information about moving objects. *Journal of Experimental Psychology: Human Perception and Performance* 7:795–810.

Todd, J. T. (1984). Formal theories of visual information. In *Persistence and Change*, W. H. Warren, Jr., and R. E. Shaw (eds.). Hillsdale, N.J.: Erlbaum Associates, 87–102.

Tolman, E. C. (1933). Gestalt and sign-Gestalt. Reprinted in *Behavior and Psychological Man*, E. C. Tolman. Berkeley: University of California Press, 77–93.

Topper, D. R. (1977). On interpreting pictorial art: Reflections on J. J. Gibson's invariants hypothesis. *Leonardo* 10:295–300.

Topper, D. R. (1979). Further reflections on J. J. Gibson's hypothesis of picture perception. *Leonardo* 12:135–136.

Torretti, R. (1978). *Philosophy of Geometry from Riemann to Poincaré*. Dordrecht, Netherlands: Reidel.

Torrey, C. (1985). Visual flow and direction of locomotion. *Science* 227:1064.

Turvey, M. T. (1977). Contrasting orientations to the theory of visual information processing. *Psychological Review* 84:67–88.

Ullman, S. (1979). *The Interpretation of Visual Motion*. Cambridge, Mass.: The MIT Press.

Ullman, S. (1980). Against direct perception. *The Behavioral and Brain Sciences* 3:373–415.

Ullman, S. (1981). Analysis of visual motion by biological and computer systems. *Computer* 14(8):57–69.

Ullman, S. (1983). Recent computational studies in the interpretation of structure from motion. In *Human and Machine Vision*, J. Beck, B. Hope, and A. Rosenfeld (eds.). New York: Academic Press, 459–480.

Ullman, S. (1984). Maximizing rigidity: The incremental recovery of 3-D structure from rigid and nonrigid motion. *Perception* 13:255–274.

Wald, G. (1950). Eye and camera. *Scientific American* 183(2):32–41.

Walk, R. D., and Gibson, E. J. (1961). A comparative and analytic study of visual depth perception. *Psychological Monographs* 75, no. 519.

Wallach, H. (1976a). The apparent rotation of pictorial scenes. In *Vision and Artifact*, M. Henle (ed.). New York: Springer, 65–69.

Wallach, H. (1976b). *On Perception*. New York: Quadrangle Books.

Walls, G. L. (1962). The evolutionary history of eye movements. *Vision Research* 2:69–80.

Warren, R. (1976). The perception of egomotion. *Journal of Experimental Psychology: Human Perception and Performance* 2:448–456.

Warren, W. H., Jr., and Shaw, R. E. (1984). Events and encounters as units of analysis for ecological psychology. In *Persistence and Change*, R. H. Warren, Jr., and R. E. Shaw (eds.). Hillsdale, N.J.: Erlbaum Associates, 1–27.

Watson, A. B. (1978). A Riemann geometric explanation of the visual illusions and figural after-effects. In *Formal Theories of Visual Perception*, E. L. J. Leeuwenberg and H. F. J. M. Buffart (eds.). Chichester, England: Wiley, 139–169.

Wexler, K., and Culicover, P. W. (1981). *Formal Principles of Language Acquisition*. Cambridge, Mass: The MIT Press.

White, J. (1957). *The Birth and Rebirth of Pictorial Space*. London: Faber and Faber.

Whiteside, T. C., and Samuel, G. D. (1970). Blur zone. *Nature* 225:94–95.

Wiener, N. (1922). The relation of space and geometry to experience. *The Monist* 32:12–60, 200–247, 364–394.

Wiggins, D. (1968). On being in the same place at the same time. *Philosophical Review* 77:90–95.

Wilcox, S., and Edwards, D. A. (1982). Some Gibsonian perspectives on the ways that psychologists use physics. *Acta Psychologica* 52:147–163.

Williams, D. R., and Collier, R. (1983). Consequences of spatial sampling by a human receptor mosaic. *Science* 221:385–387.

Yellott, J. I. (1983). Spectral consequences of photoreceptor sampling in the rhesus retina. *Science* 221:382–385.

Zadeh, L. A. (1969). The logic of inexact concepts. *Synthese* 19:325–373.

Zadeh, L. A. (1983). Commonsense knowledge representation based on fuzzy logic. *Computer* 16(10):61–65.

Zegers, R. T. (1948). Monocular movement parallax thresholds as functions of field size, field position, and speed of stimulus movement. *Journal of Psychology* 26:477–498.

Index

⅃Ⴈ Bradford Books